INDUSTRIALIZATION AND SOCIETY

INDUSTRIALIZATION

AND

SOCIETY

EDITED BY:

BERT F. HOSELITZ
Professor at the University of Chicago

WILBERT E. MOORE
Professor at Princeton University

UNESCO - MOUTON
1963

PROCEEDINGS OF THE CHICAGO CONFERENCE

ON SOCIAL IMPLICATIONS OF

INDUSTRIALIZATION AND TECHNICAL CHANGE

15-22 September 1960

Publication prepared by:

THE INTERNATIONAL SOCIAL SCIENCE COUNCIL

with the assistance of the

ECOLE PRATIQUE DES HAUTES ETUDES

(VIe SECTION)

Preface

The papers presented in this volume were prepared for the North American Conference on the Social Implications of Industrialization and Technological Change, which was one of the activities of the Department of Social Sciences of UNESCO. The North American Conference had been preceded by several other regional conferences on related topics. However, this last Conference, though nominally regional, was, in fact, international in both content and participants.

The actual planning and organization of the Conference were the primary responsibility of Bert F. Hoselitz. Wilbert E. Moore was responsible for co-ordinating the regional surveys of research results on the subject, and he served as *rapporteur général* for the Conference. As its organizer and reporter, respectively, we have joined as editors of this partial collection of the proceedings of the Conference.

The Conference was sponsored jointly by UNESCO, the Canadian and the United States National Commissions for UNESCO, and the University of Chicago. It was held at Chicago during September 15-22, 1960. Twenty-four technical papers, prepared for the Conference, were distributed in advance and discussed during the sessions of the Conference. In addition, a series of twelve "Working Papers," surveying the research results on the topic of the Conference in the major regions of the world, were part of the documentation. These reports were assembled and distributed by the Research Office of the International Social Science Council. The Working Papers, as well as a few papers prepared for the Conference that contained similar subject matter, are not reproduced in the following pages. Chapter 15 presents an extensive summary based in part on the materials relating to the several regions. The bibliographies of the regional papers are the principal source for the Classified Bibliography contained in this volume. A limited number of the Working Papers are available from the International Social Science Council; they will be of particular interest to regional specialists. These papers and their full titles are listed in Chapter 15.

There were thirty-four regular participants in the Conference, including those who prepared technical papers. The participants came from eleven countries in addition to Canada and the United States. Although the mother tongue or ordinary language of professional discourse of twelve of the participants was other than English, the discussions were conducted entirely in English. Eighteen observers, representing a variety of international and national public agencies and private organizations and foundations, also attended the Conference.

The subjects of the technical papers and of the several discussion sessions of the Conference ranged widely and deeply over the various aspects of the social implications of industrialization. Authors have had the opportunity of revising their papers in the light of these discussions; and we, as editors, have partially rearranged the sequence of the papers, so that they proceed from conceptual through substantive and theoretical to methodological concerns. The final section of the chapter, "Industrialization and Social Change," by W. E. Moore, was largely prepared after the close of the Conference, although preliminary notes were presented for oral discussion at the final session.

We wish to record our thanks to a number of persons and organizations who helped in the planning and excution of this Conference and provided financial support to make it possible. On the part of UNESCO, the advice of M. André Bertrand, Mr. H. M. Phillips, and Mr. Peter Lengyel was extremely valuable. Mr. George Mitchell of the United States National Commission and Mr. E. Bussière of the Canadian National Commission also offered great help. We also wish to express our thanks to the Carnegie Corporation of New York, the Joint Committees of the American Council of Learned Societies and the Social Science Research Council for International Scholarly Congresses in the United States, and the Fund for Adult Education Public Policy Conferences at the University of Chicago, for having made funds available that made it possible to enlarge the Conference from a small meeting to its international scope and its ample attendance. Finally, we desire to express our gratitude to Mme. Odette Charrière, Miss Ruth Kaufman, and Mr. John Hodgess Roper, who contributed, by their efficient handling of many details, to the comfort and effectiveness of the Conference's participants. The manuscript was edited and proof was read competently and carefully by Miss Selma B. Abelson.

We believe that the analyses presented here represent a substantial step forward in the understanding of economic growth and its social conditions, correlates, and consequences. Although much more needs to be learned, the areas and degrees of our uncertainty and ignorance are becoming more clearly identified. This, too, is knowledge of no mean sort.

B. F. H.
W. E. M.

February, 1961

Table of Contents

PART I

Introduction

CHAPTER 1

Main Concepts in the Analysis of the Social Implications of Technical Change

BERT F. HOSELITZ

The University of Chicago

The growing maturity and sophistication of the social sciences in the last quarter-century have brought about a great proliferation of technical terms and a multitude of new definitions and conceptualizations. Though a large number of these technical terms have chiefly specialized uses, several of them have come to be applied to quite usual phenomena in the study of social change; and many students of the process of economic and technological change and its social implications have found it useful to codify and inventory not merely the theories, but also the concepts commonly in use, to describe the generalized phenomena of social and cultural change. A recent publication produced under the guidance of the International Research Office on the Social Implications of Technological Progress constitutes one such attempt;[1] and the proposed "Dictionary of Social Sciences Terms," which is planned by UNESCO and will doubtless appear shortly, is another effort in the same vein. It cannot be the purpose of this paper either to repeat the performance of the International Research Office or to offer a selection from the forthcoming "Dictionary"; nor would this essay be a suitable vehicle for propounding an elaborate theory of social and economic concomitants of industrialization.

It appears that, perhaps, the best path to follow is to present first some aspects of the basic contrast, in social structure and cultural relations, between a society which has not yet entered the process of industrial development and a society which has passed through this process; and, after discussing some of their contrasting features, to draw attention to the principal factors which seem to be most crucial in this process of change.[2]

One may conveniently begin this task by referring to well-known contrasts in social and cultural features of differing types of society—e.g., the dichotomy between folk and urban cultures; or between "community" and "society" (*Gemeinschaft* and *Gesellschaft*); or between tradition-oriented patterns of social action and those conforming to the canons of purposive

11

and substantive rationality.[3] We need not dwell long on the dichotomies originally proposed by Robert Redfield or Ferdinand Toennies, since, whatever their merits for the comparative study of culture, reference to them has been infrequent in studies of technical and economic change. The distinction between traditional and rational action, ultimately going back to Max Weber, is much more important. We find often that action and behavior patterns in technologically and economically little developed societies are described as "traditional," and that this concept implies that these action patterns are inefficient, technologically non-complex, and strongly resistant to innovation.

Before we enter into a more detailed analysis of the concept of tradition-oriented behavior, it would be useful, however, to draw attention to two features of non-industrialized societies that have received extensive treatment in the works of Redfield and Toennies and their followers. Redfield frequently reiterated the point that social acts in a folk or folk-like society typically are not "single-interest" but "multiple-interest" actions. This means that productive activity, for example, has not only an economic purpose; it also is conceived, by the members of folk societies, as containing ritual elements, elements pertaining to social cohesion or structure, "political goals," and others. This very "multi-dimensionality" of all social behavior in folk societies it at the bottom of some of the difficulties of bringing about changes in behavior. If social behavior were uni-dimensional, change would be relatively easy. However, a given action is considered—in addition to meeting one specific objective—as simultaneously meeting other objectives. Thus, change is possible only if the new way of acting can be interpreted as comprising all these associated objectives also. In brief, behavior such as planting, or harvesting, or engaging in exchange, is conceived of not merely as productive activity, but, at the same time, as behavior maintaining the stability and relational adequacy of a person's position in his culture. Hence, if different forms of productive activity are proposed, they will prove acceptable (without strong external compulsion) only if they also fulfil in one form or another, all or most of the other objectives fulfilled by the activity to be replaced. The prevalence of many folk-like elements in the productive relations of non-industrialized societies accounts for some of the serious obstacles to economic and technical change that have been experienced there.[4]

The emphasis that Toennies and his disciples have placed on the significance of community has also played an important role in the study of conditions surrounding technological change and economic innovation. In this context, the significant point is that, for many non-industrialized societies, the small group is the relevant unit of social cohesion. This small community often has its origin in tribal or kinship groups. Its importance lies in the fact that its membership is usually strictly circumscribed—limited

12

to persons who have either long-standing face-to-face relationships or, where these are rarer, some other kind of close common identification with one another. All outsiders—i.e., all persons who do not belong to the small community—are strangers and are often regarded with suspicion. The small group, and the area within which its resides and maintains mutual contacts, form a world of their own which is regarded as opposed to the world beyond. One's loyalty is confined to the members of one's group, and everyone outside it is a stranger—regardless of whether or not he shares in a similar or closely related culture.

In many underdeveloped countries, these highly particularistic groups still exist; and in some instances, they have considerable strength. They are frequently tribal groups; but they may also constitute village communities or castes and other associations based on kinship or quasi-kinship ties, or on joint occupancy of a small area. Usually, the group lives in a regionally compact area, and its members are related by blood or marriage ties. Geography and familiarity thus reinforce one another; and the small community appears, in certain cultural contexts, as a hard-shelled unit whose main forms of social interaction occur only within the group, and whose relations to the outside are tenuous and often associated with suspicions and fears. In the development process, strong tendencies are set in motion to break up this isolation of the community and to enmesh its members in manifold social relations with the outside. Moreover, frequently those persons who have low status within the community are the ones who penetrate most easily the wall built around it and who tend to interact most with the remainder of the society. This disrupts the internal structure of the small community, and often leads its high-status members to reinforce their isolation against the outside.

Thus the small community is significant (1) in its resistance against absorption into the "great society"; and (2) as a source of conflicts which arise, on the social and personal levels, in the process in which primary loyalties to the small group gradually tend to be replaced by loyalties to the larger society. Moreover, many of the institutions which have meaning within the context of the small community lose this meaning in the framework of the larger society. The family loses its place as a productive and economic security-yielding unit in a society in which industrialization has taken place, and where economic ties are with persons outside the kinship group, and economic security is obtained through governmental or other insurance schemes. Similarly, the intimate relation with tribal or village deities loses its full import for those who enter the larger society; and the patterns of deference and authority within the small community have no force outside it. All this tends to produce conflicts within and beyond the small community, as in India, where they manifest themselves in conflicts within and between castes; in Africa, where they appear as struggles be-

13

tween centralized authorities and tribal chieftains; and elsewhere, where they assume still different forms.

The strong nationalism which permeates many industrializing countries is the chief ideological underpinning for a process of social change that leads from the ubiquity of small particularistic communities to a more uniform, structurally diversified, but more highly interdependent society. Other processes, associated with industrial development and less subject to manipulation by agitators and intellectuals, support this trend. Among them are urbanization and bureaucratization of governmental and productive procedures. The onslaught on the small community thus comes from all sides; and it is not likely that it can withstand the combined impact of these forces.

From the description of the small community and of the folk society, with its multi-faceted features of social interaction, we can see that these two concepts are chiefly different designations of the same social type.[5] A third and, on the whole, more popular, way of describing it is to point to its traditionalism—or, perhaps more correctly, to represent it as a society in which traditional forms of action predominate. In fact, the most common way to delineate societies with little industrialization and a limited application of scientific technology to production processes is simply to call them—as is done, for example, by W. W. Rostow—"traditional societies."[6] As we have seen, the concept of traditional social action ultimately goes back to Max Weber, who contrasted it with different forms of rational action. Since the concept of traditional or tradition-oriented action has gained such wide popularity, it might be considered a worth-while task to explore it somewhat more in detail. It is not my purpose to undertake an exhaustive analysis of the concept of tradition and traditional action, especially since I have presented my views on this problem in a recent publication elsewhere.[7]

The main point of this discussion relates to the definition of the concept of traditional action and its distinction from traditionalistic action. Though Max Weber did not make this distinction explicitly, it is implicit in his work. Traditional or tradition-oriented social action is found in all societies. Weber described it as action based upon "the psychic atitude set for the habitual workaday and . . . the belief in the everday routine as an inviolable norm of conduct."[8] But beyond this, the concept of traditional action may be widened by also including forms of social behavior which have been taken over from ancestors and forebearers, because all populations have a sense of their historical past and a need for continuity of behavioral norms, and because these forms of social action can appropriately be fitted into the action scheme of a society. This does not mean that traditional action excludes change. Tradition does not consist in a stereotype in external aspects of behavior; on the contrary, it is based on

14

a continuity of attitudes and states of mind. Many practices in modern, highly industrial societies are based on tradition and traditional norms. This is true of such everyday behavior patterns as forms of greetings and rules of personal conduct; and it is also true of more complex behavior in the political and economic spheres. It would be difficult to differentiate societies at different levels of economic performance by the relative "quantity" of tradition-oriented behavior that their members exercise.

Traditionalism, on the other hand, may be defined as action based on the "self-conscious deliberate affirmation of traditional norms in full awareness of their traditional nature and alleging that their merit derives from that traditional transmission from a sacred orientation."[9] In other words, traditionalistic action is a conscious revival of things past—a conscious return to a past glorious age or a past sacred lore, an ideology which looks to the great achievements of a past golden age as providing a set of norms whose revival would again lead to splendor and greatness. In the nationalisms of many industrializing countries—especially those whose roots go deeply into a great past—like the civilizations of India or the Islamic countries—we can find strong traditionalistic admixtures. Their ideologies go deeper than the mere rejection of Western values: the revival and revitalization of old values, often long dead, are demanded; and external behavior is approved that is considered to be in conformance with these norms.

Though traditional behavior may sometimes conflict with the demands of modernization and technological change, usually it is an important reinforcing element in the maintenance or support of stability in a period of rapid change. On the whole, the persistence of traditions in social behavior may be an important factor mitigating the many dislocations and disorganizations which tend to accompany rapid industrialization and technical change. Since traditionalistic action, on the other hand, tries to elevate outdated practices and values to the level of current behavioral norms, it usually has strong reactionary ingredients, and hence is a factor acting to retard economic change.

In brief, we need examination and study of the traits contributing to what is commonly described as traditional or tradition-oriented action. Weber himself was preoccupied with the analysis of rational action, which he regarded as the mainspring of economically and politically progressive societies. Hence tradition, the opposite of rationalism, became regarded as a characteristic of all that was static, stagnant, and retarded. But, as we have seen, traditions may have positive as well as negative effects; and, rather than leaving the whole body if ideas surrounding the analysis of tradition unsurveyed, we must make a more careful and precise study of the aspects of tradition that conduce to economic and technological progress, and of the aspects that may impede such progress.

One attempt to elaborate further the characteristics of tradition-oriented societies, and, in fact, to breaking the rationalism-tradition dichotomy into its components, is the description of societies at different levels of economic performance by means of the pattern variables proposed by Talcott Parsons.[10] Though the entire apparatus developed by Parsons is not often applied to the analysis of the social implications of industrialization, many of the chief pattern alternatives he describes—e.g., ascription or particularism—are frequently found in the literature. It may, therefore, be useful to present the pertinent parts of Parsons' theory and to apply it, in particular, to the problem under investigation.

Three of the five pairs of pattern alternatives stated by Parsons are more immediately applicable to our problem. These are the choice between modalities of the social object (achievement *vs.* ascription); the choice between types of value orientation standard (universalism *vs.* particularism); and the definition of scope of interest in the object (specifity *vs.* diffuseness). In applying these three pattern variables to the distinctions between industrialized and predominantly non-industrial societies, we find that the former are characterized by the preponderance of achievement standards in the distribution of economic roles and objects; that they also employ universalistic criteria in this distribution process; and that economic roles in these societies are typically functionally specific. Primitive and other non-industrial societies, on the other hand, exhibit predominantly features of ascription, particularism, and functional diffuseness in the corresponding fields of social action. Let us now consider each pair of variables in somewhat more detail.

We should begin by pointing out that we are concerned with norms of social behavior. It is true, of course, that actual social behavior often does not conform to these norms; and there may even be cases in which it would be appropriate to say that the norms are honored in their breach. In other words, the complex of pattern variables alleged to describe economic activity in a society constitutes an ideal type; and, as in other cases when ideal types are applied to the analysis of actual societies, we find that the reality presents features which are more or less deviant from the ideal-type construct.[11] But pattern variables may be used, to help discover elements of social change, for estimating the degree to which actual practice in any given society deviates from the "pure" state which a social system would have if the norms corresponding to the complex of pattern variables were actually enforced. For example: in a given society, ascription is regarded as the norm for distributing economic roles. However, we find that actually a number of these roles are assigned on the basis of achievement or performance. In such a case, we may discern an incipient process of social change, whose further ramifications may be traced by empirical inquiry.

16

Let us now return to the pattern variables. The achievement-ascription dichotomy is closely related to, though not identical with, the contrast between status-oriented and contract-oriented societies.[12] If we apply this dichotomy to economic objects, we find that, in a society in which ascription is the norm, economic roles are distributed ideally on the basis of who a person is rather than of what he can do. A practical example of a society based on ascription would be an "ideal" caste system, in which each caste is in full control of a certain occupation—that is, where only members of a specific caste are admitted to that occupation. Now the caste system—though it may have come close to this ideal in some localities, at certain times—has never, as a whole, exhibited fully ascriptive features. But it is quite clear, from the example given, that, in a society in which economic roles are assigned on the basis of status or ascription, social mobility is made difficult, and social change, to the extent to which it depends upon mobility, is severely impeded.

In contrast, if an achievement norm predominates with respect to the distribution of economic roles, then the primary criterion for attaining a certain occupation is based on a person's capacity to perform the required tasks for this occupation. In practice, an actual test may be involved in the process of allocating economic roles; in the absence of such a test, certain objective criteria—such as successfully passing through a certain number of school years, the obtaining of a degree, etc.—may be prescribed. Again, it is well known that pure performance criteria are not applied everywhere in industrialized countries—economic roles are sometimes allocated there on the basis of strong ascriptive criteria. Inheritance of property, the preponderance of extended kinship groups—especially among the upper social classes—and general impediments against social mobility, are some factors which inhibit the full application of achievement norms. But the ideal of an achievement norm is strong enough so that, even where economic roles are actually allocated on the basis of ascription, the pretense is made that the performance requirement has been met. An illustration of this is provided by the fact that, in quite a few American companies, the son of the boss must work his way to the top in the firm—though it is perhaps not doubtful from the beginning that he will succeed in this endeavor.

The next pair of pattern alternatives, particularism and universalism, are related to the first pair. They do not prescribe norms designating who is to perform a given role, but are concerned with whether the same rules of recruitment for economic roles apply to everyone. Medieval European society illustrates the application of particularistic norms to economic action —in that society, specific rules applied to peasants and burghers, to nobles and commoners. Certain markets and certain transactions were reserved to certain groups; and only an outsider's admission to an otherwise closed group could permit him to perform the functions reserved for that group. The principle of universalism, on the contrary, makes no such distinctions. The same rules apply to all; the principle of formal equality is elevated to a general norm of social behavior.

It almost follows logically that, in a society in which economic roles are distributed on the basis of universalistic performance criteria, the roles themselves are functionally highly specific. This requirement issues from the rigorous application of the principle of achievement, for the latter would be of little value unless a role could be clearly defined and circumscribed. Moreover, functional specifity flows from the increasing division of labor. Adam Smith, in his famous example of the manufacture of pins, has clearly demonstrated its economic advantages. For, as he points out:

The improvement of the dexterity of the workman necessarily increases the quantity of work he can perform; and the division of labour by reducing every man's business to some one simple operation; and by making this operation the sole employment of his life, necessarily increases very much the dexterity of the workman.[13]

Smith sees that there are other advantages that accrue from the division of labor; but he quite accurately places the development of a high degree of functional specificity first.

Functional diffuseness stands in direct contrast to specificity. The simple peasant in a non-industrial society is a characteristic representative of this type of work norms. He not only performs all work connected with producing a crop, but he also builds his house, makes his implements, and often produces his own clothes and other final consumption goods. As in cases of the ascription-achievement duality and the particularism-universalism duality, we find non-characteristic instances which seem to contradict the generalization that diffuseness is normally associated with non-industrial societies. In India, for example, the system of social division of labor under the predominance of caste has led, even in a non-industrial society, to a high degree of functional specifity. On the other hand, certain occupations, especially on the highest managerial level, are functionally diffuse, even in highly industrialized societies. In general, functional specificity has been instituted more widely for the simpler and less complex tasks; but the progressive specialization in business management, and even in scientific pursuits, indicates that this process of occupational differentiation is ubiquitous and strong in modernizing societies.

The use of pattern variables has had the advantage of putting some of the strategic mechanisms of social change associated with industrialization and technical progress into sharper focus. Universalistic norms need not generally replace particularistic ones. However, the transitions from allocating economic roles according to a system of ascription to assigning

18

them on a basis of achievement, and the replacement of functionally diffuse by functionally specific norms for the definition of economic tasks, appear to have occurred in all cases of successful modernization. Before we examine the institutional changes associated with these two processes of transition, it may be useful to relate the description of industrial and non-industrial social types, made in terms of the pattern variables, to the earlier description, made by means of the folk-urban continuum and the community-society dichotomy.

We have already seen that the folk society is characterized by the fact that economic acts have a multi-dimensional meaning—i.e., they have relevance not merely as acts of production or exchange, but also as acts of ritual, assertion of associative values, etc. Alternatively, this characteristic can be described by indicating the high degree of functional diffuseness of economic acts in the folk society. If a particular form of social behavior has meaning in several segments of social action—if it is not clearly confined to the set of adaptive, or integrative, or any other subsystem of social action—it must necessarily be diffuse. It has many meanings; and, though the actual manipulations demanded in its performance may be rigidly prescribed, its multi-dimensionality gives it the character of functional diffuseness—which, incidentally, also makes it so resistant to change.

Similarly, we may conceive of the little community as a set of institutionalized relationships, among persons, based primarily on ascriptive characteristics. The cohesion and compactness of the small community are enhanced because economic roles are tied to ascriptive status, and because, even where there is a considerable degree of specificity in different economic roles (as, for example, in the Indian village), ascriptive norms provide a stability and internal rigidity that render change from within exceedingly difficult. Only the breakup of the small community, or its infiltration from the outside, tends to reduce the significance of ascription in the distribution of economic (and other, e.g., political or deference) roles. Sometimes ascriptive norms are transferred into the wider society, but there, because of the absence of well-circumscribed boundaries for the group, they have primarily symbolic, rather than real, meaning.

The gradual destruction of the "traditional" folk-like small community thus is accompanied, in the economic and technological spheres, by a process of differentiation of economic roles and by a relaxation of the rules assigning these roles to particular actors. But the process is not a smooth one; it proceeds in spurts and jolts. During it, new institutions develop; and, as each new institution becomes established, it provides a pivotal point around which further changes gather momentum. If the juxtaposition of societies on different levels of economic modernization provided a classic case of the comparative analysis of social institutions, the analysis of the transition from one to the next level of economic performance may be regarded as a study of institutional change.

We shall now turn briefly to an examination of some of the principal concepts which have been developed in examining this process of institutional change. It must be repeated that we are not dealing here with a theory of social or cultural change, and hence it is not maintained that the concepts which will be discussed necessarily fit into a neat theoretical scheme. Nevertheless, we shall attempt to provide some indication of the relation between the various major concepts which have been employed in the description of the social implications of technical progress.

Let us begin by considering more carefully the process of institutional change and associated phenomena of social transformation. Industrial development may be regarded as requiring that two preconditions be fulfilled without which it is unlikely to start on any relatively large scale. One is the buildup of certain forms of physical overhead capital—such as communications and transport facilities; some warehouses and similar installations, especially favoring international trade; educational facilities and other public buildings. The other is the development of an institutional framework in the legal, familial, and motivational orders. Once these new institutions have been created, they provide an impetus of their own to further economic development and growth. Thus we may consider that this change in the institutional order is an important feature of social change in a pre-industrial or little-industrialized society—especially in areas which transform a society, from one in which capital formation and the introduction of modern technical devices in production are difficult, to one in which the accumulation of capital and the acceptance of innovations in production technique and economic organization appear as "natural" and unquestioned concomitants of general social progress.

Among the basic bottlenecks which have been identified in the process of modernization are shortages of capital, of skilled workers, and of entrepreneurs. Hence, from the viewpoint of industrialization, institutional arrangements which will contribute to the breakdown of any obstacles to larger supplies of these productive factors are of primary importance.

It was early recognized that the supplies of savings, of skilled labor, and of entrepreneurial talent are, in part, functions of the psychological make-up of a population. We may regard the willingness or propensity to save, as well as the propensity to run enterprises, as stemming from attitudes endemic to technically advanced societies. Some writers have been so impressed with these attitudes that they have regarded them as the chief psychological ingredients of capitalist society. For example, the main substance of Sombart's *Quintessence of Capitalism* is based upon his description of the capitalist spirit as a tension between rationalism and

20

irrationalism, between calculation and speculation, between the bourgeois spirit and the robber spirit, between prudence and venturesomeness.[14] It is quite clear that Sombart describes, in these terms, two personality types: the first type is recognizable as the embodiment of the Puritan virtues of thrift and hard work; and the other, as the visionary entrepreneur whose role in economic development has been stressed by Schumpeter. Now, it may be argued that the motivational dispositions to save and work hard and innovate are preconditions of economic and technical progress; but the impact of these traits on a society is greatly enhanced by the presence of institutions within whose framework they can be exercised. Among the chief institutions which supported these attitudes in the Western world were the legitimation of interest and the social approval of profit maximization as a goal of economic activity. Both had been present in Western societies before these societies had entered a full process of industrialization; and it is in this sense that industrialization and the exploitation of technical innovations for economic ends were given an important impetus.

In societies in which these institutions are not present or only weakly developed, others may have to take their place. One of the reasons for the predominance of governmental planning in the economic development process of the countries of Asia and Africa is the weakness or absence of these institutions and the need to find a different institutional framework —in this case, the expansion of the role of government as the custodian of economic advancement. But in some "mixed economies," for example in India, the taking of interest and profit maximization as institutionalized norms have gained a sufficient foothold to justify placing reliance on them as focal points for the mobilization of private savings and their channeling into productive investment. Given a favorable environment, these features of the social system have been observed to produce decided results in the realm of industrialization—although other institutions, e.g., the pooling of resources within the context of the extended family, have also played an important role. In India, certain communities—for example, the Marwaris, or Bhatias, or Parsees—have played a particularly strategic role in the industrialization process. This fact appears to indicate that the institutionalization of norms furthering the economic exploitation of technical innovations is distributed unevenly in the society and has stronger roots in certain communities than in others.[15]

This consideration of the conditions leading to the positive grasping of opportunities, in the economic field, provided by technical innovations brings us near to the study of entrepreneurship—a factor which has played, and continus to play, a considerable role in discussions of economic development and technological modernization. But, although entrepreneurship has often been examined, and although sometimes exaggerated claims have been made for the function of entrepreneurs in the industrialization process, there is still confusion about the exact meaning of "entrepreneurship" and there is still a good deal of ignorance about its social and psychological components. Concerning the role of entrepreneurship in economic development, the meaning which Joseph Schumpeter attributed to it is usually paramount. In a now famous passage, Schumpeter defined the entrepreneur in the following words:

We now come to the third of the elements with which our analysis works, namely the "new combinations of means of production," and credit. Although all three elements form a whole, the third may be described as *the fundamental phenomenon* of economic development. The carrying out of new combinations we call "enterprise"; the individuals whose function it is to carry them out we call "entrepreneurs." . . . The ordinary characterisation of the enterpreneur type by such expressions as "initiative," "authority," or "foresight" points entirely in our direction.[16]

In this passage, Schumpeter makes it clear that he regards the entrepreneur as an innovator, and that he considers the introduction of "new combinations of means of production" as the crucial element in giving an economic system the impetus to rise toward higher levels of productivity. In his work, Schumpeter lists in greater detail what he means by "new combinations." Among these he distinguishes: (*1*) the introduction of a new good; (*2*) the introduction of a new method of production; (*3*) the opening of a new market; (*4*) the conquest of a new source of supply of raw materials; and (*5*) the carrying out of the new organization of any industry.[17] As this list indicates, the first, third, and fourth alternatives apply primarily to commercial enterprises, whereas the second applies mainly to industrial enterprises. The fifth applies to all kinds of enterprises in industry, commerce, and finance. As a consequence, the exercise of entrepreneurship, in Schumpeter's sense, extends over the whole range of economic activity and is not confined to industrial entrepreneurship alone.

In much of the literature on the role of entrepreneurship in economic development, little or no distinction has been made about whether this activity was exercised in the commercial, the financial, or the industrial field. Yet even a superficial study of business leaders in many underdeveloped countries shows that industrial entrepreneurship is not exercised in some countries in which commercial and financial entrepreneurship flourishes. Why do we find, in so many underdeveloped countries, native moneylenders and traders, and so few native industrialists? Various arguments have been devised to explain this phenomenon; and, since we are interested in industrialization in particular, these arguments may be relevant.

The first of these arguments is the statement that native industrialists,

22

especially in former colonial areas, were unable to compete with the powerful industrial enterprises set up by foreigners. This is hardly convincing, for the same competition was equally severe in commerce and banking. And, if we examine the kinds of enterprises that native entrepreneurs did establish in the trading and moneylending fields, we find that they were supplementary to similar activities exercised by large European firms. Native traders and moneylenders found a place in the interstices of the economic system left unoccupied by larger foreign firms. They mediated between the larger urban centers and the countryside; they provisioned small and minute retailers; they serviced the needs for loans of that part of the rural population which was without capacity to offer bankable securities.

Why is no parallel phenomenon discernible in the industrial field? Clearly, small native entrepreneurs could not be expected to have entered into competition with the large foreign mining and transportation companies. But there were, and are, numerous industrial branches in which there appears to be ample opportunity for the establishment of small and medium-scale plants, which could play a role, with respect to the larger foreign-financed enterprises, similar to that of the native trader and moneylender to the foreign wholesaler and banker.

One of the reasons for the sluggish evolution of industrial entrepreneurship may be the fact that the talents required to guide an industrial enterprise differ from those needed for successful commercial or financial entrepreneurship. The small trader or moneylender can operate with few, and often without any, permanently employed assistants; whereas the industrial entrepreneur (provided he is more than a craftsman) typically must hire a group of men whose labor he must organize and direct. In addition to being motivated by the expectation of profit, and his capacity for applying innovations, he must have managerial abilities and, above all, the ability to command and organize. The chief characteristics of a small industrial entrepreneur are not so much his venturesomeness, nor his motivation to make profits, but his capacity to lead other men in a common undertaking, and his inclination to introduce technical innavations; and, in the early stages of industrialization, the vast bulk of these innovations are of a technological nature requiring the direct and immediate participation of the entrepreneur.

Finally, the capital employed by a trader or moneylender turns over much faster than that used in industrial establishments. A trader may carry on his business without ever attaining property rights in the objects he deals with. If he is a broker or commission agent, he may merely lose his earnings from a transaction, but not the capital invested in it. Moreover, a moneylender or banker deals in that commodity that has the widest currency, that is accepted by anyone, that can easily be transported or hidden, and that can be directly used to bribe officials or persons in power, if the need should arise. An industrial entrepreneur usually has more property tied up in his plant for a longer time than either the merchant or banker; he depends upon an often imperfect market to sell his output; his property is exposed to a series of dangers—destruction by fire or other accidents—which the others may escape. Other things being equal, the risks and uncertainties of putting a given amount of capital into industrial assets are much greater than those involved in trading and moneylending.

Hence, in speaking of a "favorable climate" for entrepreneurship, one must distinguish carefully whether the entrepreneurs who do flourish in this climate belong to the commercial and financial groups or are industrialists. Apparently, for industrialization to take hold and for industrial business leaders to come forward, a favorable climate for entrepreneurship by itself is not sufficient. I am not aware that the additional conditions which must be present to convert a commercial upsurge into an industrial upsurge have been investigated carefully enough to provide us with sufficient empirical data to distinguish more precisely the role which entrepreneurship actually does play in the process of industrialization. Doubtless, it plays an important role; but how this is to be fitted in with other alterations in social structure, and with changes in the institutional order and the normative prescription of a society, is as yet little explored.[18]

One additional characteristic of industrial entrepreneurs should be mentioned—i.e., that they have quite universally been regarded as "new men." Marx already talked of the accumulating capitalist in these terms; and much of the recent work on entrepreneurship has seen, in entrepreneurial activity—especially as opposed to governmental disposition over resources—a new form of economic behavior.[19] In part, the conflict about whether entrepreneurs are "new men" and whether entrepreneurial activity is a new form of social behavior depends upon what is meant by "entrepreneurship." If we adopt Schumpeter's definition and identify entrepreneurship with the introduction of innovations, we find that entrepreneurs have always existed—from the prehistorical past, when man first applied the wheel and introduced sedentary agriculture and cattle herding, to the most recent period. If we consider entrepreneurship to be exercised primarily within a contect of formal organizations, called "business enterprise"—which is itself again a unit in a group of social institutions—as does Arthur H. Cole, we come to stress the personal psychological connotations of the entrepreneurial personality less than the social setting in which entrepreneurial activity is exercised; and here we find that the social setting grows progressively more hospitable to entrepreneurship as we move to the modern period.

But if we interpret entrepreneurship in the second sense and regard it

24

as largely coincident with business leadership, then we may trace through its gradual development in an institutionalized setting. Then the application of certain sociological categories—such as deviance and social or cultural marginality—to the analysis of the gradual evolution of entrepreneurship makes sense. Of course, the concepts of social deviance and social marginality have usefulness in other areas also. They may be applied to such phenomena as the growth of scientific and technological inquiry, the development of more secular attitudes in a society, and a host of other problems—many of which may be only slightly related to the process of industrialization and technological change.

Let us consider social deviance briefly. As already stated, we are concerned primarily with those forms of deviant behavior which are relevant for economic activity and organization. Now if the concept of deviance is to have operational meaning, it cannot be interpreted as signifying simply behavior which is new; it must also imply that a set of innovating acts is opposed, in some way, to existing social norms or approved forms of behavior. In other words, a deviant always engages in behavior which constitutes a breach of the existing order and is either contrary to, or at least not positively weighted in, the hierarchy of existing social values. Applying this concept to the behavior of businessmen and merchants during the course of the economic history of Western Europe, we find that we can speak of genuine deviance in those periods and societies in which entrepreneurial behavior did not belong to the category of social actions which were considered as constituting the "good life." As late as the fifteenth century, this was true of certain kinds of financial entrepreneurship, which was always tainted by the Church's official opposition to usury. And later, when financial entrepreneurship became fully respectable, industrial entrepreneurship became regarded with some disdain because it often dirtied one's hands. These sentiments toward business or industrial activity as not quite proper for a gentleman to carry out are familiar in many underdeveloped countries today. This interpretation also provides an additional explanation for the differential response made by members of different castes in business. Since caste membership is associated with ritual status, the exercise of deviant behavior provokes different sanctions in different castes; and, most importantly, the meaning and interpretation of deviance vary between castes.

If "deviance" implies a breach with existing social norms, it is interesting to investigate further the social classes or groups from which persons come who engage in various forms of deviant behavior. Clearly, the expected rewards of their deviance must be attractive; and persons engaged in it are likely to feel a strong urge to rise in the social scale (perhaps a strong motivation for achievement), or must have resentments against some aspects of the existing order. In brief, it is quite possible to reconcile the theory of deviance with various alternative, social-psychological hypotheses—e.g., the theories of David C. McClelland or Everett E. Hagen—which have been proposed in explanation of the rise to prominence of business leaders.[20]

However, an alternative hypothesis is that persons engaging in deviant behavior are at the margin of a given culture or are in a social or cultural position in which they straddle more than one culture. In short, we may identify cases in which deviance coincides with social marginality. For example, in medieval Europe the earliest moneylenders were often foreigners. In Italy, at the time of Gothic and Lombard rule, they were Syrians, Byzantines, and Jews. Later, when Italians turned to financial entrepreneurship on a large scale, the Genoese and Pisans, Sienese and Florentines—who were all lumped together under the name of "Lombards" —became the financial entrepreneurs north of the Alps.

The role of marginal individuals in diverse economic pursuits in many economically little advanced countries is eminently manifest today. One can cite the Chinese in various South-East Asian countries, the Indians in East Africa, and the widely scattered Lebanese and Syrians who make their appearance as businessmen in West Africa, Latin America, and elsewhere in less advanced countries.

What is the mechanism which allows marginal individuals to perform the roles they apparently have so widely accepted? As Robert E. Park, the inventor of the concept and the discoverer of the significance of social marginality, has stressed, marginal men are—precisely because of their ambiguous position from a cultural, ethnic, linguistic, or socio-structural standpoint—strongly motivated to make creative adjustments in situations of change, and, in the course of this adjustment process, to develop innovations in social behavior.[21] Although many of Park's very general propositions have been refined by subsequent researchers, the theory of social marginality has not advanced sufficiently to supply convincing evidence for the role that marginal individuals may play in all episodes of social change. Even if it is admitted that marginal persons are inclined more often to make creative adjustments than to relapse into old orthodoxies or to embrace new ones, the record is not at all clear; and there are some students who warn us that marginal individuals may be more prone than others to succumb to *anomie* and thus to become carriers of trends leading toward social disorganization rather than toward creative innovations.

In circumstances in which a certain amount of deviant behavior has been displayed, the anchoring of this behavior in a new institution is of strategic significance. Once a form of deviant behavior has been able find the shelter of an institution, it ceases to be deviant, it becomes routinized, and it may display all the characteristics of highly approved forms of social

26

behavior. Thus, institutions in which deviant action is anchored form an advance post from which additional deviance becomes possible. For example, the institutions which arose in Western Europe before the industrial revolution, and in Japan before the Meiji period, were already the end products of a process of social change that had begun with deviant behavior; but by their very existence, these institutions, in turn, made possible further economic and technological change.

Whether or not any given form of deviance will lead to the elaboration of new social institutions and to the ultimate routinization of this hitherto deviant pattern of social action is contingent on several factors. Among these, the system of sanctions existing in the society may be the most important. These sanctions may be internalized, i.e., they may reside in the values and beliefs of a population; or they may be externalized, i.e., they may be imposed by persons in power, by the elite, against actual or would-be deviants. In some societies, e.g., imperial China, both types of sanctions seem to have been very strong. In pre-Meiji Japan, internal sanctions had partially broken down, and the power of the shogunate had become increasingly weak; so external sanctions had been softened to the point where they were inadequate to prevent the formation of new institutions, or at least the beginnings of these innovations.

Thus the analysis of social change may be conducted largely through considering the impact of deviance—whether exercised by marginal men or not—the gradual institutionalization and routinization of deviant behavior, and the range of sanctions opposed to it. This analysis may be carried out, in first approximation, on the "aggregate level"—i.e., it may take into account an entire complex society at once. But our insights on social change are sharpened if we disaggregate the variables in our analysis —in other words, if, in a complex society, we take account, not of changes affecting the society as a whole, but of those affecting specialized sections or classes in the society. For deviance, sanctions, and the process of institutionalization have a different place and impact among different groups. Let us use sanctions to illustrate this point. Clearly, in a society in which ascriptive norms are strong, different individuals will, according to their respective status positions, be subject to different internalized sanctions; and in a society with extensive particularisms, even external sanctions will be imposed and enforced to very different degrees on persons belonging to different special groups or classes.

This means that we are likely to discover, in any society, certain strategic groups which become the carriers of innovations. In many instances, these groups are composed of marginal men—especially if the innovations are transmitted from the outside. The role of marginal individuals in the acculturation or culture-contact process has as yet been insufficiently explored; but their prominent participation in it follows almost as a matter of definition. Another group which may, and often actually does, play a strategic role is the elite of a society. Though considerable attention has been given to the part of the elite in preserving a status quo, its impact on the introduction of organizational and technological innovations has, perhaps, been underestimated. In general, social change has been perceived as accompanied by a "circulation of elites," rather than as a process in which existing elites were capable of reorienting an entire society's goals and attempting to implement them. Yet in the present economically little advanced countries, where so much economic change is managed by the leaders of political power, the role of the elites as innovators must be acknowledged. The entrepreneurial functions—which, in Western countries, were performed predominantly by independent businessmen who often belonged to a not fully enfranchised and politically impotent bourgeoisie—have been taken over by bureaucrats who operate with the blessing, and under the protection, of the political power apparatus.

In part, the intervention of the state in the industrialization process is certainly a consequence of the greater pressures, of the greater distance between reality and aspirations, that exist in the present. In a perceptive essay, Alexander Eckstein has presented several factors which tend to enhance the role of the state in the process of economic growth. He lists the following factors: The urge for massive state intervention in the process of economic and industrial growth will be the stronger (1) the greater the range of ends and the higher the level of attainment sought; (2) the shorter the time horizon within which the ends are to be attained—that is, the more rapid the rate of economic growth desired; (3) the more unfavorable the factor and resource endowments; (4) the greater the institutional barriers to economic change and industrialization; and (5) the more backward the economy in relative terms.[22] Now, as time goes on, the fifth condition is bound to obtain—simply because the more the onset of industrialization is delayed in a country, the more backward it will be in relative terms. But if this condition holds, it is likely that the first, second, and fourth conditions will also obtain. We may conclude, from this empirically derived set of conditions, that, in the course of time, incentives and urges for state intervention in the industrialization process have constantly increased. As corollaries of this conclusion, we must assume that industrialization, as a goal, has progressively become an objective of over-all social policy; and that existing elites, whatever their primary ends may have been in the past, have reoriented the hierarchy of the systemic goals they try to implement by assigning an increasingly important place to economic development. However, the increased interest of governments in economic growth and industrialization means more than merely that they are capable of exercising control over the total resources of a society

28

to be applied to its economic buildup. It also means that a government, more effectively than any other agency, can influence the forms of social behavior by altering patterns of rewards and sanctions, by reallocating responsibility and authority, and by intervening in other ways in the social structure. But if a government is to exercise this influence successfully and beneficially, and is to avoid, as much as possible, unanticipated detrimental secondary consequences, it is necessary that the interaction between social and cultural change, on the one hand, and between economic and technical progress, on the other, be better understood. In this paper, we have presented some of the crucial concepts and ideas, mainly on the theoretical level, that have been employed in the work of social scientists in analyzing socio-cultural change in the new countries of Asia, Africa, and Latin America. It is the purpose of the papers that follow to discuss, in more detail and with greater concreteness, the mechanisms involved in the interaction of the chief categories of sociological research with the process of technical change in newly developing societies.

NOTES TO CHAPTER 1

1. See *Social Economic and Technological Change: A Theoretical Approach* (Paris: Bureau International de Recherche sur les Implications Sociales du Progrès Technique, 1958).

2. This approach has also been used in a recent essay by Charles P. Loomis, "Toward a Theory of Systematic Social Change," *Interprofessional Training Goals for Technical Assistance of Personnel Abroad* (New York: Council on Social Work Education, 1959) pp. 165-98.

3. Several other dichotomies of this nature are mentioned in the essay by Loomis. On the original statements of the folk-urban dichotomy, see Robert Redfield, "The Folk Society," *American Journal of Sociology,* LII (January, 1947), 293-308; on the *Gemeinschaft-Gesellschaft* dichotomy, see Ferdinand Toennies, *Community and Society—Gemeinschaft und Gesellschaft* (East Lansing, Michigan, 1957); on the rationalism-traditionalism dichotomy, see Max Weber, *The Theory of Social and Economic Organization* (New York, 1947), pp. 115 ff.

4. Numerous actual examples might be cited from the literature on economic relations among non-industrial peoples. See, for example, F. G. Bailey, *Caste and the Economic Frontier* (Manchester, 1957); Cyril S. Belshaw, "In Search of Wealth," *American Anthropologist,* LVII (February, 1955), Part II ("Memoirs of the American Anthropological Association," No. 80); Manning Nash, *The Machine Age Maya* (Glencoe, Ill., 1958).

5. The combined features of the folk society and the small community have been given a perhaps classic expression in the work of Robert Redfield, *The Little Community* (Chicago, 1955).

6. See W. W. Rostow, *The Stages of Economic Growth* (Cambridge, 1960), pp. 4-6.

7. See Bert F. Hoselitz, "Tradition and Economic Growth," in Ralph Braibanti and Joseph J. Spengler (eds.), *Tradition, Values, and Socio-Economic Development* (Durham, N.C., 1961), pp. 83-113.

8. See Max Weber, "The Social Psychology of the World Religions," in H. H. Gerth and C. W. Mills (eds.), *From Max Weber: Essays in Sociology* (New York, 1946), p. 296.

9. See Edward A. Shils, "Tradition and Liberty: Antinomy and Interdependence," *Ethics,* LXVIII (April, 1958), 160-61.

10. See Talcott Parsons, *The Social System* (Glencoe, Ill., 1951), pp. 58 ff. Applications of Parsons' theory to situations of social change have been attempted by William L. Kolb, "The Social Structure and Functions of Cities," *Economic Development and Cultural Change,* III (October, 1954), 30-46; and Bert F. Hoselitz, *Sociological Aspects of Economic Growth* (Glencoe, Ill., 1960), esp. chap. II.

11. On the concept and use of the ideal type, see Max Weber, *On the Methodology of the Social Sciences* (Glencoe, Ill., 1949), pp. 90 ff.

12. On the status-contract dichotomy, see Sir Henry Sumner Maine, *Ancient Law,* ed. Sir. Frederik Pollock (New York, 1906), pp. 163-65.

13. Adam Smith, *An Inquiry into the Nature and Causes of the Wealth of Nations,* ed. Edwin Cannan, (New York, 1937), p. 7.

14. See Werner Sombart, *The Quintessence of Capitalism* (London, 1915), *passim;* especially pp. 63-129.

15. On the Indian communities specially attracted to entrepreneurship, see Helen Lamb, "The Indian Business Communities and the Evolution of an Industrial Class," *Pacific Affairs,* XXVIII (June, 1955), 101-16; on the role of the extended family as a source of industrial capital, see James J. Berna, "Patterns of Entrepreneurship in South India," *Economic Development and Cultural Change,* VII (April, 1959), 343-62.

16. Joseph Schumpeter, *The Theory of Economic Development* (Cambridge, Mass., 1934), pp. 74-75. (Italics not in original).

17. *Ibid.,* p. 66.

18. Perhaps the most extensive and most systematic inquiry into the problem of entrepreneurship and its role in the industrialization process has recently been published by Arthur H. Cole, *Business Enterprise in its Social Setting* (Cambridge, Mass., 1959). Though its author does not claim that this is a definitive study, he discusses, with profound insight and great wisdom, many of the points which have been raised in the postwar period among students concerned with entrepreneurship and its social and historical dimensions.

19. See, for example, *ibid.,* pp. 99-100.

20. See David C. McClelland, "Some Social Consequences of Achievement Movitation," in Marshall Jones (ed.), *Nebraska Symposium on Motivation, III* (Lincoln, 1956), pp. 41-72; and Everett E. Hagen, "The Process of Economic Development," *Economic Development and Cultural Change,* V (April, 1957), pp. 208-15.

21. Robert E. Park, *Race and Culture* (Glencoe, Ill., 1950), pp. 345 ff., especially 375-76.

22. Alexander Eckstein, "Individualism and the Role of the State in Economic Growth," *Economic Development and Cultural Change,* VI (January, 1958), p. 83.

CHAPTER 2

Mechanisms of Change
and Adjustment to Change[1]

NEIL J. SMELSER

University of California, Berkeley

INTRODUCTION

A thorough analysis of the social changes accompanying economic development would require an ambitious theoretical scheme and a vast quantity
of comparative data. Because I lack both necessities—and the space to
use them if I possessed them—I shall restrict this exploratory statement
in two ways. (*1*) Methodologically, I shall deal only with ideal-type constructs, in Weber's sense; I shall not discuss any individual cases of development, or the comparative applicability of particular historical generalizations. (*2*) Substantively, I shall consider only modifications of the social
structure; I shall not deal with factor-allocation, savings and investment,
inflation, balance of payments, foreign aid, size of population, and rate
of population change—even though these variables naturally affect, and
are affected by, structural changes. These omissions call for brief comment.

Max Weber defined an ideal-type construct as a

one-sided accentuation . . . by the synthesis of a great many diffuse, discrete,
more or less present and occasionally absent *concrete individual* phenomena,
which are arranged . . . into a unified *analytical* construct. In its conceptual
purity, this mental construct cannot be found anywhere in reality.[2]

The analyst utilizes such ideal constructs to unravel and explain a variety
of actual historical situations. Weber mentions explicitly two kinds of
ideal-type constructs—first, "historically unique configurations," such as
"rational bourgeois capitalism," "medieval Christianity," etc.; and second,
statements concerning historical evolution, such as the Marxist laws of
capitalist development.[3] While the second type presupposes some version
of the first, I shall concentrate on the dynamic constructs.

"Economic development" generally refers to the "growth of output per

32

head of population."[4] For purposes of analyzing the relationships between economic growth and the social structure, it is possible to isolate the effects of several interrelated technical, economic, and ecological processes that frequently accompany development. These may be listed as follows: (*1*) In the realm of technology, the change *from* simple and traditionalized techniques *toward* the application of scientific knowledge. (*2*) In agriculture, the evolution *from* subsistence farming *toward* commercial production of agricultural goods. This means specialization in cash crops, purchase of non-agricultural products in the market, and often agricultural wage-labor. (*3*) In industry, the transition *from* the use of human and animal power *toward* industrialization proper, or "men aggregated at power-driven machines, working for monetary return with the products of the manufacturing process entering into a market based on a network of exchange relations."[5] (*4*) In ecological arrangements, the movement *from* the farm and village *toward* urban centers. These several processes often, but not necessarily, occur simultaneously. Certain technological improvements—e.g., the use of improved seeds—can be introduced without automatically and instantaneously causing organizational changes;[6] agriculture may be commercialized without any concomitant industrialization, as in many colonial countries;[7] industrialization may occur in villages;[8] and cities may proliferate even where there is no significant industrialization.[9] Furthermore, the specific social consequences of technological advance, commercialized agriculture, the factory, and the city, respectively, are not in any sense reducible to each other.[10]

Despite such differences, all four processes tend to affect the social structure in similar ways. All give rise to the following ideal-type structural changes, which have ramifications throughout society: (*1*) Structural differentiation, or the establishment of more specialized and more autonomous social units. I shall discuss the occurrence of this process in the different spheres of economy, family, religion, and stratification. (*2*) Integration, which changes its character as the old social order is made obsolete by the process of differentiation. The state, the law, political groupings, and other associations are particularly salient in this integration. (*3*) Social disturbances—mass hysteria, outbursts of violence, religious and political movements, etc.—which reflect the uneven advances of differentiation and integration, respectively.

Obviously, the implications of technological advance, agricultural reorganization, industrialization, and urbanization differ from society to society, as do the resulting structural realignments. Some of the sources of variation in these ideal patterns of pressure and change are described in the next paragraphs.

a) Variations in pre-modern conditions. Is the society's value system congenial or antagonistic to industrial values? How well integrated is the society? How "backward" is it? What is its level of wealth? How is the wealth distributed? Is the country "young and empty" or "old and crowded"? Is the country politically dependent, newly independent, or completely autonomous? Such pre-existing factors shape the impact of the forces of economic development.[11]

b) Variations in the impetus to change. Do pressures to modernize come from the internal implications of a value system, from a wish for national security and prestige, from a desire for material propery, or from a combination of these? Is political coercion used to form a labor force? Or are the pressures economic, as in the case of population pressure on the land or that of loss of handicraft markets to cheap imported products? Or do economic and political pressures combine, as, for example, when a tax is levied on peasants that is payable only in money? Or are the pressures social, as they are when there is a desire to escape burdensome aspects of the old order? Factors like these influence the adjustment to modernization greatly.[12]

c) Variations in the path toward modernization. Does the sequence begin with light consumer industries? Or is there an attempt to introduce heavy, capital-intensive industries first? What is the role of government in shaping the pattern of investment? What is the rate of accumulation of technological knowledge and skills? What is the general tempo of industrialization? These questions indicate elements which affect the nature of structural change and the degree of discomfort created by this change.[13]

d) Variations in the advanced stages of modernization. What is the emergent distribution of industries in developed economies? What are the emergent relations between state and economy, religion and economy, state and religion, etc.? While all advanced industrialized societies have their "industrialization" in common, uniquely national differences remain. For instance, "social class" has a different social significance in the United States than in the United Kingdom, even though both are highly developed countries.

e) Variations in the content and timing of dramatic events during modernization. What is the import of wars, revolutions, rapid migrations, natural catastrophes, etc., for the course of economic and social development?

These sources of variation render it virtually impossible to establish hard and fast empirical generalizations concerning the evolution of social structures during economic and social development.[14] Therefore, my purpose here is not to search for such generalizations, but rather to outline certain ideal-type directions of structural change that modernization involves. On the basis of these ideal types, we may classify, describe, and analyze varying national experiences. Factors like those indicated above determine, in part, a nation's distinctive response to the universal aspects

34

of modernization; but this in no way detracts from their universality. While I shall base my remarks on the vast literature of economic development, I can in no sense attempt an exhaustive comparative study.

STRUCTURAL DIFFERENTIATION IN PERIODS OF DEVELOPMENT

The concept of structural differentiation can be employed to analyze what is frequently termed the "marked break in established patterns of social and economic life" in periods of development.[15] Simply defined, "differentiation" is the evolution from a multi-functional role structure to several more specialized structures. In illustration, we may cite here three typical examples. During a society's transition from domestic to factory industry, the division of labor increases, and the economic activities previously lodged in the family move to the firm. As a formal educational system emerges, the training functions previously performed by the family and church are established in a more specialized unit, the school.[16] The modern political party has a more complex structure than do tribal factions, and the former is less likely to be fettered with kinship loyalties, competition for religious leadership, etc.

Formally defined, then, structural differentiation is a process whereby

one social role or organization ... differentiates into *two or more* roles or organizations which function more effectively in the new historical circumstances. The new social units are structurally distinct from each other, but taken together are functionally equivalent to the original unit.[17]

Differentiation concerns only changes in role structure. It must not be confused with two closely related concepts. The first of these involves the cause or motivation for entering the differentiated role. Someone may be motivated to engage in wage-labor, for instance, by a desire for economic improvement, by political coercion, or indeed by a wish to fulfil traditional obligations (e.g., to use wages to supply a dowry). These "reasons" should be kept conceptually distinct from differentiation itself. The other related concept concerns the integration of differentiated roles. For example, as differentiated wage-labor begins to emerge, there also appear legal norms, labor exchanges, trade unions, and so on, that regulate —with varying degrees of success—the relations between labor and management. Such readjustments, even though they sometimes produce a new social unit, should be considered separately from role specialization in other functions.

Let us now inquire into the process of differentiation in several different social realms.

35

Differentiation of Economic Activities

In underdeveloped countries, production typically is located in kinship units. Subsistence farming predominates; other industry is supplementary but still attached to kin and village. In some cases, occupational position is determined largely by an extended group, such as the caste.[18]

Similarly, exchange and consumption are deeply embedded in family and village. In subsistence agriculture, there is a limited amount of independent exchange outside the family; thus production and consumption occur in the same social context. Exchange systems proper are still lodged in kinship and community (e.g., reciprocal exchange), and stratification systems (e.g., redistribution according to caste membership), in in political systems (e.g., taxes, tributes, payments in kind, forced labor).[19] Under these conditions, market systems are underdeveloped, and the independent power of money to command the movement of goods and services is minimal.

As the economy develops, several kinds of economic activity are removed from this family-community complex. In agriculture, the introduction of money crops marks a differentiation between the social contexts of production and of consumption. Agricultural wage-labor sometimes undermines the family production unit. In industry, several levels of differentiation can be identified. Household industry, the simplest form, parallels subsistence agriculture in that it supplies "the worker's own needs, unconnected with trade." "Handicraft production" splits production and consumption, though frequently consumption takes place in the local community. "Cottage industry," on the other hand, often involves a differentiation between consumption and community, since production is "for the market, for an unknown consumer, sold to a wholesaler who accumulates a stock."[20] Finally, manufacturing and factory systems segregate the worker from his capital and not rarely from his family.

Simultaneously, similar differentiations emerge in the exchange system. Goods and services, previously exchanged on a non-economic basis, are pulled progressively more into the market. Money now commands the movement of increasingly more goods and services; it thus begins to supplant—and sometimes undermine—the religious, political, familial, or caste sanctions which had hitherto governed economic activity.[21] This is the setting for the institutionalization of relatively autonomous economic systems that exhibit a greater emphasis on values like "universalism," "functional specificity," and "rationality."[22]

Empirically, underdeveloped economies may be classified according to the respective distances they have moved along this line of differentiation. Migratory labor, for instance, may be a kind of compromise between full membership in a wage-labor force and attachment to an old community life. Cottage industry introduces extended markets but retains the family-

36

production fusion. The employment of families in factories maintains a version of family production. The expenditure of wages on traditional items, like dowries, also manifests the half-entry into the more differentiated industrial-urban structure.[23] The causes of such partial differentiation may lie in resistance on the part of the populace to give up traditional modes, in the economics of demand for handmade products, in systems of racial discrimination against native labor, or elsewhere.[24] In any case, the concept of structural differentiation provides a yardstick for discerning the distance that the economic structure has evolved toward modernization.

Differentiation of Family Activities

One consequence of the removal of economic activities from the kinship nexus is the family's loss of some of its previous functions, and its thereby becoming a more specialized agency. As the family ceases to be an economic unit of production, one or more members leave the household to seek employment in the labor market. The family's activities become more concentrated on emotional gratification and socialization. While many halfway houses, such as family hiring and migratory systems, persist, the trend is toward the segregation of family functions from economic functions.[25]

Several related processes accompany the differentiation of the family from its other involvements. (*1*) Apprenticeship within the family declines. (*2*) Pressures develop against nepotism in the recruitment of labor and management. These pressures often are based on the demands of economic rationality. The intervention frequently persists, however—especially at the managerial levels—and in some cases (e.g., Japan), family ties continue to be a major basis for labor recruitment. (*3*) The direct control of elders and collateral kinsmen over the nuclear family weakens. This marks, in structural terms, the differentiation of the nuclear family from the extended family. (*4*) An aspect of this loss of control is the growth of personal choice, love, and related criteria as the foundation for courtship and marriage. Structurally, this is the differentiation of courtship from extended kinship. (*5*) One result of this complex of processes is the changing status of women, who generally become less subordinated economically, politically, and socially to their husbands than they had been under earlier conditions.[26]

In such ways, structural differentiation undermines the old modes of integration in society. The controls of extended family and village begin to dissolve in the enlarged, complicated social setting which differentiation creates. Thereupon, new integrative problems are posed. We shall inquire presently into some of the lines of integration.

Differentiation of Religious Systems

Because of Max Weber's monumental thesis linking ascetic Protestantism and capitalism,[27] a disproportionate amount of attention has been devoted to the initiating role that *formal* religious values play in economic development. Although much excellent work has been done in this area,[28] insufficient emphasis has been given to the important role of secular nationalism in the industrial takeoff.

With the world organized as it is, nationalism is a *sine qua non* of industrialization, because it provides people with an overriding, easily acquired, secular motivation for making painful changes. National strength or prestige becomes the supreme goal, industrialization the chief means. The costs, inconveniences, sacrifices, and loss of traditional values can be justified in terms of this transcending, collective ambition. The new collective entity, the nation-state, that sponsors and grows from this aspiration is equal to the exigencies of industrial complexity; it draws directly the allegiance of every citizen, organizing the population as one community; it controls the passage of persons, goods, and news across the borders; it regulates economic and social life in detail. To the degree that the obstacles to industrialization are strong, nationalism must be intense to overcome them.[29]

In fact, nationalism seems in many cases to be the very instrument designed to smash the traditional religious systems—those like, e.g., the classical Chinese or Indian—which Weber himself found to be less permissive than Protestantism for economic modernization.

On the other hand, nationalism, like many traditionalistic religious systems, may hinder economic advancement by "reaffirmation of traditionally honored ways of acting and thinking,"[30] by fostering anti-colonial attitudes after they are no longer relevant,[31] and, more indirectly, by encouraging passive expectations of "ready-made prosperity."[32] We can distinguish among these contrasting forces of "stimulus" and "drag" that such value systems bring to economic development by using the logic of differentiation in the following way.

In the early phases of modernization, many traditional attachments must be modified to permit more differentiated institutional structures to be set up. Because the existing commitments and methods of integration are deeply rooted in the organization of traditional society, a very generalized and powerful commitment is required to pry individuals from these attachments. The values of ascetic and this-worldly religious beliefs, xenophobic national aspirations, and political ideologies (like, e.g., socialism), provide such a lever. Sometimes these diverse types of values combine into a single system of legitimacy. In any case, all three have an "ultimacy" of commitment, in whose name a wide range of sacrifices can be demanded and procured.

The very success of these value systems, however, breeds the conditions

38

for their own weakening. In a perceptive statement, Weber notes that, at the beginning of the twentieth century, when the capitalistic system was already highly developed, it no longer needed the impetus of ascetic Protestantism.[33] By virtue of its conquest of much of Western society, capitalism had solidly established an institutional base and a secular value system of its own—economic rationality. Its secular economic values had no further need for the "ultimate" justification they had required during the newer, unsteadier days of economic revolution.

Such lines of differentiation constitute the secularization of religious values. In the same process, other institutional spheres—economic, political, scientific, etc.—become more nearly established on their own. The values governing these spheres are no longer sanctioned directly by religious beliefs, but by an autonomous rationality. In so far as this replaces religious sanctions, secularization occurs in these spheres.

Similarly, nationalistic and related value systems undergo a process of secularization as differentiation proceeds. As a society moves increasingly toward more complex social organization, the encompassing demands of nationalistic commitment give way to more autonomous systems of rationality. For instance, the Soviet Union, as its social structure grows more differentiated, is apparently introducing more "independent" market mechanisms, "freer" social scientific investigation in some spheres, and so on.[34] Moreover, these measures are not directly sanctioned by nationalistic or communistic values. Finally, it seems reasonable to make the historical generalization that, in the early stages of a nation's development, nationalism is heady, muscular, and aggressive; as the society evolves to an advanced state, however, nationalism tends to settle into a more remote and complacent condition, rising to fury only in times of national crisis.

Hence there is a paradoxical element in the role of religious or nationalistic belief systems. In so far as they encourage the breakup of old patterns, they may stimulate economic modernization. In so far as they resist their own subsequent secularization, however, these same value systems may become an impediment to economic advance and structural change.

Differentiation of Systems of Stratification
In analyzing systems of stratification, we concentrate on two kinds of issues.

a) Are ascribed qualities subject to ranking? Ascription focuses primarily on those aspects of the human condition that touch the biological and physical world—kinship, age, sex, race or ethnicity, and territorial location. To what extent is status determined by birth in a certain tribe? in a certain family? in a certain ethnic group? in a certain place—a region of the country or "the wrong side of the tracks"? Some ascription exists in all societies, since the infant in the nuclear family always and every-

39

where begins with the status of his parents.[35] The degree to which this ascribed ranking extends beyond the family varies from society to society. In our own ideology, we minimize the ascriptive elements of class and ethnic membership; but in practice these matter greatly, especially for Negroes.

b) The degree to which all positions in society (occupational, political, religious, etc.) are consequences of status ascribed from birth. For example, the American egalitarian ideology places a premium on the maximum separation of these positions from ascribed categories; but in fact, family membership, minority-group membership, etc., impinge on the ultimate "placing" of persons. In many non-industrialized societies, the link between ascription and position is much closer. Criteria like these reveal the degree of openness, or social mobility, in a system.

Under conditions of economic modernization, structural differentiation increases along both dimensions discussed.

1) Other evaluative standards intrude on ascribed memberships. For instance, McKim Marriott has noted that, in the village of Paril in India,

Personal wealth, influence, and mortality have surpassed the traditional caste-and-order alignment of kind groups as the effective bases of ranking. Since such new bases of ranking can no longer be clearly tied to any inclusive system of large solidary groupings, judgments must be made according to the characteristics of individual or family units. This individualization of judgments leads to greater dissensus [*sic*.].[36]

Of course, castes, ethnic groups, and traditional religious groupings do not necessarily decline in importance *in every respect* during periods of modernization. As political interest groups or reference groups for diffuse loyalty, they may become even more significant.[37] As the sole bases of ranking, however, ascriptive standards become more differentiated from economic, political, and other standards.[38]

2) Individual mobility through the occupational hierarchies increases. This is indicative of the differentiation of the adult's functional position from his point of origin. In addition, individual mobility is frequently substituted for collective mobility. Individuals, and no longer whole castes or tribes, compete for higher standing in society. The phenomenon of growing individual mobility seems to be one of the universal consequences of industrialization. After assembling extensive empirical data on patterns of mobility in industrialized nations, Lipset and Bendix conclude that "the overall pattern of [individual] social mobility appears to be much the same in the industrial societies of various Western countries."[39] Patterns of class symbolization and class ideology may, however, continue to be different in industrialized countries.

40

One of Emile Durkheim's remarkable insights concerned the role of integrative mechanisms during periods of growing social heterogeneity. Attacking the utilitarian view that the division of labor would flourish best without regulation, Durkheim demonstrates that one concomitant of a growing division of labor is an *increase* in mechanisms for co-ordinating and solidifying the interaction among individuals whose interests are becoming progressively more diversified.[40] Durkheim locates this integration largely in the legal structure; however, similar kinds of integrative forces can be discerned elsewhere in society.

Differentiation, therefore, is not by itself sufficient for modernization. Development proceeds as a contrapuntal interplay between differentiation (which is divisive of established society) and integration (which unites differentiated structures on a new basis). Paradoxically, however, the course of integration itself produces more *differentiated* structures—e.g., trade unions, associations, political parties, and a mushrooming state apparatus. Let us illustrate this complex process of integration in several institutional spheres.

Economy and Family
Under a simple kind of economic organization, like subsistence agriculture or household industry, there is little differentiation between economic roles and family roles. All reside in the kinship structure. The *integration* of these diverse but unspecialized activities also rests in the local family and community structures, and in the religious traditions which fortify both.

When differentiation has begun, the social setting for production is separated from that for consumption; and the productive roles of family members are isolated geographically, temporally, and structurally from their distinctively familial roles. This differentiation immediately creates integrative problems. How is information about employment opportunities to be conveyed to working people? How are the interests of families to be integrated with the interests of firms? How are families to be protected from market fluctuation? Whereas such integrative exigencies had been faced by kinsmen, neighbors, and local largesse in pre-modern settings, modernization creates dozens of institutions and organizations designed to deal with the new integrative problems—labor recruitment agencies and exchanges; labor unions; government regulation of labor allocation; welfare and relief arrangements; co-operative societies; savings institutions.[41] All these involve agencies which specialize in integration.

Community
When industrialization occurs only in villages, or when villages are built

around paternalistic industrial enterprises,[42] many ties of community and kinship can be maintained under the industrial conditions. Urbanization, however, frequently creates more anonymity. As a result, in expanding cities there often emerge voluntary associations—churches and chapels, unions, schools, halls, athletic clubs, bars, shops, mutual-aid groups, etc. Sometimes the growth of these integrative groupings is retarded because of the movement of migratory workers,[43] who "come to the city for their differentiation" and "return to the village for their integration." In cities themselves, the original criterion for associating may have been the common tribe, caste, or village; this criterion sometimes persists or is gradually replaced by more "functional" groupings based on economic or political interest.[44]

Political Structure

In a typical pre-modern setting, political integration is closely fused with kinship position, tribal membership, control of the land, or control of the unknown. Political forms include chieftains, kings, councils of elders, strong landlords, powerful magicians and oracles, etc.

As social systems grow more complex, political systems are modified accordingly. Fortes and Evans-Pritchard have specified three types of native African political systems. These, listed in terms of their respective degrees of differentiation from kinship lineages, are as follows: (1) small societies in which the largest political unit embraces only those united by kinship—thus political authority is conterminous with kinship relations; (2) societies in which the political framework is the integrative core for a number of kinship lineages; and (3) societies with a more formal administrative organization. Such systems move toward greater differentiation as the society's population grows and economic and cultural heterogenity increases.[45] In colonial and recently-freed African societies, political systems have evolved much further; parties, congresses, pressure groups, and even "parliamentary" systems have emerged.[46] In describing the Indian village, Marriott speaks of the "wider integration of local groups with outside groups." [47] Sometimes such wider political integration is, like community integration, based on extension and modification of an old integrative principle. Harrison has argued that modern developments in India have changed the significance of caste from the "traditional village extension of the joint family" to "regional alliances of kindred local units." This modification has led to the formation of "new caste lobbies" which constitute some of the strongest and most explosive political forces in modern India.[48] We shall mention some of the possible political consequences of this persistence of old integrative forms later.

We have indicated the ways in which differentiation in society impinges on the integrative sphere. The resulting integrative structures attempt,

42

with more or less success, to co-ordinate and solidify the social structure which the forces of differentiation threaten to fragment. In many cases, the integrative associations and parties are extremely unstable: labor unions turn into political or nationalistic parties; religious sects become political clubs; football clubs become religious sects; and so on.[49] This fluidity indicates the urgent need for reintegration during rapid, irregular, and disruptive processes of differentiation. The initial response is a trial-and-error type of reaching for many kinds of integration at once.

We have outlined some structural consequences of technological advance, agricultural commercialization, urbanization, and industrialization. We have analyzed these consequences in terms of differentiation and integration. The structural changes are not, one must remember, a simple function of industrialization alone. Some of the most far-reaching structural changes have occurred in countries where industrialization has hardly begun. For instance, colonialism or related forms of economic dominance create not only an extensive differentiation of cash products and wage-labor, but also a vulnerability to world price fluctuations in commodities.[50] Hence many of the structural changes already described, and the consequent social disturbances to be described presently, are characteristics of societies which are still technically pre-industrial.

DISCONTINUITIES IN DIFFERENTIATION AND INTEGRATION: SOCIAL DISTURBANCES

The structural changes associated with modernization are disruptive to the social order for the following reasons:

a) Differentiation demands the creation of new activities, norms, rewards, and sanctions—money, political position, prestige based on occupation, etc. These often conflict with old modes of social action, which are frequently dominated by traditional religious, tribal, and kinship systems. Traditional standards are among the most intransigent obstacles to modernization; and when they are threatened, serious dissatisfaction and opposition to the threatening agents arise.

b) Structural change is, above all, *uneven* during periods of modernization. In colonial societies, for instance, the European powers frequently revolutionized the economic, political, and educational frameworks; but they simultaneously encouraged or imposed a conservatism in traditional religious, class, and family systems.

The basic problem in these [colonial] societies was the expectation that the native population would accept certain broad, modern institutional settings ... and would perform within them various roles—especially economic and administrative roles—while at the same time, they were denied some of the basic rewards inherent in these setting . . . they were expected to act on the basis of a motivational system derived from a different social structure which the colonial powers and indigenous rulers tried to maintain.[51]

In a society undergoing post-colonial modernization, similar discontinuities appear. Within the economy itself, rapid industrialization—no matter how co-ordinated—bites unevenly into the established social and economic structures.[52] And throughout the society, the differentiation occasioned by agricultural, industrial, and urban changes always proceeds in a see-saw relationship with integration: the two forces continuously breed lags and bottlenecks. The faster the tempo of modernization is, the more severe the discontinuities. This unevenness creates *anomie* in the classical sense, for it generates disharmony between life experiences and the normative framework which regulates them.[53]

c) Dissatisfactions arising from conflict with traditional ways and those arising from *anomie* sometimes aggravate each other upon coming into contact. *Anomie* may be partially relieved by new integrative devices, like unions, associations, clubs, and government regulations. However, such innovations are often opposed by traditional vested interests because they compete with the older undifferentiated systems of solidarity.[54] The result is a three-way tug-of-war among the forces of tradition, the forces of differentiation, and the new forces of integration.[55] Under these conditions, virtually unlimited potentialities for group conflict are created.[56]

Three classic responses to these discontinuities are anxiety, hostility, and fantasy. If and when these responses become collective, they crystallize into a variety of social movements—peaceful agitation, political violence, millenarianism, nationalism, revolution, underground subversion, etc.[57] There is plausible—though not entirely convincing—evidence that the people most readily drawn into such movements are those suffering most severely under the displacements created by structural change. For example:

[Nationalism appeared] as a permanent force in Southeast Asia at the moment when the peasants were forced to give up subsistence farming for the cultivation of cash crops or when (as in highly colonized Java) subsistence farming ceased to yield a subsistence. The introduction of a money economy and the withering away of the village as the unit of life accompanied this development and finally established the period of economic dependence.[58]

Other theoretical and empirical data suggest that social movements appeal most to those who have been dislodged from old social ties by differentiation without also being integrated into the new social order.[59]

Many belief systems associated with these movements envision the

44

grand, almost instantaneous integration of society. Frequently, the beliefs are highly emotional and unconcerned with realistic policies. In nationalistic movements in colonial societies, for instance, "the political symbols were intended to develop new, ultimate, common values and basic loyalties, rather than relate to current policy issues within the colonial society." [60] Furthermore, belief systems of this kind reflect the ambivalence that results from the conflict between traditionalism and modernization. Nationalists alternate between xenophobia and xenophilia; they predict that they will simultaneously "outmodernize" the West in the future and "restore" the true values of the ancient civilization; they argue both for egalitarian and for hierarchical principles of social organization at the same time.[61] Nationalism and related ideologies unite these contradictory tendencies in the society under one large symbol. If these ideologies are successful, they are then often used as a means to modernize the society and thus to erase those kinds of social discontinuity that caused the initial nationalistic outburst.

Naturally, early modernization does not inevitably produce violent nationalism or other social movements. Furthermore, when such movements do arise, they take many different forms. Below are listed the five factors which seem most decisive in the genesis and molding of social disturbances.

1) The scope and intensity of the social dislocation created by structural changes. "The greater the tempo of these changes . . . the greater the problems of acute mal-integration the society has to face." [62]

2) The structural complexity of the society at the time when modernization begins. In the least developed societies, where "the language of politics is at the same time the language of religion," protest movements more or less immediately take on a religious cast. In Africa, for instance, utopian religious movements apparently have relatively greater appeal in the less developed regions; whereas the more secular types of political protest, like trade union movements and party agitations, have tended to cluster in the more developed areas.[63] The secularization of protest increases, of course, as modernization and differentiation advance.

3) The access that disturbed groups have to channels that influence social policy. If dislocated groups have access to those responsible for introducing reforms, agitation is usually relatively peaceful and orderly. If this avenue is blocked—because of either the isolation of the groups or the intransigence of the ruling authorities—demands for reform tend to take more violent, utopian, and bizarre forms. This is the reason that fantasy and unorganized violence are likely to cluster among the disinherited, the colonized, and the socially isolated migrants.[64]

4) The overlap of interests and lines of cleavage. In many colonial societies, the social order broke more or less imperfectly into three groupings: (*a*) the Western representatives, who controlled economic and political administration, and who were frequently allied with large local landowners; (*b*) a large native population who—when drawn into the colonial economy—entered it as tenant farmers, wage-laborers, etc.; (*c*) a group of foreigners—Chinese, Indians, Syrians, Goans, Lebanese, etc.—who fitted between the first two groups as traders, moneylenders, merchants, creditors, etc. This view is oversimplified, of course; but several colonial societies approximated this arrangement.[65] The important structural feature of such an arrangement is that economic, political, and racial-ethnic memberships *coincide* with each other. Thus, *any* kind of conflict is likely to assume racial overtones and to arouse the more diffuse loyalties and prejudices of the warring parties. Many colonial outbursts did, in fact, follow racial lines.[66] In so far as such "earthquake faults" persist after independence has been attained, these societies will probably be plagued by similar outbursts.[67] If, on the other hand, the different lines of cleavage in the society criss-cross, the society is more nearly able to insulate and manage specific economic and political grievances peacefully.[68]

5) The kind and amount of foreign infiltration and intervention on behalf of protest groups.

STRUCTURAL BASES FOR THE ROLE OF GOVERNMENT

Many have argued, on economic grounds, for the presence of a strong, centralized government in rapidly modernizing societies. Governmental planning and activity are required, for example, to direct saving and investment, to regulate incentives, to encourage entrepreneurship, to control trade and prices, etc.[69] To their arguments, I should like to add several considerations that emerge from the analysis of structural change during periods of rapid development.

a) Undifferentiated institutional structures frequently constitute the primary social barriers to modernization. Individuals refuse to work for wages because of traditional kinship, village, tribal, and other ties. Invariably, a certain amount of political pressure must be applied to loosen these ties. The need for this pressure increases, of course, in proportion to the rate of modernization desired.

b) The process of differentiation itself creates conditions demanding a larger, more formal type of political administration. Thus, another argument in favor of the importance of strong government during rapid and uneven modernization is based on the necessity to accommodate the growing cultural, economic, and social heterogeneity, and to control the political repercussions of the constantly shifting distribution of power accompanying extensive social reorganization.

46

c) The probability that periods of early modernization will erupt into explosive outburst creates delicate political problems for the leaders of developing nations. We shall conclude this essay on the major social forces of modernization by suggesting the kinds of government that are likely to be most effective in such troubled areas. First, political leaders can increase their effectiveness by openly and vigorously committing themselves to utopian and xenophobic nationalism. This commitment is a powerful instrument for attaining three of their most important ends. (*1*) They can enhance their own claim to legitimacy by endowing themselves with the mission of creating the nation-state. (*2*) They can procure otherwise unobtainable sacrifices from a populace which may be committed to modernization in the abstract, but which resists making concrete breaks with traditional ways. (*3*) They can use their claim to legitimacy to repress protests and to prevent generalized symbols, such as communism, from spreading to all sorts of particular grievances. However, these political leaders should not take their claim to legitimacy too literally. They should not rely on their nationalistic commitment as being strong enough to enable them to ignore or smother grievances completely. They should "play politics," in the usual sense, with aggrieved groups, thus giving these groups access to responsible political agencies, and thereby reducing the conditions that favor counter-claims to legitimacy. One key to political stability seems to be, therefore, the practice of flexible politics behind the façade of an inflexible commitment to a national mission.

CONCLUSION

I have attempted to sketch, in ideal-type terms, the ways in which economic and social development are related to the social structure. I have organized the discussion around three major categories: differentiation, which characterizes a social structure that is moving toward greater complexity; integration, which in certain respects balances the divisive character of differentiation; and social disturbances, which result from the discontinuities between differentiation and integration.

Four qualifications must be added to this analysis. (*1*) I have not tried to account for the determinants of economic development itself. In fact, the discussion of differentiation, integration, and social disturbances has presupposed a certain attempt to develop economically. However, these three forces condition the *course* of that development once it has started. (*2*) For purposes of exposition, I have presented the three major categories in the order restated above. However, this ordering must not be inferred to mean that any one of the forces assumes causal precedence in social change. Rather, they form an interactive system. Disturbances, for instance, may arise from discontinuities created by structural differentiation; but these very disturbances may shape the course of future processes of differentiation. Likewise, integrative developments may be set in motion by differentiation; but they, in their turn, may initiate new lines of differentiation. (3) Even though the forces of differentiation, integration, and disturbances are closely linked empirically, we should not "close" the "system" composed of the relationship among the three forces. Differentiation may arise from sources other than economic development; the necessity for integration may emerge from conditions other than differentiation; and the sources of social disturbances are not exhausted by the discontinuities between differentiation and integration. (4) The "all-at-once" character of the transition from less differentiated to more differentiated societies should not be exaggerated. Empirically, the process evolves gradually and influences the social structure selectively. This essay has emphasized various halfway arrangements and compromises in order to illustrate this gradualness and irregularity.

NOTES TO CHAPTER 2

1. I am grateful to Professors William Petersen, Herbert Blumer, Reinhard Bendix, and Kingsley Davis of the University of California, Berkeley, for critical comments on an earlier version of this essay.

2. Max Weber, *The Methodology of the Social Sciences* (Glencoe, Ill., 1949), pp. 90, 93.

3. *Ibid.,* pp. 93, 101-03.

4. W. A. Lewis, *The Theory of Economic Growth* (Homewood, Ill., 1955), p. 1.

5. M. Nash, "Some Notes on Village Industrialization in South and East Asia," *Economic Development and Cultural Change,* III, No. 3, 271.

6. W. H. Beckett, for instance, distinguishes between "technical improvement" and "organizational improvement" in agriculture. See "The Development of Peasant Agriculture," in P. Ruopp, (ed.), *Approaches to Community Development* (The Hague, 1953), pp. 138-43. For an analysis of the interplay between technological advance and productive reorganization during the Tokugawa period in Japan, see H. Rosovsky, "Japanese Economic Development and the Western Model" (mimeographed), pp. 7-17.

7. For example, J. H. Boeke, *The Structure of the Netherlands Indian Economy* (New York, 1942), pp. 76-89.

8. Nash, *op. cit.*; T. Herman, "The Role of Cottage and Small-Scale Industries in Asian Economic Development," *Economic Development and Cultural Change,* IV, No. 4, 356-70; H. G. Aubrey, "Small Industry in Economic Development," in L. W. Shannon (ed.), *Underdeveloped Areas* (New York, 1957), pp. 215-25.

9. T. Hodgkin, *Nationalism in Colonial Africa* (New York, 1957), chap. ii.

10. B. F. Hoselitz, "The City, the Factory, and Economic Growth," *American Economic Review,* XLV, No. 2, 166-84; K. Davis and H. H. Golden, "Urbanization and the Development of Pre-Industrial Areas," *Economic Development and Cultural Change,* III, No. 1, 6-26; Nash, *op. cit.,* p. 277.

11. S. Kuznets, "Problems in Comparisons of Economic Trends," in S. Kuznets, W. E. Moore, and J. J. Spengler (eds.), *Economic Growth: Brazil, India, Japan* (Durham, N.C., 1955), pp. 14-19; Kuznets, "International Differences in Income Levels: Some Reflections on Their Causes," *Economic Development and Cultural Change,* II, No. 1, 22-23; A. Gerschenkron, "Economic Backwardness in

Historical Perspective," and R. Linton, "Cultural and Personality Factors Affecting Economic Growth," both in B. Hoselitz (ed.), *The Progress of Underdeveloped Areas* (Chicago, 1952), pp. 3-29, 80 ff.; H. G. J. Aitken (ed.), *The State and Economic Growth* (New York, 1959).

12. E. Staley, *The Future of Underdeveloped Areas* (New York, 1954), pp. 21-22; W. W. Rostow, *The Stages of Economic Growth: A Non-Communist Manifesto* (Cambridge, 1960), pp. 26-35; W. E. Moore, *Industrialization and Labor* (Ithaca and New York, 1951), chaps. ii-iv; Hoselitz, "The City, the Factory," pp. 177-79.

13. United Nations, Department of Economic and Social Affairs, *Processes and Problems of Industrialization in Underdeveloped Countries* (New York, 1955), chap. i; C. P. Kindleberger, *Economic Development* (New York, 1958), pp. 184-85, 315-16; N. S. Buchanan and H. S. Ellis, *Aproaches to Economic Development* (New York, 1955), pp. 275 ff.; Kuznets, "International Differences," pp. 21-22.

14. For instance, Blumer has questioned the generalization that "early industrialization, by nature, alienates and disaffects workers, makes them radical, and propels them to protest behavior." He even concludes that "industrialization . . . is neutral and indifferent to what follows in its wake" (H. Blumer, "Early Industrialization and the Laboring Class," *The Sociological Quarterly,* I, No. 1, 9). If one searches for specific generalizations like those Blumer has rejected, of course, he will inevitably be disappointed. One must not conclude, however, that the establishment of ideal-type constructs about the consequences of industrialization, and their use in interpreting national experiences are fruitless.

15. Kuznets, "International Differences," p. 23.

16. N. J. Smelser, *Social Change in the Industrial Revolution* (Chicago, 1959), chaps. ix-xi.

17. *Ibid.,* p. 2.

18. Boeke, *op. cit.,* pp. 8-9, 32-34; E. E. Hagen, "The Process of Economic Development," *Economic Development and Cultural Change,* V, No. 3, 195; B. K. Maden, "The Economics of the Indian Village and Its Implications in Social Structure," *International Social Science Bulletin,* III, No. 4, 813-21; D. F. Dowd, "Two-thirds of the World," in Shannon, *op. cit.,* pp. 14 ff.. For qualifications on the degree to which caste dominates occupation in India, see K. Davis, *The Population of India and Pakistan* (Princeton, N.I., 1951), pp. 163 ff.

19. K. Polanyi, C. M. Arensberg, and H. W. Pearson (eds.), *Trade and Market in the Early Empires* (Glencoe, Ill., 1957); N. J. Smelser, "A Comparative View of Exchange Systems," *Economic Development and Cultural Change,* VII, No. 2, 173-82; Boeke, *op. cit.,* pp. 36-39; M. R. Solomon, "The Structure of the Market in Underdeveloped Economies," in Shannon, *op. cit.,* pp. 131 ff.

20. These "levels," which represent points on the continuum from structural fusion to structural differentiation, are taken from Boeke, *op. cit.,* p. 90.

21. F. G. Bailey, *Caste and the Economic Frontier* (Manchester, 1957), pp. 4-5.

22. M. J. Levy, Jr., "Some Sources of the Vulnerability of the Structures of Relatively Non-Industrialized Societies to Those of Highly Industrialized Societies," in Hoselitz, *The Progress of Underdeveloped Areas,* pp. 116-25. The pattern variables of T. *Parsons* are also relevant (discussed in *The Social System* [Glencoe, Ill., 1951], pp. 58-67). For applications of the pattern variables to economic development, see G. A. Theodorson, "Acceptance of Industrialization and Its

Attendant Consequences for the Social Patterns of Non-Western Societies," *American Sociological Review,* XVIII, No. 5, 477-84; and B. F. Hoselitz, "Social Structure and Economic Growth," *Economia Internazionale,* VI, No. 3, 52-77.

23. Examples of these compromises may be found in Moore, *op. cit.,* pp. 29-34; *idem.,* "The Migration of Native Laborers in South Africa," in Shannon, *op. cit.,* pp. 79 ff.; A. I. Richards (ed.), *Economic Development and Tribal Change* (Cambridge, n.d.), chap. v; C. A. Myers, *Labor Problems in the Industrialization of India* (Cambridge, Mass., 1958), pp. 52, 175; S. Rottenberg, "Income and Leisure in an Underdeveloped Economy," in Shannon, *op. cit.,* pp. 150-51; Aubrey, "Small Industry in Economic Development," in Shannon, *op. cit.,* pp. 215 ff.; A. Doucy, "The Unsettled Attitude of Negro Workers in the Belgian Congo," *International Social Science Bulletin,* VI, No. 3, 442-51; G. Balandier, "Social Changes and Social Problems in Negro Africa," in C. W. Stillman (ed.), *Africa in the Modern World* (Chicago, 1955), pp. 60-61; Smelser, *Social Change,* chap. ix; Herman, *op. cit.,* pp. 357-58.

24. Non-economic barriers are discussed at length in Moore, *Industrialization and Labor,* chaps. ii-iv. On the persistence of handicrafts, see A. L. Minkes, "A Note on Handicrafts in Underdeveloped Areas," *Economic Development and Cultural Change,* I, No. 2, 156-58; Herman, *op. cit.,* pp. 362-65; T. Uyeda, *The Small Industries of Japan* (Shanghai, 1938), pp. 84-112.

25. For case studies, see M. J. Levy, Jr., *The Family Revolution in Modern China* (Cambridge, Mass., 1949), and Smelser, *Social Change.*

26. Kindleberger, *op. cit.,* pp. 59 ff.; Moore *Industrialization and Labor,* pp. 29-34, 71-75; E. F. Frazier, "The Impact of Colonialism on African Social Forms and Personality," in Stillman, *op. cit.,* pp. 76-83; UNESCO, *Social Implications of Industrialization and Urbanization South of the Sahara* (Geneva, 1956), pp. 108-09, 115-17, 187, 216-20, 369-72, and 616 ff.; K. El Daghestani, "The Evolution of the Moslem Family in the Middle Eastern Countries," *International Social Science Bulletin,* VI, No. 3, 442-51; B. J. Siegel, "Social Structure and Economic Change in Brazil," and S. J. Stein, "The Brazilian Cotton Textile Industry, 1850-1950," both in Kuznets, *et al., Economic Growth,* pp. 388 ff., 433-38; W. Elkan, *An African Labour Force* (Kampala, Uganda, 1956), chap. v; Myers *op. cit.,* p. 177; Linton, *op. cit.,* pp. 83-84; H. Belshaw, "Some Social Aspects of Economic Development in Underdeveloped Areas," in Shannon, *op. cit.,* pp. 88 ff., 191 ff.; G. St. J. Orde Browne, *The African Labourer,* (London, 1933), pp. 100-05.

27. Weber's relevant works include *The Protestant Ethic and the Spirit of Capitalism* (London, 1948); *The Religion of China* (Glencoe, Ill., 1951); and *The Religion of India* (Glencoe, Ill., 1958). For secondary treatments, see T. Parsons, *The Structure of Social Action* (New York, 1937), chaps. xiv-xv; and R. Bendix, *Max Weber* (New York, 1959), Parts I and II.

28. R. N. Bellah, *Tokugawa Religion* (Glencoe, Ill., 1957); C. Geertz, *The Social Context of Economic Change* (Cambridge, Mass., 1956).

29. K. Davis, "Social and Demographic Aspects of Economic Development in India," in Kuznets *et al., Economic Growth,* p. 294; Gerschenkron, *op. cit.,* pp. 22-25; Rostow, *op. cit.,* pp. 26-29.

30. B. F. Hoselitz, "Non-Economic Barriers to Economic Development," *Economic Development and Cultural Change,* I, No. 1, 9.

31. Cf., for example, the Indonesian expulsion of needed Dutch teachers and engineers. It has been maintained that the upsurge of regionalism in India has

led to a deterioration of English as a linguistic medium for education in Indian universities. See S. E. Harrison, *India: The Most Dangerous Decades* (Princeton, N.J., 1960), pp. 60-95.

32. J. van der Kroef, "Economic Developments in Indonesia: Some Social and Cultural Impediments," *Economic Development and Cultural Change*, IV, No. 2, 116-33.

33. *The Protestant Ethic and the Spirit of Capitalism,* pp. 181-82.

34. E. Crankshaw, "Big Business in Russia," *Atlantic,* CCII, No. 5, 35-41. For discussion of the balance among political and other elements in Soviet society, see R. A. Bauer, A. Inkeles, and C. Kluckhohn, *How the Soviet System Works* (Cambridge, Mass., 1957), Part II.

35. K. Davis, *Human Society* (New York, 1957), chap. xiv; T. Parsons, "An Analytical Approach to the Theory of Social Stratification," *Essays in Sociological Theory* (rev. ed.; Gloencoe, Ill., 1954), chap. iv.

36. Marriott, "Social Change in an Indian Village," *Economic Development and Cultural Change,* I, No. 2, 153; UNESCO, *op. cit.,* p. 152; J. S. Coleman, *Nigeria: Background to Nationalism* (Berkeley and Los Angeles, 1958), pp. 70-73.

37. In some cases, these ascriptive pegs become the basis for political groupings long after the society has begun to modernize. See E. H. Jacoby, *Agrarian Unrest in Southeast Asia* (New York, 1949), pp. 27-28, 50, 76, 91-93, 123-25, and 248; Coleman, *op cit.,* pp. 332-67. Harrison has argued that the present significance of caste in India is "if anything, stronger than before," but that this significance appears as competitiveness in the new political arena of the country (Harrison, *op. cit.,* chap. iv; also Davis, *Population of India*; p. 171). William Petersen has suggested that, in the advanced society of Holland, a process of "pillarization" has occurred, in which semi-ascribed religious groups have become the major focus of political and social competition ("Dutch Society *vs.* Mass Society," University of California Public Lecture, May 9, 1960).

38. For a study of the cross-cultural similarity in the ranking of industrial occupations in developed countries, see A. Inkeles and P. H. Rossi, "National Comparisons of Occupational Prestige," *American Journal of Sociology*, LXI, No. 4, 329-39.

39. S. M. Lipset and R. Bendix, *Social Mobility in Industrial Society* (Berkeley and Los Angeles, 1959), pp. 13 ff. Of course, the transition from collective to individual mobility is not instantaneous. See Marriott, *op. cit.,* p. 153; and Davis, "Social and Demographic Aspects," pp. 308-13.

40. E. Durkheim, *The Division of Labor in Society* (Glencoe, Ill., 1949), chaps. iii-viii. A recent formulation of the relationship between differentiation and integration may be found in R. F. Bales, *Interaction Process Analysis* (Cambridge, Mass., 1950).

41. Smelser, *Social Change*, chaps. xii-xiii; T. Parsons and N. Smelser, *Economy and Society* (Glencoe, Ill., 1956), chap. iii; also Nash, *op. cit.,* p. 275; A. Mehta, "The Mediating Role of the Trade Union in Underdeveloped Countries," *Economic Development and Cultural Change*, VI, No. 1, 20-23.

42. Smelser, *Social Change*, pp. 99-108; Myers, *op. cit.,* pp. 52-54; Stein *op. cit.,* pp. 433 ff.

43. Orde Browne, *op. cit.,* pp. 112-16; Doucy, *op. cit.,* pp. 446-50; Elkan, *op. cit.,* chaps. ii-iii.

44. UNESCO, *op. cit.*, pp. 84-85, 105, 120-21, 128-30, 220-21, 373-77, and 469-73; D. Forde, "The Social Impact of Industrialization and Urban Conditions in Africa South of the Sahara," *International Social Science Bulletin*, VII, No. 1, 119-21; Hodgkin, *op. cit.*, pp. 85 ff.; Hoselitz, "The City, the Factory," p. 183; Coleman, *op. cit.*, pp. 73-80; Harrison, *op. cit.*, pp. 330-32.

45. M. Fortes and E. E. Evans-Pritchard (eds.), *African Political Systems* (London, 1940), pp. 1-25.

46. D. Apter, *The Gold Coast in Transition* (Princeton, 1956); Hodgkin *op. cit.*, pp. 115-39; G. A. Almond and J. S. Coleman, *The Politics of Developing Areas* (Princeton, 1960).

47. Marriott, *op. cit.*, p. 152.

48. Harrison, *op. cit.*, pp. 100 ff.

49. Hodgkin, *op. cit.*, pp. 85 ff.

50. Jacoby, *op. cit.*, chap. i; R. Emerson, L. A. Mills, and V. Thompson, *Government and Nationalism in Southeast Asia* (New York, 1942), pp. 135-36; S. A. Mosk, *Industrial Revolution in Mexico* (Berkeley and Los Angeles, 1950), pp. 3-17.

51. S. N. Eisenstadt, "Sociological Aspects of Political Development in Underdeveloped Countries," *Economic Development and Cultural Change,* V. No. 4, 298.

52. P. T. Bauer and B. S. Yamey, *The Economics of Underdeveloped Countries* (Chicago, 1957), p. 64.

53. E. Durkheim, *Suicide* (Glencoe, Ill., 1951), Book II, chap. v.

54. Davis, "Social and Demographic Aspects," pp. 296 ff.

55. E.g., M. A. Jaspan, "A Sociological Case Study: Community Hostility to Imposed Social Change in South Africa," in Ruopp *op. cit.*, pp. 97-120.

56. E.g., the conflict between migratory workers and full-time resident workers; see Elkan, *op. cit.,* pp. 23-24.

57. For theoretical discussions of this relationship between strain and disturbance, see T. Parsons, R. F. Bales, *et al., Family, Socialization, and Interaction Process* (Glencoe, Ill., 1955), chaps. ii, iv; Smelser, *Social Change*, chaps, ii, ix-x.

58. Jacoby, *op. cit.* ,p. 246.

59. Emerson, *et al.*, op. cit., pp. 25-29; Eisenstadt, *op cit.*, pp. 294-98; W. Kornhauser, *The Politics of Mass Society* (Glencoe, Ill., 1959), Parts II and III; S. M. Lipset, *Political Man* (Garden City, N.Y., 1960), chap. ii; M. Watnick, "The Appeal of Communism to the Underdeveloped Peoples," in Hoselitz, *Progres of Underdeveloped Areas*, pp. 152-72.

60. Eisenstadt, *op. cit.*, p. 294.

61. M. Matossian, "Ideologies of Delayed Industrialization," *Economic Development and Cultural Change*, VI, No. 3, 217-28.

62. Eisenstadt, *loc. cit.*; J. S. Coleman, "Nationalism in Tropical Africa," in Shannon, *op. cit.*, pp. 42 ff.; Hodgkin, *op. cit.*, p. 56.

63. Hodgkin, *op. cit.*, pp. 95-150; Coleman, "Nationalism in Tropical Africa," pp. 38 ff.

64. B. Barber, "Acculturation and Messianic Movements," *American Sociological Review*, VI. No. 5, 663-69; H. R. Niebuhr, *The Social Sources of Denomination-*

alism (New York, 1929); J. B. Holt, "Holiness Religion: Cultural Shock and Social Reorganization," *American Sociological Review*, V, No. 5, 740-47; B. G. M. Sundkler, *Bantu Prophets in South Africa* (London, 1948); P. Worsley, *The Trumpet Shall Sound* (London, 1957).

65. Emerson *et al., op. cit.*, pp. 136-40; Hodgkin, *op. cit.*, pp. 60-75; C. Robequain, *The Economic Development of French Indo-China* (London, 1944), pp. 79-88; J. S. Furnivall, *Colonial Policy and Practice* (Cambridge, 1948), pp. 116-23; F. Machlup, "Three Economic Systems Clash in Burma," *Review of Economic Studies*, III, No. 2, 140-46.

66. Emerson *et al., op. cit.*, pp. 141-43; Jacoby, *op. cit.*, chap. viii.

67. J. M. van der Kroef, "Minority Problems in Indonesia," *Far Eastern Survey*, XXIV, 129-33, 165-71; Harrison, *op. cit.*, chaps. iii-vi.

68. Lipset, *Political Man*, chap. iii.

69. J. J. Spengler, "Social Structure, the State, and Economic Growth," in Kuznets *et al., Economic Growth*, pp. 370-79.

PART II

Entrepreneurship and Innovation

CHAPTER 3

The Entrepreneurial Function in Relation to Technological and Economic Change

W. T. EASTERBROOK

University of Toronto

The topic assigned to me is sufficiently broad in scope to permit considerable freedom in treating it. This freedom has its advantages, but it also raises awkward problems of presentation. I share a common dislike of lengthy methodological discussions of the sort which Tawney has likened to Chinese dramas—five hours of curtain-raising and the performance over when some might expect it to begin. Yet speculation about relationships, historically considered, demands some form of conceptual apparatus whose construction requires space as well as time. I have cut corners by summarizing two sets of concepts, with which I have been experimenting for some time, that seem to me to be of value in "placing" technological progress in the main stream of historical change. The first set includes (*1*) the entrepreneurial function; (*2*) strategies of investment; and (*3*) uncertainty responses. The second set has reference to (*1*) security zones or centers of investment; (*2*) the subsequent interaction of centers of enterprise and their margins; and (*3*) the patterns of persistence and transformation resulting from this interaction. These last lead to the consideration of the historical conditions of technological change in a few selected and contrasting "cases" of economic development. Interest is less in technology per se than in the interplay of technological and other aspects of change.

There is ample evidence that technological history is now emerging as a discipline in its own right, and the value of intensive research in this area cannot be doubted—increased knowledge and painstaking evaluation of technological progress obviously improve prospects for sound interpretation of historical change. It is also clear that these gains are giving new urgency to an old problem, namely, the need for more adequate concepts for examining the historical role of technology and the factors determining the timing, rate, and quality of innovations on the technological front. We may be able to begin by concentrating on technological advances in communication,[1] for these pervade every area of human thought and action; but the possibility has yet to be demonstrated. I turn, rather, to entrepreneurship as a focus in the study of interrelations. For this purpose, recent revisions of the concept promise to give it greater historical relevance than it has had in the past. The vision of the entrepreneur as the innovating giant, the heroic bearer of uncertainties, "the baron of a belligerently expanding capitalism,"[2] was striking and dramatic—but limited to a comparatively few historical cases. Entrepreneurial action may be viewed as a continuing process resting on a constant modification of behavior, rather than as a series of big changes wrought by the few; as such, it cannot be analyzed solely in economic terms or by limiting reference to the internal workings of a system in motion. It is unlikely that any one definition of entrepreneurship will find general acceptance. For this paper, I confine myself to considering the entrepreneurial function as noted below, and to outlining a number of related concepts useful in linking this function with the process of technological and economic change.

THE ENTREPRENEURIAL FUNCTION — INVESTMENT — UNCERTAINTY

A few propositions under this heading may be summarized at this point. (a) The primary function of entrepreneurship is the investment of time, capital, and energy in economically significant pursuits; emphasis is on decision-making in its various aspects, with little reference to the motivations or characteristics of those making decisions. (b) The investment process typically proceeds in the face of uncertainties rooted in imperfect knowledge. Uncertainty analysis provides a means of bringing together the varied and diverse elements which impinge on decision-making and makes it possible to examine the total environment in which investment decisions are made. The analysis concerns uncertainties present in every sphere of human behavior—social, economic, and political—with a tip of the hat to the psychological bases of uncertainty. (c) The entrepreneurial function, viewed in these terms, provides a focus for classifying and studying developmental patterns and their implications for technological change.

"Entrepreneurial function" refers to its varied appearances in different areas and kinds of activity—whether this function is performed by guild or corporation, Church, state, or small enterprise. However, in the matter of investment, theoretical distinctions between induced and autonomous investments—although of very limited operational meaning for the historian, and possibly for the theorist, too—suggest another and conceivably more fundamental distinction. A. J. Youngson and A. O. Hirschman, working from different points of view, have utilized this distinction; and their writings contain valuable clues for the historian.[3] Induced investment involves basically routine decisions; it tends to be gradual and relatively predictable in outcome; and it relates to growth[4] situations and to advanced economies. On the other hand, autonomous investment, in Hirschman's terms, involves "genuine decision-making"; and it has reference to investment strategies in "developmental" situations, in which qualitative aspects of action are of primary importance. It is associated with efforts to effect development that involve creative, shaping action, in contrast to more or less routine change. As such, autonomous investment draws attention to the process of capital creation and to the historical environments in which it occurs. In Youngson's terms, autonomous investment demands study of the "socio-economic milieu in which investment decisions are undertaken," and "it cannot be conveniently fitted into any theoretical system." This category of investment involves study of total situations in which technological changes take place. In this regard, the most interesting area of investment is the autonomous in its developmental aspect.

Since the distinction is fundamental in this essay, its relevance to technological change should be noted, although it cannot be elaborated at this point. It is characteristic of historical patterns of "persistence"[5]—those in which the course of development remains largely within the limits of a structure laid down in an initial phase of economic beginnings—that technological progress depends chiefly on entrepreneurial reactions to opportunities present in external market demands and internal resource endowments. This is basically a pattern of response in which technological change goes on within the framework of institutions which retain their grip on later developments. A satisfactory rate of growth may be attained in terms of increasing per capita income. However, heavy reliance on borrowing techniques and capital from external sources, and concentration on processes related to the exploitation of a limited number of basic resources, seriously restrict the possibility of creative action on the part of the entrepreneurship of "persistence" areas, whose induced investment is reflected in the more or less routine technological change characteristic of such areas. In North America, Canadian economic developments display this pattern of change; and the Southern states of the United States provide a similar illustration of the endurance of structures established in an early phase of development. Entrepreneurial leadership may change; but the basic features of entrepreneurial action in the investment function aspect remain intact over the long period. Technological progress, an accompaniment of growth, manifests little or nothing of the transforming power which, in some areas, takes us to the heart of economic change. Such an area was the northeast sector of the United States, which emerged early in the nineteenth century as a location of autonomous investment, where technological innovations brought substantial structural changes.

Consideration of the entrepreneurial investment function suggests that a sharper focus is necessary if we are to move beyond the level of abstraction. "Uncertainty" has its value in this respect, in that it makes possible the examination of the decision-making process in various situations, in initial stage or advanced phase of development, in old country or new, in long- or short-range study. It is an ubiquitous element in change, a concomitant of novelty which is the essence of change. As a key factor in entrepreneurial decisions, "uncertainty" provides a technique for exploring various environments in which choices are made and resources are committed to diverse uses. Then the entrepreneur, creative or adaptive, supplies the dynamics of change; and "uncertainty" is a means of systematically examining the interaction between man and the conditions, opportunities, and pressures to which he responds. In this paper, less emphasis is placed on the source and nature of uncertainties [6] than on the entrepreneurial responses to uncertainties that are reflected in contrasting patterns of development.

Unfortunately, the refinement and application of this concept in the social sciences have barely commenced. Although promising beginnings have been made in economic analysis, in sociology, and in psychology, there appears to be a notable lack of interest in uncertainty, in its time dimension and in its applicability to historical research. This neglect may be partially due to the difficulty of utilizing the concept of uncertainty in the search for means of predicting future developments on the basis of past experience. Expectations are fired by imagination, insight, and inspiration; they are characterized by imperfect knowledge; and they commonly involve non-insurable, non-seriable events. Thus, prediction in any "scientific" sense is precluded; men make history, and what defines good judgment in one situation may have little application in another. A purely subjective view of uncertainty comes close to excluding any use of the concept in the study of change. There are several avenues of escape from the "Shackle dilemma." [7] The complexities of change may be studied with the use of a "simplified decision model" in which it is assumed that power is dispersed and time horizons short, and in which investments are made in a given, stable setting. This is applicable to situations where the rules are unchanging and clearly defined, and where problems of power and time remain well in the background of analysis. It has value as a pedagogical device. However, its usefulness is obviously limited if the investigation goes, beyond systems of simple response, to situations in which investment strategies take the form of creative activity directed toward minimizing or reducing uncertainties to the point at which expectations may be translated into action.[8] Somehow, those conditions and events

60

must be taken into account that stabilize and structure expectations— those factors which, in reality, make decision-making possible in the face of uncertainties, which, for the entrepreneur, have their economic para- meters, their political aspects, and their implications for the status and role of decision-makers. For this purpose, historical examination of the conditions in which expectations are formed must be made in terms of the objective uncertainties encountered in investment, the techniques of mini- mizing the effects of uncertainty, and the consequences for technological and economic change.

This functional approach to investment uncertainties will be amplified later in this paper. However, a brief mention of uncertainty in relation to historical patterns may be useful here. Clearly, entrepreneurs operating in what I have called "persistence" areas—those in which investments are mainly "induced"—confront a range of uncertainties very different from those present in areas in which change has been characterized by the association of transformation with autonomous investment. In the former, uncertainties are rooted in the state of external demands and in the con- ditions of discovery and exploitation of basic resources. The typical ex- ample is the staples-producing area with its dependence on, and its vul- nerability to, external influences.[9] The dependence and vulnerability commonly give rise to strongly centralist tendencies in politics and society; and, confronting the uncertainties inherent in this satellite [10] role, enter- prise itself tends to be strongly centralist. The persistence pattern of change mirrors difficult and continuing problems, but study of techno- logical and economic change is comparatively simple: stages are clear-cut; shifts from one stage to another are easily defined; investment flows in clearly discernible channels; and techniques reflect the grip of institutions which change slowly, if at all. The perplexing problems of historical in- vestigation are not found here. The situation is very different in areas of autonomous investment, where technological change exerts a shaping in- fluence of its own, modifying and sometimes transforming the larger structures in which economic life goes on. In such areas, uncertainties cannot be enclosed in a market-resource framework of analysis, since institutional change itself must be taken into account. The interplay be- tween institutional dynamics and transforming technologies requires a more comprehensive approach than has been necessary thus far; and for this purpose, I shall present another set of concepts closely related to the foregoing.

SECURITY ZONES — CENTER-MARGIN INTERACTION — PATTERNS OF CHANGE

The following propositions indicate the course of the argument. (*1*) An essential condition of economic development is the building of security

61

zones of investment. This process entails entrepreneurial initiative exercised over a broad range, economic and non-economic, of human action. (2) This given rise to a center-margin interaction in which larger patterns reflect marked differences in the relationship that entrepreneurship may have to economic and technological change in various instances. In connection with security zones of investment, examination of initial phases of development reveals a common reliance on certain investment strategies. These take the form of group action involving the use of power in its several aspects, political, social, and economic, to promote or create the conditions in which investment may be made with prospects of adequate return—that is, with the expectation of returns commensurate with the uncertainties encountered. Entrepreneurial action during formative stages of development is usually conducted in a climate of investment that is hostile, or at best neutral, to economic motivations and strategies. Progress depends on the attainment and use of power and influences to expand the area of choice among alternatives and to insure duration or continuity of operations.

In other words, during phases of growth, investment strategies rest on positive action directed toward modifying and expanding market structures, and, in fact, toward shaping, to some degree, the whole economic environment. These strategies cannot be fitted into the temporal categories of short- and long-range change. Flexibility in organization and procedures, diversification of activity, concern for safety margins, innovational action —these and other responses reflect less the length of investment periods than they do the nature of the uncertainties encountered. These call for action beyond the economic calculus of the market place—e.g., the use of social and family influence, the utilization of political connections and power, the control of communications. This may be expressed in terms of a "universal tendency to monopolize," which Zimmerman [11] appropriately describes as a natural response to disequilibrium, although he is content to limit his analysis to changes in aggregate supply and demand conditions. Hence a prerequisite of successful action is the achievement of the stability of expectations essential to action; failure or qualified success insures a limited time horizon, a restricted area of choice.

Although building security zones of investment is a continuing process, the most difficult part of the "construction" is the building of the initial phase of investment. As a rule, it is the stage most neglected by historical inquiry, and the most difficult: motivations are usually mixed, and strategies complex. Carter Goodrich has commented on this neglect of "precondition," this "undifferentiated limbo, a sort of economic B.C." [12] Explanations commonly take the form of an eclectic listing of facts accounting for the rise of this or that center. Yet it is during this phase that investment channels become set; and it is in the light of developments

62

occurring then that subsequent change must be interpreted. One significant feature of this phase is that group effort and the use of political and social influence and connections constitute a major line of strategy in the rise of what are basically "communities" of influence. Individual initiative may be present within the security zone; but the prime condition of this initiative is the group or collectivist action which creates an environment conducive to continuing investment. Constant reliance on collective solutions to uncertainty problems is a manifestation of persevering uncertainties which demand group effort, and which, in some instances, are great enough to restrict entrepreneurial action to small-scale, temporally limited operations on the peripheries of structures on which they exert little influence. In Canada, the perseverance of these uncertainties provides much of the explanation of the durability of investment channels which were laid down in a period of "pre-conditions". In the more dynamic areas of the United States' development, the historian's task is to determine how early institutions were superseded to the point where technology could assume a transforming role in economic change.

Consideration of this divergence of patterns leads to the concept of center-margin interaction and its consequences for developments that extend beyond the initial phase of growth. Economic history contains numerous references to centers of influence—the medieval commercial town, the city-state, the metropolitan center, and, on a large scale, England at her prime and, more recently, the United States. And there is abundant literature about the impact of these centers on the areas marginal to them. Less emphasis has been placed on the impact that marginal regions have on the centers which, so to speak, set them in motion.[13] We are aware of the generative power of established centers[14] and of their stimulus to new areas of investment which, in turn, pass (or fail to pass) from the institutional arrangements of the early phase to more or less self-sustaining patterns of growth.[15] We evince much less awareness of the significance of the interaction of center and margin; and yet this interaction supplies a key to the explanation of contrast in patterns of development—patterns that emerge in the course of the interaction. Canada provides an illustration of a society where centers remain dominant over margins during a long period, where margins continue to fit into the structures in which the entrepreneurial decisions and the strategies of investment of the center are decisive. The result is a persistence pattern. In this case, "margins," in the investment sense, are not free margins; and their interaction with centers is basically a one-way relationship wherein they exert little influence on the course and character of development. They commonly display "backwash" characteristics.[16] They provide instances of "defensive expansionism."[17] Their development tends to strengthen, rather than to challenge, the control of the centers which gave them birth. We must stress that we have not thus delineated the "frontier thesis," which commonly takes a geographic form—although, significantly, the Turner hypothesis is most applicable to free margins in the investment sense as well as in the geographic sense. The "frontiers" of persistence areas display little or nothing of the dynamism of the frontiers in which Turner was primarily interested.

This center-margin interaction may be examined in various settings. Regionally, the relations of the Canadian maritime provinces with the central St. Lawrence area illustrate the defensive marginal response to strong centralist tendencies. On a continental basis, the relations of Canadian entrepreneurship to the dominant northeastern complex of the United States reflect strikingly similar tendencies. North American entrepreneurship has recently exhibited defensive reactions as new centers have arisen to challenge its leadership on a world scale. Stated in terms of uncertainty—and irrespective of the source of the uncertainties—the political and economic structures in which center-margin reaction goes on reflect the degree of uncertainty facing entrepreneurs in their role as investors. When the structure is under heavy external pressure, or is faced with serious and enduring internal tensions which threaten its stability, centralist tendencies are strong, and margins play a more or less adaptive and passive role in development. The structures evince strong resistance to change, and technological progress is usually confined within the bounds of established socio-political institutions on which change and progress exert little pressure for alterations. This is relevant for investigating an important question, namely, why do institutions and attitudes sometimes (as in some pre-industrial areas) harden and retain their control over the long period; and, conversely, why, in other instances, after the initial or "staples" phase, can a break in continuity—in the form either of a relatively sharp acceleration of change with consequent institutional and other adjustments, or of a pronounced structural change in the setting of economic life—be discerned? We have tried to explain this through the analysis of entrepreneurial response to investment opportunities as defined in uncertainty terms. And the nature of the uncertainties encountered in the investment process may provide us with clues for understanding the sequence of change that can be traced as centers build margins and as the interaction between the centers and their margins evolves.

The persistence pattern of change contrasts with the center-margin relationship in "transformation" areas. The latter is illustrated, e.g., by developments in the North Atlantic economy of the seventeenth and eighteenth centuries.[18] In the Canadian example of the persistence pattern, a centralized, continental system of development emerged very early. It was characterized by the extensive market uncertainties inherent in fluctuating demands for export commodities and heavy fixed costs of operation, and by a constant necessity to force expansion in the face of a vastly more powerful neighbor. In contradistinction to the Canadian case, the American colonies were characterized by the emergence of a number of new centers of initiative within the security system of the British Empire —centers whose rivalries, at first maritime and later continental, provided a strong impulse to expansion. Bernard Bailyn[19] has traced the rise of colonial entrepreneurs, who functioned initially within the limits imposed by a religious oligarchy, and subsequently operated within the more flexible framework of a civil officialdom in which mercantile groups attained political and social status. The appearance of a New World mercantilism by the mid-eighteenth century represents the rise of a dynamic margin—one that had its own centers of entrepreneurship, which conflicted with the old center, and that developed the strength to break loose and to devote itself to building its own margins of investment. The formative stage—distinguished by its maritime outlook, its internal dynamic of inter-urban rivalries, its flexibility and initiative in trade—laid the foundations for the the continental phase that was well along by the 1830's. The technological advances in shipping, internal transportation, and early manufacturing during the early phase were made under the mercantile leadership of centers which, by the early nineteenth century, were beginning to turn to the building of continental hinterlands of investment.

The real shift to continental expansion began under exceptionally favorable circumstances. Economic conflict with England in the Caribbean had ended; the Hamiltonian dream of an orderly, more or less controlled development had given way before the aggressive energies of more speculative interests; and numerous centers, led by New York, began the push to western margins. A period of unrestrained entrepreneurial initiative followed in the key areas of transportation and finance; a new staples area appeared in the trans-Appalachian West;[20] and another cycle of center-margin interaction emerged as new centers arose in the Great Lakes region and along the Mississippi, and led to interurban rivalries similar to those between longer-established seabord centers. This development of the United States in the west had strongly autonomous characteristics, and progress there manifested little of the one-way control, the dominance from center, operative on the western frontiers of Canada.[21] The former was not a centralized, more or less planned development; it was a spontaneous, highly competitive drive on the part of many centers of initiative. From the standpoint of uncertainties encountered, entrepreneurs invested under nearly ideal conditions. A philosophy of negative government, allowing strong government support to private investment;[22] the weakness of opposition by organized labor or agriculture; the absence of legal restraints; the freedom from external pressures, political or economic—these made for a climate of investment that encouraged the rapid

65

exploitation of the resource endowments of the West. Western centers, led by Chicago, turned early to building their own margins, with the railway as their principal strategic instrument.

Seen in retrospect, the 1830's marked the end of any propect for stable and orderly development, and the beginnings of a process in which technological change—unfettered by institutional restraints, flexible, and free of traditionalism—became the major agent in the transformation which created the national economy of the later nineteenth century. Only in the closing decades of the century did the uncertainties inherent in chaotic competition among enterprises with a large element of fixed costs, cause a shift to centralized control under private auspices in the leading sectors of industry; these uncertainties simultaneously caused a shift to organized action by the more exposed agrarian and labor groups. Technological progress assumed a more routine aspect as small entrepreneurs were superseded by big—a movement that has culminated in the giant laboratories of the present.

The South, like Canada, remained largely unaffected by this transformation of the central sector of the continent. Southern nationalism had taken shape in the 1830's, and Southern defensive tactics—reflected in states-rights claims, and in tariff, banking, and land policies—enabled basic Southern institutions to last despite Northern aggressiveness. The Civil War and its aftermath destroyed some of these defenses; but, as Douglas Dowd has shown,[23] even this period of chaotic change left the established Southern institutions largely intact. The staying power of Southern institutions has its consequence in center-margin relationships similar to those Canada has with the United States. In spite of their rich resources, each of these marginal areas of the continental investment pattern has lagged in terms of per capita income; each has been exposed to the dominance of Northern capital and entrepreneurship; and each has yet to experience the transformation essential to an independent, diversified pattern of growth.[24] In each, the dominant position of the central sector of the continent has contributed to the perpetuation of a staples phase, which, at least in Canada—possibly because of its stronger political defenses—shows few signs of weakening. It seems extremely unlikely that this pattern of persistence can be altered except through strenuous and probably costly measures. Apparently, external direct investments in extractive export industries, although creating "high productivity islands,"[25] weaken prospects for autonomous advance in the domestic economy along a number of lines. Induced expansion, through international or interregional trade based on export commodities, has not been accompanied by the domestic diversification essential to the creation of a forward momentum of growth. Technological progress remains narrowly confined, directed toward basic resources in demand for export, and relying heavily on technological borrowings from more advanced areas. Such technological change tends to prolong the persistence pattern, to increase the dependence of persistence areas, and to stress the fact that aggressive "national" policies are necessary if transformation is to become a reality rather than a vision.

In the foregoing, we have outlined the investment facet of the enterpreneurial function, and examined the climate of investment in terms of investment uncertainties. We have shown that initial phases of growth are characterized by the building of security zones or centers of investment; this occasions interaction between these centers and the margins or hinterlands of investment they promote; and this interaction, in turn, has consequences in persistence and transformation patterns of development. We shall now consider the relationship between technological change and the historical patterns which define the role that technology plays in different circumstances.

PATTERNS AND TECHNOLOGICAL CHANGE

"Persistence" has been identified with strong continuing institutional restraints on the course of technological change; "transformation," with autonomous investment and creative, innovational action on the technological front. This distinction enables us to review technological change in its "pattern" aspect.

The emphasis on historical cases of center-margin interaction has led to the neglect of more common instances of failure in this relationship. The assumption that, given time, margins would eventually achieve, under the stimulus of centers, a forward momentum of their own, was based on a belief in the strength of forces operative in transmitting growth from advanced to underdeveloped regions. This assumption was applicable to only a limited area of the nineteenth-century world economy; there are indications that these forces are even less powerfull now.[26] Preoccupations with the eighteenth-century British-dominated center-margin relationships, and with the repetition of this pattern in nineteenth-century development in the United States, probably have contributed causally to the failure to note the instances in which margins did not move into independent and more or less balanced forms of growth. "Transformation" happened only in uniquely favorable settings of investment—i.e., when entrepreneurship in the larger structure of center and margin functioned in secure environments, free from external pressures or serious internal tensions, and "uncertainties" were principally the risks encountered in "the ordinary conduct of business".[27] The actual occurrence of such freedom from the need for defensive strategies has been rare; but the few cases of it still influence much of our thinking about long-term change. It is significant that even the most favored areas of the past, when confronted with the uncertainties induced by rapid technological change and the appearance of new rivals in world markets, have shifted to a twentieth-century phase. In this, centralist tendencies in investment, and strong institutional forces working to induce technological change, suggest a return to a persistence pattern of growth. This is well under way in England, less advanced in the United States.[28]

As we have noted, this movement is not inconsistent with a satisfactory rate of growth. It does, however, have important implications for the relationships outlined in this paper. A pronounced shift to routinized technological change, and a hardening of the institutional framework in which such change proceeds, add new dimensions to the problem of inducing the active center-margin relations so crucial to economic development on a world scale. In the past, persistence areas, like Spain and eighteenth-century France, failed to promote dynamic margins of investment. There are few signs that twentieth-century powers have been much more successful in their relations with underdeveloped areas. In this respect, the past failures of margins to move into more active relationships with advanced areas of enterprise have valuable lessons for the present. When strong and persisting uncertainties invoke defensive, conservative reactions in the politico-economic sphere, and collectivist or group response in investment, then established institutions tighten their control, and technological changes reflect the "induced" investment characteristics of such patterns.

It is significant that transformation has assumed a new aspect in this century.[29] Japan and the Soviet Union provide illustrations of patterns in which investment strategies are directed toward achieving, by design, the ends that "came naturally" to the Anglo-Americans. Technological advance in key sectors of industry has been harnessed to the national interest, and spectacular gains have ensued. The ensuing progress has then given rise to uncertainties rooted in the cumulative and unpredictable effects of technological progress, in its impact on existing structures of control, and in its threats to rival powers. The enormously productive technical apparatus of advanced economies exerts a heavy pressure for institutional change, and causes tensions which are resolved more easily by external expansion than by internal adjustments. If the pressure to expand were to effect a widening area of dynamic center-margin interaction, a general rise in national incomes and living standards could be expected to occur as margins took on "a life of their own." This form of interaction does not seem to be emerging in our time. Marginal areas, confronting the expansive power of aggressive centers, have tended to stress the kind of defensive tactics characteristics of persistence patterns—in a world in which no power structures appear to be capable of sponsoring free margins in nineteenth-century style. In other words, there is little evidence that transformation in present persistence areas can be effected by rival centers—which are themselves under heavy pressure. Successful marginal reaction to the stimulus of centers rests, rather, on the rise of "native" entrepreneurial groups able to build their own security zones of investment. In the absence of such entrepreneurship, the action of modern centers is more likely to strengthen than to displace or weaken the established institutions of persistence areas.

The technological advances of the present, and their widespread effects, appear to confirm the old cliché that men make history but seldom know what they are doing in the process. Massive investment, with its dynamic, shaping impact, causes a rate and momentum of technological change that are productive of threats to institutional stability and to the leadership of the groups which set the process in motion. Such pressures can be temporarily reduced by an overflow of capital and goods into marginal areas. However, unless the latter then develop their own centers of entrepreneurial initiative, the sheer weight of technological advance invariably must create increasing tensions and a climate of political and economic uncertainty in which centralist, politically oriented action assumes progressively more importance. We find the dynamics of change in technological progress; but to tame its explosive tendencies without causing a sharp deceleration in the rate of change, we must have a better understanding of the historical role of technology than we now possess. This is only one facet of the complex interplay of variables over the long period. Since it cannot be treated in isolation, the use of a historical model, involving a limited number of relatively simple concepts, has been suggested as a feasible approach to the study of interrelationships over time. Entrepreneurial investment, both induced and autonomous, and uncertainty response, are limited concepts which serve only to start us on our investigations. However, applied in the comparative study of historical cases, they are useful tools for examining the rise of security zones of investment in diverse instances, the subsequent interplay of centers and their margins, and the consequent patterns of development.

In this inquiry, the initial phases of development—those in which security zones are built and in which entrepreneurs advance by investment strategies which may range over the spectrum of human action—are stressed. This is scarcely a neglected area of historical investigation; but for the most past, these phases have not been integrated or correlated with the study of economic development. We maintain that paying closer attention to the rise of centers and to their relationships with relevant margins would be valuable for a unified treatment of long-term change. Although considerations of space have severely limited our reference to historical evidence concerning the nature and timing of center-margin interactions, it is clear that they have crucial implications for the changing role of technology. These interactions have been mentioned in relation to contrasting patterns of development—i.e., those of persistence and of transformation, whether "classical" or twentieth-century style. Demonstrably, the more or less evolutionary expansion of the North Atlantic economy until 1860, for example, has given way, in the face of the overriding uncertainties of the present, to an emphasis on collectivist or centralist action in investment, particularly in the area of developmental research.[30] The almost explosive force now imparted to technological change, its momentum, weight, and unpredictability, produce new uncertainties in which both centers and margins are involved. Thus, new dimensions have been added to the problem of maintaining or encouraging a satisfactory rate of development, in a world in which power politics outweigh purely economic considerations. Whether technological progress will tend to strengthen established institutions, or whether it will conduce to transformation in which centers interact with dynamic margins, is a question which must rest with investment strategies now operative on a global scale.

NOTES TO CHAPTER 3

1. For a brilliant treatment of this theme, see R. L. Meier, "Information, Resource Use, and Economic Growth," a paper read at the Conference on National Resources and Economic Growth, at Ann Arbor, Michigan, April, 1960. (Mimeographed. Social Science Research Council: Resources for the Future Inc.)

2. J. E. Sawyer, "Entrepreneurial Studies: Perspectives and Directives, 1945-1958," *The Business History Review* (Winter, 1958), pp. 439-43; see also his *"Entrepreneurship in Periods of Rapid Growth," Entrepreneurship and Economic Growth* (Cambridge, Mass., 1954), pp. C1-C7.

3. A. J. Youngson, "The Disaggregation of Investment in the Study of Economic Growth," *Economic Journal* (June, 1956), pp. 236-43; *idem, Possibilities of Economic Progress* (Cambridge, 1959), chaps. iv-v; also A. O. Hirschman, *The Strategy of Economic Development* (New Haven, Conn., 1958), chaps. i-iii.

4. "Growth" as an aspect of development has reference chiefly to situations in which structural change is absent or slow and investment channels are more or less set, and where there are sufficient regularities in change to permit statistical and theoretical investigation to proceed with a minimum of historical sophistication. "Developmental situations," on the other hand, involve the complex interrelations of long-term change and cannot be "boxed" in growth theory. The economic historian has yet to come to terms with the incursions of theorists concerned with economic change but working largely in isolation from conventional economic history. Carter Goodrich raises this problem in his paper, "Economic History: One Field or Two?," *Journal of Economic History* (December, 1960), pp. 531-538.

5. See below, "Security Zones—center-margin Interaction—Patterns of Change."

6. See my "Climate of Enterprise," *Papers and Proceedings, American Economic Review* (May, 1949), pp. 322-35, and "Uncertainty and Economic Change," *Journal of Economic History* (September, 1954), pp. 346-60, for exploratory remarks on the historical aspect of uncertainty. Hans Selye's observations on specific response to "non-specifically induced" stress have much in common with this emphasis on response to uncertainties: see his *The Stress of Life* (New York, 1956), chap. vii.

7. See G. L. S. Shackle, *Time in Economics* (Amsterdam, 1958).

8. See H. A. Simon, "The Role of Expectations in an Adaptive or Behavioristic

Model," *Expectations, Uncertainty and Business Behaviour,* ed. M. J. Bowman (New York, 1958), p. 55.

9. On staple development in Canada, see R. E. Caves and R. H. Holton, *The Canadian Economy, Prospect and Retrospect* (Cambridge, Mass., 1959), chap. ii.

10. See B. F. Hoselitz, "Patterns of Economic Growth," *Canadian Journal of Economics and Political Science* (November, 1955), pp. 420-22.

11. See L. J. Zimmerman, *The Propensity to Monopolize* (Amsterdam, 1952).

12. Terms used by Carter Goodrich, *op. cit.*

13. See J. S. M. Careless, "Frontierism, Metropolitanism and Canadian History," *Canadian Historical Review* (March, 1954), pp. 1-21, for a discussion of the frontier thesis; also M. Zaslow, "The Frontier Hypothesis in Canadian Historiography," *Canadian Historical Review* (June, 1958), pp. 153-66.

14. See Youngson, *Possibilities of Economic Progress,* Part II; also G. M. Meier and R. E. Baldwin, *Economic Development* (New York, 1957), Part II.

15. The only meaning that I can attach to "self-sustaining" is that of a continuing and successful response to uncertainties, which, it seems to be assumed, are more easily met in progressive economies.

16. See G. Myrdal, *Economic Theory and Underdeveloped Regions* (London, 1957), chap. iii; also Hirschman, *op. cit.,* p. 187.

17. See H. J. Aitken, "Defensive Expansionism: The State and Economic Growth in Canada, *The State and Economic Growth,* ed. H. J. Aitken (New York, 1959), pp. 79-114.

18. See F. Thistlethwaite, *The Great Experiment* (Cambridge, 1955), chap. iv.

19. B. Bailyn, "Communications and Trade: the Atlantic in the Seventeenth Century," *Journal of Economic History* (Fall, 1953), pp. 378-87; and *The New England Merchants in the Seventeenth Century* (Cambridge, Mass., 1955).

20. See D. C. North, "Investment Capital Flows and the Development of the American West," *Journal of Economic History* (December, 1956), pp. 493-505.

21. Urban development in the West underlines this contrast. For example, Winnipeg—a western city and distribution point for eastern products—exhibits, in its history, little of the aggressive free enterprise of Chicago.

22. See Carter Goodrich *Government Promotion of American Canals and Railroads, 1800-1890* (New York, 1960).

23. See D. F. Dowd, "Comparative Analysis of Economic Development in the American West and South," *Journal of Economic History* (December, 1956), pp. 558-74.

24. On recent developments in the South, see B. U. Ratchford, "Patterns of Economic Development," *Southern Economic Journal* (January, 1954), p. 171.

25. R. Nurkse, "The Conflict between 'Balanced Growth' and International Specialisation," *Lectures on Economic Development* (Istanbul, 1958), p. 171.

26. *Ibid.,* p. 177.

27. See W. P. Strassman, *Risk and Technological Innovation* (Ithaca, N.Y., 1959), chap. vi.

28. See T. C. Cochran, *The American Business System, A Historical Perspective, 1900-55* (Cambridge, Mass., 1957), chap. ix-x.

29. A. Gerschenkron describes a mid-nineteenth-century example of this transformation in French economic history; see his "Economic Backwardness in Historical Perspective," *The Progress of Underdeveloped Areas,* ed. B. F. Hoselitz, Chicago, 1951), pp. 9-12. See also B. F. Hoselitz, "Entrepreneurship and Capital Formation in France and Britain since 1700," *Capital Formation and Economic Growth* (Princeton, N.J., 1955), pp. 304-11.

30. See the papers presented by Burton H. Klein, Irving H. Siegel, and Richard R. Nelson, at the Conference on the Economic and Social Factors Determining the Rate and Direction of Inventive Activity, May 12-14, 1960. (Mimeographed. National Bureau of Economic Research, New York.)

CHAPTER 4

The Achievement Motive in Economic Growth [1]

DAVID C. McCLELLAND

Harvard University

From the beginning of recorded history, men have been fascinated by the fact that civilizations rise and fall. Culture growth, as Kroeber has demonstrated, is episodic, and sometimes occurs in quite different fields.[2] For example, the people living in the Italian peninsula at the time of ancient Rome produced a great civilization of law, politics, and military conquest; and at another time, during the Renaissance, the inhabitants of Italy produced a great civilization of art, music, letters, and science. What can account for such cultural flowerings? In our time we have theorists like Huntington, who stresses the importance of climate, or Toynbee, who also feels the right amount of challenge from the environment is crucial though he conceives of the environment as including its psychic effects. Others, like Kroeber, have difficulty imagining any general explanation; they perforce must accept the notion that a particular culture happens to hit on a particularly happy mode of self-expression, which it then pursues until it becomes overspecialized and sterile.

My concern is not with all culture growth, but with economic growth. Some wealth or leisure may be essential to development in other fields—the arts, politics, science, or war—but we need not insist on it. However, the question of why some countries develop rapidly in the economic sphere at certain times and not at others is in itself of great interest, whatever its relation to other types of culture growth. Usually, rapid economic growth has been explained in terms of "external" factors—favorable opportunities for trade, unusual natural resources, or conquests that have opened up new markets or produced internal political stability. But I am interested in the *internal* factors—in the values and motives men have that lead them to exploit opportunities, to take advantage of favorable trade conditions; in short, to shape their own destiny.

This interest is not surprising; I am a psychologist—and, furthermore, a psychologist whose primary research interest is in human motivation, in

74

the *reasons* that people behave as they do. Of course, all people have always, to a certain extent, been interested in human motivation. The difference between their interest and the twentieth-century psychologist's interest is that the latter tries to define his subject matter very precisely and, like all scientists, to measure it. How can human motives be identified, or even measured? Psychologists' favorite techniques for conducting research in this area have always been the interview and the questionnaire. If you want to know what a man's motives are, ask him. Of course, you need not ask him directly; but perhaps, if you talk to him long enough in an interview, or ask him enough in a questionnaire, you can infer what his motives are—more or less the same way that, from a number of clues, a detective would infer who had committed a crime.

Whatever else one thinks of Freud and the other psychoanalysts, they performed one extremely important service for psychology: once and for all, they persuaded us, rightly or wrongly, that what people said about their motives was not a reliable basis for determining what those motives really were. In his analyses of the psychopathology of everyday life and of dreams and neurotic symptoms, Freud demonstrated repeatedly that the "obvious" motives—the motives that the people themselves thought they had or that a reasonable observer would attribute to them—were not, in fact, the real motives for their often strange behavior. By the same token, Freud also showed the way to a better method of learning what people's motives were. He analyzed dreams and free associations: in short, fantasy or imaginative behavior. Stripped of its air of mystery and the occult, psychoanalysis has taught us that one can learn a great deal about people's motives through observing the things about which they are spontaneously concerned in their dreams and waking fantasies. About ten or twelve years ago, the research group in America with which I was connected decided to take this insight quite seriously and to see what we could learn about human motivation by coding objectively what people spontaneously thought about in their waking fantasies.[3]   Our method was to collect such free fantasy, in the form of brief stories written about pictures, and to count the frequency with which certain themes appeared—rather as a medical technician counts the frequency with which red or white corpuscles appear in a blood sample. We were able to demonstrate that the frequency with which certain "inner concerns" appeared in these fantasies varied systematically as a function of specific experimental conditions by which we aroused or induced motivational states in the subjects. Eventually, we were able to isolate several of these inner concerns, or motives, which, if present in great frequency in the fantasies of a particular person, enabled us to know something about how he would behave in many other areas of life.

Chief among these motives was what we termed "the need for Achievement" (*n* Achievement)—a desire to do well, not so much for the sake of social recognition or prestige, but to attain an inner feeling of personal accomplishment. This motive is my particular concern in this paper. Our early laboratory studies showed that people "high" in *n* Achievement tend to work harder at certain tasks; to learn faster; to do their best work when it counts for the record, and not when special incentives, like money prizes, are introduced; to choose experts over friends as working partners; etc. Obviously, we cannot here review the many, many studies in this area. About five years ago, we became especially interested in the problem of what would happen in a society if a large number of people with a high need for achievement should happen to be present in it at a particular time. In others words, we became interested in a social-psychological question: What effect would a concentration of people with high *n* Achievement have on a society?

It might be relevant to describe how we began wondering about this. I had always been greatly impressed by the very perceptive analysis of the connection between Protestantism and the spirit of capitalism made by the great German sociologist, Max Weber.[4] He argues that the distinguishing characteristic of Protestant business entrepreneurs and of workers, particularly from the pietistic sects, was not that they had in any sense invented the institutions of capitalism or good craftmanship, but that they went about their jobs with a new perfectionist spirit. The Calvinistic doctrine of predestination had forced them to rationalize every aspect of their lives and to strive hard for perfection in the positions in this world to which they had been assigned by God. As I read Weber's description of the behavior of these people, I concluded that they must certainly have had a high level of *n* Achievement. Perhaps the new spirit of capitalism Weber describes was none other than a high need for achievement—if so, then *n* Achievement has been responsible, in part, for the extraordinary economic development of the West. Another factor served to confirm this hypothesis. A careful study by Winterbottom had shown that boys with high *n* Achievement usually came from families in which the mothers stressed early self-reliance and mastery.[5] The boys whose mothers did *not* encourage their early self-reliance, or did not set such high standards of excellence, tended to develop lower need for achievement. Obviously, one of the key characteristics of the Protestant Reformation was its emphasis on self-reliance. Luther stressed the "priesthood of all believers" and translated the Bible so that every man could have direct access to God and religious thought. Calvin accentuated a rationalized perfection in this life for everyone. Certainly, the character of the Reformation seems to have set the stage, historically, for parents to encourage their children to attain earlier self-reliance and achievement. If the parents did in fact do so, they very possibly unintentionally pro-

76

level in English history (as determined on the basis of dramas, sea captains' letters, and street ballads) rose, between 1400–1800, *twice*, a generation or two before waves of accelerated economic growth (incidentally, at times of Protestant revival). This point is significant because it shows that there is no "necessary" steady decline in a civilization's entrepreneurial energy from its earlier to its later periods. In the Spanish and English cases, as in the Greek, high levels of *n* Achievement preceded economic decline. Unfortunately, space limitations preclude more detailed discussion of these studies here.

We also tested the hypothesis by applying it to preliterate cultures of the sort that anthropologists investigate. At Yale University, an organized effort has been made to collect everything that is known about all the primitive tribes that have been studied and to classify the information systematically for comparative purposes. We utilized this cross-cultural file to obtain the two measures that we needed to test our general hypothesis. For over fifty of these cultures, collections of folk tales existed that Child and others had coded,[9] just as we coded literary documents and individual imaginative stories, for *n* Achievement and other motives. These folk tales have the character of fantasy that we believe to be so essential for getting at "inner concerns." In the meantime, we were searching for a method of classifying the economic development of these cultures, so that we could determine whether those evincing high *n* Achievement in their folk tales had developed further than those showing lower *n* Achievement. The respective modes of gaining a livelihood were naturally very different in these cultures, since they came from every continent in the world and every type of physical habitat; yet we had to find a measure for comparing them. We finally thought of trying to estimate the number of full-time "business entrepreneurs" there were among the adults in each culture. We defined "entrepreneur" as "anyone who exercises control over the means of production and produces more than he can consume in order to sell it for individual or household income." Thus an entrepreneur was anyone who derived at least seventy-five per cent of his income from such exchange or market practices. The entrepreneurs were mostly traders, independent artisans, or operators of small firms like stores, inns, etc. Nineteen cultures were classified as high in *n* Achievement on the basis of their folk tales; seventy-four per cent of them contained some entrepreneurs. On the other hand, only thirty-five per cent of the twenty cultures that were classified as low in *n* Achievement contained any entrepreneurs (as we defined it) at all. The difference is highly significant statistically (Chi-square = 5.97, p < .02). Hence data about primitive tribes seem to confirm the hypothesis that high *n* Achievement leads to a more advanced type of economic activity.

But what about modern nations? Can we estimate their level of *n* Achievement and relate it to their economic development? The question is obviously one of the greatest importance, but the technical problems of getting measures of our two variables proved to be really formidable. What type of literary document could we use that would be equally representative of the motivational levels of people in India, Japan, Portugal, Germany, the United States, and Italy? We had discovered in our historical studies that certain types of literature usually contain much more achievement imagery than others. This is not too serious as long as we are dealing with time changes within a given culture; but it is very serious if we want to compare two cultures, each of which may express its achievement motivation in a different literary form. At least, we decided to use children's stories, for several reasons. They exist in standard form in every modern nation, since all modern nations are involved in teaching their children to read and use brief stories for this purpose. Furthermore, the stories are imaginative; and, if selected from those used in the earliest grades, they are not often influenced by temporary political events. (We were most impressed by this when reading the stories that every Russian child reads. In general, they cannot be distinguished, in style and content, from the stories read in all the countries of the West.)

We collected children's readers for the second, third, and fourth grades from every country where they could be found for two time periods, which were roughly centered around 1925 and around 1950. We got some thirteen hundred stories, which were all translated into English. In all, we had twenty-one stories from each of twenty-three countries about 1925, and the same number from each of thirty-nine countries about 1950. Code was used on proper names, so that our scorers would not know the national origins of the stories. The tales were then mixed together, and coded for *n* Achievement (and certain other motives and values that I shall mention only briefly).

The next task was to find a measure of economic development. Again, the problem was to insure comparability. Some countries have much greater natural resources; some have developed industrially sooner than others; some concentrate in one area of production and some in another. Economists consider national income figures in per capita terms to be the best measure available; but they are difficult to obtain for all countries, and it is hard to translate them into equal purchasing power. Ultimately, we came to rely chiefly on the measure of electricity produced: the units of measurement are the same all over the world; the figures are available from the 1920's on; and electricity is the *form* of energy (regardless of how it is produced) that is essential to modern economic development. In fact, electricity produced per capita correlates with estimates of income per capita in the 1950's around .90 anyway. To equate for differences in natural resources, such as the amount of water power

80

available, etc., we studied *gains* in kilowatt hours produced per capita between 1925 and 1950. The level of electrical production in 1925 is, as one would expect, highly correlated with the size of the gain between then and 1950. So it was necessary to resort to a regression analysis; that is, to calculate, from the average regression of gain on level for all countries, how much gain a particular country should have shown between 1925 and 1950. The actual gain could then be compared with the expected gain, and the country could be classified as gaining more or less rapidly than would have been expected on the basis of its 1925 performance. The procedure is directly comparable to what we do when we predict, on the basis of some measure of I.Q., what grades a child can be expected to get in school, and then classify him as an "under-" or "over-achiever."

The correlation between the *n* Achievement level in the children's readers in 1925 and the growth in electrical output between 1925 and 1950, as compared with expectation, is a quite substantial .53, which is highly significant statistically. It could hardly have arisen by chance. Furthermore, the correlation is also substantial with a measure of gain over the expected in per capita income, equated for purchasing power by Colin Clark. To check this result more definitively with the sample of forty countries for which we had reader estimates of *n* Achievement levels in 1950, we computed the equation for gains in electrical output in 1952–1958 as a function of level in 1952. It turned out to be remarkably linear when translated into logarithmic units, as is so often the case with simple growth functions. Table 2 presents the performance of each of the countries, as compared with predictions from initial level in 1952, in standard score units and classified by high and low *n* Achievement in 1950. Once again we found that *n* Achievement levels predicted significantly ($r = .43$) the countries which would perform more or less rapidly than expected in terms of the average for all countries. The finding is more striking than the earlier one, because many Communist and under-developed countries are included in the sample. Apparently, *n* Achievement is a precursor of economic growth—and not only in the Western style of capitalism based on the small entrepreneur, but also in economies controlled and fostered largely by the state.

For those who believe in economic determinism, it is especially interesting that *n* Achievement level in 1950 is *not* correlated either with *previous* economic growth between 1925 and 1950, or with the level of prosperity in 1950. This strongly suggests that *n* Achievement is a *causative* factor—a change in the minds of men which produces economic growth rather than being produced by it. In a century dominated by economic determinism, in both Communist and Western thought, it is startling to find concrete evidence for psychological determinism, for

81

TABLE 2

Rate of growth in electrical output (1952–1958) and national n Achievement levels in 1950

DEVIATION FROM EXPECTED GROWTH RATE*
IN STANDARD SCORE UNITS

National n Achievement levels (1950) †	Above expectation		Below expectation
High n Achievement			
3.62 Turkey	+1.38		
2.71 India ‡	+1.12		
2.38 Australia	+ .42		
2.32 Israel	+1.18		
2.33 Spain	+ .01		
2.29 Pakistan §	+2.75		
2.29 Greece	+1.18	3.38 Argentina	— .56
2.29 Canada	+ .08	2.71 Lebanon	— .67
2.24 Bulgaria	+1.37	2.38 France	— .24
2.24 U.S.A.	+ .47	2.33 U. So. Africa	— .06
2.14 West Germany	+ .53	2.29 Ireland	— .41
2.10 U.S.S.R.	+1.61	2.14 Tunisia	—1.87
2.10 Portugal	+ .76	2.10 Syria	— .25
Low n Achievement			
1.95 Iraq	+ .29	2.05 New Zealand	— .29
1.86 Austria	+ .38	1.86 Uruguay	— .75
1.67 U.K.	+ .17	1.81 Hungary	— .62
1.57 Mexico	+ .12	1.71 Norway	— .77
.86 Poland	+1.26	1.62 Sweden	— .64
		1.52 Finland	— .08
		1.48 Netherlands	— .15
		1.33 Italy	— .57
		1.29 Japan	— .04
		1.20 Switzerland #	—1.92
		1.19 Chile	—1.81
Correlation of n Achievement		1.05 Denmark	— .89
level (1950) x deviations from		.57 Algeria	— .83
expected growth rate = .43, p <.01.		.43 Belgium	—1.65

* The estimates are computed from the monthly average electrical production figures, in millions of Kwh, for 1952 and 1958, from United Nations, *Monthly Bulletin of Statistics* (January, 1960), and *World Energy Supplies,* 1951-1954 and 1955-1958, (Statistical Papers, Series J).

The correlation between log level 1952 and log gain 1952-58 is .976.

The regression equation based on these thirty-nine countries, plus four others from the same climatic zone on which data are available (China-Taiwan, Czechoslovakia, Rumania, Yugoslavia), is: log gain (1952-58) = .9229 **log** level (1952) + .0480.

Standard scores are deviations from mean gain predicted by the regression

82

psychological developments as preceding and presumably causing economic changes.

The many interesting results which our study of children's stories yielded have succeeded in convincing me that we chose the right material to analyze. Apparently, adults unconsciously flavor their stories for young children with the attitudes, the aspirations, the values, and the motives that they hold to be most important.

I want to mention briefly two other findings, one concerned with economic development, the other with totalitarianism. When the more and less rapidly developing economies are compared on all the other variables for which we scored the children's stories, one fact stands out. In stories from those countries which had developed more rapidly in both the earlier and later periods, there was a discernible tendency to emphasize, in 1925 and in 1950, what David Riesman has called "other-directedness"—namely, reliance on the opinion of particular others, rather than on tradition, for guidance in social behavior.[10] *Public opinion* had, in these countries, become a major source of guidance for the individual. Those countries which had developed the mass media further and faster —the press, the radio, the public-address system—were also the ones who were developing more rapidly economically. I think that "other-directedness" helped these countries to develop more rapidly because public opinion is basically more flexible than institutionalized moral or social traditions. Authorities can utilize it to inform people widely about the need for new ways of doing things. However, traditional institutionalized values may insist that people go on behaving in ways that are no longer adaptive to a changed social and economic order.

The other finding is not directly relevant to economic development, but it perhaps involves the means of achieving it. Quite unexpectedly, we discovered that every major dictatorial regime which came to power between the 1920's and 1950's (with the possible exception of Portugal's) was foreshadowed by a particular motive pattern in its stories for children: namely, a low need for affiliation (little interest in friendly relationships with people) and a high need for power (a great concern over controlling and influencing other people).

---

formula ($M = -.01831$) divided by the standard deviation of the deviations from mean predicted gain ($SD = .159$).

† Based on twenty-one children's stories from second-, third-, and fourth-grade readers in each country.

‡ Based on six Hindi, seven Telegu, and eight Tamil stories.

§ Based on twelve Urdu and eleven Bengali stories.

Based on twenty-one German Swiss stories, mean = .91; twenty-one French Swiss stories, mean = 1.71; over-all mean obtained by weighting German mean double to give approximately proportionate representation to the two main ethnic population groups.

The German readers showed this pattern before Hitler; the Japanese readers, before Tojo; the Argentine readers, before Peron; the Spanish readers, before Franco; the South African readers, before the present authoritarian government in South Africa; etc. On the other hand, very few countries which did not have dictatorships manifested this particular motive combination. The difference was highly significant statistically, since there was only one exception in the first instance and very few in the second. Apparently, we stumbled on a psychological index of ruthlessness—i.e., the need to influence other people (n Power), unchecked by sufficient concern for their welfare (n Affiliation). It is interesting, and a little disturbing, to discover that the German readers of today still evince this particular combination of motives, just as they did in 1925. Let us hope that this is one case where a social science generalization will not be confirmed by the appearance of a totalitarian regime in Germany in the next ten years.

To return to our main theme—let us discuss the precise ways that higher n Achievement leads to more rapid economic development, and why it should lead to economic development rather than, for example, to military or artistic development. We must consider in more detail the mechanism by which the concentration of a particular type of human motive in a population leads to a complex social phenomenon like economic growth. The link between the two social phenomena is, obviously, the business entrepreneur. I am not using the term "entrepreneur" in the sense of "capitalist": in fact, I should like to divorce "entrepreneur" entirely from any connotations of ownership. An entrepreneur is someone who exercises control over production that is not just for his personal consumption. According to my definition, for example, an executive in a steel production unit in Russia is an entrepreneur.

It was Joseph Schumpeter who drew the attention of economists to the importance that the activity of these entrepreneurs had in creating industrialization in the West. Their vigorous endeavors put together firms and created productive units where there had been none before. In the beginning, at least, the entrepreneurs often collected material resources, organized a production unit to combine the resources into a new product, and sold the product. Until recently, nearly all economists—including not only Marx, but also Western classical economists—assumed that these men were moved primarily by the "profit motive." We are all familiar with the Marxian argument that they were so driven by their desire for profits that they exploited the workingman and ultimately forced him to revolt. Recently, economic historians have been studying the actual lives of such entrepreneurs and finding—certainly to the surprise of some of the investigators—that many of them seemingly were not interested in making money as such. In psychological terms, at least,

84

Marx's picture is slightly out of focus. Had these entrepreneurs been above all interested in money, many more of them would have quit working as soon as they had made all the money that they could possibly use. They would not have continued to risk their money in further entrepreneurial ventures. Many of them, in fact, came from pietistic sects, like the Quakers in England, that prohibited the enjoyment of wealth in any of the ways cultivated so successfully by some members of the European nobility. However, the entrepreneurs often seemed consciously to be greatly concerned with expanding their businesses, with getting a greater share of the market, with "conquering brute nature," or even with altruistic schemes for bettering the lot of mankind or bringing about the kingdom of God on earth more rapidly. Such desires have frequently enough been labeled as hypocritical. However, if we assume that these men were really motivated by a desire for achievement rather than by a desire for money as such, the label no longer fits. This assumption also simplifies further matters considerably. It provides an explanation for the fact that these entrepreneurs were interested in money without wanting it for its own sake, namely, that money served as a ready quantitative index of how well they were doing—e.g., of how much they had achieved by their efforts over the past year. The need to achieve can never be satisfied by money; but estimates of profitability in money terms can supply direct knowledge of how well one is doing one's job.

The brief consideration of the lives of business entrepreneurs of the past suggested that their chief motive may well have been a high n Achievement. What evidence have we found in support of this? We made two approaches to the problem. First, we attempted to determine whether individuals with high n Achievement behave like entrepreneurs; and second, we investigated to learn whether actual entrepreneurs, particularly the more successful ones, in a number of countries, have higher n Achievement than do other people of roughly the same status. Of course, we had to establish what we meant by "behave like entrepreneurs"—what precisely distinguishes the way an entrepreneur behaves from the way other people behave?

The adequate answers to these questions would entail a long discussion of the sociology of occupations, involving the distinction originally made by Max Weber between capitalists and bureaucrats. Since this cannot be done here, a very brief report on our extensive investigations in this area will have to suffice. First, one of the defining characteristics of an entrepreneur is *taking risks* and/or innovating. A person who adds up a column of figures is not an entrepreneur—however carefully, efficiently, or correctly he adds them. He is simply following established rules. However, a man who decides to add a new line to his business *is* an entrepreneur, in that he cannot know in advance whether his decision will be correct. Nevertheless, he does not feel that he is in the position of a gambler who places some money on the turn of a card. Knowledge, judgment, and skill enter into his decision-making; and, if his choice is justified by future developments, he can certainly feel a sense of personal achievement from having made a successful move.

Therefore, if people with high n Achievement are to behave in an entrepreneurial way, they must seek out and perform in situations in which there is some moderate risk of failure—a risk which can, presumably, be reduced by increased effort or skill. They should not work harder than other people at routine tasks, or perform functions which they are certain to do well simply by doing what everyone accepts as the correct traditional thing to do. On the other hand, they should avoid gambling situations, because, even if they win, they can receive no sense of personal achievement, since it was not skill but luck that produced the results. (And, of course, most of the time they would lose, which would be highly unpleasant to them.) The data on this point are very clear-cut. We have repeatedly found, for example, that boys with high n Achievement choose to play games of skill that incorporate a moderate risk of failure. Table 3 represents one study. The game was adapted from one used by the psychologist Kurt Lewin. Each child was given a rope ring and told that he could stand at any distance that he preferred from the peg, to try to throw the ring over the peg. The children with high n Achievement usually stood at middle distances from the peg, where the chances of success or failure were moderate. However, the children with low n Achievement evinced no particular preference for any position. They more frequently stood at extremes of distance—either very close to the peg, where they were sure to throw the ring over it, or very far away, where they were almost certain not to. They thus manifested behavior like that of many people in underdeveloped countries who, while they act very traditionally economically, at the same time love to indulge in lotteries—risking a little to make a great deal on a very long shot. In neither of the two last examples do the actors concentrate on the realistic *calculated* risk, as do the subjects with high n Achievement.

We have recently concluded a somewhat analogous study, which indicated that boys with high n Achievement tend to perform better and to work harder under conditions of moderate risk—boys not only in the United States, but also in Japan, Brazil, and India. In each of these countries, the boys with high n Achievement did not invariably perform a laboratory task better than the boys with low n Achievement. They did better only under conditions involving some degree of competition, some risk of doing worse than others or of not getting a sense of personal achievement. There was still another group of boys in the sample from each country. These boys were identified by their optimistic attitude

86

toward life in general, as manifested in their answers to a questionnaire. The members of these groups always had more success than the others, no matter what the competitive or risk situation was. I like to think of these boys as the conscientious ones, who will do their work cheerfully and efficiently under any kind of incentive conditions. They may form the backbone of the civil service, because they can tolerate routine; but they will not be the business entrepreneurs, because the latter constantly

TABLE 3

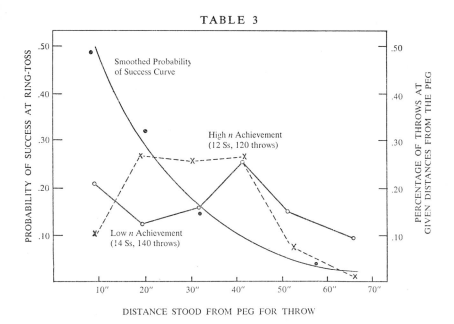

DISTANCE STOOD FROM PEG FOR THROW

Percentage of throws made by 5-year-olds with high and low 'doodle' n Achievement at different distances from the peg and smoothed curve of probability of success at those distances. 26 Ss, 10 throws each. Plotted at midpoints of intervals of 11 inches beginning with closest distance stood (4"–14", 5"–15", etc.)

seek situations in which they can obtain a sense of personal achievement from having overcome risks or difficulties.

Another quality that the entrepreneur seeks in his work is that his job be a kind that ordinarily provides him with accurate knowledge of the results of his decisions. As a rule, growth in sales, in output, or in profit margins tells him very precisely whether he has made the correct choice under uncertainty or not. Thus, the concern for profit enters in—profit is

87

a measure of success. We have repeatedly found that boys with a high *n* Achievement work more efficiently when they know how well they are doing. Also, they will not work harder for money rewards; but if they are asked, they state that greater money rewards should be awarded for accomplishing more difficult things in games of skill. In the ring-toss game, subjects were asked how much money they thought should be awarded for successful throws from different distances. Subjects with high *n* Achievement and those with low *n* Achievement agreed substantially about the amounts for throws made close to the peg. However, as the distance from the peg increased, the amounts awarded for successful throws by the subjects with high *n* Achievement rose more rapidly than did the rewards by those with low *n* Achievement. Here, as elsewhere, individuals with high *n* Achievement behaved as they must if they are to be the successful entrepreneurs in society. They believed that greater achievement should be recognized by quantitatively larger reward.

We are now investigating to learn whether business executives do, in fact, have higher *n* Achievement. Our analysis of this question is not yet finished; but Table 4 indicates what, on the whole, we shall probably find. Four conclusions can be drawn from it. (*1*) Entrepreneurs ("junior executives") have higher *n* Achievement than do a comparable group of non-entrepreneurs ("adjusters"), whose chief job was quasi-judicial (tax claim and insurance adjusters). A very careful study in the General Electric Company has confirmed this finding: on the average, production managers have higher *n* Achievement than do staff specialists of comparable education and pay. (*2*) The more successful junior executives have higher *n* Achievement than the less successful ones. (*3*) Turkish executives have a lower *average* level of *n* Achievement than American executives. This finding supports the general impression that the "entrepreneurial spirit" is in short supply in such countries. (*4*) Nevertheless, the more successful Turkish executives have a higher level of *n* Achievement than do the less successful ones. This confirms our prediction that *n* Achievement equips people peculiarly for the business executive role—even in a country like Turkey, where business traditions are quite different from those of the West.

There are two successful, and one unsuccessful, methods by which the business community recruits people with the "entrepreneurial spirit"—with high *n* Achievement. The unsuccessful way is easiest to describe and is still characteristic of many underdeveloped countries. In a study of the occupational likes and dislikes of boys in Japan, Brazil, Germany, India, and the United States, we found that (as Atkinson had predicted on theoretical grounds) the boys with high *n* Achievement usually aspire toward the occupation of highest prestige *which they have a reasonable chance to enter and to succeed*.[11] For example, their ambitions will be

TABLE 4

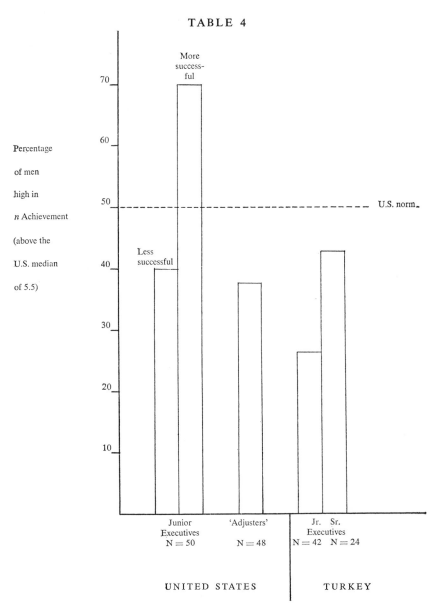

Percentages of Different Types of Executives
High in n Achievement in the U.S.A. and Turkey (after data supplied
by N. M. Bradburn)

centered on the professions, which are the highest prestige occupations in most countries—*if* the boys themselves are from the upper class and thus have the opportunity and backing to enter the professions. In other words, when the business leadership of a country is largely recruited from the élite (as it is in many countries, because only the élite has access to capital and to government), it will *not* tend to attract those with high n Achievement who are not from the upper class.

Developments in many of the Western democracies were quite different. In the most rapidly advancing countries, business leadership was drawn, at least in the early stages, largely from the middle classes. A business career was the highest prestige occupation to which a middle-class boy with high n Achievement could aspire—especially if he were a member of a disliked minority group, like the Protestants in France or the Jews in many countries, to whom other channels of upward mobility were closed. Thus a constant "natural" flow of entrepreneurial talent from the middle classes provided economic leadership of a high quality.

The other successful method of recruiting entrepreneurial talent is the one that has been adopted, for example, in the U.S.S.R. There, the central government took a severe, achievement-oriented, "pass-or-fail" attitude toward its plant managers, so that only the "fittest" survived. We believe that those "fittest" were the ones with the highest n Achievement, although we have no supporting evidence as yet. In the free enterprise system, the recruiting method may be compared to a garden in which all plants are allowed to grow until some crowd the others out. In the Soviet system, it is comparable to a garden in which plants that have not reached a specified height by a certain time are weeded out. In many underdeveloped countries, it is comparable to a garden where only certain plants are permitted to live in the first place, so that the gardener has to take them whatever size they attain. Of course, no country represents a pure type; but perhaps the analogy, oversimplified though it is, helps to illustrate my point.

What produces high n Achievement? Why do some societies produce a large number of people with this motive, while other societies produce so many fewer? We conducted long series of researches into this question. I can present only a few here.

One very important finding is essentially a negative one: n Achievement cannot be hereditary. Popular psychology has long maintained that some races are more energetic than others. Our data clearly contradict this in connection with n Achievement. The changes in n Achievement level within a given population are too rapid to be attributed to heredity. For example, the correlation between respective n Achievement levels in the 1925 and 1950 samples of readers is substantially zero. Many of the countries that were high in n Achievement at one or both times may be

90

low or moderate in n Achievement now, and vice versa. Germany was low in 1925 and is high now; and certainly the hereditary makeup of the German nation has not changed in a generation.

However, there is substantiating evidence that n Achievement is a motive which a child can acquire quite early in life, say, by the age of eight or ten, as a result of the way his parents have brought him up. Winterbottom's study of the importance of early self-reliance and achieve-

TABLE 5

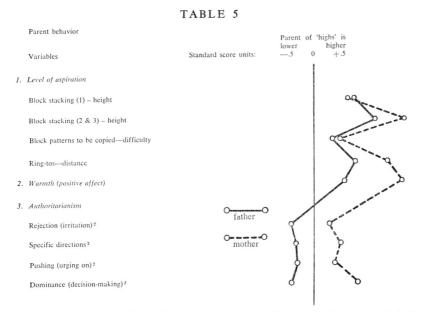

Mean differences in the behavior of parents of sons with low and high
n Achievement working in task situations [1]

ment training has been supplemented by a much more detailed inquiry by Rosen and D'Andrade.[12] They actually entered the homes of boys with high and low n Achievement and observed how the boys were treated by their parents while they were engaged in various kinds of work, e.g., stacking blocks blindfolded. The principal results are summarized in Table 5, which indicates the differences between the parents of the "high n Achievement boys" and the parents of boys with low n Achievement. In general, the mothers and the fathers of the first group set higher levels of aspiration in a number of tasks for their sons. They were also much

[1] After Rosen and D'Andrade.
[2] Parents of 'highs' predicted to be lower, permitting more independence.

91

warmer, showing positive emotion in reacting to their sons' performances. In the area of authority or dominance, the data are quite interesting. The mothers of the "highs" were more domineering than the mothers of the "lows," but the *fathers* of the "highs" were significantly *less* domineering than the fathers of the "lows". In other words, the fathers of the "highs" set high standards and are warmly interested in their sons' performances, but they do not directly interfere. This gives the boys the chance to develop initiative and self-reliance.

What factors cause parents to behave in this way? Their behavior certainly is involved with their values and, possibly, ultimately with their religion or their general world view. At present, we cannot be sure that Protestant parents are more likely to behave this way than Catholic parents—there are too many subgroup variations within each religious portion of the community: the Lutheran father is probably as likely to be authoritarian as the Catholic father. However, there does seem to be one crucial variable discernible: the extent to which the religion of the family emphasizes individual, as contrasted with ritual, contact with God. The preliterate tribes that we studied in which the religion was the kind that stressed the individual contact had higher n Achievement; and in general, mystical sects in which this kind of religious self-reliance dominates have had higher n Achievement.

The extent to which the authoritarian father is away from the home while the boy is growing up may prove to be another crucial variable. If so, then one incidental consequence of prolonged wars may be an increase in n Achievement, because the fathers are away too much to interfere with their sons' development of it. And in Turkey, Bradburn found that those boys tended to have higher n Achievement who had left home early or whose fathers had died before they were eighteen.[13] Slavery was another factor which played an important role in the past. It probably lowered n Achievement—in the slaves, for whom obedience and responsibility, but not achievement, were obvious virtues; and in the slave-owners, because household slaves were often disposed to spoil the owner's children as a means for improving their own positions. This is both a plausible and a probable reason for the drop in n Achievement level in ancient Greece that occurred at about the time the middle-class entrepreneur was first able to afford, and obtain by conquest, as many as two slaves for each child. The idea also clarifies the slow economic development of the South in the United States by attributing its dilatoriness to a lack of n Achievement in its élite; and it also indicates why lower-class American Negroes, who are closest to the slave tradition, possess very low n Achievement.[14]

I have outlined our research findings. Do they indicate ways of accelerating economic development? Increasing the level of n Achievement in a country suggests itself as an obvious first possibility. If n Achievement is so important, so specifically adapted to the business role, then it certainly should be raised in level, so that more young men have an "entrepreneurial drive." The difficulty in this excellent plan is that our studies of how n Achievement originates indicate that the family is the key formative influence; and it is very hard to change on a really large scale. To be sure, major historical events like wars have taken authoritarian fathers out of the home; and religious reform movements have sometimes converted the parents to a new achievement-oriented ideology. However, such matters are not ordinarily within the policy-making province of the agencies charged with speeding economic development.

Such agencies can, perhaps, effect the general acceptance of an achievement-oriented ideology as an absolute *sine qua non* of economic development. Furthermore, this ideology should be diffused not only in business and governmental circles, but throughout the nation, and in ways that will influence the thinking of all parents as they bring up their children. As Rosen and D'Andrade found, parents must, above all, set high standards for their children. The campaign to spread achievement-oriented ideology, if possible, could also incorporate an attack on the extreme authoritarianism in fathers that impedes or prevents the development of self-reliance in their sons. This is, however, a more delicate point, and attacking this, in many countries, would be to threaten values at the very center of social life. I believe that a more indirect approach would be more successful. One approach would be to take the boys out of the home and to camps. A more significant method would be to promote the rights of women, both legally and socially—one of the ways to undermine the absolute dominance of the male is to strengthen the rights of the female! Another reason for concentrating particularly on women is that they play the leading role in rearing the next generation. Yet, while men in underdeveloped countries come in contact with new achievement-oriented values and standards through their work, women may be left almost untouched by such influences. But if the sons are to have high n Achievement, the mothers must first be reached.

It may seem strange that a paper on economic development should discuss the importance of feminism and the way children are reared; but this is precisely where a psychological analysis leads. If the motives of men are the agents that influence the speed with which the economic machine operates, then the speed can be increased only through affecting the factors that create the motives. Furthermore—to state this point less theoretically —I cannot think of evinced substantial, rapid long-term economic development where women have not been somewhat freed from their traditional setting of "Kinder, Küche und Kirche" and allowed to play a more powerful role in society, specifically as part of the working force.

This generalization applies not only to the Western democracies like the United States, Sweden, or England, but also to the U.S.S.R., Japan, and now China.

In the present state of our knowledge, we can conceive of trying to raise n Achievement levels only in the next generation—although new research findings may soon indicate n Achievement in adults can be increased. Most economic planners, while accepting the long-range desirability of raising n Achievement in future generations, want to know what can be done during the next five or ten years. This immediacy inevitably focuses attention on the process or processes by which executives or entrepreneurs are selected. Foreigners with proved entrepreneurial drive can be hired, but at best this is a temporary and unsatisfactory solution. In most underdeveloped countries where government is playing a leading role in promoting economic development, it is clearly necessary for the government to adopt rigid achievement-oriented standards of performance like those in the U.S.S.R.[15] A government manager or, for that matter, a private entrepreneur, should have to produce "or else." Production targets must be set, as they are in most economic plans; and individuals must be held responsible for achieving them, even at the plant level. The philosophy should be one of "no excuses accepted." It is common for government officials or economic theorists in underdeveloped countries to be weighed down by all the difficulties which face the economy and render its rapid development difficult or impossible. They note that there is too rapid population growth, too little capital, too few technically competent people, etc. Such obstacles to growth are prevalent, and in many cases they are immensely hard to overcome; but talking about them can provide merely a comfortable rationalization for mediocre performance. It is difficult to fire an administrator, no matter how poor his performance, if so many objective reasons exist for his doing badly. Even worse, such rationalization permits, in the private sector, the continued employment of incompetent family members as executives. If these private firms were afraid of being penalized for poor performance, they might be impelled to find more able professional managers a little more quickly. I am not an expert in this field, and the mechanisms I am suggesting may be far from appropriate. Still, they may serve to illustrate my main point: if a country short in entrepreneurial talent wants to advance rapidly, it must find ways and means of insuring that only the most competent retain positions of responsibility. One of the obvious methods of doing so is to judge people in terms of their *performance*—and not according to their family or political connections, their skill in explaining why their unit failed to produce as expected, or their conscientiousness in following the rules. I would suggest the use of psychological tests as a means of selecting people with high n Achievement; but, to be perfectly frank, I think this approach is at present somewhat impractical on a large enough scale in most underdeveloped countries.

Finally, there is another approach which I think is promising for recruiting and developing more competent business leadership. It is the one called, in some circles, the "professionalization of management." Harbison and Myers have recently completed a world-wide survey of the efforts made to develop professional schools of high-level management. They have concluded that, in most countries, progress in this direction is slow.[16] Professional management is important for three reasons. (1) It may endow a business career with higher prestige (as a kind of profession), so that business will attract more of the young men with high n Achievement from the élite groups in backward countries. (2) It stresses *performance* criteria of excellence in the management area—i.e., what a man can do and not what he is. (3) Advanced management schools can themselves be so achievement-oriented in their instruction that they are able to raise the n Achievement of those who attend them.

Applied toward explaining historical events, the results of our researches clearly shift attention away from external factors and to man—in particular, to his motives and values. That about which he thinks and dreams determines what will happen. The emphasis is quite different from the Darwinian or Marxist view of man as a creature who *adapts* to his environment. It is even different from the Freudian view of civilization as the sublimation of man's primitive urges. Civilization, at least in its economic aspects, is neither adaptation nor sublimation; it is a positive creation by a people made dynamic by a high level of n Achievement. Nor can we agree with Toynbee, who recognizes the importance of psychological factors as "the very forces which actually decide the issue when an encounter takes place," when he states that these factors "inherently are impossible to weigh and measure, and therefore to estimate scientifically in advance." [17] It is a measure of the pace at which the behavorial sciences are developing that even within Toynbee's lifetime we can demonstrate that he was mistaken. The psychological factor responsible for a civilization's rising to a challenge is so far from being "inherently impossible to weigh and measure" that it has been weighed and measured and scientifically estimated in advance; and, so far as we can now tell, this factor is the achievement motive.

1. This paper is a summary of the author's book, *The Achieving Society,* published by Van Nostrand Co. in Princeton, N.J., in the fall of 1961.

2. A. L. Kroeber, *Configurations of Culture Growth* (Berkeley, California, 1944).

3. J. W. Atkinson (Ed.), *Motives in Fantasy, Action, and Society* (Princeton, N.J., 1958).

4. Max Weber, *The Protestant Ethic and the Spirit of Capitalism,* trans. Talcott Parsons (New York, 1930).

5. M. R. Winterbottom, "The Relation of Need for Achievement to Learning and Experiences in Independence and Mastery," in Atkinson, *op. cit.,* pp. 453-478.

6. F. Heichelheim, *Wirtschaftsgeschichte des Altertums* (Leiden, 1938).

7. J. B. Cortés, "The Achievement Motive in the Spanish Economy between the Thirteenth and the Eighteenth Centuries," *Economic Development and Cultural Change,* IX., (1960), 144-163.

8. N. M. Bradburn and D. E. Berlew, "Need for Achievement and English Economic Growth," *Economic Development and Cultural Change,* 1961.

9. I. L. Child, T. Storm, and J. Veroff, "Achievement Themes in Folk Tales Related to Socialization Practices," in Atkinson, *op. cit.,* pp. 479-492.

10. David Riesman, with the assistance of Nathan Glazer and Reuel Denney, *The Lonely Crowd* (New Haven, Conn., 1950).

11. J. W. Atkinson, "Motivational Determinants of Risk-Taking Behavior," *Psychological Review,* LXIV (1957), 359-372.

12. B. C. Rosen and R. G. D'Andrade, "The Psychosocial Origins of Achievement Motivation," *Sociometry,* XXII (1959), 185-218.

13. N. M. Bradburn, "The Managerial Role in Turkey" (unpublished Ph. D. dissertation, Harvard University, 1960).

14. B. C. Rosen, "Race, Ethnicity, and Achievement Syndrome," *American Sociological Review,* XXIV (1959), 47-60.

15. David Granick, *The Red Executive* (New York, 1960).

16. Frederick Harbison and Charles A. Myers, *Management in the Industrial World* (New York, 1959).

17. Arnold J. Toynbee, *A Study of History* (abridgment by D. C. Somervell; Vol. I; New York, 1941).

PART III

Consumption, Savings, and Investment

CHAPTER 5

Consumption, Industrialization and Urbanization

SIMON KUZNETS
Harvard University

PER CAPITA INCOME, INDUSTRIALIZATION, AND URBANIZATION

The relation between per capita income, which we use here as a crude measure of economic development, and the degree of industrialization, is illustrated in lines *1–6* of Table 1. When countries are grouped by their per capita income in the early 1950's, the non-agricultural sectors in the high-income countries—the M sector (including mining, manufacturing, and construction) and the S sector (including transportation and communication, trade, personal and professional services, government, and other services)—account for over eight-tenths of national income and of labor force, leaving less than two-tenths for the A sector (agriculture, forestry, and fisheries). In the low-income countries, as much as fifty per cent of national income originates, and close to sixty per cent of the labor force are engaged, in the A sector. Obviously, there is a positive association between per capita income and degree of industrialization, as measured by the shares of non-agricultural sectors in income and in the labor force.

Many observations have been made of this association, and we need not discuss it in detail here. However, we should not assume that its existence means that per capita income in the developed countries is high *because* the shares of the non-A sectors in income and labor force are high. Indeed, the implication could be the reverse: the shares of the non-A sectors might be high because per capita income is so high; and a high per capita income requires a high level of production and of income in the A sector also, if only to permit the release of labor force to non-agricultural pursuits. A more balanced explanation of the correlation of high per capita income with the large proportions of income originating in and labor force engaged in the non-A sectors in the developed countries is that these countries could take advantage of the potentials of economic

99

performance provided by modern technology—in *both* the agricultural and other sectors of the economy; and that the impact of technological progress on all sectors, resulting in high per capita income, shifts the structure of demand away from the products of agriculture and toward the products of the M and S sectors. The combination of high productivity in all sectors of the economy—not the least in the A sector—with low secular income-elasticity of demand for products of agriculture, accounts for the positive association between per capita income and degree of industrialization. In the low-income, underdeveloped countries, productivity is low in all sectors. In the A sector it is particularly low; and when per capita income is low, demand is concentrated on basic foods and other products of the A sector. As a result, both the share of agriculture in the labor force, and the share of its contribution to national income, are large. If the term "industrialization," applying to a basic feature of modern economic growth, is intended to signify that only the non-agricultural industries display major rises in productivity—that the revolution is limited to an industrial one—then it is a dangerous misnomer. The agricultural revolution is just as indispensable as the industrial; the agricultural sectors of underdeveloped countries are even more backward than the non-agricultural; and policies aimed at overcoming economic backwardness and facilitating the transition to modern economic growth must be concerned with the A sector at least as much as with the ohers.

However, the connection between industrialization and urbanization, and hence between the latter and per capita income, is of greater interest here. The measure of urbanization used in Table 1 is the proportion of population in localities of twenty thousand and over, because these are the data available for the largest number of countries. But the results are the same if we shift the dividing line between urban and rural. Data for fewer countries show that the proportion of population in localities of two thousand and over is between four- and seven-tenths higher than the proportion in localities of twenty thousand and over—and there is no apparent association of these differences with per capita income. Thus the share of population in localities of two thousand and over would vary, roughly, from a high of sixty-five per cent in Group I to a low of less than twenty-five per cent in Groups VI and VII.

We were interested in determining the possible effect of the size of the country's population, since a larger population presumably would permit a greater relative concentration in localities above a given *absolute* size. We therefore calculated the average population per country in each group (line *8*), and derived a *weighted* share of population in localities of twenty thousand and over (line *10*). We thus found that the differences in population size have no systematic relation to per capita income; and the weighted share of population in localities of twenty thousand and over

100

TABLE 1

Degree of Industrialization and Urbanization, Countries grouped by per Capita Income, Post-World War II Years

	Groups of Countries by Per Capita Income			
	I	II + III	IV + V	VI + VII
	(1)	(3)	(2)	(4)
1. Range of per capita income (U.S. 1952-54 dollars)	775 or more	351-775	151-350	150 or less *
2. Approximate per capita income (U.S. 1952-54 dollars)	1,000	550	250	100 *
Degree of Industrialization National Income				
3. Number of countries	7	14	19	24 †
4. Average share of non-A sectors (%)	86.8	80.8	66.9	50.9†
Labor Force, Excl. Unpaid Family Labor				
5. Number of countries	7	13	12	11 †
6. Average share of non-A sectors (%)	85.6	72.7	49.7	41.2†
Degree of Urbanization				
7. Number of countries	8	11	15	10 †
8. Average population, 1950 (millions)	30.0	30.7	20.9	42.2‡
9. Unweighted average share population in localities of 20,000 and over (%)	45.8	37.8	20.9	14.7‡
10. Weighted (by population) average share in localities of 20,000 and over (%)	47.4	35.9	27.9	12.4‡
Index of Urbanization of Non-A Labor Force				
11. Line 9 ÷ line 6	0.54	0.52	0.42	0.36
12. Line 10 ÷ line 6	0.55	0.49	0.56	0.30

* Information in lines *1* and *2* taken largely from United Nations, *Per Capita National Product of Fifty-five Countries, 1952-1954* ("Statistical Papers," Series E, No. 4, New York, 1957). For more detailed discussion of the Roman numeral groupings, see Kuznets, "Quantitative Aspects of the Economic Growth of Nations: II. Industrial Distribution of National Product and Labor Force," *Economic Development and Cultural Change,* V (Supplement), No. 4 (July, 1957), particularly p. 7 and Appendix Table 9.

† Information in lines *3-6* taken from Kuznets, *op. cit.,* Table 3, p. 10 and Table 10, p. 23. The averages for all countries, including Communist, were used.

‡ The population totals in line *8,* needed to calculate the weighted averages of shares

shows wider range than the unweighted in positive association with per capita income. In short, the association of urbanization, industrialization, and per capita income is definitely positive and marked.

That a greater degree of industrialization should produce more urbanization is hardly surprising. However, it must be emphasized that there is no *inevitable* technical connection between the two. One can, with effort, imagine a situation in which the population engaged in agriculture have living accommodations in sizable cities—although the cost of the necessary extensive transportation and urban living facilities would be extremely high. On the other hand, in many non-A sectors—e.g., manufacturing, many types of public utilities, and even some service activities (educational, curative, and business services, etc.)—economies of scale engender a large optimum plant size. Each such optimum-scale unit may require many workers—enough, in fact, to constitute in and of themselves (without counting the auxiliary service groups that would be there) urban conglomerations well above the twenty thousand mark. Yet, it is conceivable that these workers could be provided with housing facilities scattered through the countryside, with a density no higher than that of the agricultural population—if, of course, the concomitant cost of transportation and other services could be met, and if this use of the land could be reconciled with the need for land of agriculture.

Although it is technically possible to combine the pursuit of agriculture with urbanization, and the pursuit of modern industry with rural living, the economic cost of such combinations would be prohibitively high. To provide the farm population wih urban living accommodations would tax the resources of even a highly developed country. Of course, it would be quite impossible in an underdeveloped country, with its huge and widespread agricultural population, and its limited transportation and other facilities. To provide the population attached to a large-scale modern industry with rural living accommodations would require transportation, trade, and other service facilities that would strain severely the material resources and the social inventiveness of the most developed country. It is because modern industry enjoys the enormous economies of the increasing size of the optimum unit, and because the cities provide such an effective way of exploiting the technological potentials of economies of scale, that industrialization and urbanization go together. In the less developed countries, it is the relative absence of modern industry and of economies of scale that limits urbanization.[1]

in line *10*, are from United Nations, *Demographic Yearbook*, 1958 (New York, 1958), Table 4, pp. 110-21. The population for the U.S.S.R. given there is 200.2 million for 1956; we assumed it to be 190 million in 1950. The data for lines *9* and *10* are from United Nations, *Report on the World Social Situation* (New York, 1957), in particular the table on p. 115; Table 5, p. 118; and Table 6, p. 119.

The emphasis on the lack of any inevitable technical connection between industrialization and urbanization is useful, because it draws attention to the two boundaries at which such a connection may be weakened. First, only the modern industrial sectors are characterized by large optimum-size units—and then only if the transport and communication network is adequately developed. If cottage industries are extensive and the transport and communication system is underdeveloped, urbanization may be slight, even if the shares of income originating in, and of labor force attached to, the non-A sectors are sizable. It is interesting to note that in the less developed countries the ratio of the urban population proportion to the proportion of labor force in the non-A sectors is distinctly lower than in the more developed countries. In other words, in the former, a larger proportion of the non-A labor force is in the countryside (see Table 1, lines *11* and *12*).[2] Second, in the developed countries, the increase in wealth may permit a dispersion of living facilities—even with the continued concentration of population during working hours. The rapid growth of suburban areas near the larger cities in the United States—the so-called "dormitory" or "bedroom" suburbs—is a case in point. A movement like this implies the acceptance of the additional cost of decentralized living combined with centralized and urbanized production. It is resulting in an obfuscation of the lines of division between rural non-farm communities and cities. But these factors merely qualify the major association between industrialization and urbanization; they do not negate it.

PER CAPITA INCOME AND MAJOR TYPES OF INCOME USE

Differences in per capita income need to be translated into differences in per capita consumption expenditures. If they are not, the association of economic development, as measured by per capita income, with industrialization and urbanization, need not be translated into an association with per capita consumption and with the correlated differences in *structure* of consumption. Hence, it is important to examine the connection between per capita income and the uses of income—particularly its use for consumption.

Table 2 presents a simple comparison, for countries grouped by per capita income, of the major types of income use for the post-World War II years (mostly 1951–57). In lines *2–4*, gross domestic expenditures are apportioned among three use-categories: consumption (or, rather, expenditures for consumption purposes) by households and non-profit associations; consumption by government, i.e., governmental expenditures on non-capital goods; and gross domestic capital formation, i.e., retention

TABLE 2

Distribution of Gross Domestic Expenditures and Net National Product by Major Type of Use, Countries grouped by per Capita Income, Post-World War II Years

	Groups of Countries by Per Capita Income			
	I	II + III	IV + V	VI + VII
	(1)	(2)	(3)	(4)
1. Number of Countries	8	12	17	16*
Average Share in Gross Domestic Expenditures (%)				
2. Consumption by households and non-profit institutions	64.6	66.5	72.0	74.1*
3. Government consumption	14.1	13.4	11.4	10.3*
4. Gross domestic capital formation	21.3	20.1	16.6	15.6*
5. Net balance of current foreign transactions (capital exports or imports)	—0.3	—3.3	—1.6	—2.7*
Average Share in Net National Product (%)				
6. Consumption by households and non-profit institutions	71	75	79	81†
7. Government consumption	15	15	12	11†
8. Net national capital formation	14	10	9	8†
9. Approximate per capita consumption (U.S. 1952-54 dollars)	710	413	198	81‡

* The basic data for lines *1-5* are from United Nations, *Yearbook of National Accounts Statistics, 1958* (New York, 1959), and earlier issues when needed. The totals for each country were cumulated for 1951-57 (or some period close to it, if all seven years were not given), and the percentage shares were calculated from these cumulated totals. Then the percentages for countries belonging to the same Roman numeral group were averaged (arithmetic means, unweighted).

† Lines *6-8* were derived by assuming, on the basis of post-World War II data, a ratio of capital consumption allowances to gross domestic capital formation of 0.4, in each group in columns *1-4*; subtracting capital consumption so calculated from gross domestic capital formation in line *4*; adding the entries in line *5*; and recomputing the percentages in lines *2-4* (line *4* now combined with line *5*, after subtraction of capital consumption) to the new total (which is the percentage of net national product to gross domestic expenditures).

‡ Line *9*: the product of line *6* and Table 1, line *2*.

within the country of goods to be added to fixed capital stock or to inventories. Data on the distribution of gross domestic expenditures are available for the largest number of countries. However, we had additional data, for many of these and for some other countries, from which we could infer the average ratio of capital consumption to gross domestic capital formation. Having, in line 5, the proportional weight of the net balance of current foreign transactions (capital imports or exports), we derive the distribution of net national product (lines 6–8)—a total not very different from the national income concept used in Table 1.

Private consumption takes a larger share of net national product in the poor, low-income countries in Groups VI and VII than in the high-income countries in Group I—over eighty per cent, compared with over seventy per cent (line 6). This leaves a greater residual for government consumption and capital formation in the high-income countries than in the low—an expected response to the smaller supply of goods per capita in the latter. It is not surprising that Table 2 shows that lower per capita income is accompanied by a higher proportion of income spent on consumption and a lower proportion on capital formation. What may be surprising is that the differences in the distribution of income by major uses are not much greater—the proportion saved, or consumed by governments, is not much larger in the higher-income, developed countries. As the data stand, the share of total net product *not* devoted to consumption of households varies only from twenty-nine to nineteen per cent. As a result, the international differences in per capita consumption expenditures are not much narrower than those in per capita income: the range in the former is roughly from about nine to one (Table 2, line 9), while the range in the latter is from ten to one (Table 1, line 2).

Before speculating on the factors that produce this result, we must consider two specific aspects of Table 2. First, the table excludes Communist countries, for which it is not easy to distinguish precisely between household consumption and government consumption, as we do for other countries. And yet, on the basis of the available data, we may infer that the inclusion of Communist countries would not change the pattern much. Net capital formation proportions in most Communist countries ranged about fifteen per cent—give or take a few percentage points—but in none was the per capita income high enough for its inclusion in Group I (they would all be distributed among Groups II–VI).[3] If we assume that government consumption (as defined in non-Communist countries) would not account for more than fifteen per cent, the inferred share of consumption of households in total net product would be about seventy per cent or somewhat lower. The inclusion of Communist countries might reduce the range in line 6 of Table 2 slightly, because of the addition of shares of household consumption of about seventy per cent in Groups II and III,

105

IV and V, and VI and VII. But clearly, the range in line 9 in per capita consumption expenditures would remain almost as wide as it is now.

Second, we might ask whether government consumption, which includes defense expenditures, is not more heavily dominated by the latter in the developed countries than in the underdeveloped. If so, is the share of civilian government consumption accordingly proportionately greater in the low-income, less developed countries? As a consequence, is the component of government consumption that might be considered an addition to personal consumption (e.g., expenditures on health, education, recreation, etc.) proportionately (to national income) greater in the less developed than in the more developed countries? Whatever scanty data are readily available do not support this conjecture. We could find a distribution of government consumption between civilian and defense in the post-World War II years (1951–57) for only eighteen countries. The average share of defense for the seven in Group I was about forty per cent of total government consumption, compared with twenty-three per cent for the six in Groups II and III, and thirty per cent for the five in Groups IV–VII. Discounting the low ratio for Groups II and III (caused by bias introduced by the inclusion of West Germany, Austria, and Ireland, and the omission of other countries with much heavier defense burdens), we cannot infer that civilian government consumption would account for a higher share of net product in Groups VI and VII than in Group I. Nor can we infer that, of such civilian government consumption, a larger share would go to ultimate consumers in the less developed than in the more developed countries. Since the absolute volume of civilian government expenditures is much smaller in the low-income countries, a far higher share may have to be devoted to indispensable administration, justice, police, etc.; and a lower share, to services, like health and education, that are net additions to ultimate consumption. A more detailed analysis is not feasible here; in its absence, I would conclude that the inclusion of the proper part of government consumption with the consumption share of households would, at best, leave the range in per capita consumption expenditures in line 9 unaffected—and it might well widen it.

Why do the developed countries devote such a large share of their total product to household consumption? Ignoring, for the moment, the share of government consumption, one can argue that, in view of the high income levels of the developed countries and the rapid rate of rise in their per capita income, the net capital formation or savings proportions could be much higher than fifteen per cent. The effect that changes in the latter would have on the range in per capita consumption expenditures would be immediate. To illustrate this, let us assume that the net capital formation proportion in Group I is fifty, not fifteen per cent, and that the share of government consumption remains fifteen per cent; then the residual

106

share of consumption by households becomes thirty-five per cent. The implicit approximate per capita consumption expenditures of the population would then amount to $350—still more than four times that of Groups VI and VII. But this range of 4.4 to one would be much narrower than the ten-to-one range in per capita income in Table 1, line *2*, and than the nine-to-one range in Table 2, line *9*. Obviously, there are major factors that substantially raise personal consumption when the per capita product of an economy rises. These factors become evident when we consider the relation between the level of per capita consumption expenditures and the structure of personal consumption.

PER CAPITA CONSUMPTION EXPENDITURES AND STRUCTURE OF CONSUMPTION

Table 3 summarizes the easily available evidence, for post-World War II years, on the distribution of consumption, among various categories of consumer goods, for the two groups of countries at the extremes of the range of per capita income, and hence of per capita consumption expenditures. The data on the low-income countries are largely for those in Group VI; consequently, the distribution in column (2) is not for countries in the lowest income group. Also, because the samples are small, the comparison is subject to some errors. Finally, the distribution is of totals in current prices; and the differential in the relative prices of various categories of consumer goods makes for a distribution different from one based on the identical price structure for the two groups of countries. Nevertheless, the results of the comparison are clear, and conform sufficiently with information from other sources (such as budget studies) about the relation between per capita consumption expenditures and the structure of consumption, to reveal the major aspects of this relation. These are summarized in the paragraphs that follow.

a) The proportion of total consumption expenditures devoted to the basic food necessities is far larger in the low-income, underdeveloped countries than in the developed (line *2*). In the one country in Group VII for which we have data, this proportion is well above fifty per cent. In general, in the underdeveloped countries it is about double that in the developed countries. The contrast would be even greater if we took differences in relative prices into account. Prices of food to ultimate consumers, relative to prices of other consumer goods, are lower in the underdeveloped countries than in the high-income countries. This obtains because, in the underdeveloped countries, a larger share of food is retained by farmers for their own consumption, and thus does not carry the heavy load of transportation and distribution charges. It is also partially due

TABLE 3

Distribution of Consumer Expenditures by Major Categories of Goods, two Groups of Countries at the Extremes of the Range of per Capita Income, Post-World War II Years

	Average Share in Total Consumer Expenditures (%)		Approximate Expenditure per Capita U.S. 1952-54 dollars		
	I	VI + VII	I	VI + VII	Ratio (3) to (4)
	(1)†	(2)†	(3)‡	(4)‡	(5)
1. Number of countries	5 or 6	6*			
Categories of Consumer Goods:					
2. Food	27.2	49.8	193	40	4.8
3. Beverages and tobacco	9.4	7.2	67	5.8	11.6
4. Clothing	11.8	11.5	84	9.3	9.0
5. Household operation	26.0	18.6	185	15.1	12.3
a. Rent, water, fuel, and light	14.4	10.8	102	8.7	11.7
b. Furniture and furnishings	7.4	4.4	53	3.6	14.7
c. Household services and operation proper	4.2	3.4	30	2.8	10.7
6. Other specified services	20.2	10.1	143	8.2	17.4
a. Health and personal care	4.7	3.3	33	2.7	12.2
b. Transportation and communication	9.3	3.8	66	3.1	21.3
c. Recreation and amusement	6.2	3.0	44	2.4	18.3
7. Miscellaneous services (residual)	5.4	2.8	38	2.3	16.5
8. Total	100.0	100.0	710	81	8.8

* Includes only one country in Group VII.
† The data for columns (1) and (2) are from United Nations, *Yearbook of National Accounts Statistics, 1958* (New York, 1959), supplemented, when needed, by earlier issues. For each country, the cumulative totals of consumer expenditures, for specific categories and the total, were computed for 1951-57; the percentage shares were calculated from these cumulative amounts for the seven-year period; and then the percentages were averaged for the countries included in each group (arithmetic means, unweighted).
‡ In columns (3) and (4), lines *2-7* are the products of line *8* and columns (1) and (2), respectively. Line *8* is from Table 2, line *9*.

to the fact that, even at the retail level in the cities, food prices are lower, relative to the prices of many other consumer commodities (particularly, highly fabricated ones), in the less developed countries. Hence, if we were to shift to a comparable relative price structure (say, that of the developed countries), the proportion spent on food in the low-income countries in column (2) would be much higher than the percentage now shown.

b) The shares of all categories of consumer goods, except food, in total consumption expenditures are lower in the low-income countries than in the high-income, developed countries. But the relative differences in these shares vary considerably among the several categories. The greatest disparity is in the shares of transportation and communication (which includes purchases of automobiles), recreation and amusement, miscellaneous services (which include education and travel), and furniture and furnishings—categories either dominated by expensive durable consumer goods, or representing the more dispensable types of consumer goods, or both.

c) If we combine the percentage shares in columns (1) and (2) with the rough approximations to per capita consumer expenditures in Table 2, to derive an approximation to the absolute per capita expenditures on various types of consumer goods, we find that these absolute levels are far higher in the developed than in the underdeveloped countries for all categories (columns [3]–[5]). However, the relative range between high- and low-income countries, in this crudely estimated measure of absolute expenditures per capita, differs widely among the various categories. It is narrowest for food, where it amounts to less than five to one—and an allowance for the differential price structure might well reduce it to between two and three to one. By contrast, in categories like transportation and communication, furniture and furnishings, recreation and amusement, and miscellaneous services, the range is between 14 1/2 and twenty-one to one; and, in the first two categories at least, making an allowance for the differences in relative price structure would probably widen, rather than narrow, the range.

Some of the detail in Table 3 is subject to question and further testing —e.g., the small difference in the share of clothing and in the share of rent and water charges (the major component in line 5a, which is understated because of restrictions on rents in several countries in Group I). But the major conclusions—the income-elasticity of expenditures on food that is much lower than one; the income-elasticity of expenditures on clothing that is close to one; and the very high income-elasticity of expenditures on consumer durable commodities, transportation, recreation and amusement, and miscellaneous services (including education and travel)—are corroborated by many other studies. Furthermore, a more detailed analysis of the structure of expenditures *within* the broad food

109

category indicates that the low-income countries adapt themselves to the low level of expenditures by concentrating on the "cheap" sources of calories. It also reveals the ways, in general, in which the whole structure of consumer expenditures adjusts itself to the relative supply of various commodities and services, so that, if the total supply of goods per capita is low, the most economical utilization of the available resources is made —subject, to be sure, to many institutional and cultural traditions that may impose non-economic constraints of their own.[4]

But our main interest is not in the detail of Table 3. We are, rather, concerned with the bearing that the differences in structure of consumption between high- and low-income countries may have upon the large proportion of their income that the former devote to household consumption and not to capital accumulation. The evidence in Table 3 suggests that, as per capita income rises, and the concomitant processes of industrialization and urbanization take place, some factors *require* a higher per capita consumption expenditure. It also indicates that other factors may make the latter possible—although it would be difficult to prove that higher outlays on some goods are a prerequisite either of higher per capita income or of the industrialization and urbanization shifts associated with it.

If a larger consumer outlay on a given type of goods is necessary so that human beings are to perform efficiently as members of the productive system, and thus assure higher income per capita, then clearly the higher consumer expenditures per capita are an indispensable prerequisite of higher per capita income, industrialization, and urbanization. On the other hand, if the rise in consumer outlay can be foregone without any concomitant reduction of human efficiency or without precluding a higher per capita income and the associated processes of economic growth, then, presumably, it is not necessary, and may be called discretionary or voluntary.

We can find examples of both types of consumer expenditures easily by looking at cases in history or by comparing the expenditures of high- and low-income countries. When larger per capita outlays on food are necessary to maintain a healthier and more vigorous population, and to provide nourishment to the population in the cities where the people must live so that they can work in modern industry, then such outlays are compelled by the economic logic of economic growth. In that sense, they are not merely a consequence, but also a cause, of higher per capita income. In other words, the high-income countries consume more food per capita because their income is high; but, also, their income is high because they consume more food per capita. By contrast, a greater expenditure on certain types of amusement—or, for that matter, on certain types of food—which are not only non-essential for greater economic and social efficiency, but may even be harmful, is no prerequisite of economic growth. Thus, it is valid to say that the high-income countries spend more per capita on such items because they have a high per capita income; but we cannot say that they have a high per capita income because they spend more per capita thereon.

Before considering the broader problems raised by the distinction between required and discretionary components in consumer expenditures, I am inclined to argue that, in the high-income countries, much more of the larger per capita consumer expenditure is required, not discretionary, than in the underdeveloped countries. In the latter, the per capita food supply is poor and inadequate. It is clear, then, that in the developed countries, providing enough food, of balanced composition, to the rural and particularly to the urban populations is indispensable for maintaining a healthy and efficient labor force. In the high-income countries, the urban population is a much greater proportion of the total population; and this necessitates a far larger input of resources per capita for adequate shelter, light, sanitary facilities, etc., than that involved in providing for the large rural populations of the underdeveloped countries. Greater per capita expenditure on housing, etc., is a prerequisite for the higher income of the developed countries. The greater degree of literacy and education of the labor force, in all sectors of a country with advanced technology, necessitates larger expenditures on these services. Given the strain of urban life and the desirability of relieving it by more decentralized living and by organized recreation and amusement, the higher outlay on these consumer goods is not necessarily a frivolity permitted by higher income per capita—it may well be a necessity, if the latter is to be realized in the long run.

These are all judgments. They do not tell us *how much* of the difference between the per capita consumption of the developed countries and that of the underdeveloped countries is truly required for the higher per capita income of the former. The answer can hardly be ascertained without much detailed work. Even then, I am not sure that the answer would be valuable if it had been obtained only on the basis of restrictive assumptions that had deprived it of much interest. The whole distinction between required and discretionary consumption entails some problems that must be emphasized in the concluding section of this paper.

SOME BROAD PROBLEMS

We can attain a balanced view of the interrelation between economic growth (as reflected in per capita income), industrialization, urbanization, and consumption—an interrelation that is central to the distinction between required and discretionary consumption—only if we keep three propositions before us.

1) The economic growth of nations in modern times is not merely a process of accumulating material capital and increasing the numbers, and even the skills, of the labor force. The major source, the permissive base, lies in the increased knowledge applicable to practical problems of economic production. This large and growing potential of technological knowledge can be tapped only if economic and social institutions have been properly adjusted to permit capital accumulation and an efficient labor force, and their effective combination in economic production. Given the growth of useful knowledge, and the increasing capacity of the social system to utilize it, patterns of consumption and life in general can affect, in a wide variety of ways, a country's success in realizing the potential available. These ways differ with size of the specific country, its natural endowments, the phase of world history in which it exists, its initial economic position, etc. Thus, one can maintain in general terms that higher consumption outlays on *some* goods are a prerequisite of economic growth; however, the specification of required consumption clearly involves consideration of the divers ways in which it affects that growth. In an underdeveloped country, which can tap a vast accumulated potential in the existing world stock of technological and social knowledge, the change in consumption required to stimulate economic growth would assume a certain magnitude and content. These would be different from the ones in a developed country that has already attained a high per capita income and consumption level. For example, in the latter an increase in consumption outlay directed toward further research, and in the former an increase directed toward more food, health, and education services, would perhaps be the stimuli and prerequisites for respective further growth. And changes in consumption must be viewed not only in their simple relation to the efficiency of the economic sectors engaged in the production of goods, but also in relation to the effectiveness of the groups engaged in the production of knowledge.[5]

2) The supply of material goods represented by consumption expenditures is not the only requirement for efficient participation in economic activity. Provided that the minimum consumption requirements necessary for physical health and comfort are satisfied—and temporarily omitting consideration of consumption expenditure in specialized training (which is more properly capital investment, although in human beings)—it is possible to maintain that, beyond such minimum consumption requirements, greater consumption outlay is only one of many inducements. In other words, once the physiological and professional minimums have been fulfilled, greater consumption per capita is not the sole inducement to effective co-operation in the economic process. It follows from this that various societies may differ widely in the degree to which *economic* incentives are emphasized more than others. In some societies, levels of consumption well above the minimum universally required levels may be essential as a base for effective participation in the economy and for higher income per capita; whereas in other societies, the needed levels of consumption may be relatively lower. In fact, even those countries where markets and consumers are by and large free differ widely in their respective apportionments of income, at similar per capita levels, between consumption and saving.

3) Even if we deal only with the economic magnitudes, the use of countrywide proportions and macro-coefficients can be misleading. To avoid being misled, we must also pay attention to the distribution of the countrywide totals among different groups within the population, and to the variation of the proportions among the sectors. For example, a rise in the countrywide per capita consumption may not constitute the prerequisite for higher per capita income, if it is produced by augmenting the consumption of those members of society who do not contribute to economic growth, while reducing the consumption of members whose contribution is large. In this connection, it is important that the low average per capita consumption of the underdeveloped countries is accompanied by rather marked disparities in income and expenditure per head among various groups in the population. On the other hand, in the developed countries, inequalities in both income and expenditure are relatively smaller.

The foregoing comments indicate the reasons why it is difficult to determine just how much of the higher per capita consumption of the developed countries is a prerequisite of their higher income. They also show why, in the policy consideration of economic growth in underdeveloped countries, it is difficult to decide what amount of increase in per capita consumption is an indispensable prerequisite for attaining a specified growth in per capita income. It is easy to demonstrate that certain factors—the long-term rise in per capita income that we consider to be the index of economic growth, industrialization, urbanization, the rise in per capita consumption expenditures, and the change in structure of consumption—are all inextricably interrelated and sustain each other in the sense that the failure of one is bound to affect the others. But it is well-nigh impossible to measure the degree of interdependence, the levels at which these various trends become discretionary rather than required.

However, awareness of these broader problems is useful, if only as an indication of the wider framework within which any statistical comparisons between income per capita, industrialization, urbanization, and consumption must be viewed and interpreted. Even simple comparisons of these several aspects of the economic and social system, like those in our tables, illuminate the interplay between structural shifts within the process of economic growth and the rate at which this growth proceeds. We can learn much from such simple comparisons. We can learn more when they are carried through in detail, both among countries and over time. And we can learn still more when we associate the similarities and differences observed with the specific characteristics of the economies and societies involved. The principal purpose of raising these broader problems is to emphasize that economic growth is a process of social as well as of economic change; that it calls for adjustments over and above those in the economic aspects of social life and in the countrywide magnitudes. The interplay between rise in per capita income, industrialization, urbanization, and consumption can be most effectively studied and interpreted if the economic analysis is tested against the political background, the social structure, and the cultural milieu, each of which modifies to some degree the associations among the economic variables proper.

NOTES TO CHAPTER 5

1. Economies of scale affect not only the production of goods in modern industry, but also (and possibly even more important), the production of knowledge—whose accumulation and application to production are the basis of modern economic growth. Cities are, therefore, important both as loci for the large optimum size units of modern industries and as foci for the production and spread of knowledge. It is difficult to envisage great advances in science and applied knowledge as being generated by isolated thinkers, scientists, and inventors scattered through the countryside. It is equally difficult to imagine that advances in the representative and literary arts could be made without the intensive interchange and economies of scale of artistic pursuits that only the larger cities make possible. The discussion in the text omits consideration of these broader aspects of the relation between urbanization and economic growth. For extensive discussions of the role of cities in economic growth, see the series of papers in *Economic Development and Cultural Change*, III, Nos 1-3 (October, 1954; January, 1955; and April, 1955.)

2. The same results would be obtained if we lowered the division line. At the 2,000 line, the ratio in Group I would rise to almost 0.8; that in Groups VI and VII would not be much above 0.5.

   We should also note that the labor force in the A-sector in the underdeveloped countries may include a larger *proportion* of people engaged part- or even full-time in non-agricultural production than would the labor force in the A-sector in more developed countries. Thus even more of the non-agricultural activity in the lower-income countries is non-urbanized than the figures in Table 1 suggest.

3. See my paper on capital formation proportions in recent years in *Economic Development and Cultural Change*, VIII, No. 4 (July, 1960), Part 2, 19-21.

4. See, in this connection, my paper, "Regional Economic Trends and Levels of Living," in Philip M. Hauser (ed.), *Population and World Politics* (Glencoe, Ill., 1958), in particular Tables 3 and 4, and the discussion in Section 2, "Differences in Per Capita Consumption Levels," pp. 85-92.

   More detail on the structure of consumption and on its share in national product is provided in my paper, written after the present, and published in *Economic Development and Cultural Change*, X, No. 2 (January, 1962), Part. 2, 3-92.

5. This is true even of the underdeveloped countries, which presumably can "borrow" from the existing stock of knowledge. Technological knowledge that has originated elsewhere and is transferred to a given country may need to be modified. The modifications must be made largely with the skilled resources of the "borrowing" country. Thus an underdeveloped country must, as a prerequisite of growth, allow for a certain amount of consumption directed toward training and research, in order to maximize the effectiveness of the adopted modern technology.

115

The Social and Psychological Determinants of Savings and Investments in Developing Societies

RICHARD D. LAMBERT

University of Pennsylvania

The fundamental question posed by this paper [1] is: To what extent do attitudes and values intrinsic to the cultures of the countries from Pakistan to the Philippines determine the amount, the components, the demand for, and the use of savings? It seems clear that differences among countries in their current level and pace of economic development are imperfectly correlated with the rate of savings alone.

Kuznets [2] reports that the range of differences among nations in the proportion of their national product they devote to capital formation is fairly narrow, much narrower than either differences in per capita income or in gross national product.

Throughout South Asia, an annual national savings rate of eight to nine per cent is common. A recent estimate [3] for India's savings from 1951–57 found them to range from 7.6 to 5.9 per cent of the national income. This was accompanied by a capital formation rate of 5.1 per cent of the net domestic product, compared with 10.2 per cent for the United States, 8.3 per cent for the United Kingdom, and a massive 23.2 per cent for Japan. [4] Latest reports indicate that India may have reached eleven per cent. However, these rates of savings and capital formation can be misleading. In the first place, they are based on aggregate data in which as much as forty per cent of the value of the national output must be imputed, since it never reaches the market. In the second place, a large part of the savings, perhaps twenty to twenty-five per cent in India, is in non-monetized form; and this part is expended on direct investment, particularly in agriculture and small-scale enterprise, where replacement consumes an indeterminate, but sizable, amount of investment. Malenbaum [5] estimates that seventy-five per cent of investment in the private sector in India may have been directly invested, that is, expended by the individual saver on his own assets. Two-thirds of the private investment went into agriculture and housing, where such difficulties are greatest.

116

For these reasons, I shall not be primarily concerned with the volume of total national savings, i.e., income less consumption. I shall concentrate on other variables, both qualitative and quantitative, that influence the degree of effectiveness with which savings create the greatest possible additions to the national product. These variables comprise, in part, the factors relating to the separate schedules for savings and investment. They also include both structural features and attitudes relating to the demand side and to the effective utilization of savings. I shall omit consideration of a whole host of variables, such as interest rates, inflation, and other financial covariables of savings and investment,[6] even though these may be the primary implements available to government policy-makers seeking to manipulate the over-all rates. I shall examine ideologies and broad cultural features, some of them outside of the economic sphere proper, that are not so subject to short-run fluctuations or easy manipulation. As one consequence of the emphasis on cultural abstractions, the discussion will have more relevance to the private household sector of savings, where individual decisions are more directly influenced by cultural norms. I shall direct most of my remarks to the interaction between governmental development strategies and the attitudes and values in the rural areas where the greatest need for change occurs.

This emphasis is given in spite of the fact that aggregate national savings include, in addition, a sizable contribution provided by business corporations, where the ratio of savings to income is about the same in most countries whether developed or underdeveloped. These limitations, however, while they must be explicitly stated, do not undermine the importance of the attitudes and values of which I am writing.

In the countries of southern Asia, a high proportion of saving comes from the household sector—about eighty-seven per cent in India in 1956–57. Then, too, it is the scarcity of household savings that sets a limit to the domestic capital formation proportion.[7] In addition, one of the most important problems in underdeveloped countries is the conversion of household savings into corporate investment, particularly in the manufacturing sector, whose relative contribution to the gross national product can serve as a good index of domestic capital formation proportions. This problem involves the discouragement of direct investment in the household sector, greater monetization of savings, and the transfer of savings to the corporate sector, where the marginal propensity to save and invest is highest and where savings will be allocated to producer goods rather than to inventory or housing.

There is a tendency to use the experience of Western Europe and the United States as a model against which to contrast and measure the progress of developmental efforts in the underdeveloped countries. In some ways, the situation facing the underdeveloped countries—in particular the southern Asian countries—is very different from that which the West confronted at the outset of its period of rapid growth.

For instance, there was no parallel in the West to present Asian subsistence levels and rural population densities; and these factors make savings and accumulation for industrial investment more difficult for Asian countries. Also, at the important stage in the development of Western industrialism, wealth became concentrated in fewer and fewer hands. Today, in Asia, this would be politically dangerous in democratic countries, at least. Moreover, while Western capitalism and industrialization were based on the great trade of the eighteenth century and its accompanying capital accumulation, no similar virgin markets and favorable terms of trade await the developing countries today.

These and similar contrasts are essentially situational and more or less directly related to economic affairs. Most observers would admit their relevance to economic growth. We are on much more treacherous ground when we include the attitudinal and non-economic variables.

Max Weber's venture into the relationship between religion and economics provoked a fulsome and sometimes acrimonious controversy. The dispute involved not only his attempt to attribute the rise of capitalism to the tenets of the Protestant ethic, but also similar efforts to show that non-economic factors lay behind economic phenomena. The attempts to find non-economic causes for economic events have graced the development of economics as an art and have permitted scholars from other disciplines to work happily in the economists' vineyards; but within the field of economics itself, the battle lines are still drawn. In the report of a recent set of conferences sponsored by the National Bureau of Economic Research on the comparative study of economic growth and structure, the editor remarked:

The exact nature of the relationship between economic and non-economic factors in economic growth, and in particular the best method of studying this interrelationship, turned out to be possibly the most controversial point in our conferences and in comments on a preliminary draft of this report.[8]

Most economists would, I suspect, agree with an additional statement in the report that said, in effect, that non-economic factors should be given second priority, since most of them cannot be quantified, their connection with economic aspects is uncertain, and there is enough work to go around just with the economic factors without including others.

In spite of these arguments, this paper is on the attitudinal and valuational side of the line. Taking full cognizance of the Bureau's considered judgment, however, we must say that we too can argue only plausibility for the discussion to follow. One of the intentions of the UNESCO study

118

is to generate the careful research necessary to test the propositions arising from this exploratory stage.

The classic way to study the problem is to match the elements that contrast in our own society before and after its period of rapid growth with contrasts between the West and the Orient today. This method rests upon the assumption, most clearly stated by Max Weber, that the development of "the rational capitalistic organization of free labour" in the West was a unique historical emergent, and that other countries wishing to emulate the rapid economic advance which accompanied that historical process must supply the same cultural ingredients which produced it. Bert Hoselitz and I, in another paper,[9] have argued that the broad changes described below were crucial to the growth process in the West.

First, the domain of economic decisions became greatly enlarged so that, when an economic and a familial or religious value are in disagreement, the economic value wins out. To put it another way, the institutional limits of the economy, vis-à-vis the state, the family, and religion, were greatly extended. The second major factor was the evolution of a particular economic ideology of rational profit maximization. This, of course, follows Max Weber. The words *rational, profit,* and *maximization* should each be emphasized. The search for gain is ubiquitous in all societies; but rational profit maximization involves the principles that whatever brings the greatest monetary gains will be engaged in, and that science and technology will be used to the utmost in the reckoning and pursuit of this end. The third element crucial to the growth of the advanced economies of the West was the legitimation of the pursuit of maximum profits for all segments of society and not for just a limited few. In medieval Europe, subsistence was the fundamental motive for economic activity for the vast bulk of the populace. Traders who sought gain and accumulation were generally ethnically separate—Syrians, Greeks, Jews, Italians, Provençals, etc.; for others, this was not a worth-while endeavor. In the economic transformation of the West, profit became a generalized motive, legitimately sought by all members of the society. The fourth factor was the transformation of labor into a commodity, subject to the same market mechanisms as goods, however circumscribed the operation of the market.

If Weber's conception of the unique historical emergent is adopted, to what extent do the contrasts distinguishing the period before from the period after rapid economic growth in the West also distinguish the societies of the Orient from those in the West today? Weber chose the impact of religion on economic behavior as the starting point for his analysis. We are not interested in the specific validity of the Weber-Troeltsch theory [10] about the role of Protestantism in the West; but Weber's characterization of the Asian religions as lacking the attributes which had induced the rise

119

of rational capitalism in the West is relevant to our purpose. He wrote of Asian religions:

The unrestricted lust for gain of the Asiatics in large and in small is notoriously unequalled in the rest of the world. However, it is precisely a "drive for gain" pursued with every possible means including universal magic. It was lacking in precisely that which was decisive for the economics of the Occident: the refraction and rational immersion of the drive character of economic striving and its accompaniments in a system of rational, inner-worldly ethic of behavior, e.g., the "inner-worldly asceticism" of Protestantism in the West. Asiatic religion could not supply the presuppositions of inner-worldly asceticism.[11]

Weber's concern was primarily historical. He maintained that the religious philosophies of the East made unlikely the *indigenous* development and ascendance to power of an elite like the Western bourgeois class. The problem with which we are concerned is somewhat different. The countries of southern Asia are currently governed by elites who are committed to rational profit maximization, albeit for national rather than for private units; and the important question is whether the religions present an obstacle to such development. The most common assumption in this regard is that priority's being given to spiritual rather than material ends presents a major handicap. This thesis, like the story of Mark Twain's death, is highly exaggerated.

The two most extreme cases of "other-worldly" religions, Hinduism and Buddhism, consider personal salvation as the highest goal, but conceive of it as attainable only by a limited few. The doctrines of self-denial or the cessation of desire were applicable only to religious professionals or, for the ordinary man, confined to a stage in life in which worldly obligations had already been met. Among the Hindus, most of the traditional literature concerns the soul and is a glorification of the practice of religion; but some of it is highly secular. For instance, Kautalya's *Arthashastra* is explicitly a primer on means of maximizing wealth and power. An entire stream of literature, sometimes called the *banya* or merchant literature, which was most highly developed among the Jains, gives religious sanction to what would elsewhere be called secular ends. Laxmi, the goddess of wealth and good fortune, is a favorite in the Hindu pantheon. Even in the most sacrosanct of all Hindu literature, the *Rig-Veda*, the patronage of the sacred ritual was intended to advance the wealth and power of the kings. Later, the particularistic nature of duty included in the concept of *dharma* meant that each man carried out his *vrata*, his function— which, for all but the ascetic few, meant the pursuit of secular goals. Thus, while the search for wealth was not the highest of purposes, it was a perfectly respectable one. There is, moreover, a great gap between the religion sponsored by this priestly literature and popular Hinduism, which

120

is full of magic, deities, devils, and spirits both benign and malevolent; and the extent to which the Brahmans historically enjoyed the ascendancy they depict in their literature is an open question.

The same is true for Buddhism, where the denial of worldly pleasures is even more marked. Salvation and release from the pain of worldly existences and cycle of rebirths is a possibility only for *bhikkus,* or monks. For the rest of the populace, the emphasis rests upon the accumulation of merit through good deeds, *Karma,* which, for the laity, are in the main socially visible forms of piety and dedication to the Buddhist *Sangha.* For many of these deeds it was useful, even imperative to be wealthy. For instance, merit derives from supporting monks, constructing monasteries, wells, and ponds. The rewards for good deeds were secular riches, a good caste in the next life, good name, good friends. Nirvana was pictured as a land of splendor, wealth and happiness. In popular Buddhism, asceticism is not associated with the laity. The rewards for the deeds of the *upasaka,* or lay disciple, were not release but mundane pleasure in this life and the next.

The esoteric doctrines of Taoism contained no injunctions against trying to acquire wealth, and Confucianism is most secular in its orientation. Islam is not an other-worldly religion, and the *Koran* and *Hadith* do not depreciate the pursuit of wealth. In fact, Muslim law lays down a definite code for business activity, regulating purchases, sales, contracts, partnerships, loans, deposits, etc. But Islam does prohibit certain means of attaining wealth. Unlike Hinduism, in which the defiling occupations are largely menial, Islam prohibits the taking of usury, which is distinguished from permissible interest in that the latter involves risk-bearing or return on capital for productive activity. There are, in fact, some professional Muslim moneylenders in South Asia, like the Pathans, the Memons and the Khojas, but they either operate outside of their home regions or are descendants of Hindu trading castes. One of the most powerful incentives for the creation of Pakistan was that trading and credit facilities were monopolized by Hindus and Jains in areas where the populace was overwhelmingly Muslim; but Pakistan is still having difficulty in filling the gap created by their departure.[12] The recent expulsion of the Chinese minority from rural Indonesia is another case in point.

While the major religions of Asia do not denigrate wealth, they do tend to place the responsibility for the acquisition or lack of wealth on forces other than the individual's own efforts. In the Philippines, success is attributed to "swerte," or luck. In Islam, each man is apportioned at birth a certain *risq,* or share in life. True, he must work for it; but the amount is not set by his own efforts. In Viet Nam, the astrological rules of Tu Vi and the astral cycle determine one's destiny. In all the Asian societies where one's chances in life depend upon ascriptive characteristics,[13] the cultures bear a heavy burden of fatalism. I do not argue that fatalism destroys either the aspirations or the striving. It does provide an explanation for success and a consolation for the lack of it. It removes the necessity of seeking rational means for manipulating one's fate.

The removal from rationality is reinforced by the ubiquitous dependence in popular religion upon the intercession of minor deities and spirits who must be pleased—or, in the case of lesser ones, even magically manipulated. In fact, the behavior of villagers throughout southern Asia clearly shows that to them the only form of investment likely to produce the spectacular change in their fortunes that is necessary to bring them to a surplus standard of living is the investment of money, time, and food in the service of some supernatural power. If this investment is unproductive, the drain upon any small increment in income, particularly monetized income, may be substantial. In general, I would argue that the inhibition to economic growth engendered by religions in Asia lies not in their other-worldly orientation but in their institutional characteristics—especially in their ability to absorb accumulations of wealth that might otherwise be put to more economically productive uses. Even in a Christian country like the Philippines, increments in family wealth call for increased expenditures on religious rituals. Wedding ceremonies, burial ceremonies, and feasts for the dead are sharply graduated by cost. In a wedding, the proximity of the bride and groom to the altar, the use of an embroidered pillow, the celebration of high mass, the prolonged ringing of the bells, are all a function of expenditure. In death ceremonies, the priest's going to the house where the body lies, instead of waiting at the church; an elaborate ceremony at the church, complete with choir and church bells, the priest's going to the cemetery to make offerings for the dead; a choir singing and a band playing at the grave—all these can increase the cost of a funeral ten to fifteen times. Graduated cermonials are common in all countries. What is important in Asia is their priority in allocating expenditures and the high ratio of expenditures to both income and wealth.

Another of the institutional aspects of the religions that impede the transformation of the society to fit Max Weber's model are the support of social structures such as the caste system, the feudal economy, or the heavy family dependency—structures which inhibit incentives, prevent the entrance of many groups into the maximization competition, and make it less likely that concentration of savings will occur in the hands of a single person where rational economic decisions might dispose of it productively.

Religions provide the broad unifying cultural tradition in the countries of southern Asia. However, there are, in each of these countries, more secular ideological streams which also define the proper modes of economic activity. In the different countries, the relative strengths of these

122

streams vary considerably; but in all of them, the friction between the different clusters of attitudes has proved a major obstacle to the successful implementation of development plans.

The first and most important of these competing streams might be described as the "caretaker elites," committed to governmentally induced, planned economic growth. In each of the newly independent countries, the post-World War II years have witnessed the accession to power of these caretaker elites, who are remarkably similar, in their motivations, ideologies, and relationships, to the rest of the people in their countries. I call them "caretakers" because their legitimating principle is an instrumental ideology in which the material benefits of their efforts are to accrue to all members of their society. An ancillary, and in part contradictory, aim is to diminish the inequalities in the societies by letting the state champion the rights of the less powerful and less wealthy. Such a principle of legitimacy can operate as strictly in defining membership in the elite as blood kinship, lineage, or piety did in earlier eras. It provides the means for denying membership to such groups as business leaders or the landed aristocracy, who presumably operate in their own interests. In general, its goal is modernization—those elements of Westernization that suit indigenous valuational tastes. In particular, this includes: national unification, i.e., the supersession of all secondary, non-economic sources of power; nation building, i.e., acquiring the format and the hardware of an industrialized economy; equalitarianism, i.e., reducing the power of non-governmental economic organizations and individuals, and removing the more visible signs of poverty among the masses; and mass participation, i.e., legitimating centrally conceived and adopted plans by involving the largest number of people in their implementation. Briefly characterized, the economic ideology of the caretaker elite is a sort of *ad hoc* Fabianism. Their general attitudes toward wealth and savings include the notion that wealth is best when it is most evenly distributed. They consider that both wealth and savings in the economy as a whole will be most effectively increased and best utilized for national growth to the extent that they are controlled by government. The history of the private sector in their economies, and what they consider the anti-social acquisitiveness of both foreign and indigenous business groups, do nothing to dissuade them from this viewpoint.

The economic ethic of this elite, in a way, fits our concept of rational profit maximization. The fact that planners in "socialistic" societies seek their profits in national income totals, rather than in the assets and liabilities of an individual concern, does not weaken the fact that their action is predicated above all on a rational calculation of achieving a final surplus, measured in terms of money, and those actions are chosen which presumably will maximize the return. There are, of course, many other

123

factors which intrude in policy decisions— political favoritism, broad social welfare considerations, equalitarianism, etc.—but these are competing streams of thought that engender imperfections in, not negations of, the orientation toward rational gain-producing activities. The emphasis in the plans on the distribution of capital outlay, and the reckoning of the rewards in terms of per capita income, confirm our point.

Partly in agreement with, and partly in juxtaposition to, the caretaker elite are the Western-based or Western-oriented industrial and commercial houses. While they share the ethic of rational profit maximization, the unit to be benefited is more limited. To the extent that they are joint-stock companies, their ideology is also instrumental. However, it has none of the egalitarian, welfare-state motif, although the best do tend to exercise a paternalism toward their workers. They are less committed than the caretaker elite to the process of altering the traditional society at large, being interested primarily only in those segments which directly affect them—their market and labor force.

The caretaker elite, on the other hand, is committed to making sweeping changes in their efforts to increase the economic well-being of the populace. Hence, to them, almost all elements of the traditional society appear to be obstacles to modernization and economic growth. At the same time, the difficulty of effecting the desired changes is underestimated. In connection with agriculture, Charles E. Kellog writes:

Perhaps the greatest handicap to agricultural improvement in many underdeveloped areas is the false notion that this improvement is a relatively simple matter. This unhappy idea has even been supported by some American and European advisors. The notion implies, firstly, that improved farming results from emphasizing a few simple practices; secondly, that "someone" knows what these should be; and thirdly, that it is necessary to find this "someone" and have him pass the "good word" on to the cultivators. None of this is approximately true for the most underdeveloped parts of the world.[14]

The reasoning of the caretaker elites about the alteration of the traditional society is much the same as that Kellogg criticizes. Often, the economic motivations and organization necessary to implement plans do not exist or are contravened in the culture. All too frequently, planners expect cultural attitudes and values which might impede progress to (1) disappear as a consequence of changes in the economic structure; (2) be altered by the universal solvents of education and enthusiasm; or (3) be changed by multi-faceted community-development projects at the local level. It is by no means inevitable that these desired results will obtain; and one might hazard a guess that the most important obstacle to development programs has been the slippage in which programmatic inputs are dissipated as they filter through the traditional agrarian society.

124

Just as the caretaker elites in the various countries of southern Asia seem to share a remarkably similar ideology, so too the agrarian societies are remarkably similar in the broad outlines of their economically relevant attitudes and values. Considerable variations of detail occur, but the complex in each country is very much the same. The conceptions of what constitutes wealth and property, and of the priorities of most valued possessions, are strikingly alike. There is general agreement about the desirable und undesirable methods of acquiring wealth, about the appropriate means for transforming wealth into status, and about the responsibilities of the wealthy man. Taken together, these attributes form an interlocking system which provides a pattern of motivation for gain. Its touchstone is a particular form of property, land; but its rewards lie within a much more complex framework of mutual obligations and legitimation of status.

In all of the countries of the area, land heads the list of approved possessions. Where tenancy forms are simple, as in the Philippines and parts of South-East Asia, land rights may approximate our own conception of private property. Elsewhere, tenancy practices are an intricate system of graduated rights and privileges, as in India, Pakistan, or Ceylon. In the latter case, the drive for more land takes the form of maneuvering upward in the complicated labyrinth, enhancing one's security of tenure and share of the harvest, and diminishing the onerousness of the duties and services owed to the landlord. Recent tenancy legislation has had the effect of foreshortening the hierarchy, but it has by no means abolished it. Status and power differentials within rural areas are dependent upon land rights, and even wealth earned in non-agricultural pursuits must be converted into landholding to be fully legitimate. This overwhelming emphasis on acquiring land is partly understandable, since it is the primary agricultural producers' goods; but often it is pursued even when the return from it is marginal and alternative investments are demonstrably more rewarding. This is also true of the peasant's preference for growing food crops, particularly the staples like paddy or wheat. Even in areas of the highest commercialization of agriculture, peasants want to keep enough land in food staples so that they can avoid the whimsies of the market mechanisms. From Ceylon to Viet Nam, paddy land is sold last, and has a special significance for family prestige beyond that of land in other crops. One result of this emphasis is that, with increasing densities and general inflationary trends, the price of land rises rapidly. In the Philippines, the Japanese occupation and the guerrilla opposition during World War II exhausted most forms of portable wealth; land values spiralled; and today even uncultivated lands are held as investments by speculators. In 1960, the price of land is eight to ten times more than in 1939, and its costs more than can normally be earned on it in fifteen to twenty years. The conception of land as the primary form of wealth is also enhanced by the growing proletarianization of agricultural labor in many countries.

The demand for other forms of producers' goods in agriculture is essentially inelastic, in that the relatively crude implements, the small sizes of the holdings, and the commitment of agriculturists to traditional methods of cultivation, leave little scope for expansion. One can increase the number of buffaloes or oxen or implements when the amount of land increases; aside from that, there is little status-giving wealth in agricultural producers' goods. Improvements in agriculture, such as the digging of wells and canals for irrigation, are heavily labor-intensive, and tend to take the form of direct investment with payment in kind or reciprocal services rather than monetary rewards.

The same inelasticity is discernible in most rural consumption items, particularly the necessities like housing and clothing. Except for the very wealthy, who are usually absentee owners, the range of expenditures on housing and clothing is relatively narrow. The peasant is prepared to consume luxury items, like bicycles, flashlights, radios, and clocks; but these are not considered normal wants and come far down the list in wealth. In some places, sumptuary laws or customs limit the consumption of certain luxury goods to individuals whose high status is ascriptive rather than achieved.

If accumulation takes a form other than landholding, it is in currency or coins hidden in trunks or buried in a corner of the house, in jewelry and precious metals—the lower classes' insurance—and in stores of grain. The last may be used not only to safeguard a supply for consumption, but also to speculate on mid-seasonal fluctuations in prices.

In Viet Nam, an interesting distinction is made that confirms the general point. Hidden goods (*cua chim*) are distinguished from goods on display (*cua noi*). The former include houses, rice fields, cattle, rice in storage, money at the bottom of a trunk, and money on loan. The latter include clothing, jewelry which is worn, furniture, vehicles, etc. Items in the first category are highly valued; those in the latter are not.

Various permanent crops are important in rural wealth—coconuts, rubber, coffee and tea, fruit. In general, however, lands devoted to these are supplemental to, rather than in place of, land sown with food staples. After annual cash-crop land, they are the first to be sold in times of economic distress.

As a rule, the status dividends of rural wealth vary in ways which are directly opposed to the principles of rational profit maximization. This is not to say that the peasant is insensitive to economic incentives, nor that wealth in and of itself is not status-enhancing. However, differentiations are made among forms of wealth that are based on traditional hierarchical relationships where the holding of property was only part of the

126

stratification principle, where the isolation of consumers from producers' goods was at a minimum, and where the incentive to place gain above the other obligations was weak.

The primary bases for the legitimation of wealth in the rural areas are (1) how it is made and (2) how it is spent. In the first category, there is a distinct preference for wealth accumulated in the agricultural sphere rather than in commerce or moneylending. In the second category, each culture establishes a set of traditional philanthropies and dependencies which become part of behavior required of the wealthy man.

The preference for the landed aristocrat over the wealthy trader is deep. This is partly due to the special status value of land, which in South Asia is correlated highly with caste rankings. It is also due to the fact that the landholders are bound, by a set of traditional obligations, to their economic dependents. They should lend work animals, money, or seed free or at reduced costs; they should support the village festivals, assist in court cases, allow free grazing on their lands, help in times of family crisis, etc. At the same time, economic transactions between them and their inferiors in status are hedged about with non-economic controls which limit the permissible degree of exploitation—controls which grow out of the whole network of customary relationships in the village.

The paternalistic role described above is most clearly applicable to inherited landed wealth. As in all cultures, the *nouveaux riches* are on trial. An interesting illustration of this was the public pressure on war widows in the Philippines, who were suddenly wealthy with insurance payments, to invest the money in land, and the criticism of any conspicuous consumption. The conversion of wealth into status is an expensive process. In an extreme form, it may provide for the circulation of fortunes within three generations.

The example of a newly rich man in Viet Nam in trying to "wash his face" is instructive. He begins by giving help, chiefly financial, to his relatives and friends. He must own rice fields and a comfortable home in his native village; he must "purchase" a place of honor in the community hierarchy; he must organize a major banquet to which all villagers are invited; and his sons must be trained for a job higher in the social hierarchy, that of a scholar or a government official. By this time, any surplus has been dissipated and his children are in no position to renew it.

Moneylenders, storekeepers, and traders who mediate between the village and the outside world are considered to be parasitical, since, in the view of the peasants, their work does not contribute to the agricultural process. Moreover, they represent the point at which assets are monetized; and the peasant's general expectation in monetary transactions is that he will be swindled. Peasants are, of course, encouraged to find the best selling price for their grain. However, attempts made by merchants and

127

traders to maximize their return or to respond to market considerations are considered to be cheating and exploitation of the agriculturists. This attitude is partly due to the fact that the peasant usually has dealings with the trader and moneylender at a time when he is at a disadvantage in bargaining. Merchants are doubly suspect; since they are not bound by the customary code of inferior-superior relations, their rapacity, as the villagers see it, is uncontrolled. Where rapid accumulation occurs, violation of the economic norms is assumed to have preceded it.

The hostility toward the presumed exploiter in most societies results in the insulation of the non-agriculturist profit maximizers. Consequently, when this function is a full-time occupation, it is usually performed by groups outside of or immune to the normal system of sanctions and status gradations of the society. Their isolation is also necessary to them because it enables them to raise their children with a set of norms in direct contrast to those of the rest of the society. This is easy in a society like India's, where the distinctiveness of the ethics and style of life of each group is encouraged; but in other countries, it requires those with the motivation of gain to be ethnically separate from the rest of the society—in fact, traders and merchants are often alien in origin. Good illustrations are provided by the South Indian Chettiars and the overseas Chinese in South-East Asia; and by the diffusion of Marwaris and western Indian *banya* castes in India. The trading groups, thus insulated, develop a strong cohesion within heir own community, and evolve their own traditions, which are highly resistant to change. The ethnic discreteness of the trading community also induces low permeability; i.e., it inhibits the entry of newcomers into trading activities.

What are the consequences of this peasant complex for savings and investment?

The primary economic motivation in the village is the provision of security and status for the family—what Sombart would have called the principle of subsistence rather than the principle of gain. Economic activity is carried on to supply consumption needs. It is true that when a family is living close to or below the subsistence level, the two motivating principles are indistinguishable in actual behavior. The important differences are in the preference for production of one's own consumption goods, especially food; in the low marginal propensity to save when the subsistence level has been reached; in the unwillingness to forego present consumption for future gain; in the lack of motivation to invest more effort once the comfort level has been reached; and in the low degree of responsiveness to rapidly changing rates of return on investment of effort and money. Savings which do occur are drained off—into the inflationary pressure on land; into enhanced consumption of better quality, if not more, foodstuffs and consumers goods; into economically unproductive

128

investments in status; into own-account expenditures on housing that are entered in the investment and capital formation column by courtesy only; and into hoarding of foodstuffs and currency. To a great extent, savings remain in non-monetized form. This is partly because the most common outlets for them do not require monetization, and partly because the peasant expects that he loses every time his assets are turned into cash. This expectation is reinforced by his thorough distrust of the personnel through whom he monetizes his product. Not the least of those whom he distrusts are the government's tax assessors. One of the major problems confronting the planners is the fact that, the more they try to reach some of the incremental income accruing to the rural sector as a result of national development efforts, the more it is likely to recede into non-monetized own-account expenditures on marginally productive investments like housing.

The chief savers and accumulators in the rural areas are the traders, brokers, moneylenders, and shopkeepers. Their savings do somewhat enhance the rural economy, in that they provide credit in the traditionally money-short countryside. Generally, however, only a small part of this credit is used for capital investment in agriculture, and even less for improvement of production techniques. Some traders and moneylenders become involved in the peasant complex in trying to legitimate their wealth by traditional means, a process which is rarely completely successful. One of the most explosive issues in southern Asia is the progressive alienation of land into the hands of non-agriculturists.

It might be asked why these groups have not spurred the kind of economic growth that occurred in the West; why petty capitalism has not taken the next step toward rationalizing the organization of production. These questions take us far afield, into the origins and role of entrepreneurs in these societies—a topic much too extensive to be considered here. It is relevant, however, to comment that custom defined the horizons of their activities, just as it did those of other groups in the traditional society. Their urban counterparts were, in fact, productive of highly developed commercial and handicraft economies; but the conservative nature of tradition within these insulated groups kept them in commerce and finance and out of manufacture.

With a few exceptions, the modern sectors of the economy were built by foreigners or "new men" not drawn from the traditional mercantile houses. Currently, as the new generation is increasingly educated in a Westernized fashion, some of its members are passing over into the Western-oriented business and industrial elites. This entails a consequent loss in the solidarity of the traditional communities. Their status and role in the rural areas make it unlikely that they would exercise much influence on the techniques of production, even if they cared to.

Leverage, if it is to come, must come from the caretaker elites. Apparently, at least in the rural areas—and it is there that the basic changes in the society must be made—the task of creating the characteristics of the "unique historical emergent" that spurred economic development in the West is a gigantic one. Too many other demands take precedence over economic ones. Rational profit maximization is laid very lightly on top of traditional economic attitudes and values. The pursuit of profit maximization is highly circumscribed. A large part of mutual rights and obligations lies outside of the market mechanism. Perhaps southern Asia will develop a unique historical emergent of its own.

NOTES TO CHAPTER 6

1. This paper grows out of a project sponsored by UNESCO and the Conference on Economic and Cultural Affairs. Participants in the project were Professor Bert Hoselitz of the University of Chicago, Professor A. F. A. Husain of Dacca University in East Pakistan, Professor Agaton Pal of Silliman University in the Philippines, Professor Michael Swift of the University of Malaya, Professor S. J. Tambiah of the University of Ceylon, Professor V. Q. Thuc of the University of Saigon in Viet Nam, Professor Marjorie Topley of Hong Kong, Professor T. K. N. Unnithan of the School of Town and County Planning in New Delhi. I have drawn heavily upon their work for these comments. The Asian countries covered, as indicated by the participants, are those in South and South East Asia (what used to be called Southern Asia), from Pakistan to the Philippines and excluding China and Japan.

2. Simon Kuznets, "Capital Formation Proportions: International Comparisons for Recent Years," *Economic Development and Cultural Change,* VIII, No. 4, Part 2 (July, 1960).

3. V. V. Bhatt, "Savings and Capital Formation," *Economic Development and Cultural Change,* VII, No. 3, Part I (April, 1959), 318-42.

4. Kuznets, *op. cit.*

5. Wilfred Malenbaum, *East and West in India's Development* (1959).

6. For a review of current findings, see Irwin Friend, "Determinants of the Volume and Composition of Saving with Special Reference to the Influence of Monetary Policy" (to be published).

7. Kuznets, *op. cit.*

8. Wilfred Malenbaum, *The Comparative Study of Economic Growth and Structure* (New York, 1959), p. 31.

9. Hoselitz and Lambert, "The Acquisition and Uses of Wealth in Western Societies," to be published in forthcoming UNESCO symposium.

10. For a good summary of the controversy see Ephraim Fischoff, "The Protestant Ethic and the Spirit of Capitalism: the History of a Controversy," *Social Research*, 11 (1944), 61-77. For a sampling of excerpts in the dispute, see

131

Robert W. Green, *Protestantism and Capitalism: The Weber Thesis and its Critics* (Boston, 1959).

11. Max Weber, *The Religion of India,* trans. Hans H. Gerth and Don Martindale (Glencoe, Ill., 1958), p. 337.

12. See Richard D. Lambert, "Religion, Economics and Violence in Bengal," *Middle East Journal,* IV (July, 1950), 307-28.

13. In a recent study I made of factory labor in Poona, I found that some of the workers seemed to have genuine aspirations to become supervisors—but it soon appeared that these were more expectations than aspirations, and that those workers who had social characteristics similar to the present supervisors expected to reach that post. Their own efforts were to be confined to minimal job performance until the position came to them.

14. Charles E. Kellog, "Transfer of Basic Skills of Food Production," *Annals of the American Academy of Political and Social Science*, September, 1960.

PART IV

Government and Public Administration

CHAPTER 7

System, Process and the Politics of Economic Development

DAVID E. APTER

The University of California, Berkeley

THE APPROACH TO THE PROBLEM

Economic development and technological change are among the most desired goals of political leaders in contemporary new nations. Countries which have achieved independence from colonial status since 1945—and it is to these nations that this analysis is addressed—share urgent needs in both areas. The new nations have embarked on programs which they hope will help them to ameliorate their material standards. As a result, the relationship of political development to economic development is extremely relevant. What political forms are best suited to economic growth?

Of course, the role of the government varies considerably from one new nation to another. Depending on the role of the specific government, one nation's approach to technological change and economic growth will also vary from another's. The practitioner of economic aid must have a fuller understanding of the nature of the political systems emerging in new nations, if he is to understand—and, indeed, to anticipate—the probable uses and abuses to which economic aid will be put. Nor are such matters purely practical. Scholars, too, need to give special attention to the relationship between government and economic growth, if they are to understand both normative and analytical theories applicable to new nations.

I hope to show the relationship between politics and economics in new nations, by exploring some of the properties of systems and processes at work, so that applications of policy and ideas of politics about new nations can be seen more realistically. My focal problem centers around the political strategies used to induce technological change and economic development. I have deliberately omitted any discussion of programs of investment and capital formation, technical training, or utilization of

135

economic and technical elites. Nor have I discussed the adaptations of outlook and ideas that are necessary for technological change and innovation. I am aware of these factors, as is everyone involved in research concerning new nations—indeed, the immensity of these problems is blinding. This makes it imperative to attempt to build new theories, ones with a general design but admitting of specific applications.

Many choices in theoretical approach are available to the observer of development in new nations. One approach can appropriately be called "behavioral." The behavioral approach examines several variables to infer, from their relationships, an explanation of individual actions, motivations, and perceptions. Principles are established determining significant roles, their allocations and linkages. However, the larger context within which action occurs is not satisfactorily dealt with.

A second common approach is *ad hoc* analysis. In the problem of development, we can assess levels of growth, especially from a comparative point of view, if we introduce three useful factors of development: (*a*) the goals of economic and social development set by political leaders and others significant in the system; (*b*) the state of technology or resources and skills available for achieving those goals; and (*c*) the degree of outside support available. This suggestive and stimulating approach is, essentially, that of W. W. Rostow, as distinct from that of W. Arthur Lewis, in discussing economic growth.[1] By determining the nature of economic growth—or insisting on a standard of goals—and evaluating the resources, human and material, made possible by the state of technology, as well as the external contributions in investment funds and technical assistance, we are enabled to indicate conditions necessary for self-sustained growth and rapid economic development.

For our inquiry, which focuses on the relationship between government and economics, neither the behavioral nor the *ad hoc* approach is entirely satisfactory. In attempting to evaluate patterns of change through examining the phenomena of development, they fail to account for the "system" needs of governments. However, these system needs are in urgent need of analysis. This is illustrated by the fact that new nations are not very stable entities, and, second, that their governments are rarely effectively institutionalized in relation to the society at large.

The alternative approach I am suggesting here is structural analysis utilizing comparative method. The concrete units of analysis are society and government. Economic development is a problem both of government and of members of society. To deal with these units in interaction, with respect to technological change and economic development, we want a theory which indicates the *properties* of the system that form the basis of the relationship between the two units. Moreover we want to indicate the processes which will result from action between systems when con-

136

fronted with the problems of economic development and technological change.

I have written this long preamble because I wish to lay the foundation for what may appear an obscure way of dealing with readily discernible problems. The behavioral and the *ad hoc* approaches lend themselves to *probabilistic* theories; the third, to *systemic* theories. Each has its respective emphasis. The first two lead to an evaluation of behavior and efficiency in the development process. The structural analysis approach, as used here, leads to a theory of "properties" and relationships deriving from the needs of government—these needs having profound effects on the course of technological change. The specification of relationships is, thus, the purpose of this paper; and the problems of economic development and technological change are treated as of strategic importance for governments of new nations.

I propose to deal with these problems in two steps. First, we must specify the differences, from the range of characteristics distributed among the rapidly growing number of new nations, in the natures of political systems. Second, we must investigate the kinds of response to the problems of technological innovation that these differing systems evoke. Some of the immediate problems are (*a*) whether the role of political entrepreneurship is greater or smaller; (*b*) the degree to which reliance will be placed on state enterprise for economic development; and (*c*) the extent to which talents will accumulate in the central organs of government or will become dispersed and decentralized throughout the system. If this form of analysis proves useful—and, for the present, it must remain experimental—it should provide a more systematic basis for the three problems of growth mentioned above; namely, setting realistic goals, technology and its application, and the use of outside aid.

This discussion brings together two dimensions of analysis developed elsewhere and used independently.[2] The first dimension concerns the natures of the various authority systems that have emerged in the new nations. Three developmental types have appeared. Each type manifests characteristic mechanisms for determining goals and for applying and using available technological and other resources. I have used such types because, while many of the acts and activities in which new nations engage are ostensibly common to many or all of them—and, indeed, many of the instrumentalities and mechanisms of political and economic development are essentially similar—nevertheless, their implications for a given society differ markedly, depending upon the type of political system that is predominant in it. Hence, if we can specify a useful set of systemic properties for political systems, we shall be better able to predict the preferences of political leaders for types of entrepreneurship and economic growth. In addition, more formally, the meaning and social implications

137

of these mechanisms will become more apparent. Our first concern, then, is to define the properties of developmental types that are sufficiently differentiated to illustrate the vast differences in the approaches to economic development in the new nations.

The second dimension concerns the processes of change within each of these types of systems. Having enlarged on the qualities of each of the types, we determine which processes are characteristic in each.

The two dimensions are structural and dynamic. The models presented here are not complete, since extremely important elements are not within the scope of this discussion. Much material has, therefore, been excluded from this paper, because the integration of the dimensions of social analysis in a larger systematic theory must always be coupled with practical field work and research—if not, it is likely to become a sterile and arid system of formal theory-building. Moreover, the integration of dimensions of social analysis inevitably results in considerable overlapping and duplication. Therefore, I believe that the process of building a general theory should consist of taking a limited series of steps, which enable us to piece together theoretical statements and propositions in a careful but necessarily tentative manner.

I should like to emphasize a point I made earlier, namely, that the new nations are different from older and more stable ones in at least one way. One distinguishing characteristic of the former is that the rules of politics and the actions of governments take place in a less institutionalized framework than in the latter. Political leaders, however, popular, are acutely aware of the fact that when the institutionalization of governmental structures remains weak, they are particularly vulnerable to public whim and fancy. Hence it is useful to have a dynamic approach to the relationship of government to society.[3] This form of structural analysis has many merits. First, general technological change can be considered in relation to its effects on political organization and on the needs and structure of governments in new nations. In addition, it enables us to indicate the role that government is likely to play in technological change, in terms of reliance on political entrepreneurship and government intervention in the economic process. By examining some of the characteristics of governments in new countries, we can provide a framework for determining the levels of development goals that decision-makers will choose, the uses and applications they will make of technology, and the terms under which they will seek and apply outside aid. In other words, I am attempting here, though dealing with the fundamental system properties of governments in developing areas, to establish general guides for the analysis of more immediate empirical phenomena. We shall now turn to structural types. First I shall indicate their properties, before going on to discuss process variables and relationships.

138

Three developmental types have been considered here. Each represents a form of regime. We are defining them in order to examine, dynamically, the relationship of government to society. The critical question centers around the capacity of each type to absorb change and generate further innovation. All three types have emerged with lightning speed as a result of the extension of political freedom to Asia and Africa.

These types are, of course, analytical, deriving from a larger structural system of variables. They are "constructions" from typical clusterings of variables which appear frequently in the empirical universe. In that limited sense, they may be regarded as developmental profiles. They were developed primarily with respect to emerging African systems, although it is my contention that they can be applied to the governments of other new nations.[4] They are intended to be similar to Lasswell's "developmental types," the most celebrated of which was "the garrison state." Unlike Lasswell's types, which are not rooted in a wider structural base, these are derived empirically by means of a more elaborate comparative scheme.[5]

Our investigations centered around the observation that each new country in Africa faces a series of choices; in making its choices, it defines its political machinery. Some countries, e.g., Mali, Guinea, and Ghana, have chosen to mobilize their political energies and resources for a grand assault on poverty, ignorance, and backwardness. Others, like Nigeria, have tended toward some union of important constituent parts. They seek, in political unity, a common denominator to serve all the main groups within the country. Others, e.g., Ethiopia and Uganda, represent something perhaps more rare. In them, change is filtered through the medium of traditional institutions—i.e., innovation itself is traditionalized and rendered compatible with traditional institutions.

The first type we have called a *mobilization system*; the second, a *reconciliation system*; and the third, a *modernizing autocracy*. Examples of the mobilization system include Guinea and Ghana, and, in a more extreme form, the Soviet Union and Communist China. The reconciliation system is operative in Nigeria; it has also been characteristic of the United States and other federal systems. The third, the modernizing autocracy, type may be found in Buganda, Morocco, Ethiopia, and, in its sharpest form, in Japan, particularly after the Meiji Restoration.

Each type comprises five categories: (1) patterns of legitimacy; (2) loyalty; (3) decisional autonomy; (4) distribution of authority; and (5) ideological expression.[6] We can now indicate how each of the three types of regime reflects these categories. Each is an effort to examine structurally the consequences of actual political arrangements in the politics of new nations. The crucial point on which we are examining each type is whether or not it has the capacity to absorb technological change, and, in addition, to generate new political forms.

Let me now consider the types of political systems in more detail. The mobilization system is most clearly described in Selznick's description of an "organizational weapon." [7] Characteristically, mobilization systems try to rebuild society in such a way that both the instrumentalities of government and the values associated with change are remarkably altered. In Africa, countries whose regimes are of this type incline toward the belief that, to produce "the new Africa," the structural precedents of African society must be altered, and a new system of loyalties and ideas must be created, focused around the concept that economic progress is the basis for modern society.

The characteristics of a mobilization system are as follows: (*a*) hierarchical authority; (*b*) total allegiance; (*c*) tactical flexibility; (*d*) unitarism; and (*e*) ideological specialization.[8] Party or government becomes the central instrument of change.

The reconciliation system is considerably harder to define than the first. Its outstanding characteristic is the high value it places on compromises between groups which express prevailing political objectives and views. As we are using the term, a reconciliation system evolves with the formation of a simple political unit from constituent political units which do not lose their political identity on uniting. In practical terms, reconciliation systems can include relatively loose confederations which have recognized structure or highly organized parliamentary regimes. The reconciliation system is characterized by (*a*) pyramidal authority; (*b*) multiple loyalties; (*c*) necessity for compromise; (*d*) pluralism; and (*e*) ideological diffuseness.[9]

The third type of system is the modernizing autocracy, where hierarchical authority is buttressed by traditional concepts of legitimacy. One crucial typical feature of the modernizing autocracy is its ability to absorb change as long as the system of authority is not affected by it. For example, in Uganda, the Buganda Kingdom can employ new skills, modernize the school system, and expand social-welfare activities; a civil service has replaced the patrimonial bureaucratic system while retaining intact its traditional modes of authority. The modernizing autocracy manifests a profound internal solidarity based on ethnicity or religion, by means of which support is retained for the political leaders or king who makes claims on the members of the system and controls them. Its characteristics are: (*a*) hierarchical authority; (*b*) exclusivism; (*c*) strategic flexibility; (*d*) unitarism; and (*e*) neo-traditionalism.

I shall further discuss these types before going on to the second stage of this analysis, in which I shall include the consequences of economic

140

development in each of them. As I have said, the role of the government in a country's economic development varies in terms of goals of development, the level of technology and available resources, and the degree of outside support which the country is both willing and able to enlist. The way that these aspects of economic development are handled depends largely on the nature of the political system in the given country. The three forms of political structure of new states are alternative types of systems that are different in the ways in which they cope with these facets of economic growth.

If the functioning of new nations is regarded in terms of these types, the following characteristics are discernible. In mobilization systems, the goals of economic growth are very important. Also, they tend to be unrealistic; many of them are just beyond the normal capacities of technology and resources. Consequently, the effort to achieve them requires considerable discipline. New institutions must be created for the purpose of removing all those social institutions which restrict the processes of economic development. Typically, mobilization systems are inclined toward the ideology of socialism as a contemporary expression of Puritanism. They emphasize discipline and hard work for the attainment of economic goals. This emphasis implies that economic development will re-structure society so that those roles and tasks which are functional to the establishment of a modern economic order will become the dominant ones, while older roles will be obliterated. This is why the mobilization system places great stress on militancy and party organization. Governmental enterprise becomes the major mechanism for economic growth. Correspondingly, high investments are made in education and social welfare, on the grounds that an efficient labor force is the *sine qua non* of economic development. Such systems need a powerful organizational nucleus which takes the major responsibility for the establishment and achievement of goals. They are usually "autocratic" in an organizational sense.[10]

In the reconciliation system, economic growth is more diffuse. Just as political authority is widely dispersed, so there is greater reliance on private entrepreneurship than there is in the mobilization system. Political and economic decision-making is more widespread throughout the society. For example, government shares of the gross domestic product of Nigeria represent roughly only ten per cent compared to the government shares of Ghana, which are almost twenty-four per cent and rapidly rising. Politically, the reconciliation system pays far more respect to cultural separatism and local parochialism than does the mobilization system. In so far as the reconciliation type is limited in its decision-making processes by the need to find some "lowest common denominator" which will appeal to its constituent units, its progress toward goals of economic development,

141

and the goals themselves, tend to be very moderate. The relationship between internal resources and the state of technology is closer than in the mobilization type. In the mobilization system, an effort is made to effect the quickest and closest approximation of the material cultures of the technologically advanced nations of the world. Goals are thus endowed with a symbolic quality which is lacking in both the reconciliation or modernizing autocracy systems. Contrasting examples which illustrate the differences between a reconciliation and a mobilization system (where both are concerned with economic growth) are India and Communist China. The respective strategies of development, and their consequences for the people, are vastly different in the two.[11]

The modernizing autocracy exhibits structural similarities to the mobilization type, but it is distinguished by its stability within the context of rapid economic growth. Economic goals are usually more restricted and less symbolic than those of the mobilization system. Also, they must not be insuperable obstacles to the maintenance of crucial traditional institutions. For example, in a modernizing autocracy, it may be possible to change a patrimonial chieftancy system under a king into a more rationalized civil service system; however, it would be considerably more difficult to absorb an emerging system of party politics—especially when the latter would alter the patterns of recruitment to posts of political power. Strong restraints are usually placed on changes that might lead to party politics. The modernizing autocracy may inhibit certain activities of economic development if they seem threatening to the autocratic principle of rule. In Uganda, the government of Buganda is willing to restrict foreign capital investment in commercial establishments when it feels that certain of its traditional institutions would thereby be altered. In other words, the goals of economic development are filtered through the screen of traditional institutions. To be accepted, economic goals must show some positive relationship to the existing system of authority. However, this does not prevent a great deal of modernization from taking place.[12] From this point of view, one of the intriguing aspects of Japan and Morocco—two traditional modernizing autocracies—is the alacrity with which they respond to the objectives of economic development.

Although the mechanisms of political and economic growth may seem very similar in all three types, each shows a different focus and emphasis. In the mobilization system, the problem of control is central; in its effort to transform society in order to attain economic objectives, it drives opposition underground. Local separatist tendencies must be smashed. Symbolic loyalties to the political leaders and to the state must take precedence over any others. Political leaders find that they are the managers of a society in transition and must take steps to safeguard their tenure and efficiency. Policy derives from finding a balance between the

142

need to insure managerial success and the maintenance of political rule, on the one hand, and the actual achievement of economic goals, on the other. This is characteristic in the mobilization system. Usually, there is a government or party representative on all local development projects. He is there not only to initiate and stimulate local spontaneity but also to safeguard government or party control over the group—local groupings must not become sources of opposition.

In contrast, the spontaneous development of new groups is an important feature of the reconciliation system. The new groups may or may not contribute to the efficient achievement of economic goals; they do enlarge the degree of pluralism in the system. In the mobilization type, much of the spontaneity of local and rural development is eventually lost, because every new center of organization is usually controlled by government. Reconciliation systems not only accept opposition; in addition, the government, by catering to opposition and separatist points of view, is profoundly affected and shaped in its goals and in the methods of fulfilling those goals. In the mobilization system, potential sources of opposition are immediately attacked and either eliminated or effectively silenced. In the reconciliation system, local development more easily retains its vitality. This has important implications both for development and for democracy.[13]

The reconciliation systems are immediately concerned with the mechanics of establishing useful and acceptable economic priorities and with the means of achieving them in conformity with existing political practices. In this sense, they are far less flexible tactically than the mobilization system, while also being less doctrinaire. In reconciliation systems, the problem is to bring the goals advanced by the government into accord with the public desires. Both the consent and the support of the constituents of the national society are required. This is one reason that reconciliation systems rely heavily on outside sources of assistance. A government in such a system also prefers talent to be dispersed rather than concentrated at the center. Reconciliation systems in new nations are usually moderately socialist, and consequently extensive planning agencies are part of their governments. Nevertheless, planning is essentially of the "enabling" variety, i.e., it provides opportunities for private enterprise and local self-help by manipulating strategic sectors of the economy.[14]

In the modernizing autocracy, as we have indicated, considerable political stability is likely throughout the process of change. Less reliance on control and coercion is evident than in the mobilization system, while more efficient means of achieving goals are available than in the reconciliation systm. Traditional values are not destroyed; rather, they are modified and extended. Typically, the modernizing autocracy is bureau-

143

cratic. Traditional loyalties and the bureaucracy coincide. In the modernization system, on the other hand, the civil service bureaucracy is in conflict with the party bureaucracy which, having captured the organs of state power, is inclined to consider the internal needs of the party above all others. Party eventually comes to represent the state.[15]

In each type of system, the most important issue is economic development. It is economic development which either becomes the means to rapid change or else presents the greatest threat to the prevailing system. In most new nations, there are mixed feelings about the consequences of economic development. While few disagree with the material benefits of a rising standard of living, many are bitter about the organizational consequences and the demands upon individuals that such a process involves. The mobilization system is clearly willing to ride roughshod over more parochial interests. Economic development then attains the same symbolic meaning as a national goal that freedom and independence had during the nation's colonial period. Under the banners of "freedom from want" and "increased opportunity," the population can be "mobilized" for change.

The modernizing autocracy may proceed in great leaps toward modernization. However, its periods of rapid advance must be followed by periods of digestion during which the changes effected may be absorbed into the traditional political framework.

Thus economic development produces different problems, depending upon the nature and needs of the political systems. We can now extend our analysis and attempt to indicate some of the underlying factors which determine political responses to economic change. We are concerned not only with the degree to which each of the three systems responds to the achievement of economic development, but also with the consequences of such development for the future of each system itself.

Summary
All three types of systems discussed here have certain characteristics in common. Their political leaders are trying to achieve some balance between a desired level of public satisfaction, the attainment of goals of development, and the strengthening of political power. One important difference among the three types is the degree to which, in each, public satisfaction can be achieved immediately or must be postponed—a factor which has a great effect on the selection of goals. The mobilization system operates on the principle that immediate satisfaction must be sacrificed for the sake of future fulfilment. In such a system, there is a concept of forced saving in the most real sense of the term—i.e., the immediate benefits to which people aspire become limited, while postponed real gratifications through economic development become the goal of

144

government. As a consequence, a system of government is produced in which savings for investment, in the widest sociological sense, become possible. Other things being equal, we would, therefore, expect the most rapid economic growth to occur in the mobilization system.

In the reconciliation system, the goals must be moderated to conform to current demands, and the degree of forced saving is also more moderate. The degree of change is dictated chiefly by the availability of talents and resources that are widely dispersed throughout the system. If rapid technological change and economic change are to proceed, non-political means must be used to fulfill the same objectives which, in the mobilization system, are maximized through political entrepreneurship and state enterprise.

In the modernizing autocracy, it may be possible to achieve greater forced savings if the government chooses to do so. On the other hand, private sources of investment and public enterprise are likely to collaborate effectively in a close-knit relationship.

However, each type of system manifests internal conflicts and contradictions in connection with the variables listed.

To determine why each type responds in the ways generally described so far, we require a set of variables which can show the process consequences of system. Otherwise, discussion will remain at the phenomenological level, and information will be illustrative rather than explanatory. In the next section of this paper, we shall consider some process variables which apply to all three of the developmental types discussed.

In our remarks, the idea is implicit that all of the types exhibit two characteristic decisional outputs. One comprises developmental decisions; the other comprises system-maintenance decisions. Analysis of these outputs necessitates a discussion of process, and it is to the process variables that we turn for further investigation.

THE PROCESS VARIABLES

Having described the characteristics of the three developmental types of systems in new nations, we can now undertake an analysis of the political processes characteristic of each type.

Four variables are used in this analysis. They are (a) goals, defined as operative purposes of government including economic and social development; [16] (b) costs, which are the allocations of real income which must be made with respect to the achievement of such goals; (c) coercion, or government actions to insure some specific level of conformity; and (d) information, or the knowledge available to decision-makers, on the basis of which future decisions may be made.

These process variables can now be linked to our developmental types. Then we can determine, on the basis of empirical data, the political consequences of technological change and economic development that seem characteristic.

Process in the Mobilization Type of System

A mobilization system involves government in active intervention in technological change and economic development. The organizational characteristics of government become a central feature of its activities. Organization qua organization is always somewhat autocratic; and the organizational work of the government becomes pervasive, extending over wide ranges of the social and economic life of a new nation. As a result, people are "acted upon" by an "outside" system, i.e., government. In turn, this leads to a strengthening of the hierarchical and ideological facets of control over society at large. Leadership and the state tend toward identity. Goals assume the characteristics of (*a*) inviolability, and (*b*) satisfaction postponed to a future period. Goals are thus profoundly evolutionary and often symbolic.

Hence we can assume that increasing organizational control, for the purposes of mobilization and goal achievement, inevitably runs into public conservatism. A manifestation of increasing control is reliance on coercion to reach objectives that are established for the system. Coercion requires ideological justification. Technological change and economic development become symbolically important because they emphasize future social benefits. If developmental goals are very unrealistic, they may strain the available resources and technology within a new nation so much that mobilization systems may rely on external means to attain them —seeking to maximize their goals by political bargaining with industrialized powers or by acts of territorial expansion. The new nations have not yet indulged in the latter enterprise; but there are signs, in some mobilization systems, that agitation for territorial aggrandizement is beginning.

Third, we can assume that, as coercion increases, there is a corresponding decline in free information—or, in other words, in the information about public support and interests that is readily available to government. When coercion is increasing, the public tend to supply government with information that will please it. This decreases the reliability of information on which action may be based. It also makes it difficult for government to create sub-goals proximate to public needs. Government then acts in an atmosphere of greater uncertainty. To compensate for this, government leaders are inclined to increase coercion still more to insure compliance; and a new cycle of reactions is introduced.

Such a pattern has a number of effects on economic development. First, government becomes progressively more enmeshed in investment and in

146

seeking to control its side-effects in the society. Furthermore, the costs of coercion result in diverting revenue, hitherto available for investment, into military and police activities and other punitive institutions. Third, bargaining in external relations intensifies the need for stronger standing armies and better military technology, since in any bargaining relationship between independent nations, threats to one another are inherent in any interactions. Consequently, the costs of government rise continuously, and difficulties in spending investment funds for the expansion of government enterprise are met by raising public revenues and by the intensification of the mobilization process. Simultaneously, an increasing proportion of revenue is diverted to non-productive enterprise, i.e., to system-maintenance rather than to development.

In the mobilization system, the need for increasing governmental supervision and the effort to eliminate sources of major opposition result in a decline of cheap and valid information available to decision-makers. As this information declines, decision-makers find it more difficult to predict accurately the degree of public support that they have and the relationship of economic goals to public desires. To bridge the growing gap between the government and the people, there is an emphasis on ideological conformity. The highly centralized system of authority, in order to insure the allegiance of the people, continues to rely more and more on coercion. All voluntary organizations, trade unions, the military, and the bureaucracy must be increasingly devoted to the political leaders. The consequence is an even greater loss of free or inexpensive information, and, in extreme cases, the press and other media of public expression are controlled by the government.[17] The costs of coercion rise, and resources available for development, in part, are diverted to pay the rising expenses for the military and police. The optimal balance between economic growth and public desire becomes more and more determined by the actions necessary to secure the position of the government. In order to compensate for the diversion of funds which would ordinarily have been used for development, there is a tendency to use raw labor and "volunteer" labor for primary development. Talent accumulates at the center. The processes of administration are closely linked to the political control over economic development. Political leaders of the second rank and administrators are fearful of being posted far from the centers of power and intrigue.

Most new mobilization systems are autocratic rather than dictatorial. For one thing, dictatorship is inefficient without a substantial technology. In addition, dictatorship produces a control problem—not only are economic resources diverted, but, more important, many of the scarce managerial skills are consumed by the miilitary and police. Most of the new nations of Africa and Asia, however, are more concerned with utilizing

147

these scarce talents to attain economic and social goals. Therefore, typically there is a relatively mild autocracy, in which, frequently, nominal opposition or opposition within a single party remains possible. Thus, fairly inexpensive information is available to the political leaders. They can retain a closer relationship to the public and to public needs than would be possible in a totalitarian system. A mild autocracy becomes a relatively efficient means of implementing economic development and socio-political control simultaneously, by achieving equilibrium between high goal achievement, moderate coercion, and quite cheap information. This is possible in so far as the leaders are willing to modify goals in the light of information. If leaders are fanatical or inflexible about their objectives, they rely on coercion. The optimal balance of our four variables is upset; development becomes very expensive and totalitarian. Hence autocratic mobilization systems can be regarded as more efficient than totalitarian mobilization systems.

Process in the Reconciliation Type of System

In both the reconciliation system and the modernizing autocracy, the leaders are more willing to accomodate goals to public demands than are the leaders in the mobilization system. In trying to effect economic development, the mobilization system seeks to overhaul society in general through technological change. Precisely because of the ideological needs incurred by that process, the mobilization system attaches great symbolic meaning to such general goals, which become the moral basis of coercive politics.

Neither the reconciliation system nor the modernizing autocracy faces this difficulty. The modernizing autocracy derives its "morality" from tradition. The reconciliation system, when defining its objectives, is immediately concerned with gaining some agreement among its constituent units. I shall discuss this before examining process in the modernizing autocracies.

We have made several assumptions about reconciliation systems. First, in such a system, goals are based on information rather than on an image of the future. Then, too, they are high-information systems. Inexpensive information is made available to decision-makers by the variety of interest groups, voluntary associations, and political parties that express their demands to government. Third, reconciliation systems are low-coercion systems. Goals are in closer relation to resources and public desires, and government has less need to rely extensively on coercive techniques. In addition, since reconciliation systems are based upon the restrictions on government power inherent in this structural form, the government can rarely gain sufficient political consensus to enact coercive measures.

148

Fourth, reconciliation systems cannot easily act autocratically except under very extreme circumstances, such as war.

Information is cheap because any efforts to use coercive measures would call forth expensive and strenuous opposition by local and nongovernmental groups. Acting on the basis of information rather than through coercion, the government must evolve flexible strategies that enable it to win compliance. A high proportion of available resources can be utilized for economic development. However, there is one practical limitation inherent in the situation: a high rate of forced savings is politically impossible. The rate of capital investment is lower than that in the mobilization system. The government's efforts take the form of stimulating non-governmental development or local entrepreneurship. This may be done through providing sources of credit for private entrepreneurs, through expanding the possibilities of joint government and private enterprise through industrial development corporations and similar projects, and through encouraging outside investment.

The role of government is not organizational. The government's need is to reconcile diverse interests; it is mediating, integrating, and, above all, co-ordinating, rather than organizing and mobilizing. The mobilizational system fights society; the reconciliation system is a prisoner of society. Government may show that goals required by public expectations cannot, in the absence of forced measures, be achieved. The public are unwilling to sacrifice current consumption for the sake of future consumption and otherwise to modify their behavior in order to attain these goals. For this reason, while the government may be democratic, it may also break down in unfulfilment, corruption, and compromise. Thus the degree of economic development in a reconciliation system depends on the steadfast motives of the top political leaders, and on the public's determination to enforce self-discipline and to insure, through local participation in economic enterprise, a high level of development. When there are lags in the acceptance of economic goals or voluntary means of achieving them (and where, also, great cultural discontinuities may persist long after a new government has established itself), governments of the reconciliation type may be condemned to slower economic progress than would a mobilization system—at least in the short run;[18] the long-run prospects may, of course, be vastly different.

The reconciliation system must make constant efforts to find local sources of talent and engage them in the development process. When technical elites are being trained, for example, there must be a concomitant effort to maximize their services in a decentralized manner. Thus the processes of economic growth are dispersed, not only between the private and the public sectors of the economy, but also in the provinces as well as in the main center. Local decision-making and local capital investment

149

mean a great dependence on village and local communities. Hence, rapid economic growth is possible in a reconciliation system if and only if there are extensive self-discipline, popular participation, and great civic devotion. These preconditions occur only very rarely in new nations.[19]

Process in the Modernizing Autocracy Type of System
The modernizing autocracy presents a curious balance between the positions in the mobilization and reconciliation systems. First, the modernizing autocracy is able to modify its goal more easily than the mobilization system. In addition, modernizing autocracies have open to them certain coercive techniques, by traditional means, that do not result in restrictions on the flow of information.[20] Third, in so far as modernizing autocracies are autocratic, the coercive techniques available to political decision-makers have had a long tradition and are thoroughly understood by the public. Regularized means of public expression persist because, typically, modernizing autocracies have traditional limits placed on the power of decision-makers by custom and belief. Finally, the public have means for expressing their preferences about actions of government. These means are sufficiently institutionalized not to appear to government as dangerous forms of opposition within the society. The difficulty that the modernizing autocracy confronts is the possibility that changes effected in the economic sphere may eventually threaten the principle of hierarchical authority, with consequent demands for the substantial alteration of the system.

Normally, modernizing autocracies are monarchical or bureaucratic systems of rule. The symbolic position of the ruler is heavily emphasized. Opportunities for patrimony are available to him. As economic development proceeds, larger numbers of educated and technically trained personnel are absorbed into the traditional hierarchy. Those who express the desire for greater participation in the decision-making process pose the major problem. The political, rather than the economic, consequences of technological change and development create the most serious difficulties for the modernizing autocracy.

The most important feature of the modernizing autocracy is that it is a low-cost coercion system. Precedent, custom, and traditional behavioral prescriptions, having persisted through time, are central mechanisms of control over both leaders and led. At the same time, the principle of hierarchical authority and autocracy makes leaders relatively less accountable to the public than they are in the reconciliation system. Hence the leaders play an important role in innovation. Modernizing autocracies can advance technological change and require public acceptance precisely because such assertions from government are validated in the traditional patterns of authority. In so far as the government sets realistic economic goals, considerable compliance and acceptance can be assured with-

150

out increasing coercive costs and, equally important, without losing cheap information. It is interesting to speculate on the reasons for this.

The typical modernizing traditional autocracy centers around a monarch with two characteristics. He embodies complete and awesome power; he is the state personified; he is the personal lord of every citizen—the relationship between king and subject is direct and immediate. From this relationship, two contrasting forms of behavior can ensue. First, the use of authority is itself acceptable. Second, it is possible for the subject to feel that he can personally lay his complaints at the feet of his king and expect remedial action in his favor. This is the reason that modernizing autocracies are low-cost information systems, whereas in all other circumstances coercion and information have an inverse relationship to one another.[21]

One consequence of this set of circumstances is that modernizing autocracies can experiment with goals without paying the penalties of immediate instability. The modernizing autocracies, in distinction to the mobilization and reconciliation systems, have well-institutionalized regimes. In this, they show the greatest parallel to the historical experience of Western Europe, where, particularly in England, vast changes in economic and technological development during the nineteenth century were in accord with modifications in the political sector. Despite the magnitude of the changes, England was able to retain great stability—a factor not unrelated to the economy's ability to expand as rapidly as it did. Economic development also enabled England to change from a modernizing autocracy to a parliamentary unitary reconciliation type of system. Other examples, however, show a different pattern. Tsarist Russia was clearly a modernizing autocracy, at least after the emancipation of the serfs in 1861. But the excesses of the bureaucracy, and corruption, war, and poverty, required more effective and drastic structural reorganization than the government could provide. The Russian case can be regarded as a shift from a modernizing autocracy to a mobilization system. However, as a modernizing autocracy it sought economic development through war and expansion, as did Japan and Prussia. In these respects, the modernizing autocracies of Russia, Japan, and Germany at the turn of the century have many features in common.

The modernizing autocracies in the new nations are subject to tendencies similar to those operative in the examples given above. They can promote economic development along with stability only in the short run, because they cannot absorb the new elites sufficiently into the traditional hierarchy. The new elites become the spearhead of political reform, a situation which the modernizing autocracy can suffer only on a limited scale. (The rare exception, England, transformed the practice while retaining the form.)[22]

151

In our earlier remarks, we indicated that economic development and technological change could be viewed as a relationship between goals, resources, and outside aid. Although we did not analyze our material in terms of these three factors, they are obviously of central importance to the problem we are discussing. We must now draw them into our analysis, in order to specify the theoretical relationships which have been elicited here. The three factors can be distributed by means of a variety of institutional variables which, in effect, compose the inheritance of each new nation. Such institutional variables could be extended further, but we shall incorporate the following as most relevant: (*a*) administration; (*b*) technology; (*c*) per capita income; and (*d*) entrepreneurship. These affect the nature of political goals. They also indicate the possibilities for development that derive from the given state of available resources and skills and the degree of structural flexibility which a new nation inherits upon independence. Although I have not discussed these factors, they are crucial as independent variables. Moreover, they are germane to any discussion of the origins of the development types. They must therefore be added to the system under discussion. If they are considered as independent variables, the theoretical system appears as follows:

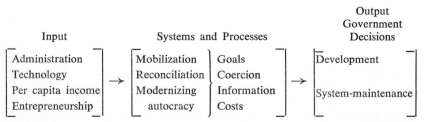

We would, of course, indicate a large number of possible situations which, logically derived from the model, have their counterparts in reality. We could also consider a set time period for a country, in which we evaluated the inputs, the operations of the system and process variables, and the decisional outputs, for their effect on the institutional inputs in a succeeding time period. Systemic analysis could then serve as a basis for probabilistic theories.

Limitations of space, however, preclude a more extensive discussion of this model. Nonetheless, it should now be clear that the heart of this analysis lies with the relationship between system-maintenance (politics) and development (economics). If politics is a conserving and protecting force, development must somehow strengthen and conserve the system. Hence the best test of development is a system-maintenance test.

We can now recapitulate some of the essentials of this discussion.

a) The mobilization system must find the optimal balance between the achievement of forward-looking goals and the allocation of real income between coercion and information. The degree of coercion is restricted by its cost on the processes of economic growth.[23] In the mobilization system, hierarchical authority seeks not only to maintain itself but to intervene in all aspects of social life. Economic development becomes the rationale for demanding total allegiance. Tactical flexibility is essential for assuring the immediate control over problems which may emerge in the economic process; its chief characteristic is that it requires a minimum amount of public accountability.

b) The reconciliation system must rely heavily on information when it defines its goals and the means of achieving them. It cannot utilize much coercion—if it does, it will be transformed into a mobilization type of system. Its distinguishing features are its participation in different aspects of group life and its stimulation of the public to participate more fully in economic processes.

In the reconciliation system, collective legitimacy results from a representative principle shared by the entire collectivity. However, the danger of separatism, and even secession, by one or more of the constituents imposes a real limitation upon the degree of freedom the political leaders have. Since multiple loyalties exist, economic development is by no means seen in terms of the state. Instead, its perspectives tend to be transformed into special interests. Development must be diffused widely throughout the system. For example, in India, the political demands of various local interests made it necessary to construct an oil refinery in a less advantageous part of the country in order to build a refinery in the most economically desirable location.

Since compromise is innate in a reconciliation system, the pace of development is determined by the willingness of the political leaders and of the public to follow a policy of the central government. The pace of growth is never more dramatic than that which the public is prepared to accept, since policy must agree with public desires. Frequently, the result is a greater degree of superficial instability in the system, with much spontaneous conflict and expressions of bitterness among the parts. In spite of this, coercive techniques remain at a minimum; and it can be argued that the strength of the reconciliation system lies, in some measure, in the perpetuation of the conflicts themselves. Each group finds a loyalty to the system determined by parochial interests and hopes to satisfy such interests. The hypotheses of both Simmel and Gluckmann concerning the social utility of conflict are relevant here. Conflict is not necessarily destructive of the social fabric.[24] On the contrary, under a reconciliation system, conflict gives people a vested interest in the system as a whole.

c) Modernizing autocracies are suspicious of advanced, dramatic programs for economic development. However, they tend to isolate those aspects of economic reforms that seem capable of being absorbed without causing too many authority problems.

In the modernizing autocracy, goals are restricted by the implications they have for the system of hierarchical authority. Those which seem to entail substantial alterations of the political framework of the society are necessarily abhorred by the government. Others, which allow the system to continue while at the same time satisfying the public—particularly with respect to expanding material standards and raising income levels—are adopted.

At the beginning of this discussion, we pointed out that many of the mechanisms of development are often similar in each of the three types. In the same sense, certain processes in the modern business enterprise in the United States and in the Soviet Union are similar. The problem of economic growth, however, poses very different problems for each kind of political system. In some, the goals of economic and technological growth become a rationale for mobilizing an entire society, and coercion is heavily used to implement mobilization. The optimal level of mobilization is reached when the costs of coercion appreciably limit the achievement of goals. The reconciliation system decides on those goals for which there is already considerable public support, so that it need employ a minimum of coercion. However, in a reconciliation government the large amount of available information may inhibit decision-makers from attaining economic growth. In the last analysis, the determination of goals, and their achievement, depend on the public willingness to work on a spontaneous and decentralized basis.[25]

The mobilization system can be efficient if it does not need to divert a large proportion of its revenues and talents to the system-maintenance sphere instead of the development sphere. In so far as it is successful in concentrating on development, it feeds out satisfactions in the social structure at large that have system-maintenance consequences. Its ability to do this is partially dependent on the urgency with which political leaders seek to develop the country and on the time which they allow for the process. If these leaders are flexible and not quick to fall back on coercive measures, they probably represent the most efficient means of creating political stability and the most rapid possible economic growth. In some mobilization systems, outside development aid may result in larger allocations of internal resources being made to system-maintenance. The dangers of this are obvious. On the other hand, suitable outside aid may effect non-coercive goal achievement without causing grave system-maintenance probems. Under such circumstances, outside aid may ultimately be the decisive factor in whether a mobilization system becomes totalitarian or democratic.[26]

154

An equally interesting situation occurs when the system-maintenence decisions of a modernizing autocracy become enlarged precisely because of the political problems posed by development achievements. As a rule, in such cases one can predict great instability for the regime, foreshadowing its change from a modernizing autocracy to one of the alternative types. Essentially, these conditions obtained in Iraq prior to the Iraqi revolution. Under such circumstances, outside developmental aid to the regime can only intensify the internal difficulties and is, therefore, ill advised.

Similar conditions obtain in a reconciliation system. If system-maintenance decisions become the major decisional burden of the government, this is a manifestation of an exceedingly unhealthy internal state; in addition it would hardly be likely that developmental decisions would help the situation. Under such circumstances, one can anticipate that, in a reconciliation type of system, there will be an increase in public expectations that is far beyond the capacity of the regime. Reconciliation systems are particularly vulnerable to this problem.

Each type of system under discussion represents a different set of relationships between goals, costs, coercion, and information. The evaluation of data about these variables should indicate the limits within which economic development and technological change can occur in each nation. Consideration of these variables should elicit the preferences which decision-makers will demonstrate by virtue of the system variables within which they must operate. It should indicate the effects that economic development will have on the systems themselves—including the transformation of one type into another.

To conclude: By means of systematic analysis of structure and process, I have attempted to provide a framework in which the study of technological innovation and economic development can be related to the politics of the developing areas. In addition, it should make it possible to draw inferences about the prospects of democracy in the context of social change.

1. See W. W. Rostow, *The Politics of Economic Growth* (New York, 1952); and W. Arthur Lewis, *The Theory of Economic Growth* (London, 1955).

2. David E. Apter and Carl Rosberg, "Some Models of Political Change in Contemporary Africa," In D. P. Ray (ed.), *The Political Economy of Contemporary Africa* (Washington, D.C., 1959); and David E. Apter, "Political Development and Tension in New Nations" (unpublished background Paper for the Conference on World Tensions, Chicago, 1960).

3. By "government," I mean here the most generalized membership unit possessing (*a*) defined responsibilities for the maintenance of the system of which it is a part; and (*b*) a practical monopoly of coercive powers. By "political system," I mean society (or other unit whose government conforms to the definition above) viewed in terms of government.

4. The initial effort to develop these types was made in an earlier monograph, written with Professor Carl Rosberg of the University of California at Berkeley. While we share the responsibility for the development of these types, he is not responsible for their application here. See Apter and Rosberg, *op. cit.*

5. See D. E. Apter, "A Comparative Method for the Study of Politics," *American Journal of Sociology*, November, 1958.

6. I am indebted to the participants of an informal seminar at the University of Chicago who helped derive these categories. They are Rodger Masters, Aristede Zolberg, Leo Snowiss, and Louis Cantori. Their perceptive comments were very useful during the preparation of this manuscript.

7. Philip Selznick, *The Organizational Weapon: A study of Bolshevik Strategy and Tactics* (New York, 1952), p. 2.

8. Although mobilization systems tend to have very pronounced ideological views on the main issues of development, in a peculiar sense such a system is less ideological than utopian—to use Mannheim's distinction between ideological and utopian thinking. In fact, in mobilization systems the party or the state will act on grounds of expediency and necessity, using ideology to give perspective and justify what appears necessary. It can be argued that opportunism remains more compelling than ideology. The most overwhelming commitment

is either to the party or to the state. See Karl Mannheim, *Ideology and Utopia* (New York, 1946), pp. 49-93.

9. See P. T. Bauer and B. S. Yamey, *The Economics of Underdeveloped Countries* (Cambridge, England, 1957), chaps. xi and xii.

10. The term "autocracy" is somewhat misleading. Such systems can be firmly "populist" and popular. See Donald G. MacRae, "Totalitarian Democracy," *The Political Quarterly*, XXXI, No. 4 (October-December, 1960).

11. See the brief discussion by C. Bettelheim, "Les exigences fondamentales d'une croissance accélérée de l'économie africaine," *Présence africaine*, June-September, 1960.

12. See David E. Apter, *The Political Kingdom in Uganda: A Study in Bureaucratic Nationalism* (Princeton, N.J., 1961); and D. Anthony Low and R. Cranford Pratt, *Buganda and British Overrule* (London, 1960). See also the effects of modernization in Japan, as described in the Introduction to *Kokutai No Hongi* (Cambridge, Mass., 1949).

13. For a discussion of these problems in Guinea, see "Democracy in Guinea," *The Economist* (London), November 14, 1959.

14. This is particularly true in those ex-colonial territories where the colonial civil service or administration had been both the planning and the administrative arm, and traditions of service and skill reside in the bureaucracy. See Ignacy Sachs, "Patterns of Public Sectors in Under-developed Economies," *The Indian Economic Review*, IV, No. 3.

15. In the reconciliation type, the bureaucracy is normally subordinate to the political arm and does not pose this problem. See D. Apter and R. Lystad, "Party, Bureaucracy and Constitutional Government," in G. M. Carter (ed.), *Transition in Africa* (Boston, 1958).

16. An extremely difficult but important factor in goals is creativity. Although discussion of creativity is beyond the scope of this paper, a case can be made for greater creativity in the mobilization type than in the other two.

17. For example, in Mali, the two newspapers are owned and controlled by the government and regarded as party instructional and informational sheets. The single party, the Union Soudanaise, considers the newspapers as agents of ideological communication to the local party cadres.

18. One need only compare India and China in this regard. See the discussion of economic growth and planning in the *Report of the Commission of Enquiry on Emoluments and Conditions of Service of Central Government Employees, 1957-9* (Delhi, 1959), pp. 35-45.

19. See the excellent discussion of this problem in Edward Shils's "Political Development in the New States," *Comparative Studies in Society and History*, II (1960), Part II.

20. i.e., through religious, clan, familial, and other pressures.

21. Both the mobilization system and the modernizing autocracy tend toward "personal" government. In the former, ideologized justifications cover up capriciousness; in the latter, custom restrains it. See Thomas Hodgkin, *Nationalism in Colonial Africa* (London, 1956), chap. v. See also William Kornhauser, *The Politics of Mass Society* (Glencoe, Ill., 1959), chap. iii.

22. Thus the prognosis in a modernizing autocracy is political trouble. In the short run, it is a stable system. In the long run, its success in the economic field

creates elites who prefer either a reconciliation or a mobilization alternative. When this occurs, economic goals may be restricted by the monarch to prevent change which he cannot control; opposing groups can easily charge the system with being feudal and archaic. Political difficulties are inherent in the system. Turkey remains one of the most interesting examples to study. There the shift to Kemalism can be described as one from a modernizing autocracy of the traditional variety to a mobilization system after the downfall of the Ottoman Empire, with a move toward a reconciliation system in the decades since the war. This has now reversed itself in an abrupt transition back to a modernizing autocracy of the secular variety. See T. Feyzioglu, "Les partis politiques en Turquie," *Revue Française de science politique,* I, No. 1 (January-March, 1954).

23. If this situation persists so that coercion becomes the primary means of assuring compliance, then there may be a change from a mobilization system employing a mild autocracy to a mobilization system employing more totalitarian methods. Should this occur, then for all practical purposes coercion and information coincide, and the perfect information system is the perfect coercive system.

24. See George Simmel, *Conflict* (Glencoe, Ill., 1955); and Max Gluckman, *Custom and Conflict in Africa* (Glencoe, Ill., 1955).

25. An important task for the government is the crystallization of economic goals— presenting them to the public in such a way that the people respond enthusiastically to the difficulties inevitable in economic development.

    There is, of course, a different but related problem of information. If information is to be effective, it must be translated into goals by efficient decision-making. If so much information is available that it cannot be "processed," decision-making suffers and the system becomes "inefficient."

26. See Charles Wolf, Jr., *Foreign Aid: Theory and Practice in Southern Asia* (Princeton, N.J., 1960), chap. viii. It can be maintained that the dilemma posed by the Lumumba government in the Congo about outside aid was of this nature.

CHAPTER 8

Problems of Emerging Bureaucracies in Developing Areas and New States

S. N. EISENSTADT

The Hebrew University

I

In all developing countries, bureaucracies very rapidly tend to develop and extend their scope. As the post-colonial new states attained independence, and as some of the older states (e.g., Latin America or the Middle East) surged toward modernization and expanded the range of state activities, they took over many organs of public administration remaining from the former period; the scope of their activities greatly expanded, and new organs were created. Each became a very important part of the political framework in these countries. Since, in most of these countries, the government plays a great role in economic development, the bureaucracies also began to engage significantly in the activities of the economic sphere. The bureaucracy's activities could then have great influence on the direction and tempo of the country's economic development.

What will this influence be? What part will the bureaucracies play in the political life of these nations? Will they help in the establishment of viable modern political systems? Or will they contribute mostly to the development of unstable, tension-ridden, and inefficient political structures? And what is the structure of the bureaucracies? How is it related to their functioning in these societies? To what extent is it similar to the major bureaucratic organizations that can be found in the West, and how does it differ from them? To what degree are the bureaucracies capable of efficiently implementing various social, political, and economic policies? Finally, how will they affect the process of economic development—will they facilitate or hinder it?

159

II

One of the striking facts about the bureaucracies of the developing areas is that, in most of these areas there exist not one but usually two or three, bureaucracies—or, at least, different layers of bureaucratic organization and structure. First, there is what may be called the "pre-modern" or "pre-development" layer, which had developed before the attainment of independence or the introduction of modernization. The second stratum has, as a rule, developed since World War II. It was engendered by the dual impacts of the attainment of independence and of modernization and of establishing new social, political, and economic goals.

In the post-colonial new states, the "old" colonial civil service still survives in remaining personnel, organizational structure, and tradition. The structure and organization of the old civil service provided the basic framework for the extension and development of bureaucratic administration after the attainment of independence.

Within these societies, the initial emergence of bureaucracies had been rooted in the need of the colonial powers for various resources and for the maintenance of law and order. The bureaucracy was based on over-all political control by the metropolitan powers; the administration participated minimally in the indigenous political and social life of the community. This necessarily limited its activities, confining them to the basic administrative services. It also dictated some of the bureaucracy's structural characteristics, such as the high degree of centralization, the great adherence to legal precepts and rules, and the relatively small internal differentiation. Thus the pre-independence bureaucracies helped establish the framework of modern, universalistic legal and administrative practices and organizations. On the other hand, they were highly apolitical. They did not meddle in politics, and they kept up the ideal of a politically neutral civil service. They were also apolitical in that they never really participated in the indigenous political life of the countries in which they served. Their very limited goals were prescribed by the colonial powers, who were not responsible to the political groups and opinions of the countries which they ruled. They did not perform any important functions in the regulation of internal political interests and activities among the "colonial" population, or in the articulation and aggregation of the political interests of that population.[1] Whatever "internal" political activities they undertook were perceived mostly in terms of administrative injunctions and enforcement of law. It is significant that the scope and impact of the activities of the colonial civil service were much greater in countries, such as India, in which "direct rule" was applied, than in countries governed according to precepts of "indirect rule," where the native population was left more or less alone to manage its own affairs, especially on the local level.

160

The second main layer of the bureaucracies in the new states consists of those departments and echelons which were developed after the attainment of independence. Here a new civil service—"new" in personnel, goals, departments, and activities—evolved. This stratum had to be staffed with new recruits—frequently with inadequately trained recruits whose chief claim to or qualification for office was their former participation in the nationalistic political movements. These new bureaucratic organs have had new types of goals, like economic development, social betterment, educational advancement, or community development.

Unlike members of the "colonial" civil service, most of the recruits to the new have usually had a clear and articulated political orientation and sense of political responsibility. They have very often perceived themselves as representatives of their respective movements, parties, or sectors. Moreover, they frequently have seen themselves as fulfilling chiefly political functions—either as implementing political goals, or as representing, articulating and regulating the political interests and activities of different groups and social strata.

The relations between the older bureaucracy and the new echelons have not always been easy. In the first period after independence, particularly, the nationalist leaders' prevailing attitude toward the remnants of the older colonial services was distrust. In some cases, this led to the almost complete destruction of the older structure. In most instances, however, some sort of *modus vivendi* has been evolved between the older and newer echelon. One or the other is usually predominant; but necessarily the implementation of new social, political, and economic goals has been strongly emphasized, and the involvement in the political process has been much greater than before.

An even more explicitly politically oriented type of bureaucracy has tended to emerge in most of the new states. This type consists of the different "party" bureaucracies which grew out of the leading nationalistic movements which became dominant parties—e.g., the Congress in India, the PCP in Ghana or the Neo-Destour in Tunisia. These party bureaucracies have been oriented more to the political manipulation of groups of population and to the provision of political support and loyalty to the new regime than to the upholding of universalistic legal norms, the development of public services, or the creation of new public administrative services. In personnel or over-all political supervision, the party bureaucracy has often been very similar to the new echelons of the governmental bureaucracy, and has sometimes also been closely related to it, especially through the activities of prime ministers and cabinet ministers. However, the basic patterns of activities and orientations of the members of the party bureaucracy have frequently differed to a very great extent from those of the governmental bureaucracy, and have sometimes clashed.[2]

161

III

The bureaucracies in developing countries which have not been under colonial rule exhibit a somewhat different, although not entirely dissimilar, pattern. Within each there existed, first, a traditional bureaucracy —whether "royal" (as in the Middle Eastern countries) or "oligarchical-republican" (as in most Latin American countries). These bureaucracies usually dominated the political scene until the end of World War II. Within them, some traditional elements were mixed with more modern ones. Frequently, the modern elements were copied from some European country—for example, the French pattern had strong influence in most Latin American countries.

These administrations were usually concerned with supporting the interests of the ruling oligarchies, and with implementing rather limited social and economic objectives. Whatever tendency to modernization they may have exhibited—e.g., in the fields of military affairs or education—their major political aim was to restrict modernization to those minimal spheres in which it was necessary to maintain the viability of the then existing system.

With increasing modernization, with the growing impact of internal democratization, and with the development of new social, political, and economic goals, these bureaucracies had to extend the scope of their activities and to recruit new personnel. However, the older pattern usually continued to leave its imprint on the new echelons and departments, in administrative training, organization, and to some extent also in social and political orientation.[3] Only in a few older countries, like Mexico, widespread, well-organized semi-revolutionary parties succeeded in upsetting the oligarchy and established a stable and viable modern political framework. There, a somewhat new pattern of bureaucratic organization was established, not dissimilar from those of new states.

In most of these older countries, the party bureaucracies were usually less important than in the new states. This was mainly because the oligarchical or monarchical elements were much stronger in the political structure, and because several major institutional interest groups, especially the armed forces, developed as important channels of political struggle and often constituted hotbeds of politics and influential pressure groups.

Both within the formerly colonial societies and in the states with longer traditions of independence, another distinct type of new bureaucratic organization has also emerged—the big economic or business corporation. Within the older countries, these corporations are usually more concentrated in the private sector; in the new states, more in the public or mixed sectors. In all these societies, however, the corporations play an important role in the economic and political life of the country.

162

IV

We see thus that, in each emerging country, the pattern of development of bureaucracies has been very mixed and heterogeneous. Each part of the bureaucracy developed under somewhat different conditions and in response to different types of needs and pressures. It was only after the attainment of independence, and/or the development of goals and programs of modernization, that these parts were brought together into a common framework and confronted with the need to find some *modus vivendi* in order to deal with the new tasks which they faced.

Perhaps the most important general problem which faced all the bureaucracies was the necessity to adapt themselves to the goals, new spheres of activity, and new social needs that arose from the growing differentiation and diversification of the social structures, the extension of the scope of social and political participation of many groups in the society, and the development of new social and political goals. In trying to adapt themselves, the emerging bureaucracies developed several characteristics which were greatly influenced by their heterogeneous origins and by the conditions in which they found themselves.

In almost none of these countries has the bureaucracy evolved into the "classical" Weberian type of legal-rational organization or an entirely neutral civil service. True, in several of the post-colonial countries— notably in India and Ghana, and, to a lesser extent in the countries which were or are under French colonial rule—the ideal of such a service was transmitted and still has a strong hold on the developing civil service. But even in these countries, events have occurred that have greatly changed the major political orientation of the bureaucracy. Similarly, the structural characteristics and the patterns of activities of these bureaucracies differ, in varying degrees, from those of the usual Western pattern.

The first and most important development in the social and political orientations of these bureaucracies is their high involvement in the political process in their respective countries. This is manifested in several ways.

In many of these countries, for example, the bureaucracy becomes not only the administrative arm of an executive, supervised by the legislature; it also constitutes itself as an effective executive or a component thereof, and plays a basic part in establishing, determining, and implementing political goals and major policy directives. In many nations, the bureaucracy may be the main or the only body which, apart from the head of the executive, is capable of formulating clear political and administrative goals and objectives.

The second major aspect of the bureaucracy's involvement in the political process is grounded in the fact that it tends to evolve as one of the principal instruments of political regulation—one of the main channels of political struggle in which and through which different interests are regulated and "aggregated"—and it tends to be very important, even predominant, in this facet of the political process. In some cases, e.g., in some Latin American countries, the bureaucracy also becomes a powerful pressure and interest group in its own right, strongly allied to other oligarchical groups.

Thus, in all these countries, the bureaucracy may tend to fulfill different types of political functions and—like parties, legislatures, and executives—become a center of various kinds of political activity. Although, through such activities, it may establish some of the basic frameworks of modern politics, it may also minimize the extent of differentiation of divers types of political roles and activities. In the latter case, it would greatly impede the development of autonomous and differentiated political activities, organizations, and orientations.

The second basic characteristic of the social orientations of emergent bureaucracies is that they are also major instruments of social change and of political socialization in their respective countries.

These bureaucratic organizations are (at least initially) based on universalistic and functionally specific definitions of the role of the official and the role of the client. The majority of the population of these countries, however, have a different orientation. In social life, their traditional orientations and structures, such as the extended family, are predominant. In these societies, most of a person's role relations are set within traditional groups; and rights and duties are defined in terms of personal relationships. Previous experience with bureaucratic organizations was restricted, and was rarely of any great significance.

Thus, the contacts of the public with governmental organizations provided a framework for a wider process of political socialization. The public's accomodation to the new political structure became, to a considerable extent, dependent upon its successful learning in these situations of contact. This has very often forced the bureaucracies to go beyond their proper specialized roles and to assume various roles of social and political leadership and tutelage—without which they could not have effected the necessary changes in the behavior of the population at large. This need to foster change often extended the scope of the activities of bureaucrats beyond their specific goals, and made them reach also into the realm of family, kinship, and community life of wide strata of the population.

V

What are the causes of these developments in the structure of bureaucracies? And what can be their possible impact on the processes of political modernization and economic development?

Generally, two types of causes can be discerned. One basic cause, often mentioned in the literature, is the difference between the general cultural values and social setting of the developing areas and those of Western countries where "modern" bureaucratic organizations originated. Presthus has illustrated these problems:

In sum, the dominant educational philosophy tends to devalue practical training and this constitutes a barrier to bureaucratic evolution. Middle East youth prefer to become white-collar rather than blue-collar workers. This inapposite value has an immediate impact on technical and economic development, since it becomes difficult to build up the required force of skilled technicians. In the universities, subjects like statistics and research methods are resisted since they, too, tend to undercut the existing theoretical and subjective conception of learning. Such beliefs deny the demands of modern bureaucratic organizations for precision, specialization, and scientific method.[4]

For our purposes, the relevant point is that subjective, political values outweigh objective, bureaucratic demands of skill and experience.

In so far as recruitment and the locus of bureaucratic loyalties are concerned, it is well known in Middle Eastern countries that subjective, "particularistic" considerations compete strongly with objective standards in appointment and in policy determination. Western "universalistic" concepts of impersonality, technical supremacy, and loyalty to some abstraction, such as the "public interest," remain alien in societies in which primary loyalties are directed to members of one's family and to personal friends. A recent observer of the Egyptian civil service concluded that people in the Near East are not yet accustomed to looking upon others impersonally in any situation. They tend to regard others as individuals, with families, friends, and communities behind them; this trend is carried into realms where recent changes have established different formal requirements.

These general cultural values and social settings undoubtedly influence the nature of administrative structure and behavior in the new countries, and must be taken into account in their analysis. The cultural traits may explain many of the different patterns of bureaucratic behavior which have been mentioned above. However, in themselves, they cannot explain the basic common political problems of these bureaucracies, nor the great variety of administrative structures and behavior that can be found in these societies.

165

It seems that consideration of these general cultural traditions and social orientations is not enough. It is necessary also to analyze some basic social aspects of the processes of political development and modernization in these societies.

VI

What are these processes? Perhaps the common central facets of the problem are the crucial role, in the process of modernization, of the state or of political leaders, and the internal contradictions which have necessarily developed in their activities in this context.

The first important fact in this respect is that—although the new ruling elites have attempted to establish frameworks of modern polities, have developed new political goals, and have tried to find the instruments for their implementation—the extent of general participation in the political process has been relatively small. There have existed few groups and strata capable of engaging in the process of modernization on their own, and able to articulate their political interests in a modern, differentiated way.

Many ascriptive (communal, tribal, and caste) groups existed. Their chief political orientations were traditional and restricted either to passive supplication and petition or to the old kind of court politics.

On the other hand, there were many small, splintered interests, such as divers small business groups, that were not able to articulate and aggregate their political interests. In some countries, especially in Latin America and the Middle East, there were also major institutional interest groups (churches, army groups) which monopolized most of the political positions and impeded the growth of modern independent political forces.

In general, in all of these societies, there developed only few and weak functionally differentiated groups and general responsible public opinion capable of generating an independent and diversified political leadership and organization.

Thus, the articulation, aggregation, and regulation of political activities and interests became mostly concentrated in the hands of the ruling elite —the leaders of the old nationalist (and military) movements. At best, they became concentrated in one major party which was able to establish a unified framework of modern polity. In other cases, they were splintered among different small parties and did not crystallize into more stable patterns.

With the attainment of independence, or with growing modernization, the elites faced several tasks in the area of political organization. They could not confine political participation to its former level; they had to

166

extend it to the politically more passive or inarticulate groups from whom new types of allegiance, political involvement, and loyalties were being demanded. The new regimes could not maintain themselves entirely on the passive allegiance that had predominated in colonial times, since they themselves had undermined this allegiance. Through their emphasis on governmental activities in many spheres of society, they penetrated more and more into various social layers. Somehow, they had to foster the development of new social and political motivations and participation. Schemes for community development, for new industrial and agrarian organizations, and for agrarian reforms whenever these were undertaken —all implied the necessity for new orientations, incentives, and the development of many new motivational patterns.

By engaging in these, however, the new political rulers found themselves in a series of new dilemmas.

In most countries under discussion, a double contradiction developed in the activities of the ruling elites, and in their efforts to activate the various strata of the population toward participation in the common collective goals. First, there was the contradiction between the traditional forces and the development of relatively modern, "free-floating" resources and divers professional, economic, and cultural groups. Second, there was the contradiction between the tendencies of the more modern forces to coalesce in relatively independent and autonomous centers of power, and the aims of the ruling elites to control as many of these forces and centers of power as possible.

Simultaneously, the elites confronted another problem or contradiction. The new goals which they proclaimed often contained various implicit or explicit promises to the population, particularly in the economic field. Many social groups were ready to present this bill to the elite for payment, especially when their support was demanded. In this way, the government could, through the distribution of various goods and services—which it controlled—to its own supporters, maintain its position and attempt to control other social forces. However, the elite could thus arrive at an impasse, in which the implementation of the various societal goals, and its own ultimate claims to legitimation, would become seriously impeded by the necessity to spend many of its resources as emoluments for its supporters. The very need of the elite to control the traditional and, especially, the modern forces, and its ambivalent attitude toward many of them, can aggravate this problem.

VII

One of the main consequences of these contradictions—an outcome in which the political elites and the bureaucracies both co-operated—was the intensification of the inherent tendency of the political elite and bureaucracy to enhance their monopolization of power and prestige. This tendency is closely related to the social transformations attendant on the attainment of independence. It has manifested itself in: (*a*) attempts to create a strong hierarchy of status in terms of political power; (*b*) efforts to subject most processes of social mobility to the control of the political elites; and (*c*) efforts to subject a large number of economic, professional, and cultural activities to political control.

The political elite and the bureaucracy were inclined to belittle the importance and efficiency of purely economic activities and the claims of economic groups toward social autonomy. It tended to superimpose extra-economic criteria on economic activities and on their bearers—not only by stipulating broad, general "social goals," but also by the daily regulation and direction of activity. Moreover, the political elites sometimes attempted to undermine the autonomous development of the middle and working classes, and of cultural and professional elites, and link their positions entirely to directives.

The efforts of the political elite and bureaucracy to direct and control all the main avenues of local mobility are closely associated to these developments. Through such efforts, they tend to maintain their hold on potential centers of power and to control their evolution. But these attempts are often self-contradictory; the close control exercised by the bureaucracy undermines efforts for economic development. More aspirants are created for new posts than there are posts available, and thus the bureaucracy itself is put in an insecure position.

This process took a somewhat different direction in the non-colonial countries. While the extent of political articulation and organization of wider groups and strata was relatively small and weak, the picture was different. In these countries, a much stronger competition between the older oligarchy and some of the new groups and parties usually emerged.

However, some modern political frameworks—even though born by a relatively restricted oligarchy—already existed. They were the main organs of political activity and regulation, and their very existence impeded both the "political" articulation of new social groups and, often, also any further political modernization. Hence the social and political expansion of the bureaucracy was often blocked by the political predominance of these groups, which frequently also impeded the efficiency and rationalization of the structure of the bureaucracy.

VIII

These characteristics of the process of modernization were most influential in the development of bureaucracies in emerging countries. The most crucial facts are that this process was greatly fostered by the political elites; that political movements, and later the state, played such an important role in the breaking up of the framework of traditional society and in advancing growing social and economic differentiation; and that there were only a few other groups which participated autonomously in this process and were able to help in the implementation of new goals. These factors necessarily gave the bureaucracy a vital place in the political process and social structure of these societies: it had to become one of the major agents of change in all spheres of social life. But, just because it became such an agent of change, it had also to generate new types of interests and activities and to undertake many functions of political aggregation and articulation.

As a result, the bureaucracy in these countries was involved in dilemmas similar to those faced by the new rulers. Efficient implementation of goals and the establishment of viable frameworks of modern political institutions depended greatly on political stability and on the development of new political and administrative attitudes and activities. However, these same conditions could create pressure for certain kinds of activities on behalf of the bureaucracy that could easily undermine its efficiency and its ability to implement goals and services while withstanding the demands of many potential political supporters.

In this context, we also must analyze the relation between certain economic processes in these countries and their developing bureaucracies. The most important aspect is that, in these countries, the bureaucracies constitute one of the principal channels of economic and social mobility and advancement. Several factors account for this. One is the central place of the government in the sphere of economic development. Another is the great prestige of white-collar work that is widespread in most of these countries—a prestige which was only enhanced by political developments and the growing social importance of the political elites. The third factor comprises the growing aspirations to mobility that emerged under the impacts both of political and economic modernization and of the need of the rulers to satisfy the aspirations to mobility and to minimize their political explosiveness. The fourth factor is the structure of the educational system, with its strong emphasis on literary, as distinct from technical, education, and its influence on the structure of the labor force and occupational choice. For all these reasons, great pressure developed on governmental and civil service jobs. These pressures, obviously, potentially could have grave repercussions on the economic and the political developments. From the economic point of view, the demands and aspirations could easily create a lack of adequate manpower for technical jobs and widespread white-collar unemployment and underemployment. Politically, these tendencies created many potential pressures and tensions.

169

Moreover, they could weaken the efficiency of the bureaucracy, by making it into a sort of system of sinecures in which there was little relation between job security and performance, and in which extraneous (political and personal) criteria could become the main determinants of recruitment and advancement. In these combined economic and political pressures, one can find the roots of the widespread tendency to corruption that has emerged in these bureaucracies.

IX

All these forces—the cultural orientations prevalent in these societies, the political and economic processes and pressures—necessarily have their repercussion on the structure of the bureaucracies and on their ability to implement major political and social goals and to provide continuous services to the population.

Among the most important of such structural problems, the following have often been noted:[5] (a) the low density of administrative structure, i.e., the relatively small ratio of officials to population and tasks; (b) the lack of fully qualified and adequate personnel; (c) the small extent of diversification of functions, and consequent overlapping between different organizations; (d) inadequate communication between different echelons and departments; and (e) overcentralization, poor co-ordination, and lack of autonomy and initiative of the linestaff.

Riggs has aptly summarized some of these problems, especially as they apply to older independent countries:

Obstacles to identification of personal with program goals are especially conspicuous in the way the work load and responsibilities of different officials are allocated, that is, in "organization and management." These often make it impossible for anyone to carry out a constructive project without waiting for the concurrence of many others, whereby many people have the power to block action. One result is often to elevate the level of settlement of even minor disputes to ministerial, cabinet, and chief executive levels. Top administrators become embroiled in continual interagency conflicts while subordinates piddle away their energies waiting for requisite approvals. Moreover, because many persons far from the scene of action become involved in decision making, questions are often referred to persons with only remote interest in them, it becomes difficult to assign responsibility for action, and final decisions hinge on the outcome of power struggles among individuals only indirectly concerned.[6]

In some countries, elaborate ministerial secretariats, staffed by generalists, who rotate frequently between headquarters and district assignments, have been placed in the line of communication and command between ministers and executive or administrative departments and divisions. Invariably,

170

great delay ensues while secretariat officials review more and more of the work nominally assigned to and originating in the departments. We may quote the words of a distinguished former civil servant in India about the result:

The head of the department is deprived of all initiative and instead of being allowed to attend to and make progress with his own work, has to spend a great deal of time submitting unnecessary reports, explaining the position in individual matters to the Ministry and getting its orders on points which lie well within his own sphere of authority.

Because of overcentralization and lack of delegation, those close to the goals of action cannot easily cooperate with their colleagues in other agencies whose work directly affects the success of their own efforts. Characteristically, to overcome this stagnation, new agencies are often set up in the hope that, outside the bog of established structures, action may be possible. But the new agencies simply add to the intra-bureaucratic conflict and competition, increasing the burden on the top of the hierarchy to impose coordination.[7]

The relative importance of these problems naturally varies in different countries. In the post-colonial countries, the most critical problems seem to be lack of adequate staff, overcentralization, and too little diversification. In the independent countries, the most vital problems are the excessive control, rigidity, and lack of initiative of the officials, and their regarding their offices as sinecures. However, there is much overlapping between these different structural aspects. And beyond all these, there always hovers the double specter of corruption and growing inefficiency of the bureaucracy.

X

The patterns of activities, organization, and political and social orientations of the bureaucracies in developing areas differ greatly from those of Western countries. However, it does not suffice to stress the differences between the new emerging bureaucracies and the older bureaucracies of Western countries or to point out the former's structural deficiencies and problems. Except for their common characteristics, outlined above, the exact ways in which they will develop differ greatly between countries. These differences may be of crucial importance in their implications for political and economic development.

In evaluating the effect of these bureaucracies on political modernization and economic development, we must again stress the fact that they have become major agents of social and political change, and examine what influence they may have on such change. Generally, there are two major, and sometimes overlapping, possible influences the bureaucracies can have on processes of change and development in the developing areas.

The first major possibility is the development of relatively efficient frameworks of modern administration; the upholding of legal norms and rules and the maintenance of basic services, even if this is effected through the bureaucracy's monopolization of many political functions; the bureaucracy's extension of its scope of activities; and the assumption, by its officials, of many social, political, and leadership roles. These bureaucracies may generate through the establishment of new political frameworks and through the development of such activities, many new social organizations and activities on both the central and local level, and may contribute both to the establishment of viable political frameworks and to conditions conducive to economic development.

The evolution of this type of orientation and activities of the bureaucracy depends greatly on two conditions. (1) Some basic, unitary political framework, a relatively unified political elite, and a degree of political consensus must exist. (2) Purely institutional interest groups (e.g., army, churches, etc.) must be relatively weak in comparison to ecological strata and certain functional groups.

The main issues facing the elites are the extent to which they can overcome the pressures for a higher level of consumption, and the degree to which they can advance wider educational schemes capable of providing adequate training for personnel in technical fields and thus alleviating the pressures on the white-collar jobs.

The structure and patterns of activities of the bureaucracies which develop under these conditions differ greatly from those of "classical" bureaucratic organizations. However, the very fact that the scope of their activities is relatively wide, combined with a firm political orientation and a high measure of political consensus, may facilitate the maintenance of relative stability and continuity, induce and generate new types of economic entrepreneurship, and generate professional activities and political leadership on the local and even on the central level. Furthermore, the bureaucracy also may gradually generate diversification of functionally specific groups and independent public opinion and leadership. It is interesting to note that, in these cases, there usually exist also rather strong party bureaucracies. While, initially, there may be conflicts between them and the civil service, the very fact that there is some initial diversification of functions within a relatively unified political framework may help generate change and economic development.

The second important kind of possible bureaucratic development is characterized by the bureaucracy's contributions mainly to what Riggs has called "negative development."[8] Here the bureaucracy tends to monopolize some central political functions; in addition, it tends to become a major interest group, usually closely allied with some institutional interest

172

groups and with various oligarchical strata. Because of this alliance, the bureaucracy is inclined to become a center of attraction for various "white-collar" aspirants, and thus overstaffed. On the other hand, it necessarily becomes a "narrow" interest group, which tends to stifle any development of independent political action. It may easily obstruct schemes of economic development that threaten its level of relative income and other vested interests. In such cases, the bureaucracy usually becomes an active participant in the narrow political and economic struggle. Corruption usually becomes rampant; the stability of the basic administrative services, universalistic legal framework, and economic activities may be broken down. Such processes are facilitated when there is no unified political framework and consensus; when the rift between traditional and modern elites, or the lack of consensus within the modern elite, is very great; and when institutional interest groups, like a church, army, and other narrow oligarchical groups, predominate in the social and economic structure.

As indicated above, both possible developments within the bureaucracies are inherent in the basic conditions of economic and political evolution in the developing areas. In any concrete case, these tendencies can overlap, but the bureaucracy itself often influences, to some degree at least, the concrete outcome of these developments, through its own adherence to common political goals or through educational policies.

1. For the terms used here, see G. A. Almond, "A Functional Approach to Comparative Politics," in G. A. Almond and J. S. Coleman (eds.), *The Politics of the Developing Areas* (Princeton, N.J., 1960), pp. 26-58.

2. See D. Apter and R. A. Lystad, "Bureaucracy, Party and Constitutional Democracy," in G. M. Carter and W. O. Brown (eds.), *Transition in Africa* (Boston, 1958).

3. See the papers by G. Blanksten and D. Rustow in Almond and Coleman, *op. cit.* See also the papers by W. R. Sharp (on Egypt), A. Lepawsky (on Bolivia), F. Heady (on the Philippines), and J. N. More (on Thailand), in W. J. Siffin (ed.), *Toward the Comparative Study of Public Administration* (Bloomington, Ind., 1957).

4. Robert V. Presthus, "The Social Bases of Bureaucratic Organization," *Social Forces,* XXXVIII, No. 2 (December, 1959), 103-09.

5. See, for instance, J. L. Quermonne, "La sous-administration et les politiques d'équipement administratif," *Revue française de science politique,* IX, No. 3 (Septembre, 1959), 629-67.

6. F. W. Riggs, "Public Administration—A Neglected Factor in Economic Development," *Annals of the American Academy of Political and Social Science* (May, 1956), pp. 70-81.

7. A. D. Gorwala, *Report on Public Administration* (New Delhi, 1951), p. 39. See also Paul H. Appleby, *Public Administration in India; Report of a Survey* (New Delhi, 1953), Sec. II, especially p. 21.

8. F. V. Riggs, "Economic Development and Local Administration" *The Philippine Journal of Public Administration,* III, No. 1 (January, 1959), 86-146.

CHAPTER 9

Transference of Social and Political Loyalties [1]

GEORGE I. BLANKSTEN
Northwestern University

I

I shall attempt in this paper to relate economic growth to changes in social and political loyalties in the underdeveloped areas. Our problem is to determine whether or not transformations in the economy are accompanied by changes in attitudes and loyalties. If they are, what is the nature of these changes? What directions might they be expected to take?

Probably, in the underdeveloped areas, political alterations go hand-in-hand with economic growth. Yet we have hardly begun to scratch the surface in inquiring after the properties of these changes, and we know virtually nothing about the political implications and consequences of economic development. Elsewhere, I have suggested that the study of political groups might provide a fruitful point of departure in determining the relationship between economic and political change.[2] A group may be regarded as a system of patterned or regular interaction among a number of individuals. The interaction is sufficiently patterned to permit the system to be viewed as a unit, which may be called a "political" group when its action is directed toward some phase of the operation of government. Every political group has an interest. Essentially, this is the central and continuing type of activity that endows the group with its identity as a system or a unit. A sizable sector of the literature of political science is devoted to the elaboration of what is usually termed "the group theory of politics." In general, this holds that government and politics can best be understood as the products of the behavior of groups and of the patterns of the relationships among them. I shall not restate the elements of this theory here. Much has already been written about it; I shall merely mention a few of the leading books and articles on the group theory of politics.[3]

Before the group approach is applied to an analysis of the politics of the underdeveloped areas, a few prefatory points should be made. For one thing, the identity and the relative weight of interest groups appear to vary according to level or stage of economic development. Thus land-owning, military, and religious groups, to select a few examples, are more influential in the politics of less developed areas than, say, industrialists and organized labor, which are among the more powerful political groups in the more advanced economies.

Further, the manner in which interest groups perform political functions also seems to vary with levels of economic development. In dealing with the transference of loyalties, we are concerned primarily with two political functions of groups. The first is the aggregation of interests. In the more developed economies, groups tend to be aggregative. That is, each political group attempts to raise its umbrella over a wider range of interests than does the typical group in the less developed areas. In the latter case, groups are often non-aggregative, representing isolated interests separately and making little or no effort to combine them. Probably no phenomenon illustrates this more clearly than does the political party. Compare the all-things-to-all-men or catch-all appeal of either major party in the United States, of the Radical party of Argentina, or of similar parties in more advanced economies, on the one hand, with, on the other, the non-aggregative appeal to exclusive and sharply identified sectors of society exercised in underdeveloped areas by groups like the *Mau-Mau* of Kenya or the *Apristas* of Peru. The second political function of groups that is especially relevant to the transference of loyalties is the articulation of interests. The performance of this function also appears to correspond to levels of economic development. Thus, in the more advanced economies virtually all interests are represented by organized groups which are generally in a position to voice those interests in a national political forum. In contrast, in the less developed economies, the articulation of interests is far less effective. Indeed, often significant interests go unheard on a national political level, and in some instances they are not even represented by effectively organized groups.[4]

The interests of groups are particularly related to the question of loyalties. I have already mentioned that every political group has an interest, and how that interest may be viewed. "The interest and the group are the same phenomenon observed from slighty different positions, and an 'interest group' is a tautological expression," it has been said. "The interest is not a thing that exists apart from the activity or that controls activity."[5] Thus interest is abstracted from the observed pattern of inter-action, and cannot conflict with it. It seems reasonable to view a loyalty as the identification of an individual's own interest with that of a group. This would imply "the associated necessity of furthering both the larger

176

purpose which the group fosters and the integral unity of the individual himself with the group and the group purpose."[6]

The process of economic development alters the nature and the relative political influence of groups. Economic growth thus affects the distribution of interests, attitudes, and loyalties. "By virtue of the patterning demanded by a particular technological development, people come to have different occupations and roles, to have different amounts of wealth, and different amounts of economic and political power."[7] In the change process, some groups weaken, some are lost, some gain in influence, and some new ones appear. Let us call the last two classes of interests—those gaining in strength and those of the newly emerging groups— "ascendant interests." We may then be able to gain some insight into the transference of social and political loyalties from data about attitudes toward ascendant groups. We can discern three categories of such attitudes in the underdeveloped areas. First, in some cases there are no identifiable attitudes toward ascendant groups as such. Second, there are centers of definitely negative or hostile attitudes toward the expanding interests. Finally, there are the positive or receptive attitudes—loyalty or potential loyalty—toward the ascendant groups.

II

Among indigenous peoples, where elements of traditional systems are prominent in continuing ways of life, no articulated attitudes toward ascendant interests exist. This does not mean that change does not occur in these less developed areas. Indeed, quite the contrary is true. "One of the enduring questions about man is his inventiveness," a recent anthropological study has pointed out. "We know that man invents; we know that primitive man invents."[8] Moreover, the proposition that technological change alters the life circumstances of communities is as true of traditional systems as it is of others.

Yet traditional peoples, even when they are aware of such changes, often have neither positive nor negative attitudes toward the expanding groups and interests. There are two chief reasons for this. The first lies in the manner in which the political functions of groups are performed in the underdeveloped areas; and the second, in the nature of the process of economic development itself.

Much has been written about the unintegrated character of the political systems of the less developed areas. Many terms have been coined— "pre-national communities," "non-national states," "cultural heterogeneity," and "plural societies," to mention but a few—to describe the same fundamental condition. The central lack of political integration may assume any of a number of forms. In one country, it may be a caste

177

system; and in another, a class structure that separates social units from each other and minimizes the interaction between them. In many cases, cultural differences, including the speaking of different languages, contribute to the isolation of communities. Illiteracy also reduces the possibilities of contact and communication. Geographic barriers—impenetrable jungles, almost impassable mountains, forbidding deserts—similarly increase the difficulty of transportation and communication. Writers of monographs about the traditional communities often overemphasize the significance of the physical or geographic isolation of the societies studied. Though physical isolation, where it is found, poses no theoretical problem in the analysis of unintegrated political systems, it should also be stressed that neither does the absence of isolating geographic conditions. In Guatemala, for example, "although travel among Indians is extremely common, they have customs which 'insulate' them from regarding new ways as adaptable to themselves. The social relationships in which an Indian participates make the customs and habits of a stranger not desirable, but simply 'another way' of doing things."[9] The problem of such insulation is charmingly illustrated by this tale drawn from Burmese folklore:

The master of the house said to his servant, "Look out of the window. I hear footsteps of some people." The servant looked and replied, "Sire, there are no people in the street, only three foreigners." [10]

These social separations in underdeveloped areas are in large part the product of the non-aggregative nature of their interest groups. Rather than combining together elements of different castes or classes or cultures in aggregative systems, isolated groups represent them separately if at all. No doubt, the task of penetrating a jungle or crossing a high mountain or traveling across a terrifying desert or even negotiating a dirt road during rainy season would be easier to perform if common interests joined the points of departure and destination of these journeys. Why should the rural dweller travel to the city, let alone have articulated attitudes toward the interests to be found there, in the absence of some such aggregative device?

Perhaps it would be sufficient to note that, in traditional systems, there are few positive or negative attitudes toward ascendant interests with which there is little or no communication or integration. But the process of economic development itself adds still another facet to the situation. In most forms of culture change, frontal attacks are made against traditional and dearly held values. These attacks constitute formidable and quickly recognized threats against long-established ways of life. But economic development does not promote the conflict of values in quite this way. Essentially, economic development is technological change:

178

It is in the realm of technology that innovations are most apt to be acceptable, because of the particular character that technology has as distinct from, say, family organization or religion. Technology is a goal-directed aspect of culture. ... The direct impact of technological results can usually be seen in terms of explicit, commonly held goals in the society. ... The chances for technological innovation to prove itself are relatively good.[11]

Non-technological changes, in other words, present almost immediate conflicts of values. Technological change, on the other hand, introduces a more efficient method of realizing an already established value. This innovation is likely to bring other changes, to be sure; but these frequently are not perceived in traditional systems.

It may happen, then, that in such systems economic development may not necessarily lead to changing attitudes or loyalties toward interest groups, or even to change or conflict of values. Thus we find, in a study of the political modernization of Uganda, that "the organization of political life, which had been the crucial social structure in Buganda, was regarded as continuing from the past, with each innovation simply perfecting and strengthening an established system. All novelty came to be regarded as a device for strengthening tradition."[12] In Uganda, "innovations, it is widely believed, have come not from an alien source, but through the Buganda government itself."[13]

Similar situations are to be found in other underdeveloped areas of the world. Among them, the case of Guatemala is instructive. There are two major classes in the country. The ruling group, the *Ladinos*, are essentially Westernized; the other class—the overwhelming majority of the population—are the Indians, whose ways are largely traditional. During most of the history of Guatemala, government has been by and for *Ladinos*. During the decade between 1944 and 1954, however, a movement dedicated, among other things, to extending the fruits of economic development to the Indians, was in power. An intriguing survey of political changes in selected Indian communities during the revolutionary decade has been published. Some of the findings are discussed below.

In the Indian town of Santo Domingo Xenacoj, for example, "the classic form is still the ideal, and that which is believed ... Traditional *principales*[14] are still the authorities."[15] In another village, the local governor representing the revolutionary national government "complained about the apathy of the rural Indians."[16] In the *municipio*[17] of San Luis Jilotepeque, "the large bulk of the Indian population remained relatively passive ... The Indians, four years after the revolution, showed no openly expressed effort to seize total political power or to carry into effect such measures as seizure and redistribution of privately owned lands."[18] And in Cobán:

179

There was only one Indian elected official in the municipality. . . . Indians have the idea that their lone alderman is a sort of ambassador to "protect the race." . . . Cobán's Kekchi [19] population has always been politically inert, or at least ineffective. . . . A political behavior-social structure questionnaire run in Cobán in 1953 indicates that over 90 per cent of the Indians queried would express no opinions on political matters at all. There are no words in Kekchi for "nationalism" or "imperialism" or other catchwords of modern political interplay.[20]

We may thus conclude that, among indigenous peoples, when traditional features are still prominent in the prevailing ways of life, frequently no articulated attitudes toward ascendant interests exist.[21]

III

The second broad category of social and political loyalties embraces the centers of definitely negative or hostile attitudes toward the ascendant interests. These arise under three major types of circumstances in the underdeveloped areas. (1) A traditionally governing elite, if it feels that its ruling position is threatened by economic development, may express attitudes of hostility toward the ascendant and emerging groups. (2) Members of indigenous societies may perceive economic changes as destructive of their traditional systems and, in resisting detribalization and otherwise struggling to preserve them, may develop hostile attitudes toward the expanding groups. (3) Groups may accept economic development but believe that its fruits are being denied or withheld, and, in frustration, harbor attitudes of resentment and hostility toward the ascendant interests. Let us devote a word to each of these types of circumstances.

1) One of the earliest propositions developed in elite analysis says, in effect, that governing groups resist change likely to displace them from their ruling positions. I shall return to this proposition later in this paper. Here, however, I shall merely observe that, in so far as it is thought to be in the interests of ruling groups to preserve the status quo, economic development is often considered to be a threat to the established order and to the security and power of governing elites. In many sectors of the Arab Middle East and of Latin America, governments resist economic development as dangerous to themselves. Noting that "some Latin-American leaders don't want technological change," one observer has pointed out that "those people with the maximum status, dignity, power, and influence in Latin-American society have not seen fit to spend their time and money in studying science, technology, and administration for adaptation to their own cultures."[22]

180

Latin-American politics abound with instances of the desperate opposition of landowning aristocracies, in the process of being displaced, against such emergent groups as developing industrialists and organized labor. Thus the Argentine landowning "Oligarchy," the nucleus of the Conservative party, was bitterly opposed to both new industries and the expansion of organized labor.[23] In Brazil, the coffee interests resolutely opposed President Getúlio Vargas. In power from 1930 to 1945, and again from 1951 to 1954, he pursued policies which, together with the economic development of Brazil, strengthened industrialists and labor groups as major political threats to the older landowning elites.[24] A variation of this pattern has long characterized Ecuadoran politics. The traditional landed aristocracy of the mountainous Sierra region has long viewed the commercial and emergent industrial groups of the Coast as deadly political enemies.[25]

During Guatemala's revolutionary decade, 1944–54, a similar situation was much in evidence. Whether or not the governments of Presidents Juan José Arévalo and Jacobo Arbenz succeeded in achieving the emancipation of the Indians, many elements of the traditionally ruling *Ladino* elite feared that this might indeed come to pass. A trained observer noted that, in the *municipio* of San Miguel Acatán, long controlled by appointed *Ladino* officials, "most *Ladinos*—and all the older ones—resent the political emancipation of the Indians."[26] This account was given of the fear that change might engulf the village of Chinautla:

The *Ladinos* felt threatened. . . . The psychological impact was obviously one of great threat, insecurity, and, perhaps most of all, insult to the "dignity of the individual." . . . The traditional political superordination of the *Ladinos* . . . has now suffered a reversal. The result . . . has intensified the degree of threat to the *Ladino* status. Displaced, thus, from the former leading sociopolitical rank, they are now seeking security by associating with the "reform Catholics" and by taking a middle-of-the-road political position.[27]

2) Historic elites fearing to be superseded in their ruling positions do not have a monopoly on hostile attitudes toward the expanding interests. Negative attitudes are also often held by members of traditional systems similarly threatened by economic development. Struggling against detribalization and other manifestations of the passing of their societies, they are likewise sharply resentful of the ascendant groups.

The recent political histories of underdeveloped areas abound with instances of "liberal" or reform governments which have come to power with the avowed purpose of speeding the distribution of the benefits of economic development among the "downtrodden" indigenous peoples of the countries involved, only to find these efforts bitterly opposed by the intended beneficiaries themselves. Often the latter regard such attempts

181

on their behalf as unwarranted interference in their affairs by the ruling outsiders. Manuel Estrada Cabrera, who was President of Guatemala from 1898 until 1920, headed a "liberal" government dedicated to the economic amelioration of the Indians' living conditions and to the reduction of the temporal power of the Roman Catholic church. Today, many Guatemalan Indians "still recall the days of Cabrera—and the man himself—as thoroughly bad. These were years of an active deterioration of [indigenous local] institutions." [28]

Similar circumstances have been found in Ghana. "What was the effect of innovation?" a recent student of the politics of that country has asked. "Traditional chieftaincy and social organization increasingly became a focus for internal resentments. ... Considerable friction developed between chiefs who took their seats not only in traditional councils, but on the legislative council and other conciliar bodies set up by the Government, and the urban educated elites which emerged with the spread of modern commerce." [29]

In situations involving either insecure or displaced traditional elites or disintegrating indigenous systems, hostile political attitudes may assume a number of forms. Nationalism is among the more significant of these. Indeed, nationalism may be viewed as "the striving of a society threatened by the intrusion of alien forces to reconstitute itself in order to achieve a new place of dignity and equality in a changing world." [30] In the case of nationalism in Ghana, attempts to preserve the disappearing systems were rejected both by the British and by the developing Western-educated elites. "Such rejection gave fervor to the nationalists of the Convention Peoples Party who by adherence to the party gave a new coherence to Ghana as a national society. ... A fraternity of the disadvantaged was encouraged to turn society in their favor by means of national political institutions and political freedom." [31] Some observers believe that similar elements exist in the contemporary struggles in Algeria. There, it has been argued, a desperate attempt to preserve disappearing systems has fed a violent nationalism. In any case, traditional elites and their indigenous subjects—often historically opposed to each other—on occasion make common, and frequently nationalistic, cause in their joint bitter hostility toward ascendant interests.

3) Another major center of negative attitudes consists of groups which have broken with their traditional pasts to accept economic development, but who believe that its fruits are being denied to, or withheld from, them. In frustration, they feel resentment and hostility against those whom they believe to be the beneficiaries of economic development.

Where a wronged group feels that it is being denied the benefits of economic growth, there is often a time lag between the rate of secularization and the changing functions of groups. Thus an individual may be

182

carried far enough along in the process of change to have lost his loyalties to a traditional or indigenous system and to have acquired some desire to participate in, and benefit from, newly emerging interests. But it is possible that the realignment of groups might not have kept pace with that change, and their functions might still be more non-aggregative than aggregative. The emergent or ascendant interest might not yet spread its umbrella widely enough to cover many who seek its benefits. Frustrated aspirant entrepreneurs may, for example, find business careers virtually closed to them, because of prevailing class or caste systems, or because of dual economies in which the interest groups in one sector are closed to applicants from the other. Frequently, those whose aspirations are so impeded develop attitudes of hostility toward the interests closed to them. When such situations evolve within the contexts of class systems, strong class consciousnesses often arise among the disadvantaged groups.

Few studies of political attitudes in such situations have been published.[32] What has appeared, however, suggests a strong correlation between political attitudes and the extent to which it is believed to be possible to acquire emergent interests. Allan B. Cole's *Political Tendencies of Japanese in Small Enterprises*, for example, indicates a marked relationship between identification with ascendant interests and political attitudes. Significant percentages of entrepreneurs are affiliated with the Liberal (i.e., "conservative") party; many industrial workers, and white-collar workers with unfrustrated aspirations to economic mobility, gravitate to the Social Democratic party; and militantly class-conscious political radicalism—including significant percentages of Communists—is prominent among those who believe they are excluded from ascendant groups. "Class-consciousness increases among workers who lose hope in ever becoming entrepreneurs. This trend has been underway for decades as the master-apprentice system has declined."[33]

IV

The third, and last, broad category of social and political loyalties comprises the positive or receptive attitudes—loyalty or potential loyalty—toward the ascendant groups. In so far as I have been able to determine, such attitudes occur in four major types of situations in the underdeveloped areas. (*1*) The "revolution of rising expectations" may be accompanied by positive attitudes toward the expanding interests. (*2*) Some controlling elites—notably the governments of new nations—identify their own interests with those of the ascendant groups. (*3*) Newly emerging industrializing and entrepreneurial groups—small in most of the underdeveloped regions—tend to associate their interests with those of the rising groups. (4) Ethnic minorities performing commercializing functions in many of the countries appear to be similarly oriented. Let us examine each of these types.

1) A good deal more has been said than written about the so-called "revolution of rising expectations." I understand this term to refer to the process by which people on a lower standard of living become acquainted with the benefits of a higher standard, and, in consequence of this "demonstration effect," come to desire or demand the goods of the higher level. I suggest that this change in demand encourages receptive attitudes toward emergent interest groups.

In Africa, south of the Sahara, for example, most of the "peoples have been the beneficiaries of programs of positive social, economic, and political development initiated and carried through by colonial powers not only chastened and reformed by imperial disintegration elsewhere but subject to ever-increasing pressure of a critical world opinion and growing African nationalism." [34] Benefiting from such development programs and positively oriented toward many of the directions of change as seen through sub-Saharan eyes, situations have developed in Africa in which "each emerging group thought itself destined to inherit political power." [35] In South-East Asia,

The rapid growth of urban centers . . . produced a great increase in the number of informal associations. . . . As Asians, they came to represent and articulate what was accepted as "Asian opinion," but which, in fact, was the opinion of only a segment of the society. . . . Their interests were those of a stratum of the total society that was seeking admission into the culture and society of the national elite. [36]

The concept of the "revolution of rising expectations" has been advocated as "more meaningful for elites than for masses." [37] There has been some evidence to support this proposition. I have already referred to of Guatemala, and the movement there, 1944–54, that tried to confer the benefits of economic development to the Indians while it was in power. A survey of political changes in selected Indian communities during that period suggests that, where Indians did react positively to the values of the ascendant groups, these attitudes were held by elites or by peculiarly selected sectors of the Indian population of Guatemala. Thus, in the *municipio* of San Luis Jilotepeque "the large bulk of the Indian population remained relatively passive, but all of the few literate and 'enlightened' young Indian men were taken into the [revolutionary] movement." [38] Literacy, "enlightenment," and secularization were similarly selective in the *municipio* of Cantel. [39]

In some cases, the existence of labor unions may perform the function of selecting an elite to undergo a revolution in expectations and become

184

positively oriented toward ascendant interests. Guatemala again provides an illustration:

The concern of the revolutionary government and its ideology had no meaning or effect in Cantel until a union of factory workers was organized in 1945. . . . Cantel has in its midst a modern textile factory which employs nearly a fourth of the community's economically active persons. It is this special circumstance which provided the ambit in which the forces of the national revolution could be effective in modifying the structure and function of the hierarchy. For it was the local factory workers' labor union, a consequence of both the presence of the factory and the labor laws of the Arévalo and Arbenz governments, which acted as a funnel to the local community of the ideas of political democracy and social equality which formed an important part of the early days of the revolution against Ubico.[40]

A similar function of organized labor has been noted in South-East Asia. "So long as trade union leaders see themselves as occupying a position from which they can move into the ranks of the national elite," Pye has observed, "they will tend to articulate . . . the demands and ideas which will make them appear to be appropriate members of the national elite." [41]

2) In any case, elites constitute perhaps the most significant center of changing attitudes and loyalties in the underdeveloped areas. Early elite analysis maintained—and, indeed, it has long been believed—that governing groups resist change likely to displace them from their ruling positions.[42] Yet one of the most widespread contemporary phenomena in the underdeveloped areas is the spectacle of controlling elites—especially the governments of new nations—dedicated to change, encouraging it, and identifying their own interests with those of the ascendant groups. A recent study has demonstrated that, in India, Pakistan, and Ceylon, "Westernized intelligentsia . . . dominate the governments of all three countries and . . . dominate the policies of these governments. . . . In general the leaderships of all of them are dedicated to 'modernization' in some form or other." [43] In another part of the world, "segments of the leadership in Jamaica . . . are particularly committed to rapid social, economic, and political change. They feel that they have a mission to perform for their country. They push for ordered, rationalistic plans of economic development. . . . They are deeply dedicated." [44] In Israel, recent realignments within the Mapai, the governing political party, suggest "that rapid attitudinal changes are taking place. Given the need to manage the economy and to increase its efficiency, previously held norms and ideas are being swept away." [45] Indeed, one general characterization of new nations has it that "all show a passion for technology. All desire to expand the welfare state. They are concerned with efficiency and rapid change. In short, the characteristic of new nations is their desire for social mobilization, planning, and rapid change." [46]

I believe that this is the core of one of the most crucial questions in research into the political implications of economic development. Perhaps it is true, as was argued in a recent article, that, since their separation, political science and economics have drifted so far apart that it has become extremely difficult for them to make a joint approach to a common problem.[47] Yet I believe that this issue is sufficiently significant to warrant the attempt, however difficult, at a joint attack. In the underdeveloped areas, three phenomena—the first fundamentally economic, and the other two essentially political—appear to be integrally interrelated; and the problem is to discover the nature of this interrelationship and the mechanism of its operation.

The first phenomenon is what W. W. Rostow calls the "takeoff" in economic growth. This has been defined as the decisive transformation, or

the interval during which the rate of investment increases in such a way that the real output *per capita* rises and this initial increase carries with it radical changes in production techniques and the disposition of income flows which perpetuate the new scale of investment and perpetuate thereby the rising trend in *per capita* output.[48]

I realize that this is a controversial formulation and that there is no generally received theory of the stages of economic growth. All this is clearly a matter for economists, and it is no doubt foolhardy for a political scientist to get himself involved in it. However, I strongly suspect that, whether the Rostow formulation eventually stands or falls,[49] there *is* a phase, largely economic in character, of decisive transformation in economic development, and that this is a time of rapid change. A number of economies in the underdeveloped areas are currently in this stage—whether it is called "take-off" or not.

It seems likely that two political phenomena accompany the takeoff stage in economic growth. One has to do with the nature of political parties and party systems. During this stage, countries usually have what have been called "dominant non-dictatorial" political parties. These, frequently comprehensive and nationalist, resemble one-party systems in that the dominant groups are not seriously challenged by rival political parties; but they differ from dictatorial systems in that other political parties may and do coexist legally with the "dominant" organizations.[50] Illustrative of dominant non-dictatorial political parties in the underdeveloped areas are the Congress party of India, the Party of Revolutionary Institutions (PRI [51]) of Mexico, and, until 1957, the Republican People's party of Turkey.

The second political characteristic of takeoff is the commitment of governing elites to change. Thus, the dominant parties appear to be similarly oriented toward economic development and other forms of

186

change. India's Congress party is "dedicated to 'modernization,' " [52] the Mexican PRI is devoted to an impressive drive toward industrialization,[53] and the Turkish Republican People's party has been committed to the Westernization of Turkey.[54] The clear, sometimes passionate, devotion of these ruling elites to change is inescapable, as are their receptivity and potential loyalty toward ascendant groups. The conventional conception of a ruling elite struggling to preserve the status quo for fear that change might spell displacement seems curiously irrelevant to an analysis of the attitudes and loyalties of many of the governing groups of the underdeveloped areas. In a study of the attitudes of Jamaican elites, for example, Bell has found that over sixty per cent of those who believed that their careers would be affected by change expected to *benefit* from it! [55]

How does this come about? I can only suggest some ingredients for a hypothesis. These would run to the effect that in the period prior to takeoff—during the stage of "preconditions," to borrow another of Rostow's terms [56]—the ruling groups harbor attitudes and loyalties in conformity with what the bulk of elite analysis has led us to expect; i.e., they are conservative about the status quo and they resent and resist change.[57] With the coming of takeoff, however, change appears to be irresistible. Indeed, change at this point seems to be the chief characteristic and the main preoccupation of the society. Early in this period, the ruling elite's orientations are dramatically reversed. Those who once stubbornly opposed change now become dedicated to it and attempt to lead the society toward economic development. I do not mean that a cynical attitude of "if you can't beat them, join them" is at work here. Rather, I suspect that a more fundamental process, which we have hardly detected, much less understood, is involved. The decisive transformation in economic growth tends to galvanize the governing elite in a dominant political party dedicated uncompromisingly to change. In such groups, we find the "push for ordered, rationalistic plans of economic development. . . . They are deeply dedicated to the welfare of the common people . . . but . . . become impatient and irritated with the masses when the people reject their candidates at the polls or their representatives elsewhere." [58] Such elites develop attitudes—however non-democratic—and loyalties that are receptively and positively toward ascendant groups and newly emerging interests.

I have discussed governing elites at this length because I regard them as the most significant of the groups in the underdeveloped areas with such positive or receptive attitudes. Other groups are so oriented, however, and they also deserve of some attention.

3) Newly emerging industrializing and entrepreneurial groups—small in most of the underdeveloped regions—usually associate their interests with those of the rising groups. Little has thus far been published about

187

the industrializers or entrepreneurs in these economies, and terminology is far from settled in this field. I have seen these groups called "industrializing elites," "the emerging middle class," and the "middle sectors," among other things. Whatever the terms, these groups are important in some of the countries, and appear to hold positive and receptive attitudes toward ascendant interests.

A recent study of political change in selected parts of Latin America ascribes some significance to the role of the "middle sectors," which are identified as "politically ambitious middle groups" active in commerce and developing industry.[59] As a rule, these groups locate in major urban centers like Mexico City, Buenos Aires, Rio de Janeiro, and São Paulo; they are strongly nationalistic and active in political parties; and they are firmly committed to industrialization. There is some evidence that these middle sectors are increasing in significance in the more developed parts of Latin America, and that they are important centers of positive attitudes and potential loyalty toward ascendant interests.[60]

Similarly oriented entrepreneurial or industrializing groups exist in other areas. "Managerial positions are held in high esteem" in Japan, where "membership in the managerial elite in itself gives one a high life-time status." [61] The available data also suggest that, in some portions of the Middle East, the industrializers not only have a political role of growing importance but also hold considerably militant attitudes and loyalties. Thus, Israeli management "is perceptibly gaining in economic power and becoming a functional entity." [62] In Israel, a

General awakening of a management *élan* ... has been manifested recently in the increasing militancy of the technical, administrative, and managerial groups. This militancy has concerned basic issues on which managerial and professional needs have been in conflict with older socialist and egalitarian norms. These conflicts have produced either abandonment of, or compromises in, the original ideology.[63]

Similarly,

Egypt's bright young men are now strongly attracted by managerial careers. ... These ... have contributed to the emergence of a more vigorous and enthusiastic managerial elite in both public and private enterprise. ... Egypt's industrial progress is not retarded by a conservative patrimonial elite. ... Her careerist managerial class, both in private as well as in public enterprise, is comparatively free of allegiance to an old order and thus inclined to be receptive to new ideas and to concepts of organization appropriate to modern technology.[64]

We may thus identify the newly emerging industrializing and entrepreneurial groups, dubbed "middle sectors" or "emerging middle classes," as positive or receptive toward ascendant groups.

188

4) Finally, there is a curious class, with possibly great significance, in the underdeveloped areas. I refer to ethnic minorities who perform commercializing functions in many of the countries. Great numbers of Chinese have emigrated to other countries of the Far East. Similarly, Levantines and others have left their homelands in the Middle East to live in parts of sub-Saharan Africa and portions of the Caribbean area. Of course, these patterns of emigration are not a recent phenomenon. Levantine and Chinese communities have existed in sub-Saharan Africa and Asian countries for generations; and it may well be that the ages of some Chinese communities in Burma, Indonesia, and Thailand could be computed in centuries.

The position of these Levantine and Chinese communities is intriguingly reminiscent of that of the Jews in early modern Europe. Indeed, today there is a widespread tendency in the Far East to refer to the Chinese minority as the "Jews of the East." Typically, the indigenous ethnic groups in countries like Nigeria, Ghana, Burma, Indonesia, Thailand, and the Philippines are engaged primarily in agricultural pursuits; their elites are attracted into politics and government service. The Levantine and Chinese communities, on the other hand, provide a merchant and trading class. In general, they do not become industrial entrepreneurs on any significant scale. Their economic function is essentially to commercialize rather than to industrialize. However, the analysis of the contribution of such merchant and trading groups to the economic development of the countries involved is a task I leave to others. What concerns us here is the relationship of the merchant and trading ethnic minorities to the patterns of social and political attitudes and loyalties in the countries in which these groups function.

In the first place, these minorities are strongly disliked—in some cases, "hated" is probably not too strong a word—in the countries in which they play commercializing roles. They are often accused of monopolizing trade and commerce and of exploiting the indigenous groups—in this, too, these communities recall the Jews of Europe. The prevailing dislike of the Levantine trader in countries like Nigeria and Ghana, and the strong anti-Chinese attitudes in states like Indonesia, Thailand, and the Philippines, have assumed the proportions of an underdeveloped area's version of anti-Semitism. A Burmese tale illustrates this:

The quiet of a village was broken by shouts of "A man has fallen into the well!" The villagers came out in alarm, but the first to reach the well looked into it and cried out: "Be calm, my friends, it is not a man but a Chinese!" The Chinese from the bottom of the well shouted back in anger, "If I am not a man, am I a bird? Am I a bird?"[65]

In Indonesia, anti-Chinese sentiment has gone so far as to become official

189

policy in recent restrictive legislation against the merchant and trading group.[66]

What of the attitudes and loyalties of the Levantine and Chinese communities in such situations? I regret that in the Levantine case I am familiar with virtually no data on this question. I can report only that many of the Levantines in Colombia, where they are called *turcos*, are affiliated with the Liberal, rather than the Conservative, party and, within the context of Colombian politics, are markedly anti-clerical and devoted to land reform programs calculated to reduce the number and influence of large landed estates. A *turco*, Gabriel Turbay, was for a time regarded as the leader of the left wing of the Liberal party, and was its unsuccessful presidential candidate in the election campaign of 1946.[67]

A little—but only a little—more is known of the political attitudes and loyalties of the "Jews of the East." Disliked, hated, and in some cases persecuted, where do they turn? Some renew their loyalty to the homeland, to be sure; but there is some evidence that Chinese Communists, while they exist, are not representative of a dominant tendency within the minority communities. Figures gathered during the anti-Chinese campaign in Indonesia, for example, indicate that of approximately three million ethnic Chinese resident in the country, the overwhelming majority had become Indonesian citizens; only about four hundred thousand remained Chinese citizens.[68] Questionnaires administered indicated that significantly greater percentages of ethnic Chinese than of indigenous Indonesians favored private enterprise and sought careers in it, and that the former had a greater tendency to become Christianized and pro-Western.[69] Not only in Indonesia, but also in Thailand and the Philippines, Chinese businessmen feel themselves to be in politically weak positions. They almost never take open stands on national political issues, seldom participate directly in politics and government, and rely upon bribery when it is thought necessary to influence politicians or government officials.[70]

The present state of our knowledge about ethnic minorities performing commercializing functions in the underdeveloped areas is far too sketchy to permit generalizations about their social and political attitudes and loyalties. It may not be unreasonable to suspect, however, that these, too, might be centers of positive attitudes toward ascendant interests.

V

I shall devote my concluding remarks to two matters. First, I wish to summarize what I think I have said about the transference of social and political loyalties in the underdeveloped areas. Then, I shall suggest priorities in needed research on this problem.

190

I believe that the study of political groups might throw considerable light on the mechanisms of change in attitudes and loyalties. The identity, nature, and relative weight of interest groups vary according to level or stage of economic development. Transformations in the economy thus alter the nature and relative political influence of groups. All groups have interests. A loyalty may be regarded as the identification of an individual's own interest with that of a group. Thus, economic growth affects the distribution of interests, attitudes, and loyalties.

During economic development, some political groups weaken, some vanish, some gain in influence, and some new groups appear. The problem then becomes one of identifying the attitudes and loyalties toward the ascendant interests and emergent groups. I have suggested that, in the underdeveloped areas, these attitudes may be classified as neutral, negative, or positive.

Neutral attitudes toward ascendant interests are common among peoples in traditional systems where the political groups are so non-aggregative that these peoples have little or no contact or interaction with them. Negative attitudes toward ascendant groups arise among traditionally governing elites who feel threatened by change; members of indigenous societies resisting the destruction of their traditional systems; and groups who accept economic development but believe that its benefits are being denied or withheld from them. Positive attitudes—loyalty or potential loyalty—toward the ascendant groups may be expected to appear where the "revolution of rising expectations" has been effective; among some controlling elites, particularly the governments of new nations; among newly emerging industrializing and entrepreneurial groups; and possibly among ethnic minorities performing commercializing functions in some underdeveloped countries.

Investigation of the nature of social and political loyalties in the under-developed areas has hardly begun, and the need for knowledge and under-standing is critical at a great number of points. It is not easy to establish a limited number of priorities in an area where much research obviously must be done. The needs are great both in the construction and devel-opment of theory and in the accumulation of raw empirical data. While I do not wish to underestimate the value of empirical research, I would place a somewhat higher priority on theoretical work at this stage.

The need for theoretical effort appears to be especially critical in two spheres. The first is the extension of the group theory of politics to research on the underdeveloped areas. Interest groups vary according to level or stage of economic development, and ascendant or emergent groups are especially significant for the study of the transference of social and political loyalties. It would thus appear that these latter groups them-selves must be subjected to a closer and harder examination. This would entail, not so much the compilation of an exhaustive list of the groups to be found in developing areas, but rather the identification and rigorous analysis of what is probably a small number of especially critical emergent groups that might become indices to the progress of economic and political development. If these groups—they might include such entities as professional associations, industrializing elites, organized skilled labor, and bureaucracies—were identified, and the mechanisms through which they emerge in the underdeveloped regions analyzed, this work might well constitute a major contribution to this field. Some research, of course, has already been done on industrializing elites,[71] labor organizations,[72] and bureaucracy;[73] but many questions have yet to be answered. Theory identifying the especially significant ascendant groups and relating them more precisely to the course of economic growth is sorely needed.

A second area where the theoretical need is especially great involves the relationship among the decisive transformation—the takeoff—in economic development; the commitment of some controlling elites, especially the governments of new nations, to rapid change; and the attitudes and loyalties stemming from that commitment. I have observed that I believe these to be integrally interrelated. I cannot overemphasize the significance I attach to the necessity for an early breakthrough on this question. I think this would make vitally important contribution to our understanding of the interrelationship between economic development and a wide range of political changes, including those in attitudes and loyalties.

Finally, empirical research is also needed. I mention this last, not because I think it of lowest value, but rather because I believe that it would be most useful if it were to follow rather than to precede theoretical refinement. Obviously, we have very little data on the political groups in underdeveloped areas and on the nature and status of attitudes, opinions, and loyalties there. This does not mean that we should dash immediately into the field to compile exhaustive telephone-directory-style lists of the interest groups to be found there, or that we should be conducting public-opinion polls or attitude and loyalty surveys in the absence of a clear formulation of the theoretical problems on which such empirical findings might be expected to throw light. The literature of political science is already regrettably cluttered with cases in which the energy expended in gathering data so far outstripped that devoted to the development of theory that the data gatherers arrived at the point where they forgot—if they ever knew in the first place—why they embarked upon this activity and what their findings might be expected to prove or disprove. I am, therefore, not alarmed by the present short supply of empirical data on social and political loyalties in the underdeveloped areas. I hope that our knowledge here might follow our theoretical progress, to which I assign the leading priorities at this stage in our endeavors.

192

NOTES TO CHAPTER 9

1. This paper grew out of a larger inquiry into the interplay between economic development and political change in the underdeveloped areas. During the academic year 1959-60, that project was supported by a fellowship from the Ford Foundation, whose assistance is gratefully acknowledged.

2. See George I. Blanksten, "Political Groups in Latin America," *American Politi cal Science Review,* LIII, No. 1 (March, 1959), 106-27, especially pp. 124-27.

3. The most complete recent statement of the theory is in David B. Truman, *The Governmental Process* (New York, 1951). A noteworthy formulation may also be found in Charles B. Hagen, "The Group in a Political Science," in Roland A. Young (ed.), *Approaches to the Study of Politics* (Evanston, Ill., 1958), pp. 38-51. For a provocative critique of the theory, see Stanley Rothman, "Systematic Political Theory: Observations on the Group Approach," *American Political Science Review,* LIV, No. 1 (March, 1960), 15-33.

4. See Gabriel A. Almond, "A Comparative Study of Interest Groups and the Political Process" (unpublished; Committee on Comparative Politics, Social Science Research Council, 1957); Almond and James S. Coleman (eds.), *The Politics of the Developing Areas* (Princeton, N.J., 1960), *passim*; and Henry W. Ehrmann (ed.), *Interest Groups on Four Continents* (Pittsburgh, 1958), *passim.*

5. Hagen, *op. cit.,* p. 44.

6. Herbert A. Bloch, *The Concept of Our Changing Loyalties* (New York, 1934), p. 36.

7. H. J. Eysenck, *The Psychology of Politics* (New York, 1955), p. 15.

8. Walter Goldschmidt, *Man's Way* (Cleveland, Ohio, 1959), p. 111.

9. Richard N. Adams (ed.), *Political Changes in Guatemalan Indian Communities* (New Orleans, 1957), p. 48. See also Douglas H. K. Lee, *Climate and Economic Development in the Tropics* (New York, 1957), *passim.*

10. Htin Aung, "Commentary," in Urban G. Whitaker (ed.), *Nationalism and International Progress* (San Francisco, 1960), p. 44.

11. Goldschmidt, *op. cit.,* p. 113.

12. David E. Apter, "An Analysis of the Consequences of Traditionalism in the

Political Modernization of Ghana and Uganda" (Unpublished Chicago, 1959), p. 8.

13. *Ibid.*, p. 23.

14. *Principales* are traditional officers of local government in many of the Indian communities of Guatemala.

15. Raymond L. Scheele, "Santo Domingo Xenacoj: 1944-51," in Adams, *op. cit.*, pp. 38-39.

16. K. H. Silvert and Arden R. King, "Cobán: 1944-53," *ibid.*, p. 46.

17. The *municipio* is an administrative subdivision more similar to the institution in the United States of the county than of the municipality. Although they have been established throughout Guatemala, *municipios* have far greater cultural and political significance in the rural than in the urban areas.

18. John Gillin, "San Luis Jilotepeque: 1942-55," Adams, *op. cit.*, p. 26.

19. Kekchi is the indigenous language of the majority of the Indians of Cobán.

20. Silvert and King, *op. cit.*, pp. 44-45.

21. See Daniel Lerner, *The Passing of Traditional Society* (Glencoe, Ill., 1958), *passim.;* and Julius H. Boeke, *The Interests of the Voiceless Far East* (Leiden, 1948), *passim.*

22. William S. Stokes, "Some Latin-American Leaders Don't Want Technological Change," in Lewis Hanke, *Mexico and the Caribbean* (New York, 1959), p. 123. Also see Stokes, "The Drag of the *Pensadores*," in James W. Wiggins and Helmut Schoeck (eds.), *Foreign Aid Reexamined* (Washington: Foreign Affairs Press, 1958), pp. 76, 79, 56-57, 62-63, and 68.

23. See Blanksten, *Perón's Argentina* (Chicago, 1953), *passim.*

24. See Karl Loewenstein, *Brazil under Vargas* (New York, 1942), *passim.*

25. See Blanksten, *Ecuador: Constitutions and Caudillos* (Berkeley, California, 1951), *passim.*

26. Morris Siegel, "San Miguel Acatán: 1938-53," Adams, *op. cit.*, p. 43. See also Zbigniew Brzezinski, "The Politics of Underdevelopment," *World Politics*, IX, No. 1 (October, 1956).

27. Ruben E. Reina, "Chinautla: 1944-53," Adams, *op. cit.*, p. 35.

28. Raymond G. Amir, "Magdalena Milpas Altas: 1880-1952," *ibid.*, p. 13.

29. Apter, *op. cit.*, pp. 14-15.

30. Rupert Emerson, "The Progress of Nationalism," Whitaker, *op. cit.*, p. 34.

31. Apter, *op. cit.*, p. 15.

32. See Daniel Lerner and A. J. Weiner (eds.), "Attitude Research in Modernizing Areas," *Public Opinion Quarterly*, XXII, No. 3 (Fall, 1958), *passim.*

33. Allan B. Cole, *Political Tendencies of Japanese in Small Enterprises* (New York, 1959), p. 55.

34. James S. Coleman, "The Politics of Sub-Saharan Africa," Almond and Coleman, *op. cit.*, p. 320.

35. Apter, *op. cit.*, p. 15.

36. Lucian W. Pye, "The Politics of Southeast Asia," Almond and Coleman, *op. cit.*, p. 121.

194

37. Wilfred Malenbaum, "Political Stability and Economic Development: The Case of India" (Unpublished Cambridge, 1959), p. 7.

38. Gillin, *op. cit.*, p. 27.

39. Manning Nash, "Recruitment of Wage Labor Development of New Skills," *Annals of the American Academy of Political and Social Science,* CCCV (May, 1956), 30.

40. *Ibid.*, pp. 28-29.

41. Pye, *op. cit.*, p. 120.

42. See p. 6 above.

43. Myron Weiner, "The Politics of South Asia," Almond and Coleman, *op. cit.*, p. 212.

44. Wendell Bell, "Images of the United States and the Soviet Union Held by Jamaican Elite Groups," *World Politics,* XII, No. 2 (January, 1960), 237-38.

45. Frederick Harbison and Charles A. Myers, *Management in the Industrial World* (New York, 1959), p. 202.

46. David E. Apter, "Steps toward a Theory of Political Development" (Unpublished Chicago, 1959), p. 8.

47. See Joseph Cropsey, "On the Relation of Political Science and Economics," *American Political Science Review,* LIV, No. 1 (March, 1960), 3-14.

48. W. W. Rostow, "The Take-off into Self-Sustained Growth," *The Economic Journal* (March, 1956), p. 25.

49. In addition to the article cited immediately above, Rostow's leading writings on the stages of economic growth are *The Process of Economic Growth* (London, 1953); "Trends in the Allocation of Resources in Secular Growth," in Léon H. Dupriez (ed.), *Economic Progress* (Louvain, 1955); "The Relation between Political and Economic Development" (Unpublished Cambridge, 1956); "The Stages of Economic Growth," *The Economic History Review,* Series 2, XII, no. 1 (August, 1959), 1-16; and *The Stages of Economic Growth* (New York, 1960).

50. See Almond and Coleman, *op. cit.*, pp. 40-41, 479-81, 397-98, 188, 114, 286-94, and 295.

51. After the initial letters of *Partido Revolucionario Institucional.*

52. Weiner, *op. cit.*, p. 212.

53. See Robert E. Scott, *Mexican Government in Transition* (Urbana, Ill., 1959), *passim*; and Sanford A. Mosk, *Industrial Revolution in Mexico* (Berkeley, Calif., 1950), *passim*.

54. See Dankwart A. Rustow, "The Politics of the Near East," Almond and Coleman, *op. cit.*, pp. 397-98.

55. Wendell Bell, "Attitudes of Jamaican Elites toward the West Indies Federation," *Annals of the New York Academy of Sciences,* LXXXIII (January, 1960), 862-79, especially p. 874.

56. Rostow, *The Stages of Economic Growth,* pp. 4-35.

57. See pp. 6-8, above.

58. Bell, "Images of the United States and the Soviet Union," periodical p. 238.

59. John J. Johnson, *Political Change in Latin America* (Stanford, Calif., 1958), p. vii, and *passim*.

60. See George I. Blanksten, "In Quest of the Middle Sectors," *World Politics,* XII, No. 2 (January, 1960), 323-27; and Orrin E. Klapp and L. Vincent Padgett, "Power Structure and Decision-Making in a Mexican Border City," *American Journal of Sociology,* LXV, No. 4 (January, 1960), 400-06.

61. Harbison and Myers, *op. cit.,* p. 260.

62. *Ibid.,* p. 204.

63. *Ibid.,* p. 200.

64. *Ibid.,* pp. 160-62. See also Harbison, "Entrepreneurial Organization as a Factor in Economic Development," *Quarterly Journal of Economics* (August, 1956), pp. 364-79.

65. Htin Aung, *op. cit.,* p. 44.

66. See Guy J. Pauker, "Southeast Asia as a Problem Area in the Next Decade," *World Politics,* XI, No. 3 (April, 1959), 325-45.

67. See Vernon L. Fluharty, *Dance of the Millions* (Pittsburgh, 1957), *passim.*

68. See Pauker, *op. cit., passim.*

69. Interview with Professor Leonard Doyle, Graduate School of Business Administration, University of California, Berkeley, April, 1960.

70. See G. William Skinner, *Chinese Society in Thailand* (Ithaca, N.Y., 1957), *passim.*; and Skinner, *Leadership and Power in the Chinese Community of Thailand* (Ithaca, N.Y., 1958), *passim.*

71. See Harbosin and Myers, *op. cit., passim*; and Harbison, "Entrepreneurial Organization."

72. George C. Lodge, "Labor's Role in Newly Developing Countries," *Foreign Affairs,* XXXVII, No. 4 (July, 1959), 660-71; and Karl de Schweinitz, Jr., "Industrialization, Labor Controls, and Democracy," *Economic Development and Cultural Change,* VII, No. 4 (July, 1959), 385-404.

73. Lloyd A. Fallers, *Bantu Bureaucracy* (Cambridge, 1957).

PART V

*Urbanization, Population,
and Family*

CHAPTER 10

The Social, Economic, and Technological Problems
of Rapid Urbanization

PHILIP M. HAUSER
University of Chicago

A world demographic revolution has been under way since at least the middle of the seventeenth century. Accompanying the observed explosive increased rates of population growth have been profound changes in the distribution of population. Perhaps the most dramatic of these during the modern era is the increasing concentration of population represented by the huge and still growing urban agglomerations. In fact, urban population has increased more rapidly than world population for as far back as reliable data are available, i.e., at least since 1800. Moreover, the rate of world urbanization has been accelerating and this acceleration is undoubtedly still going on.[1]

TABLE 1

Comparison of world's urban population growth rates and world's total population growth rates, 1800–1950 *

Period	Total world population	Percentage increase in		
		World population in cities		
		5,000 and over	20,000 and over	100,000 and over
1800–1850	29.2	175.4	132.3	76.3
1850–1900	37.3	192.0	193.5	222.2
1900–1950	49.3	227.7	239.6	254.1

* Source: Kingsley Davis and Hilda Hertz, "Patterns of World Urbanization" to be published by Macmillan & Co.

During the nineteenth century, world urbanization was largely the result of the large concentration of population in the cities of Europe and North America. In the twentieth century, however, the rate of world urbanization has been sustained by the rapid growth of urban populations in the

199

economically underdeveloped areas of the world, particularly in Asia, Latin America, and Africa. During the course of this century, the economically advanced areas of the world had already reached near-saturation points of urbanization; the economically underdeveloped areas were still experiencing the flow of people from the rural countryside to the cities. Despite the present relatively rapid rate of urbanization in the economically underdeveloped areas of the world, they still have comparatively small proportions of their populations living in cities. In 1950, for example, the world average showed twenty-one per cent resident in cities of twenty thousand or more; but only nine per cent of Africa's population lived in such cities, and only thirteen per cent of Asia's. Twenty-one per cent of Central America's population, and twenty-six per cent of South America's, lived in cities of twenty thousand or more. In contrast, forty-seven per cent of the population in Oceania, forty-two per cent in North America, thirty-five per cent in Europe (excluding the U.S.S.R.), and thirty-one per cent in the U.S.S.R., lived in cities of this size.

TABLE 2

Percentages of urban population in major world areas, 1950 *

	Percentage of total population in cities of 20,000 and more	Percentage of population in cities of 100,000 and more
World	21	13
Oceania	47	41
North America †	42	29
Europe ‡	35	21
U.S.S.R.	31	18
South America	26	18
Central America §	21	12
Asia	13	8
Africa	9	5

* Source: Kingsley Davis and Hilda Hertz, "The World Distribution of Urbanization," *Bulletin of the International Statistical Institute*, XXXIII, Part 4, 227-42.
† Includes U.S.A. and Canada.
‡ Without U.S.S.R.
§ Includes Mexico, countries of Central America, and Caribbean Islands.

A large urban population is appropriately identified as characteristic of an economically advanced area, the advent of industrialization, and the development of Western civilization in general. Yet, despite the relatively low rate of urbanization in the economically less advanced areas, they have more people living in cities of twenty thousand or more, or cities of one hundred thousand or more, than do Europe and North America combined. In 1950, forty-one per cent of world population living in cities of twenty thousand or more was in Europe (excluding the U.S.S.R.) and

North America; whereas Asia, Latin America, and Africa combined contained over forty-five per cent of the world's residents in cities of this size.[2] The U.S.S.R. contained about twelve per cent of the world's urban population, and Oceania the remaining one or two per cent.

The rate of world urbanization, and particularly that of the areas with low proportions of urban populations at the present time, may be expected to continue to accelerate. In 1950, about 502 million persons lived in cities of twenty thousand and over. By 1975, should the rate of urbanization as observed between 1900 and 1950 continue and total world population increase in accordance with United Nations projections, urban population in places of this size will have more than doubled, to reach a level of 1.2 billions.[3] Similarly, under the same conditions, population in cities of one hundred thousand and over—314 million, in 1950—could reach a level of 745 million, i.e., also more than double, by 1975. Even if the proportion of the world's urban population remained fixed from 1950 to 1975, the population in places of twenty-thousand and over would increase by about fifty-five per cent simply because of total population increase alone. If the trend continues, by 1975 thirty per cent of the world's peoples will live in cities of twenty thousand and over, and nineteen per cent will live in cities of one hundred thousand and over. The large share of the increase in the world's urban population will occur in the economically underdeveloped areas. Asia, alone, will account for over half of the increase during the 1950–75 period.

Urban problems and the problems of rapid urbanization are quite different in the economically advanced and the economically underdeveloped areas of the world respectively. In the economically advanced nations, urbanization is both an antecedent and a consequence of high levels of living. It both makes possible and is a manifestation of great increases in division of labor and specialization, in technology, in skill, and in productivity. In the economically underdeveloped areas, it does not usually have these properties. There, large concentrations of urban population are only to a minor degree symbols of man's mastery over nature—they represent more the transfer of underemployment and poverty from an overpopulated rural countryside to an urban setting. In consequence, the social, economic, and technological problems of rapid urbanization must be considered separately for the underdeveloped and the developed areas of the globe respectively.

ECONOMIC PROBLEMS

The economic antecedents of urbanization in the economically more advanced areas differ greatly from those of the less advanced areas. Although much remains to be learned, the emergence of the urban agglomeration has been reasonably well traced for Western civilization. Permanent settlement was not possible at all until after the Neolithic revolution. Beginning with relative small village and town settlements, advancing technology, together with evolving economic, social, and political organization, permitted human agglomerations to increase steadily in size from ancient times down through the Greek and Roman civilizations.[4] With the collapse of the Roman Empire and the onset of the Dark Ages, the European world reverted to population agglomerations of relatively small size. Only with the Renaissance and the agricultural, commercial, and industrial revolutions did the large city again become possible in Europe. A city of a million or more was not achieved (with the possible exception of Ancient China, for which adequate documentation does not exist, and Tokyo) until the beginning of the nineteenth century. Continued technological and organizational developments have made possible even larger clumpings of economic activities and peoples, and have given impetus to the rapid rates of urbanization during the nineteenth and early twentieth centuries in Europe and in North America.[5] In the West, urbanization is both an antecedent and consequence of rapid industrialization. There are no highly developed economies in the world in which large cities and a high degree of industrialization are not present.

Urbanization in the economically underdeveloped areas of the world is the product of very different forces. The "primate" cities in South and South-East Asia are less the result of indigenous economic development than they are the product of economic development oriented essentially to one or more foreign countries. They developed as links between the colonial and mother country. Today, they usually still have an external orientation, serving as a link between the local elite and the outside world, rather than as an economic outpost of the national economy.[6] Urbanization in Latin America is characterized by the hypertrophy of capital cities. These, reflecting unique aspects of Latin American history, are concentrated on the seaboard, or in the mountain districts in the tropics.[7] In Latin America—as in Asia and Africa—prior to World War II, economic and urban development was largely directed toward external markets in the framework of patterns established under colonial administration. Moreover, the process of urbanization in the underdeveloped areas has been accelerated by the low land-population ratio arising from excessive population growth in relation to agriculture resources; by the disruption and disorganization produced by the last war, which forced refugee populations to choke already swelled populations in cities; by the lure of urban existence, to which large parts of the peasant population were exposed as the result of military service and other wartime dislocations; and by various other forces which pushed population to the city instead

202

of attracting it by economic opportunity of the type experienced in the West.[8]

Thus, the underdeveloped areas of the world are "over-urbanized," in that larger proportions of their population live in urban places than their degree of economic development justifies. In the underdeveloped nations, a much smaller proportion of the labor force is engaged in non-agricultural occupations than was the case in the West at comparable levels of urbanization.[9] Furthermore, during the postwar period, the rate of urbanization in the underdeveloped areas has continued proceeding more rapidly than the rate of economic development.

To say that the underdeveloped areas of the world are over-urbanized is to pose the major economic problem with which they are confronted, namely, that they do not at the present time have an adequate economic base to support present urban populations by the standards of the Western world. They must find a way of achieving higher levels of economic development to support their present, let alone their prospective, urban population. Continued rapid rates of urbanization are, therefore, likely to aggravate, rather than alleviate, present urban poverty and distress. In general, the outlook for the remainder of this century is a dismal one indeed. It is very doubtful that, over this span of time, the underdeveloped nations can attain economic development of adequate dimensions to meet Western standards of living for their present and future city dwellers.[10] The fundamental economic objective of the underdeveloped areas is that of increasing productivity; and the many difficulties they meet in their efforts to attain this objective are likely to be exacerbated rather than ameliorated by present and prospective rapid rates of urban growth.[11]

This general problem may be analyzed into a number of components.[12] Virtually all of the underdeveloped nations have ambitious programs for economic development. The cores of these programs generally consist of plans to increase industrialization. At the present levels of productivity and limited savings, a central problem is that of allocating resources for development between the agricultural and industrial sectors of the economy. If the criterion of maximizing product per head be accepted as the objective of economic development programs, then it is possible, at least in the short run, that the advancement of the agricultural sectors of the economy may be more productive than efforts to induce industrialization. The achievement of adequate balance between agricultural and industrial development is a major difficulty which confronts almost all of the economically underdeveloped nations.

Another issue involves the allocation of scarce investment resources between "social investment" and "productive investment." This problem, although it exists both in the urban and rural sectors, assumes its most acute form in the cities. Cities in the underdeveloped areas are charac-

203

terized by inadequate infrastructure development, precluding the usual amenities of urban existence found in Western cities. The temptation to devote scarce savings to social purposes—e.g., piped water, sewerage, better housing, etc.—is great, particularly in view of the expectations which have accompanied political independence and the opportunity for self-determination. Yet social investment of this type, badly needed as it may be, is possible only at the expense of decreased productive investment —investment in power plants and factories, or in tractors and fertilizers, designed to increase productivity.

Another difficult problem posed by the continued accelerated rates of urbanization in the underdeveloped areas is that of the location of industry. At the present time, numerous small commercial towns serving agricultural areas are widely dispersed, largely in accordance with the location of agricultural activity and the density of agricultural population. Larger towns are superimposed on the widespread distributional pattern of the smaller commercial centers. They are usually near transport nodal points—river and road junctions and, more recently, railroad junctions. These centers, and the seaports, are the "break-of-bulk" points; their essential function is the transshipment and distribution of goods between land and water and within the interior. Such cities have increasingly become convenient points of location for processing and light manufacturing industry. In most underdeveloped areas, the growth of towns and cities and industrialization, apart from primate and capital cities, have gone little beyond this point.

Efforts to increase industrialization, and to deal with the many pressing problems of swelling urban populations, are forcing decisions about the location of economic development projects. In the economically more advanced nations, the locations, as well as the size and function of urban places, were largely the products of the play of market forces. In the economically underdeveloped areas, these decisions are usually centrally administered. They involve considerations of raw materials, power sources, availability of labor, the location of consumer markets, national policy concerning centralization or decentralization of industry, regional development, and general national economic development. In centralized decision-making about the location of new industry, there are dangers of serious dis-economies.

Decentralization is necessary because the "great city" tends to be "parasitic," in that it usually retards the development of other cities in the nation, and may contribute relatively little to the development of its own hinterland because it is oriented primarily to the contribution of services abroad or to the indigenous or remaining Western elite inhabiting it. On the other hand, the decision to decentralize industry may produce dis-economies by ignoring the productive factors already available in the

204

larger urban agglomerations. The larger cities in the underdeveloped areas represent already available labor supply, markets, and a wide variety of public services which may be utilized for industrial and business development. To duplicate such agglomerations of population in efforts to decentralize may well be redundant and wasteful.

Underdeveloped areas with rapidly growing urban populations face another difficulty in making policy with respect to employment opportunities. To provide work for hordes of unemployed and underemployed immigrants to urban centers, there is a tendency to emphasize labor-intensive techniques. If carried too far, this tendency may adversely affect the growth of the nation's net aggregate product by retarding labor-saving technological developments. In general, policy determination presumably must aim toward obtaining balance in industrial development between employment opportunities, in the short run, and technological advance to insure maximum product per head, in the longer run.

Low productivity and poverty are distinguishing traits in both rural and urban areas in underdeveloped nations. Because internal migratory flow from agricultural to urban centers is a major factor in the present and prospective increase in urban populations, programs designed to keep rural people in agricultural areas may be important in any effort to deal with urban, as well as national, economic development problems. Programs that raised the level of living of rural populations would undoubtedly moderate the excessive flow of migrants from rural to urban areas. In a number of underdeveloped nations, outmoded land tenure systems contribute to rural poverty. Agrarian reform resulting in higher productivity, giving the agricultural population a stake in the land and an opportunity to raise its level of living, may well be an important means of alleviating urban problems by helping to reduce the flow of city-bound migrants. Similarly, the establishment of cottage industries and small industries in rural areas may keep their population from emigrating.

Western cities have undergone development and transformation with changing industrial technology. Economically underdeveloped areas today have the choice of adopting twentieth- or nineteenth-century types of industrial equipment. The extent of actual choice depends, of course, on the availability of electric, as contrasted with steam, power; on cost factors for older, as against more modern, equipment; and on the emphasis placed on labor-intensive rather than automated equipment. The adoption of twentieth-century industrial technology would undoubtedly create patterns of urban development quite different from those which characterized the West during the nineteenth. Moreover, the problem of maintaining balance in economic development is also at stake in the decisions made with respect to the types of technology adopted in different sectors of the industrial economy.

205

Urbanization has an impact on income, levels of living, savings, and capital formation that requires brief mention, even though most of what can be said is necessarily speculative. Urban residents in the underdeveloped areas, in spite of underemployment and low productivity, are generally engaged in non-agricultural activities which provide them with a relatively higher money level of income and expenditure than is achieved in rural areas. While it is a moot point whether urban real income is higher than rural real income in such areas, the higher urban money income is undoubtedly one of the factors attracting populations to cities.

The transition from the rural to the urban economy involves a shift, of course, from a subsistence to a monetary economy in which mobilization of savings can be facilitated. Urbanization produces alteration in consumption patterns, in which the proportion of consumer expenditures for food tends to decrease below the rural level; while expenditures on amusement, education, transport, services, footwear, rent, and taxes tend to rise. Consumption in cities tends also to rely more heavily on imported commodities. This trend, while it increases the drain on foreign exchange, may also provide incentives for industrial types of work. Because of low national productivity and poverty, it is difficult to analyze the effect of urbanization on saving propensities; however, in underdeveloped nations, there is some evidence that propensity to save is reduced in the city as compared with rural areas. In general, despite the fact that poverty characterizes urban as well as rural dwellers in the underdeveloped areas, there is probably some gain in marginal productivity in the cities, and the concentration of purchasing power serves as a stimulant to developing industry.

Finally, in the underdeveloped nations another crucial decision is necessary: the interventions of government and of market forces respectively, in dealing with the economic problems of the nation as a whole, as well as with the specific industrial and urban developments, must be determined. For a number of reasons, historical and contemporary, central decision-making and management of economic affairs inevitably must play a more important role in the economically underdeveloped nations than they did in the history of the economically advanced nations. If the mix of central planning and government interventionism is increased, it may be expected that patterns of economic, as well as urban, development are likely to follow different routes than they did in the West. Some types of problems engendered by Western industrialization and urbanization may be avoided or ameliorated; but it is also possible that new and critical kinds of problems will be encountered, and that the dangers of serious dis-economies will be increased. The interplay of forces most conducive to efficient and balanced economic development and orderly urbanization is far from being fully understood. In the West, the major role of the market mechanism in determining division of labor, resource allocation, and economic development in general, largely compensated for ignorance about these factors. In the economically underdeveloped nations, such ignorance may conceivably have deleterious consequences. In the play of market forces in the West, risk, as well as decision-making, were decentralized. Central planning centralizes risk along with decision-making, and may increase and concentrate the cost of bad decisions.

Economically Advanced Nations
Rapid rates of urbanization also cause economic problems for the more advanced nations, but of a quite different order. The economic problems of the advanced urban areas do not involve the basic problems of poverty and extremely low productivity. However, the size and rate of urban growth can and do affect the level of living. There is increasing evidence that urban development in the West has produced cities beyond "optimal" size and that economic functions of cities, and particularly of central cities in metropolitan area complexes, may be undergoing significant change.

There seems to be some evidence that there is an optimum city size at which external economies and economies of scale are maximized.[13] The limited data available about suggest that such an optimal point may lie between one and two hundred thousand rather than at levels well above a million. The changing economic functions of the central city undoubtedly vary for different nations and for cities within nations. In the United States, explosive metropolitan growth and the rapid obsolescence of central city plants are precipitating a number of problems, which all are clearly exacerbated by high urban growth rates. There is some evidence that there may be a decline in intensive use of space both for residence and for industrial or commercial purposes in central cities. Consideration of these problems is elaborated elsewhere;[14] it will not be pursued further in this paper, concerned, in the main, with problems relating to the underdeveloped areas.

PHYSICAL PROBLEMS

The most visible consequence of overurbanization and rapid rates of urban growth is the decadence of the urban environment in underdeveloped areas.[15] The physical city is characterized by a large proportion of shanty towns and tenement slums; inadequate urban services, including housing, water supply, sewerage, utilities, and transport; uncontrolled land use; excessive population densities; deficient educational and recreational facilities; and inefficient commercial and marketing services. Rapid urbanization in the underdeveloped areas is accompanied by not only a defective but, also, by a deteriorating urban environment. It is estimated that, in

Latin America alone, some four or five million families live in urban shanty towns and slums. The miserable physical conditions of cities create great pressure for "social" instead of "productive" investments. However, many of the public housing and physical improvement programs which have been undertaken in such areas have necessarily tended to benefit families with moderate incomes rather than to meet the needs of the lowest-income families—the residents of the shanty towns and slums.

Of course, the underdeveloped nations are very aware of the need for city and regional, as well as national, planning. But the city planner in the underdeveloped country is confronted with insuperable difficulties. These stem largely from low income levels; from rapid population growth, including hordes of immigrants from rural areas who are il–adapted to urban living; from inadequate urban infrastructure development–all in all, from a bewildering array of needs, each of which seems to have first priority.

Although urban agglomerations of the size of Western cities are to be found, the physical amenities associated with such in the West have not yet developed—at least, not for the mass population. The amenities of urban existence are available only to very small fractions of the total urban population. It is in the impact on the already inadequate urban physical plant that the rapid rate of urbanization produces some of its more serious consequences.

Economically Developed Areas [16]

Economically advanced urban centers also have acute physical problems. Although these vary from nation to nation, we may focus here on those most apparent in the United States. The urban plant of the United States —residential, commercial, industrial, and governmental—has been constructed rapidly in response to rapid urbanization. Land-use patterns have been largely the product of market forces which have caused remarkable physical development but have also permitted swift obsolescence and decay. Much of the contemporary urban plant in the United States today is blighted or threatened with blight. Although the physical plant of cities in the West in general, and in the United States in particular, is incomparably superior to that in the underdeveloped areas, Western *cities* include, by Western standards, relatively large proportions of substandard housing and are pockmarked by slums. The urban United States has only recently begun to try to cope with these physical problems on a major scale, through programs of "urban renewal," public housing, and extended efforts at city planning. The worst slums in many of the cities in the United States have now been razed; but the larger portion of the task of urban renewal still lies ahead. Moreover, it is doubtful that urban renewal is, at the present time, advancing as rapidly as the process of decay. In the United States, as in some other Western countries, it has yet to be demonstrated that the urban plant can be maintained—i.e., that blight and slum can be prevented. There can be little doubt that problems of urban renewal and urban maintenance are made much more difficult by continued rapid growth.

Rapid growth is also aggravating acute difficulties of circulation in cities in the United States. Although the automobile has been a leading factor in the growth of the urban center, it is beginning to strangle the city with congestion, and is causing large portions of it to be converted into highways and parking space. Rapid growth is augmenting the "commuter crisis" [17] and is forcing metropolitan areas to re-examine the role of mass transportation in the circulation of persons and goods. This paper cannot elaborate on the physical problems of economically advanced cities; but there *are* such problems, and these problems are aggravated by rapid urbanization.

SOCIAL PROBLEMS

The city represents not only a new form of economic organization and a changed physical environment. It also is a profoundly modified social order affecting man's conduct and thought. Urbanization produces the city as a physical and economic artifact, and also produces "urbanism as a way of life." [18] The size, density, and heterogeneity of population— aspects of "social morphology"—affect the nature, intensity, and frequency of contact, and, therefore, influence the nature of the process of socialization and human nature itself. The city is a type of mutation in culture that has far-reaching effects on social structure and process and on social institutions, including the structure and function of government. The transition from pre-urban to urban living necessarily involves frictions, which are manifested in social and personal problems. Rapid urbanization exacerbates these frictions.

The effects of living in large urban agglomerations have frequently been treated in the sociological literature. A number of frameworks for the analysis of the impact of urbanization on the social order and on the person have emerged. Among these are the distinction between "organic" and "mechanical" solidarity (Durkheim, 1893); between "community" and "society" (Toennies, 1897); and between "folk" and "urban" ways of life (Redfield, 1930; Wirth, 1938). The chief effects of urban living on the personal level are, probably, discernible in the changed nature of interpersonal relations and in the relative flexibility of personal patterns of behavior. On the cultural and social level, they are to be found in the changed nature of the forces making for cohesion, in the changed genesis

209

and function of social institutions, and in the changed structure and role of government.

On the personal level, contacts in the urban setting become secondary, segmental, and utilitarian, rather than primary, integral, and sentimental as in the traditional social order. Personality tends to change from a relatively rigid structure molded by the traditional social heritage to more fluid flexible patterns, arising from the necessity to exercise choice and from rationalism in behavior, as the hold of tradition loosens and new urban problems emerge. On the social level, cohesion in the urban social order becomes a function of interdependence engendered by increased specialization and division of labor; it is no longer the product of the constraint of convention in a relatively homogeneous and closed traditional order. Social institutions in the urban setting become "enacted" rather than "crescive" as older functions become attenuated or disappear and new instrumentalities arise to cope with unprecedented situations and problems. Even the basic social institutions—the family and the church —are subjected to forces which modify their structure, their role, and their hold on the behavior of the person.

In the urban setting, the role of government is one of increasing interventionism as organizational complexity and interdependence increase. In the West, the transition from a feudal to an industrialized and urbanized order has been characterized by the emergence of complex formal organization—bureaucracy—not only in government, but also in business, labor, voluntary associations, and virtually all organized aspects of the mass society.

In this macrocosmic consideration of the impact of urbanization, we must emphasize that the transition from the traditional to the urban society does not proceed in an orderly and synchronized manner. The process of urbanization and its impact proceed with different tempos in different sectors of the society and among the several nations. In fact, one of the basic social problems of urbanization is to be found in the coexistence, at any one time, of different stages and of differential impacts of urbanization on the social order. Moreover, the more rapid the rate of urbanization, the greater becomes the probability that divers sectors of the social order will be characterized by anachronistic relationships.

These general elements provide a framework for more specific manifestations of the social problems associated with rapid urbanization.[19] The acute as well as chronic aspects of social problems that result from rapid urbanization are, perhaps, most discernible in the adjustment of in-migrants to urban living. The rural in-migrant to the city is typically from a relatively homogeneous origin. In the city, he is confronted with a bewildering and almost incomprehensible vastness and heterogeneity. He usually lives for some time with his fellow villagers or relatives and only gradually becomes accomodated to city life. He must adapt to new and unfamiliar ways of making a living; a money economy; regular working hours; the absence of warm family living; large numbers of impersonal contacts with other human beings; new forms of recreation; and a quite different physical setting, often involving new kinds of housing, sanitation, traffic congestion, and noise. One of the greatest adjusment problems centers around the transition from a subsistence to a monetary economy, and dependence on a job for subsistence.

Furthermore, the in-migrant often finds his area of first settlement is the shanty town, in which the decadence of the underdeveloped urban environment is manifest in its most extreme form. Consequently, superimposed on problems of adjustment there may be severe problems of health and nutrition, and of extreme poverty and squalor in living conditions. In such a setting, the in-migrant frequently displays personal disorganization as the subjective aspect of social disorganization. It is in the in-migrant family that the greatest incidences of personal and social pathology are found—delinquency, crime, prostitution, mental illness, alcoholism, drug addiction, etc.

Another element contributes to the social problems and is source of severe problems for the economy as well. This is the fact that rural in-migrant workers often lack rudimentary skills for industrial work, possess high rates of illiteracy, and are otherwise ill-prepared for city living. Throughout the underdeveloped countries, the need to increase literacy and to provide minimum vocational training for urban employment is acute. In fact, the provision of adequate educational and vocational training, both to the in-migrant and to the more permanent inhabitant of urban places, is among the most critical social problems which confront the underdeveloped areas.

Rapid urbanization is accompanied by increasing tempos of cultural, social, and personal change. A number of scholars have maintained that underdeveloped areas with non-Western cultures possess ideologies and value systems that tend to resist change in general and, therefore, changes of the type induced by urbanization. A rapid rate of urbanization, as contrasted with a slow one, conceivably increases the frictions of transition from non-Western to urban (and presumably Western) value systems. It is, of course, disputable whether Western values identified with urbanism as a way of life are an antecedent or a consequence of industrialization and urbanization; and whether they are the only values consonant with urban living. Conceivably, the difference between non-Western outlooks produces different kinds of "urban mentality" and interpersonal and social relations in the urban setting. Whatever the answer to this question may be, it *is* true that rapid urbanization increases the tensions and frictions of adjustment in value systems from pre-urban ways of life.

Also among the more pressing social problems in the urban setting are the series constituting "the population problem." As dramatically demonstrated in Ceylon, contemporary public health methods permit startlingly rapid decreases in mortality to be effected in short periods of time, while fertility rates and aggregate product remain relatively unchanged. In consequence, the underdeveloped areas of the world are just beginning the type of "population explosion" which the economically advanced nations have undergone over the past three centuries. Since the capacity to decrease mortality rates is growing more rapidly, the population-explosion potential of the underdeveloped areas is of considerably greater magnitude. Urban growth rates are fed by immigration from rural areas, as well as by the natural increase resulting from lower death rates; but the large streams of migration from rural to urban areas are a function of the national explosions in the underdeveloped nations. Rapid rates of urbanization could, in the longer run, contribute to the solution of the population problem in so far as urbanization can accelerate literacy, change value systems, and prepare the populace for limiting fertility.

Another group of serious problems created or augmented by rapid rates of urbanization are those of internal disorder, political unrest, and governmental instability fed by mass misery and frustration in the urban setting. The facts that the differences between the "have" and "have not" nations, and between the "have" and "have not" peoples within nations, have become "felt differences," [20] and that we are experiencing a "revolution in expectations," have given huge urban population agglomerations an especially incendiary and explosive character. In the domestic and international settings in which many underdeveloped areas find themselves, huge and rapidly swelling urban populations constitute supersensitive tinderboxes with explosive potential. Newspaper headlines of the last few months provide adequate documentation of this observation.

Another major social problem that is precipitated by rapidly increasing urbanization is the task of planning and devising programs designed to deal with urban social problems.[21] Planning agencies, health and welfare services, educational, vocational training, and recreational facilities, etc. are either inadequate or non-existent in many of the underdeveloped nations. In particular, agencies for receiving and dealing with the problems of the in-migrant are inadequate or non-existent. Planning and programming the solution of social problems entail difficult decisions involving national planning, in general. They involve, among other things, the complex task of maximizing the participation of the urban dwellers themselves by motivating them to play a major role in helping to solve their own problems.

212

Economically Advanced Areas

Rapid urban growth is not without its accompaniment of social problems in the economically advanced nations. Although hardly assuming a magnitude comparable with the social problems of the underdeveloped areas, rapid urbanization in the United States, for example, is aggravating or creating a number of social problems. Among these are the problem of intergroup relations arising from the changing composition of newcomers to American cities; the problem of providing urban services; the problems of local governmental structure; the problem of the role of government in general. This listing is not by any means exhaustive; but it may suffice to illustrate such problems in the more advanced nations.

In the United States, rapid urbanization has historically meant both larger and more heterogeneous urban population. During the nineteenth and twentieth centuries, the United States was the foremost recipient of emigrants, mainly from Europe. Immigration contributed materially to urban, as well as to total national, growth. Rapid rates of urbanization were accompanied by increased diversity of ethnic groups in American cities and, therefore, by difficult problems of adjustment incident to the acculturation and assimilation of foreign stock.[22] This process, by no means finished yet, has created many melting-pot problems in urban areas. The difficulties of these intergroup relations have, in recent years, been in part augmented, and in part replaced, by the adjustment problems of great streams of internal migrants who, since the passage of restrictive immigration legislation, have replaced the immigrants who formerly fed urban growth in the United States. The in-migrants include white and Negro rural populations and, in some cases, appreciable numbers of Puerto Ricans as well. The adjustment problems of these in-migrants, largely unprepared for urban living, are compounded, in the cases of the Negro and Puerto Rican by the racial differences which make them more conspicuous than was the white immigrant.[23]

At present rapid urbanization in the United States involves the absorption of new streams of in-migrants with difficult problems of adjustment to urban life. The in-migrant to the American city, like the immigrants before him and like the in-migrant to the city in underdeveloped areas, also experiences the highest incidence of personal and social disorganization. Although the social problems engendered by streams of newcomers to American cities are not so intransigent as those in underdeveloped areas, they are by no means insignificant. The difficulties of intergroup relations—especially that of white-Negro relations—are particularly troublesome; and they are being greatly aggravated by the high rate of in-migration and by rapid urban growth.

As American metropolitan populations continue to grow explosively, it has become increasingly difficult to provide adequate urban services.

213

Although the problems are of an entirely different order than those in the underdeveloped nations, urban services—including water, sanitation, drainage, police and fire protection, courts, education, and recreation—have not kept pace with growing population in many areas.[24]

Explosive urban growth has created many problems in local government structure and relationships. The structure of local government inherited from the eighteenth and nineteenth centuries is evincing increasing strain under the pressure of metropolitan area problems. This is manifested by the growing number of elections about consolidated, or metropolitan, forms of government; and by the emergence of special agencies for dealing with specific metropolitan planning or administrative functions. Rapid urbanization in the United States is tending to add to pressure for "home rule," and to aggravate "upstate-downstate" conflict. It is also accelerating the trend toward direct relationship between the federal and the city governments, wherein state governments are by-passed.[25]

Finally, this metropolitan growth in the United States is unquestionably a major factor in the proliferation and expansion of government functions —on the federal and the state, as well as the local, levels. For metropolitanism, as a way of life, is synonymous with increased complexity and interdependence of living, and necessarily engenders greater interventionism.

CONCLUDING OBSERVATIONS

Forces now in motion point to the future increased industrialization and increased urbanization of the world as a whole, and particularly of the economically underdeveloped nations. In their urban centers, the social, economic, and technological problems that accompany urban living are already acute; and they are becoming even more inflamed by the accelerated pace of urbanization. Important among the forces contributing to this acceleration are explosive total population growth, forcing the migration of population from the impoverished rural countryside to urban centers; and the efforts of underdeveloped nations themselves to induce economic development by means of increased industrialization.

The patterns of urbanization in the underdeveloped nations have not followed the Western lines, and are not likely to do so in the future. The differences in the patterns of urbanization and the nature of the problems which emerge are, in large measure, attributable to the differences between present domestic and world situations and those which obtained when Western nations were first experiencing industrial and urban transformation. Some of these differences arise from the fact that in many underdeveloped areas, urban development is largely an outgrowth of colonialism and thus to a great extent reflects the troubled conditions of postwar

214

adjustments and newly won independence, or chronic political unrest and governmental instability. Others derive from the extent to which central planning and government interventionism, as contrasted with the play of free market forces, are necessary in the underdeveloped areas. There are contrasts between the state of industrial and agricultural technology in the twentieth century and that in the eighteenth and nineteenth centuries. There are differences in the ratio of population to resources, and in the availability of open land for surplus population emigration. The basic outlooks and value systems in the underdeveloped nations differ from those of the West. Finally, there are extremely important differences between the total world situation—economic, social, and political—at the present time and that during the eighteenth and nineteenth centuries.

Despite these differences, however, it may be anticipated that the urban environment in the underdeveloped nations, as in the West, will produce economic, social, physical, and personal changes. They will not necessarily take the same forms as they did in the economically advanced countries; but changes there will be—and, accompanying them, will be the frictions of change.

It must be emphasized, in closing, that the total impact of the city is far from a negative one. Urbanization, and particularly rapid rates of urbanization, precipitate many economic, social, and technological problems. However, it is also true that the city, and urbanism as a way of life, have paved the way for the great achievements of civilization. They have done more than to advance technology, increase productivity, and raise levels of living. In addition, they have stimulated intellectual and cultural developments of the type represented by the universities, the development of science, the creation of new art forms, and, in general, the increased mastery of man over nature. Hence, although rapid urbanization is producing acute problems, it is undoubtedly challenging the ingenuity of man to find solutions for these problems.

NOTES TO CHAPTER 10

1. The materials in this introductory section are drawn largely from United Nations, *Determinants and Consequences of Population Trends* (New York, 1953), chap. ii; Philip M. Hauser (ed.), *Urbanization in Asia and the Far East* (Calcutta, 1957), chaps. iii, iv. World urbanization statistics are based on the work of Davis and Hertz, "Patterns of World Urbanization" (forthcoming).

2. Hauser, *op. cit.*, p. 99.

3. Projected urban populations from Philip M. Hauser, "Implications of Population Trends for Regional and Urban Planning in Asia and the Far East," *Regional Planning* (New York, 1959), pp. 21-31.

4. Ralph Turner, *The Great Cultural Traditions,* I (*The Ancient Cities*) New York, 1941); V. Gordon Childe, *Man Makes Himself* (London, 1941).

5. Eric Lampard, "The History of Cities in the Economically Advanced Areas," *Economic Development and Cultural Change,* III, No. 2 (January, 1955); Adna F. Weber, *The Growth of Cities in the Nineteenth Century* (New York, 1899).

6. Hauser, *Urbanization,* pp. 86 ff; Mark Jefferson, "The Law of the Primate City," *Geographical Review* (April, 1939); Norton S. Ginsburg, "The Great City in Southeast Asia," *American Journal of Sociology* (special issue on "World Urbanism"), LX, No. 5 (March, 1955), 455-62.

7. UNESCO, *Report by the Director-General on The Joint UN/UNESCO Seminar on Urbanization in Latin America* (Paris, 1960), p. 6.

8. Hauser, *Urbanization,* pp. 33 ff; UNESCO, *Report by the Director-General,* p. 15.

9. Kingsley Davis, "Urbanization and the Development of Pre-Industrial Areas," *Economic Development and Cultural Change,* III, No. 1 (October, 1954).

10. Philip M. Hauser, "Demographic Dimensions of World Politics," *Science,* CXXXI, No. 3414, 16-43.

11. United Nations, *Determinants,* chap. xv; United Nations, *Report on the World Social Situation* (New York, 1957), chaps. ii, vii, viii, ix; Joseph J. Spengler, "Population and World Economic Development," *Science,* CXXXI, No. 3412, 20.

12. Discussion of economic problems is drawn largely from Hauser, *Urbanization,* chaps. i, ii, vi, vii, UNESCO, *Report by the Director-General*; and *United Nations Seminar on Regional Planning* (New York, 1958). These publications

216

summarize the UN/UNESCO Seminar considerations of economic problems associated with urbanization.

13. Sidney G. Suffrin, "Over-Urbanization and Economic Growth" (Hectographed. Presented to National Academy of Economics and Political Science, December 30, 1959, Chicago).

14. Raymond Vernon, *The Changing Economic Function of the Central City* (New York, 1959).

15. The materials on "physical problems" are drawn largely from Hauser, *Urbanization,* chaps. i, ii, xi; UNESCO, *Report by the Director-General;* and Philip M. Hauser (ed.), *Urbanization in Latin America* (UNESCO, 1961).

16. The materials in this section are drawn largely from Philip M. Hauser, "Urban Boom and Crisis in the Sixties," in Harry C. Betters (ed.), *City Problems of 1960, The Annual Proceedings of the United States Conference of Mayors* (Washington, D.C., 1960), pp. 22 ff.

17. Wilfred Owen, "Transportation," *Metropolis in Ferment, Annals of the American Academy of Political and Social Science* (November, 1957), pp. 30 ff; and W. S. Rainville, "Transit—the Traffic Engineer's Opportunity," *Traffic Engineering* (June, 1958).

18. Louis Wirth, "Urbanism as a Way of Life." The framework materials in the introductory part of "social problems" are drawn from the general sociological literature, and particularly from the works of the men to whom reference is made in the text.

19. Discussion of specific social problems is drawn largely from Hauser, *Urbanization,* chaps. i, ii, iii, viii, ix, x; UNESCO, *Report by the Director-General;* UNESCO, *Social Implications of Industrialization and Urbanization in Africa South of the Sahara* (1956); materials from a volume on "Urbanization in Latin America" edited by Hauser; and United Nations, *Report.*

20. W. S. Thompson, *Population and Progress in the Far East* (Chicago, 1959), chaps. i and xviii.

21. Hauser, *Urbanization,* especially chap. iv.

22. Oscar Handlin, *The Uprooted* (Boston, 1951).

23. Oscar Handlin, *The Newcomers* (Cambridge, Mass., 1959); O.D. and Beverly Duncan, *The Negro Population of Chicago* (Chicago, 1957); Stanley Lieberson and O.D. Duncan, "Ethnic Segregation and Assimilation," *American Journal of Sociology,* LIV (January, 1959), 364-74; Karl E. Taeuber, "Residential Segregation of Urban Nonwhites" (Ph. D. dissertation, Harvard University, 1960); Stanley Lieberson, "Comparative Segregation and Assimilation of Ethnic Groups" (Ph. D. dissertation, University of Chicago, 1960).

24. Luther Gulick, "Metropolitan Organization," *Metropolis in Ferment, The Annals of the American Academy of Political and Social Science* (November, 1957), pp. 57-65.

25. *Ibid.* In the same volume, see also Frank P. Zeidler, "Urbanism and Government 1957-1977;" Wallace S. Sayre, "Urbanism and Government, 1957-1977: A Rejoinder"; Lyle C. Fitch, "Metropolitan Financial Problems."

CHAPTER 11

The Impact of Technological Change
on Demographic Patterns

NATHAN KEYFITZ

University of Toronto

The title of this paper, selected by the Conference, has directed my attention towards some issues of keen practical concern. For the word "impact" suggests a collision, in which one object has enough momentum to change appreciably the course of another. No image could more clearly indicate that what is wanted is a causal analysis, an interpretation which goes beyond the correlation of statistical variables. Such a correlation, representing the passive examination of past history, is the starting point of any study of causes; but, unless one hopes that history will repeat itself, one must find not only which elements increased and decreased together in the past, but which among them were the operative causes of which others. The developing countries today in some features resemble, and in others, contrast, with Europe and America of the eighteenth and nineteenth centuries; Western history must thus be disentangled before its lessons can be applied to the present world.

Among demographic patterns, that of the death rate is the least problematic. It is worth mentioning here only because in one sense it created the problems of overpopulation with which the remainder of the paper deals. The death rate has been declining steadily in Europe for the last two hundred years. Before then, and in most of the ancient civilizations, an expectation of life at birth of about thirty years was typical. A United Nations publication [1] mentions a life table for Greece, *ca.* 400 B.C., that shows thirty years; Pearson calculated the expectation of Egypt about the first century B.C. to be 22.5 years; Halley found the expectation in Breslau in 1687–91 to be 33.5 years. During the past century, improvement has been rapid; a table constructed for six European countries and one state in the United States shows an increase for males from 39.6 in 1840 to 63.3 in 1940.[2] The extension of life which became considerable in the nineteenth century accelerated during the twentieth century; a United States life table for 1905 shows forty-eight years, and one for

1945, sixty-four years [3]—an average improvement in expectation of four years per decade. The first Canadian life tables calculated for the deaths of 1930–32 showed an expectation at birth, for males, of exactly sixty years; this had increased to 62.96 years by 1940–42; to 66.33 years by 1950–52; to 67.61 years by 1956. The improvement is steady at three years per decade.[4]

The tables cited above are for males. Usually the increases were similar for both sexes, with women living about two or three years longer than men. Recently, however, the expectations for women have moved sharply upward; for 1952, we have, for the white population of the United States, 66.6 years for men and 72.7 years for women, and in Canada, for 1956, 67.6 years for men and 72.9 for women.[5]

Similar changes have taken place in Asia during more recent times. Thus Ceylon's expectation for males remained at about thirty-five years from the 1890's to 1920, and then increased to 46.8 by 1945–57.[6] By 1952, Ceylon males had reached 57.6.[7] Japanese males had reached 42.1 years by 1935–36,[8] and 61.9 by 1953.[9] Thailand had reached 48.7 by 1947–48.[10]

It is not difficult to list factors which could have been responsible for the lengthening of life. The United Nations' *Determinants and Consequences of Population Trends* suggests that increases in income were primarily responsible in Europe; but it does not try to distinguish the separate effects of nutrition, housing, environmental sanitation, personal hygiene, medical services, or the increasing health consciousness of people and their desire for longer life. I am no more able to discriminate among their separate effects. But if increasing wealth were responsible in Western countries—so far as this is separable from scientific methods for the control of individual diseases—the reverse is true for the presently underdeveloped countries: with negligible increase in wealth, and sometimes with actually declining amounts of food per capita, death rates have fallen even more sharply than they did in Europe. It is easier to make unequivocal statements about the new and recent declines than about those of Europe: in Ceylon, for instance, the eradication of malaria reduced the death rate sharply within a matter of months. Ceylon showed twenty-nine deaths per thousand of population in 1920–24; twenty per thousand in 1946; fourteen per thousand in 1947; and ten per thousand in 1954.[11] These figures present a saga of the use of DDT in World War II and early postwar years. Other countries of Asia do not have such good statistics and have attacked malaria more gradually; but what is true for Ceylon today is either already true for the rest of Asia or will be within so short a time that we are justified in talking of it as actuality.

Though it seems that the use of DDT was decisive in Ceylon, we cannot distinguish everywhere between the effects of medical attention

219

and those of common sanitation, between the effects of inoculations and those of vitamins; fortunately, there is no need to do so. We can tolerate confused and overlapping notions of cause, and say that the death rate was brought down mostly by increasing wealth in Europe and by direct attack on disease in Asia, since no practical issue hinges on our finding the one cause. The shift from an expectation of life of less than thirty years to one of over sixty years is now world-wide, or will be shortly; and no one need quarrel about whether doctors, sanitarians, legislators, chemists, or bacteriologists take the credit for it. Whatever the route through which it found application, technology in one form or another underlies the improvement in both the West and the East: vaccines prevented contagion; DDT destroyed the infectious anopheles; agronomy improved food supplies in quality, quantity, and regularity; transport provided the means for feeding people stricken by local famines. In terms of expectation of life, Ceylon and other advanced parts of Asia are "contemporary" with the United States and Canada of the 1920's.

They are not contemporary in wealth nor in births, both of which have barely changed from ancient Asian levels. It is this disparity between the achievement of control in the field of death, on the one side, and in births and wealth, on the other, that sets the problem. A surprising result of technological evolution has appeared: a small amount of wealth has sufficed to bring enough technology to effect low death rates in all parts of the world; this amount of wealth has evidently not sufficed to affect births. The resulting imbalance may prevent the spread of Western levels of income around the world. Western technology, applied one-sidedly to the control of deaths, now threatens to prevent the increase of income per head which technology produced in the West. This is the point which I shall amplify in the main body of this paper.

Data for births prior to 1800 are not extensive, but it appears that Scandinavian rates in the eighteenth century were between thirty-one and thirty-four per thousand population, while those for Finland were about forty-one.[12] These were maintained until the 1870's. Meanwhile the rates in America, starting from the figure of about fifty-five per thousand which persisted to 1800, dropped steadily to eighteen in 1933.[13] France stood at thirty-two at the beginning of the nineteenth century; by the 1870's, she had fallen to twenty-six, and by the 1930's, to sixteen. The British rate remained at its plateau until the 1870's and then started the fall that brought it down to fifteen in the 1930's. The less industrialized countries of eastern Europe were slower in falling than those of western Europe; however, since Ireland began to fall before England, the connection with industrialization is not a tight one. Japan's birth rate in the early 1920's was about thirty-five; in 1938, it was twenty-seven; it rose to thirty-four in 1947, and fell to seventeen by 1958.

220

To get at the causes of these changes is as difficult as it is urgent. If time and resources were available, one could presumably find the answer by experimentation. One might, for instance, select a number of village people, arrange them in pairs whose members resembled one another, and, for one member of each pair, chosen by the toss of a coin, provide a technological environment; the other would be left in the village. The individuals who had won the toss would receive the sort of urban education, home, and job that are so widely desired in the underdeveloped world today. To distinguish the effects of working in an urban job from those of education, one would offer some of the subjects schooling but not urban jobs, and some, urban jobs but no schooling. Such a design could be used to ascertain the respective effects of technology in the presence of and in the absence of education. The experiment would take a generation or more; but except for this element of time, all its other difficulties would be removable if there were sufficient interest in determining the impact of technology on the birth rate. The failure to ascertain causation in such aspects of human affairs is not intrinsic in the problem; it is a function of the unwillingness to undertake the experiment.

In lieu of such an experiment, we must resort to the inexact inference of cause by the use of historical data. The basic principle is to clutch the most substantial straws we can find. The passive observation of nature is subject to difficulties which cannot be removed, but the more closely we can make our observation resemble experiment the better. I do not mean this only in the superficial sense that we should try to be quantitative. There are three other, and more important, lines along which we can try to circumvent the difficulties of passive observation:

1) We ought to assemble as wide a range of data as possible.

2) We ought to be especially interested in preventing variation in extraneous factors from being confounded with the one being studied.

3) We ought to make all possible use of available social theory to specify possible causal chains, and then to try to obtain the data to tell us which of them seem to apply.

At every point, we are likely to find help in Max Weber's recommendation that we think away possible causes and then see if the phenomenon we are trying to explain disappears out of our heads. Our skill in doing this presumably improves with practice—though no amount of practice will eliminate all components of habit and ideology.

To begin, we should determine the causal chains through which technology could affect the birth rate. It might be that people who move to factory work have fewer children simply by virtue of the change from farm life. The daily and annual cycle of the factory, working specified hours, being surrounded by machinery, might directly result in fewer children than the cycle of farm work and being surrounded by nature. Fertility rites based on some such magical connection between the fruitfulness of nature and that of humans are widespread in preliterate and even in literate societies. But our greater sophistication is unconvinced by any notion that connects the physical environment with human reproduction in a causal relation.

It is more plausible that technology requires educated workers, that workers cannot be educated in technological matters without developing individual aspirations for material things and some degree of willingness to follow rational means for their attainment, and that children are regarded as competing with material things. Most of the world's people, during periods of history, have been relatively unconscious of their individual careers and of the choices that affect them. They do not separate, so sharply as we have become accustomed to separating, their work from their play, their secular education from their religious observance, their individual fate from the collective fate of their group.

In Western Europe between the fifteenth century and today, there was an extraordinary focusing of art and thought on the individual. This helped him to separate, from the complex of living, certain distinct elements of means and ends. He could distinguish them, not wholly, but sufficiently to apply rational thought to a much wider range of human affairs. Such individual decision-making found many forms of expression: the Reformation with its insistence that everyone read the Bible and judge for himself what was right behavior; the development of the novel, in which hypothetical decisions by individuals, and their consequences, were amplified for the amusement and instruction of widening circles of readers; philosophies of individual perception, such as those of Locke, Hume, and Kant; many extensions and applications of the Protestant way of looking at life, from the classical economists to existentialism. The behavior of individuals became a subject of scientific study; the fantastic and unprecedented praise of selfishness in classical economics developed people's self-consciousness along lines which religion had previously tried to cover; and the effect of all this education was the unlikely achievement of a society based principally on selfishness. Selfishness was no new phenomenon in the world; it has been expressed in every kind of immoral and illegal activity through all history. But now it became moral; trade, profit, lending at interest, price-cutting, using shortcut methods of production—these were regarded as both moral and legal. The new society which encouraged them actually worked, and in some ways worked better than any previous society.

If the change to the new society was a single social movement, that movement must be perceived as consisting in interaction among its many elements. Education and technology depended on each other. Formal education, in earlier societies, had been a means of acquiring status and had had little reference to individual productive performance. The largest amount of education was reserved for those who were farthest from production work. In the new society, education never ceased to be a means of acquiring status, but it additionally became a means to better work. The shops in which the education was to be used acquired better machines, as there were skilled people to invent and operate them; the better machines made greater output possible; and this enabled more people to devote time and resources to the invention and further improvement of machines. The success of machines spurred the educational system to giving more attention to technology; and smaller portions of classroom time became devoted to teaching people to repeat the sacred books and to discussing the traditional foundations of society. Teaching that would make people more righteous and more human was superseded by the teaching of the practical calculations of the workshop and the counting-house, and to applying thought to nature so that each might take part, according to the measure of his ability, in the process of technical innovation. The natural conservatism of education could withstand neither the growing success of technology nor the insistent demand of students to be taught the new and powerful mysteries in place of the old and seemingly impotent ones.

Christianity found its first believers among the artisans of the Near East, and Protestantism was especially strong among the new kinds of artisans and organizers whose enterprise created the industrial revolution. It was in the towns and cities that technology flourished most strongly and that the individualistic outlook on life was first and most clearly expressed. It is inevitable that we see social change as starting from certain "advanced" elements of society and then spreading to other elements. Depending on the speed of these currents of movement and on how strongly they are pushed by individual emulation and by the pursuit of status and its symbols, it takes a shorter or a longer time for individual culture traits to permeate society. A new dress or a popular song may take only a few weeks or months; a new phrase or anecdote a few days or weeks; a new approach to having children may take a century.

Fortunately, the matter of family size is so thoroughly documented that, through its statistics, we can learn something about the process of social diffusion in general. Family size, made visible by statistics, is like a radioactive tracer that, in the study of physiology, reveals the movement of other elements. The differences in the birth rates of the several statistically identifiable groups in society have been remarked for almost as long as statistics has existed, and are evident in any census report. In the 1956 Census of Canada, for instance, 335,652 children through four years of age are shown within a total farm population of 2,631,587—a ratio of

.128. The corresponding ratio for the cities of over one hundred thousand population was .111. As measures of fertility, these figures fail to take account of the age distribution of the population, or of mortality among children between birth and the census date; but they serve our purpose by indicating a rough relation of family size to city life.

Using the same rough measure of fertility and going back over the series of censuses, we learn that in 1881, Ontario showed a ratio of children to total population of .131, and Quebec, of .152. By 1911, Ontario had fallen to .104, while Quebec, at .146, had scarcely changed. During the next thirty years, Quebec dropped considerably more than did Ontario—to .106, compared to Ontario's .079. The subsequent rise was smaller for Quebec than for Ontario—the two provinces reached .134 and .112 respectively in 1951. These figures suggest a drop of both provinces from pre-industrial to industrial levels, with Ontario leading. However, it is not possible to attribute the earlier fall of Ontario entirely to the industry which actually was developed; one would have to utilize a notion such as that Ontario had acquired an industrial outlook earlier than Quebec.

The 1951 Census provides a cross-section of change. We find a ratio for the English-language people of .128, and for the French-language people, of .137. One would like to analyze these figures further, for fear that a larger proportion of the French may be on farms, and the farm-urban dichotomy thus confounded with the French-English. It is easy to find the ratios for farm and urban separately: English-speaking farm persons show a ratio of .132, French on farms, of .154; English-speaking urban shows .121, French-speaking, .125. The greater difference between French and English for farm (.022) than for urban (.004) suggests that the trend to smaller families comes to the French after it comes to the English, and that the speed with which it moves from the English to the French is greater for urban than for farm families.

The same point can be made for religion. The ratio on farms is .150 for Roman Catholic, .120 for United Church (the largest Protestant group). In urban areas, it is .129 for Roman Catholic, .113 for United Church.

A scanning of the data suggests that the several religions, the several education groups, etc., are beginning to approach one another in Canada. It is as though they are dropping from the pre-industrial level, which was especially high on the North American frontier, to the lower level appropriate to the machine age and its low death rate. Elements of personal motivation mediate between the machine and the birth rate. I have mentioned the change in style of thought associated with the Reformation. In addition, parents take account of the fact that now almost all their children will live to maturity; to this extent, a lowering of the birth rate follows the lowering of the death rate. But the matter is, of course, more involved: companionship becomes more important in marriage, as E. W. Burgess and others have pointed out, and this tends to lower the birth rate; on the other hand, there is a move to suburban homes, in which children fit very well. It is typical of the difficulty of distinguishing cause from effect in such matters that no one has been able to say whether suburban living and home ownership encourage people to have children or whether their desire for children takes them to the suburbs. But in either case, presumably children come when people want them. Children are one of the many phases of human life which Westerners have been able to place more or less at the disposal of a decision-making process within the small nuclear family whose sole adults are husband and wife.

Frank Lorimer [14] suggests that the emphasis of Christianity has always been on the nuclear rather than the extended family. In entering marriage, "shall a man leave father and mother, and shall cleave to his wife, and they twain shall be one flesh" (Matt. 5 : 5). This concept differs greatly from the idea of family in Rome or of Asia, that considered respect for ancestors, living and dead, as the paramount virtue, and required that the group working together and living together comprise several generations and, generally, be much larger than husband and wife and their own children.

In the smaller group, the actions of each member are not lost, as they are in the extended family; instead, they have the sharpest effect on the welfare of all. This probably had much to do with developing the sense of individual responsibility so prominent in Western thought and behavior. Because the industry or sloth of husband or wife has such immediately evident results within the nuclear family, it becomes natural to think of individual decisions as the most important facet of life, as the subject of soul-searching which no outsider can relieve.

What happens in the psychological matrix of the extended family is not clear, but at least in some cases, as Morris Carstairs shows,[15] the Rajput son, until he is forty or older, is dominated and frustrated by his father; when the latter dies, he is too old for any other means of satisfaction than applying the same treatment to his own son. No one knows to what extent the Western sense of individual responsibilty has caused the industrial urban life we know, and to what extent the urban life supported the nuclear family and hence individual responsibility. We must accept Max Weber's evidence that religiously sponsored worldly asceticism affected the spread of technology, individual responsibility, and urban life.

Within this framework of individual responsibility, what is the reason for having children at all? Not to perpetuate our line and achieve a kind of immortality through offspring, says Ruth Benedict: "We have children, not because our parents are sitting in judgment, not because of the necessity of having an heir, but because we personally want them—whether as company in the home or to show our friends we can have them." [16]

However, our concern is not only city life and the direct presence of advanced technology. In the countryside there are differences as well. The people who live nearer to the city have the smaller families; those farther away are less affected. In any attempt to document this point, it is necessary to hold constant income, education, occupation. This was done for a sample of farm families from the 1941 Census of Canada, where the comparison was made of number of children ever born to women forty-five years of age and over. Holding constant some sixteen extraneous variables, we found that the families far from cities in Quebec were larger by 1.28 children on the average than the families near cities; in Ontario, the difference was .70 children in favor of the distant families.[17]

People who live farther from the city are more distant in a psychological as well as in a spatial sense. They not only employ simpler technology themselves, but they know fewer people who work in factories or whose lives are otherwise affected by economic organization utilizing advanced technology. Evidently, they do not engage in discussion with neighbors about a new way of life that makes a kind of accounting point of view become more or less explicit and brings the advantages of smaller families to their attention. They have not yet begun to have the restless personal ambitions which the city inculcates in so many ways.

However, the differential birth rate, firmly established as it has seemed to be, represents only a cross-sectional view of the process of diffusion of the new small family associated with technology. This becomes evident as the end of this historic phase comes into view in Western countries. Edin and Hutchinson have been, perhaps, the first to notice this in an advanced Western country. They found that the usual relation of births to income was a direct and not an inverse one for the three non-industrial groups in Stockholm.[18] The rise in the North American birth rate during the 1940's seems to have largely the same significance. Previously, it had been feared that some groups in the population were increasing so rapidly that they would eventually dominate all others. Thus Lorimer and Osborn point out that, in 1925–30, rural farm women had enough children for an increase of sixty per cent per generation, while those of the large cities showed a loss of twenty per cent per generation.[19] Since the time in which they wrote, there have been both a fall in city and country births, and then a rise, from the 1930's to the 1940's. Comparing 1935–40 with 1942–47, we find that the urban net reproduction went up by forty-nine per cent, while the rural farm rose by twelve per cent.[20]

The differential in the birth rate associated with the factory system eliminates itself as the new mode of thinking spreads through the population. The differentials of income, education, city, and country, have

226

been created only to be eliminated two or three generations later. But the result is not a mere reversion to the status quo. The family which is forming as North America reaches the full flowering of its machine age seems likely to be more uniform than in any previous epochs. How can this be? Until recently, the number of children people had was determined for them—they were somnambulistic creatures of nature or of their primitive means of birth control. Now, individual responsibility determines family size. Should not individual decisions cause a greater range of variation than appeared in times when nature did the deciding? Evidently not. Individuals do decide for themselves, according to their own notion of the life they wish to lead, whether children will support or interfere with other personal ambitions; and each couple comes up with its own answer. The answers turn out to be almost the same—they all want about three children. American Institute of Public Opinion samples have shown that about ninety per cent of American women want two, three, or four children; negligible numbers want fewer than two children; and less than ten percent want more than four.[21]

Though, at a given time, the individual decisions are the same, and the number of children that people want and have vary less about the average than they did in earlier epochs, the average itself may fluctuate widely from time to time; for instance, with the trade cycle. So far we have been spared the experience of a sudden drop in income across the whole country that has continued over a long enough period to test this point.

We have suggested that a complex chain of events has engendered today's birth rates in the West: technology, individual choice, the market, cities, and education support one another, and the fall in family size is a part of the total change. This does not occur simultaneously in all levels of society, but diffuses through the layers in an order largely determined by the degree of involvement in the new kind of society. The process includes new attitudes on a host of matters, among which are a consciousness of the explicit cost of having children as of other goods, and data on these costs that make possible individual judgment and responsibility within a rational scheme. Resources do not become scarce until they have alternative uses; alternative uses increase with income; hence scarcity—a sense of cost attached to children—rises with increasing income in the family and in the community.

This increasing income both arises from and itself accentuates a steadily increasing responsiveness of people to price and wage signals generated either spontaneously by the production-employment system, or imposed by policy of government. A dramatic instance of the latter is the decline in the Japanese birth rate from thirty-four per thousand in 1947 to eighteen per thousand in 1958.[22] The decline was partly explained by Japan's having attained a high postwar peak in 1947; however, Canadian births were also at a postwar high in 1947, and yet they later increased further instead of declining. How did the Japanese engineer this decrease? Evidently their city dwellers and peasantry alike responded, by controlling their families, to wages which were low enough to reflect the fact that their islands were crowded; government sponsorship of birth control followed the abandonment of ambitions for imperial conquest. No more in Asia than in the West, in an autocracy than in a democracy, can one make good urban workers, organizers, and enterprisers, without making people more rational in their personal choices. But in addition, the technology of communication and the technology of birth control—the former utilized to make the latter freely available—were of crucial importance. The methods of birth control used in Japan evidently ranged from those acceptable to everyone everywhere, such as abstinence, to those that can only be regarded as a temporary makeshift, such as abortion. No doubt, the same process of communication and rationality that brought the first change will now be capable of producing a change from less acceptable to more acceptable methods.

Of all the subjects which affect the welfare of individuals and communities, population is the one to which the notion of responsibility is most readily applied. The reason for this is the exceptional degree of foresight needed in the matter of the birth rate; the welfare consequences of decisions to have children do not appear either to the parents or to the community until many years after the decisions are made. The sudden drop in the death rate in Ceylon has shown this. The excess children— i.e., those who would have died under the old mortality conditions but whose deaths were prevented by the eradication of malaria about 1945–47 —do not seem a heavy cost to the families which are supporting them, at least in their first years. Parents collectively reveal, through the birth rate, that they make almost no allowance for the larger proportion of children who now live to maturity. Ceylon shows 36.6 births per thousand population in 1957, a trifling drop from pre-World War II rates. Malaya showed 43.2 births per thousand in 1957. It is safe to say that a net increase of two-and-one-half to three per cent per year is in sight for all the world's underdeveloped areas.

At present rates of increase of income, this is bound to mean a decline in goods per person. Yet the decline in income per capita seems to many to be a mere statistical indication and not to be taken seriously when people feel themselves better off. Nevertheless, those children now born whom DDT has saved from dying represent a commitment of the nation, if not of their parents, for their subsequent clothing and education, and, most important, for their ultimate establishment as full earners and consumers. The somewhat intangible figure of national income per capita surely does give a better indication of the future position than people's feelings about whether they are better off or not. The fact that the individual commitment is made fifteen to twenty years before the material consequence is actually felt is what makes population the most difficult of all political problems. It is more difficult than an increasing national debt—which, in a democracy, it resembles in that either must somehow be "understood" by a majority of voters before policy can deal with it properly. Pending its widespread understanding, the nation is menaced by every kind of inappropriate action. The popularity of "nationalization" of land by which the food surplus, formerly extracted by landlords and placed on the market, now stays on the peasant holding and goes to raise more children, is an example of the need for an electorate able to weigh consequences.

The fact that the provision of land to peasants may, in some circumstances, be nothing but a signal to them to have children—as they will interpret it, in the absence of contrary messages—indicates something of the complexity of the problem. Progress can occur only if what is dear to the nation is also held dear by the individual. Underdeveloped nations must stimulate the attitudes of foresight, alert interpretation of incentives, and other aspects of personal behavior by which people can be signaled. In addition, if their development is to be democratic, there must be yet another layer of foresight and responsibility: people must be willing to create, through their representatives in government, the signs to which they will then respond in their individual lives.

The above discussion of the impact of technology on population has barely mentioned the appliances of family limitation called "mechanical." I have assigned these a subordinate place, for human behavior is not pushed this way or that by the mere convenience of devices. It is directed by the way in which these devices are interpreted as serving or failing to serve some larger purpose.

Norman Himes brings contraception to the very center of the population stage. He sees that "the human race, in all ages and in all geographical locations, desired to control its own fertility." [23] To him, the wish to escape from the Malthusian predicament is a constant of human motivation. Himes virtually interprets history as the development of more efficient means of contraception. My thesis is that the number of children people want can vary greatly from one time to another, and that the clarity of their perception of family size and its consequences is a recent phenomenon. They seemed to want fewer children in the 1930's than they have before or since. The humanitarians who speak, not of contraception, but of responsible parenthood, of the spacing of children, of the planning of families, are not using euphemisms for having as few children as possible—rather, they are urging that the size of the family be proportionate to what parents think will constitute the good life.

While we repudiate the simple technological causation implied by Himes, we must not throw out the element of truth in it. Under certain circumstances, there is a given motivation to keep down the size of the family; and at this psychological and social point, the lower the hurdle of practical

TABLE 1

Hurdle, repugnance or moral difficulty in practising a method that an individual wishes precisely to make use of.

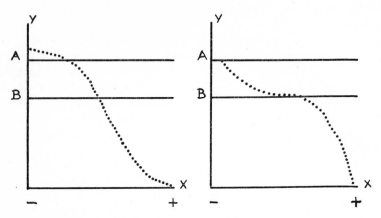

Individuals according to their diminishing wish for birth control.

POPULATION I   POPULATION II

Members of both populations were set on X according to the strength or the weakness of their motivation in controlling the size of the family. Y represents hurdle, repugnance or moral impossibility to accept a method that an individual wishes precisely to make use of. The A method could be abstinence, B method the use of pills. In population I, the invention of a pill that makes the line fall from A to B, adds few people to those practising control; in population II, it adds many people. In population II, we can speak of the invention of B as the c a u s e of the falling-off of the birth rate, but not in population I.

and moral difficulties is, the more easily and frequently it will be surmounted. The individual motivation is generated by such social elements as we have discussed, but the actual use of any means of contraception is private within the family. The easier and more reliable the method is and

230

the more it can be utilized by the more strongly motivated partner, the less it is made to seem morally repugnant or to call for inhuman powers of abstinence, the more often will the wish for fewer children be translated into actuality. Scientists are probably on the verge of devising a pill, to be taken orally, that would meet every requirement.

If the social motivation is such that most individuals would not use method A but would use method B, then in a sense the discovery of method B is the necessary and sufficient condition for family limitation in the given population. In these circumstances, the discovery of B may be described as the technological cause of limitation. If a large part of a population lies between the two methods in the strength of its motivation, then to this population (represented by Sociey II in Table 1) a technological theory of the birth rate would seem to be appropriate. For a population in which the curve is like Society I, the difference between methods A and B has less consequence; and, for theoretical understanding and practical action, something other than this difference of methods will have to be sought. Thus, aside from the mental orientations of our society that encourage a technological model of social change, the appropriateness of such a model varies according to circumstances.

We have discussed the effect of technology on the death rate and on the birth rate in terms whose complexity we have tried to match to that of the subject itself. The social and psychological elements in migration will not be similarly developed here. However, we should mention the possibility that the treatment in this paper, which considers population as affected by human motives, is entirely irrelevant. Could it be that the increase of population, consisting of births less deaths plus net migration, is determined in a fashion wholly different from the result at which one arrives by considering the terms separately? Such a model is easily imagined for a single country, and was seriously proposed for the United States by Francis Walker and, before him, by Benjamin Franklin. According to this view, the number of people that a country will add to its population is fixed by its capacity for maintaining them. If it admits more immigrants, either its birth rates will fall or its death rates will rise; the addition to its numbers will be thus held constant whatever its immigration policy. The immigration policy is capable only of deciding whether the increment of population shall be natives or foreigners.

This static Malthusian model, with its automatic controls, is rendered obsolete by the interconnectedness of the world economy and the advance of technology. It is worth discussing only to indicate the instability introduced into it by technological advance. The carrying capacity of land for human population is increased when mineral oil begins to be used to provide lighting, so that ghee and sesame oil are released for food; it is increased when tractors replace draft animals for power. There is a long series of improvements in technology—artificial fertilizers are the most obvious, and the atomic distillation of sea water is, perhaps, the most far-reaching—that will increase the number of people that the soil can support.

However, most technological advance is possible only for people with capital; and the citizens of crowded countries lack capital as much as they lack land. Technology may be a free good, but capital which embodies technology is not free. The fifty-five million people in Java or the greater number in the delta of the Ganges—occupying lands that once were covered by teak or other forests, and with their soil washing into the sea —are now at the point where they cannot feed their cities. They will soon reach the point where their countrysides will be unable to feed themselves, even if their cities are provided by foreign sources of food. What chance is there of securing the capital that would provide goods which these people could trade for food?

To people in these circumstances, technology, instead of seeming a friend, appears as an enemy, for it devalues the labor which is the only resource of the crowded areas. People who once lived by buying raw cotton, and spinning, weaving, and dyeing it by hand, and then selling it abroad, now find a foreign market whose prices are low because they are dictated by the cost of spinning, dyeing, and weaving in North American, British, or Japanese factories. Factory production has already reached such a degree of efficiency that, at the difference between the price of raw cotton and that of cotton cloth as determined by it, even if people worked at their cottage looms twelve hours a day they could not buy enough rice to live on. Of course, rice also is produced by mechanical means in America, and its price accordingly lowered—but not lowered to the point where peasants can trade handmade cotton goods for the food they need to subsist. These facts can be hidden in various ways— for example, by tariffs and by a subsidy to cottage industry, as in India —but imminent further increases in population will make them visible in the hunger of millions.

It may seem exaggerated to say that, for the people crowded into these densely populated areas, the technology which has developed in the world is no boon but a disaster. If the existence of capital lowers the return to people who are selling their bare labor in the world market in exchange for food, why do they not either borrow capital or invite foreign investment? I cannot engage in amplifying this matter here. However, I shall state that recent foreign investment in the overcrowded areas has been negligible. This is partly because world capital seems more attracted to natural resources than to labor; and, in any case, the unskilled labor of these areas does not turn out to be cheap. Furthermore, the peoples of the crowded areas are inclined to regard foreign capital as exploiting them,

232

and to impose conditions and risks which have, thus far at least, made investment uninviting.

What, then, is the chance that forms of technology involving little cost —technology without capital, as it were—will be brought to the relief of these crowded areas? Professor Ping-ti Ho demonstrates that China has had two agricultural revolutions during the past millennium—and that, in each of them, the population more than doubled.[24] The first revolution was caused by the introduction of rice that matured in two months rather than in five; the second, by the introduction from America of maize, sweet potatoes, Irish potatoes, and peanuts. The first innovation made possible multiple cropping; the second made it possible to use a variety of upland soils unsuited to rice. If each agricultural innovation enabled China to support another hundred million people, are not improvements in agricultural technology the answer for South Asia? All one can say is that they are coming—but that, so far, the rate of their introduction has been matched by the rate of erosion of the soil plus the increase of population, so that per capita food supplies have changed very slightly.

If capital does not come to the dense populations building up in certain parts of Asia, can the people not go to capital or to land? The efforts that Indonesia has made to move Javanese to nearby Sumatra show that this is not easy. Professor Higgins describes the difficulties that have prevented any substantial movement.[25] When an area has reached an annual increase of the order of a million persons per year, their relocation would require transport and other facilities on an impossible scale. Thus, before long, certain areas of high density will contain condemned populations: any one or any few persons among them may escape, but a point will come beyond which there is no exit for the great mass.

It has been suggested that the world can be fed from Western storehouses; if this were possible it would be cruel not to make the food available. But to feed people in such fashion as to increase their numbers further would be no kindness, but only an intensification of the difficulty. And this is already being done, not regularly, but in critical years. The intermittent character of the shortage of food tends to conceal it; each shortage seems to be due, not to too many people, but rather to some particular circumstance, such as the failure of the monsoon in the famine area.

I have described how the growing population within the villages of Java climbs up on its food supply. As it does so, there is a steady decline in the food with which the villages can buy the products of urban industry. And, as the amount of food available to maintain the employees of city industry diminishes, industrial growth is throttled. Furthermore, the populations of the cities and the densely settled provinces require foreign exchange to buy food. This may well conflict with the wish of the less dense areas, whose exports provide the foreign exchange, to use this for their own development—they are increasingly reluctant to divide their wealth with the denser, poorer provinces. In these conditions, the unequal growth of population within a country can subject it to political strains which can rend the fabric of nationhood.

To avoid creating within themselves such high-density areas—veritable graveyards of the living—should be the first objective of policy in underdeveloped countries. The impact of technology, if it were arrested at the point now reached in Asia, i.e., at the point of death control only, would be disastrous. One likes to assume that technology will continue, that death control will be followed by birth control, and that the creation of the sense of individual responsibility through industry and education will come. The process will begin in some elements of the population—it has, indeed, already started—and proceed to others. Once the creation of industry and a responsible citizenry has progressed to a certain point, the population problem will offer no more difficulty than it has in Japan.

We must, therefore, think of this as a race between the growth of industry and the growth of population. Within any nation, it is a race which one or the other can win decisively. Population can increase so rapidly that it prevents the emergence of a liberal industrial society which would subject it to rational control.

NOTES TO CHAPTER 11

1. *The Determinants and Consequences of Population Trends* (New York, 1953), p. 50.

2. *Loc. cit.*

3. *Ibid.,* p. 54.

4. *Canada Year Book,* 1959.

5. United Nations, *Demographic Yearbook, 1955,* p. 742.

6. Sarkar, "A Note on Abridged Life Tables for Ceylon, 1900-1947," *Population Studies,* IV, No. 4 (1951).

7. United Nations, *Demographic Yearbook, 1955.*

8. *Determinants and Consequences of Population Trends,* p. 55.

9. United Nations, *Demographic Yearbook, 1955,* p. 744.

10. *Loc. cit.*

11. *Ibid.,* p. 657.

12. *Determinants and Consequences,* p. 71.

13. *Ibid.,* p. 72.

14. *Culture and Human Fertility* (UNESCO, 1954), p. 190.

15. *The Twice Born* (London, 1957).

16. "Are Families Passé?" *Saturday Review of Literature,* XXXI, No. 52 (December 25, 1948).

17. N. Keyfitz, "Differential Fertility in Ontario: An Application of Factorial Design to a Demographic Problem," *Population Studies,* VI, No. 2 (November, 1952).

18. *Studies of Differential Fertility in Sweden* (London, 1935).

19. *Dynamics of Population* (New York, 1934), p. 341.

20. U.S. Census Bureau, *Current Population Reports,* P-20, No. 18. (June 30, 1948), Table 4.

21. Hadley Cantril (ed.), *Public Opinion 1935-46* (Princeton, N.J., 1951).

22. United Nations, *Demographic Yearbook, 1958.*

23. Norman Himes, *Medical History of Contraception* (Baltimore, Md., 1936), p. 185.

24. *Studies on the Population of China* (Cambridge, Mass., 1959).

25. Benjamin Higgins, *Indonesia's Economic Stabilization and Development* (New York, 1957), pp. 60-63, and *passim*.

CHAPTER 12

Industrialization and Family Change

WILLIAM J. GOODE

Columbia University

The latter half of the nineteenth century witnessed two great attempts to analyze social change. One was a complete intellectual failure. The other was a considerable political success; its intellectual contribution was in part the result of its being limited to one country at one time in history— England in the mid-nineteenth century. The first attempt was, of course, evolutionary theory; the second was Marxian theory.

Evolutionary theory is the only comprehensive theory of social, and therefore family, change that social science has developed. Shortly after the turn of this century, we had advanced beyond it; but we have never been able to develop an adequate substitute. Evolutionary theory aspired to explain both the history of family systems and the observable differences among them. Imbued with a naïve assumption of progress, even in its biological form, evolutionary theory asserted that man's family systems had evolved from the primitive sexual promiscuity of a semi-animal horde, through group marriage, matriarchy, and patriarchy in some polygynous form, to the highest spiritual expression of the family, Victorian monogamy.[1]

Less sanguine philosophers doubted that European family and religious systems represented man's highest moral level. Sober scientists attacked the glittering edifice at its base, and gradually came to believe that such reconstructions of man's past could not be demonstrated. "Survivals" could not be used to write man's social history.[2] Anthropologists, especially in the United States, eventually saw that contemporary primitive societies were not primeval. Perhaps they were no closer to the social patterns of Neolithic man than to those of European society. The family systems of both Neolithic and Paleolithic man are forever lost to us.

Equally prosaically, the attempt to relate family patterns with economic or technological systems indicated that, even if the latter might be arrayed in some type of "evolutionary series," no specific family form seems to

237

be associated with specific "stages" of economic and technological development. For example, the Eskimo type of kinship is close to that of the United States.[3] Indeed, as I commented in an earlier paper, "no theorist has been able to state, let alone prove, any set of systematic propositions about the relations between the family and other institutions."[4]

One attempt to locate underlying variables by scalogram analysis found that two "variables" would not "fit" into a scale of societal complexity; these were family and religion.[5] There has been no evolutionary pattern discovered in family systems—i.e., no determinate sequence of changes. Nor have we been able to show that any determinate relations exist between family variables and industrialization variables.

Marx's methodological position prevented him from attempting any such grandiose reconstruction; and his followers in sociological economics have also confined themselves to the analysis of recent historical changes in the industrial world. In the past decade, however, a more massive analysis of social change has begun. It has been stimulated by the fact that, for the first time in world history, the forces of urbanization and industrialization are affecting all societies; they are no longer confined to the unique case of modern capitalism. Thus, we can observe a wide variety of social systems that are undergoing industrialization. Eventually, the data thus acquired will permit us to develop more precise and valid propositions than were possible to formulate when we had to extrapolate from a single case.

MYTHS OF THE PAST

The renewed interest in social change has the additional advantage of being based on recent or contemporary observations. American sociology has been properly criticized for its failure to exploit historical data; and doubtless that failure is partly rooted in the fact that the citizen of the United States feels that his country's history began only recently. However, this apparent bias is also generated by the greater research sophistication of the American sociologist, who knows that reliable facts even about the present are hard to acquire.

The sociologist who investigates the family is especially prone to avoid analyzing change over long epochs, since good data about the past vanish quickly. It is a field in which familiarity is often confused with knowledge. Not a single general history of the family can meet even loose canons of validity; and there is no adequate analysis of the family systems of the two historical societies about which we know most, namely Greece and Rome. Thus, it is useful that our modern investigation of social change concentrates on the recent past.

Descriptions of family systems of even a generation or so ago are likely

238

to be stereotyped or idealized. This characteristic of family data can best be illustrated in the United States, for which our data surpass those for any other country. The usual description of the American family of the recent past really refers to "the classical family of Western nostalgia" (for, to some extent, the feeling about it is shared by Europeans); and it presents a pretty picture of life down on Grandma's farm.[6] When we try to penetrate the mists of history, we frequently discover that, in *each* generation of the past, this "classical family" is described, but is thought to have existed in a generation *still* more remote.

Those who believe there is progress often present the same stereotype, but evaluate its characteristics differently. The movement toward the urban, industrial world has, they say, freed the young from the arbitrary power of the elders, eliminated cold marriages based on economic arrangements while granting freedom of choice in marriage to the young, weakened class barriers between children, erased the subjugation of the wife, and permitted children to express themselves.

Although the classical family of the American past is still to be found in textbooks and in amateur social science, the serious sociologist of the family views it with some skepticism—just as he now knows that the classical Chinese family was an ideal, a myth, whose exact relation to reality we shall probably never learn.[7] It seems likely that, as we learn more facts about each major family system; we shall learn, or at least begin to suspect, that some mythical elements have been substituted for facts in each of them.

THE CONJUGAL FAMILY AS AN IDEAL TYPE

World changes in family patterns suggest that industrialization must indeed contain the prime social variables, since, wherever any movement toward industrialization occurs, the family system moves toward some kind of "conjugal" pattern—i.e., few kinship ties with distant relatives, and an emphasis on the nuclear family unit of husband and wife with their children. Most analysts, confronted with this phenomenon, have succumbed to the temptation to assume that industrialization is the independent variable and that family change is the dependent one. Let us, before yielding to this temptation, examine the problem more closely.

Both the *degrees* and the *types* of these family changes have not yet been charted adequately. The *processes* by which they occur have not been revealed. The detailed facts necessary for the first task, and the rigorous theory necessary for the second, are as yet insufficient. I have been engaged in trying to summarize many of the facts; but space forbids their presentation here,[8] though, later in this paper, I shall describe a few of these trends. At this point, let us consider the theoretical problem.

We must remember that, in current family theory, "conjugal family" (sometimes, "nuclear family") is used to refer to three very different notions.[9] Most commonly, it is technically an ideal type, in the Weberian sense.[10] Second, it is an *ideal*, since attitude or value surveys would show that a substantial (but unknown) percentage of American, or European, or other populations would view certain of its characteristics as legitimate, proper, or good. Third, some percentage (at present unknown) of families in the Western culture complex and elsewhere, do, in *fact* and behavior, conform to the structurally defining characteristics of this family type.

It is crucial, however, to understand that the conjugal family, as commonly described, is not a summary derived from empirical studies of the family. Usually, it is a theoretical construction, in which several central variables have been combined to make a hypothetical structural harmony, and other characteristics have then been "derived" from them sociologically.

The most important characteristic of the ideal-type conjugal family is that it excludes a wide range of affinal and blood relatives from its everyday affairs—there is no great *extension* of the kin network.[11] Most of its other characteristics can be inferred from this complex trait. Omitting the derivation itself, we can list them as follows:

1) The couple cannot count on a large number of kinfolk for help, just as these cannot call on the couple for services.

2) Neither couple nor kinfolk have many *rights* with respect to one another; thus their reciprocal obligations are few.

3) Necessarily, then, they have few moral (or other) controls over one another.

4) Kinfolk do not choose the couple's residence location—which is, therefore, "neolocal," and reinforces the couple's independence (by lowering its rate of social interaction with kin).

5) The couple's choice of one another as mate was dependent on them, not based on the rights or interests of the kin; in turn, marital adjustment is primarily between husband and wife.

6) When this system emerges, the age at marriage will change; but theory does not permit a prediction of its direction—youngsters must be old enough to take care of themselves.

7) Fertility is based on the needs of the couple, and may be high (frontier) or low (urban industry).

8) The system is omnilineal;[12] neither kin line has great weight.

9) The small nuclear unit is the chief place where the emotional input-output balance of the individual spouses must be maintained, since there is nowhere else to go.

240

10) Consequently, the divorce rate will be high—though again, we cannot predict whether it will fall or rise when such a system emerges.

11) Remarriage, after the death of one's spouse or after divorce, is highly probable.

Such an ideal-type construct should be compared with family behavior and ideals in various cultures where approximations to the conjugal system are thought to exist. To my knowledge, no such comparison has been made. We do know that, in both England and the United States, the lower-class family—presumably the least extended of families—does recognize and interact with a range of kin other than those contained in the nuclear unit.[13]

The ideal-type construct fails to fit both reality and social theory in one important respect. The family system *cannot* be limited to the nuclear unit without the application of political force. Grandparent-grandchild ties are strong; sibling ties are strong; and, therefore, parents-in-law interact relatively frequently with their children-in-law, and married people interact frequently with their siblings-in-law. The most common kind of "visiting" and "social occasions," even in the United States, remains that of seeing relatives. They are inextricably linked to the nuclear unit, since they cannot be rejected without their rejection simultaneously hurting or angering a member of *one's own* nuclear family—e.g., the child cannot ignore his uncle without hurting one of his own parents. This theoretical and empirical point is important in assessing the relations between industrialization and social change, since it (*a*) emphasizes some of the *limits* of the family's adjustment to ouside pressures, and (*b*) raises the problem of how the industrialization process—as in Russia, Israel, and China—must adjust *to* the family.

The "Fit" Between the Conjugal Family and the Industrial System
We can ignore the theoretically empty argument about whether political and economic variables determine family patterns, or the reverse. Our concern is to discover *any* determinate relations among any particular family variables and those of other institutional orders. However, we can investigate the theoretical "harmony" or "fit" between the ideal-type construct and industrialization. A second, equally important, task is to determine their empirical harmony or discord with one another. Third, we must eventually see *how* or through which processes each affects (or has affected) the other.

The second task has been attacked primarily by those who are interested in labor supply in primitive or peasant societies. In general, some investigators have noted that family systems *other* than the conjugal usually do not always yield an adequate labor pool—though they may do so if the existing economic or family system is under stress.[14] Head taxes were used to separate men from their families in Africa. Men's objections to women's leaving home for outside jobs still limit the female labor supply in various parts of Islam. On the other hand, certain primitive societies, like Palau and Manus, have willingly supplied labor to the new system.[15] In our own system, the strains between the conjugal family and the industrial system have not been empirically measured—though this matter is the subject of innumerable sermonizing essays by moralists both literary and religious.

It will be relevant to our subsequent consideration of an important point if we examine the demands of industrialization pertinent for family change. Bureaucratization can occur without industrialization (T'ang China, for example), and so can urbanization (Dahomey, Tokugawa Japan). However, neither occurs without a rise in the technological level of the society; and the modern system of industry never emerges without both bureaucratization and urbanization. The social characteristics traditionally used in analyses of both these processes also apply to industrialization.

The prime social trait of modern industrial enterprise is that—ideally, and to a considerable extent empirically—the individual obtains a position on the basis of his achievement, relative to the demands of the job. His achievement is measured universalistically—i.e., the same standards apply to all job-holders of the same status. His link with the job is functionally specific: the enterprise may not dictate his behavior except in so far as it is directly relevant to getting the job done.

Structurally, such a system is necessarily open-class; it requires both geographical and social mobility. These characteristics are intensified, under industrialization, by the smaller percentage of jobs based on land (and thus on inheritance).

Various analysts have derived certain relations, some of them intuitive, between industrialization and the conjugal family. These, familiar to the social scientist, may be summarized as follows:

1) The neolocality of the conjugal system frees the individual from specific geographical ties.

2) An individual with a limited kin network is facilitated in selecting the industrial job best suited to his skill. He can invest only in himself, not in his kin. He can change his style of life more easily.

3) Family can be separated from enterprise, so that the achievement, universalistic, and functionally specific criteria of the latter are free to operate without interference from the ascriptive, particularistic, and emotionally diffuse criteria of the former.

4) The necessarily individual ownership in a conjugal system permits mobility of capital for investment.

5) Limiting the kin networks prevents them from interlocking to form a set of closed class strata.

6) The unremitting discipline or—in the upper-level professional, managerial, and creative positions—overly demanding requirements of modern technology are psychologically burdensome. The emotionality of the conjugal family helps to restore a psychological balance—at least, the technical system has no moral responsibility for it.

7) Omnilineal in pattern, this system maintains no lineage and does not concentrate a family's land or wealth in the hands of one son or daughter.

8) The talents of both sexes are given greater scope for development to fit the manifold demands of a complex technology.

9) The small size of the family unit, and its emotional diffuseness, preclude much specification of the status obligations of each member. As a result, more individual variation in conforming to role obligations is permitted, and each individual is better able to fit the range of possible industrial demands.

10) Since youngsters choose their own spouses and should be economically independent, a long period of family dependence is legitimated. This enables each individual to find a niche appropriate to his talents in the industrial system.

We must emphasize that these "harmonies" do not explain either why industrializing countries seem to move toward some form of the conjugal system, or through which pressures they do so. Before examining this point further, we shall note some "disharmonies" and class variations.

Non-adjustment between Industrial and Familial Demands

The fact that disharmonies exist suggests again the independence of the two sets of variables. For example, child care is typically given over to one person, the wife; as a rule, there are no additional female kin who might free the young woman for work in the industrial system. Second, the substantial development of labor-saving devices interacts with the specialization of a *highly* industrialized system; the consequence is that the modern American mother is overburdened—to use the case which is so often cited to prove the opposite. These devices for the most part save no labor at all; they merely raise the standards of cleanliness, repairs, freedom from germs, etc.—an ironic confirmation of Marx's gloss on Mill's nineteenth-century doubt about whether mechanical inventions had lightened man's toil. These inventions had, Marx asserted, no such *aim* in the modern system.[16] Among modern inventions, I think, not even detergents and the dish-washing machine "save" any labor for the housewife. The housewife must spend most of her time in creating time-and-place utility—i.e., acting as chauffeur, purchaser, administrator, etc.

In consequence, American women have not become much more "career-minded" over the past half-century. Polling data indicate that the same

243

is true of women in Western Europe.[17] Except for those teaching in colleges, the proportion of women in the established professions in the United States did not change greatly from 1910 to 1950; doubtless the percentage of college-educated women who have gone into these professions has actually dropped.

Furthermore, the amount of housework is great, and husbands and wives are presumably equal—so, generally, the husband has to help with it after his working hours. This diverts much of his energy from his occupation.

The strains between industrialization and the family system which it is thought to fit are discernible in certain class differences. By definition, the middle and upper strata are more "successful" in the industrial system but, in fact, their kin pattern is *less* close to the conjugal pattern than the kin pattern of the lower strata. Upper strata recognize the widest extension of kin, maintain most control over the courtship and marriage choices of their young, and give and receive help from one another most often.

Consequently, the "freedom" that the lower strata have from their kin is like their freedom to sell their labor in an open industrial market. They are less encumbered by the weight of kin when they are *able* to move upward in the occupational system; but they also get less help from their kin when they *try* to move. Like the English peasants who, from late medieval times through the early nineteenth century,[18] were "freed" from the land by the various enclosure movements, or the nineteenth-century workers who were "freed from their tools" by machinery, the lower strata have fewer family ties and less family stability, and enjoy less family-based economic and material security.

To that degree, the "integration" of the lower-class family pattern—i.e., the most conjugal—is greatest, primarily in the sense that the individual is forced to enter the labor market with far less family support. He may move where the system needs him—hopefully, where his best opportunity lies—but he *must* fit its demands, since no extended-kin network will interest itself in his fate. His job moves him about and pays him little, so that he cannot keep his kin ties active; on the other hand, since his kin are *also* in the lower strata, his loss from relinquishing them is not great.

A further inference may be drawn. The middle and upper strata have (a) more *resources*, in any system, with which to resist the undermining pressures of the industrialization process (e.g., capital with which to support their youngsters through long professional training); and (b) a considerable *interest* in holding their family system intact against those pressures (because their existing kin network is more active and useful). We assume, then, that, in an industrializing process, both the peasant and primitive proletarians are forced to adjust their family patterns more

244

swiftly to the industrial system, and find at least more immediate opportunities in it. By contrast, the middle and upper strata can utilize these new opportunities best by loosening their kin ties more slowly. Thus, changes in middle- and upper-strata family systems are more likely to occur later in the process.

We must express one important caution. The inference last made applies, only if a non-conjugal, or extended, family pattern actually existed in the lower strata *before* industrialization. I am inclined to believe that the conjugal system will be found, *empirically*, to be more widespread than has been supposed in the lower strata of Japan, China, India, and the Arab world.

Occupational Merit and Family
We deliberately made our list of apparent harmonies general, to open the possibility of additional examples beyond the Western culture complex.

In the Western world there have been several periods—to my knowledge, not yet examined in this context—during which there was relatively high class mobility, based to a substantial extent on achievement. One of the most striking examples occurred during the twelfth and thirteenth centuries in Europe. These centuries constituted an era of marked economic expansion and increased trade. During the era, numerous buildings were constructed, and hundreds of convents, churches, and monasteries were founded. All these enterprises called for a range of administrative and even philosophic talent. Then, as in all epochs, a large proportion of the high-ranking clerical jobs went to the members of the privileged classes; but the expansion of job opportunities, and certain Church policies, engendered a considerable amount of class mobility. However, during that period, there is no evidence to indicate there was any remarkable change in the family systems of Europe; without question, there was no real movement toward a conjugal system. On the other hand, to the extent that the Church succeeded in its recurrent, and ultimately successful, effort to eliminate the family from its clergy, that group was marked by some steps toward the ultimate system of pure merit—the system in which each individual ideally stands alone, without a family; the system whose first eloquent prophet was Plato.

A second case, too complex to analyze here in detail, has obvious relevance. The data about Chinese class mobility are more reliable than those about the High Middle Ages in Europe, because each Chinese dynasty accepted the task of compiling the biographies of important men in the preceding epoch. Knowing the historiographic customs of China, we know that these biographies were formalized; but they do contain enough data to enable us to make rough guesses about the various

245

dynasties from the T'ang through the Ch'ing. Each study has shown that one-third to three-quarters of the men of high position in any given generation were "new men," with no apparent family base in the upper stratum. Hsu, using local district biographies, found that only one-fifth of the men had three generations of higher-class position behind them.[19] The Chinese laid great stress, ideologically, and in fact, on achievement. They had, compared to Europe, a relatively high level of technological and industrial development, at least until the beginning of the nineteenth century; but they did not move toward the conjugal system.

Ideology of Family and Industrialization

There is an ideology of "economic progress" and industrialization, and an ideology of the conjugal family; spokesmen for both appear in non-Western countries before any great changes are discernible in either industrial or familial behavior.

Although elders may deplore them, both appeal to the intelllectuals, to the young, to women, and to the disadvantaged generally. The ideology of the conjugal family, I suggest, is critically important in the current family changes taking place in the world. It is a radical philosophy—it is destructive of the older traditions, while having its roots in more general radical principles which arouse its adherents *politically*. It asserts equality, against class, caste, or sex barriers. It advocates the individual's right to choose his or her spouse or place to live, and his right to select which kin obligations he will respect, independent of the decisions of kin. It asserts the worth of the individual, against the kinship-controlled elements of wealth or ethnic group. It even encourages love as a right, opposing the marriage prearranged among kin. It proclaims one's right to change one's family life if it is unpleasant.[20]

Of course, no conjugal family system actually lives up to its principles. However, these express values which, at some levels of consciousness and in many strata, *arouse* peoples the world over—even when they are not yet ready to accept these notions fully. Everywhere, men and women have some resentments against their family system, to which this pattern offers a beguiling alternative.

The ideology enters the society through some spokesmen *before* industrialization; I shall suggest below that it prepares individuals somewhat for their adjustment to industrialization. Its first proponents are usually from the elite. But the debate spreads; and changes in court decisions and laws implement both the political and the family ideology. Most of the major family legislation in the past two decades has moved toward a conjugal pattern. Such legal actions shape both custom and the terms of the ideological debate, whether in Africa or China.[21]

246

Family as an Independent Causal Element in Industrialization

Progress toward a conjugal system may facilitate industrialization in non-Western countries, and may have been instrumental in Western industrialization. Let us entertain this thesis a moment, since it seems to have no champion at present.

We cannot view non-Western family systems as basically like the Western systems of some undefined earlier historical phase just before industrialization. The evolutionary model may be in error. For the past thousand years, the family systems of the West have been very different from those of China, India, Japan, Africa, or Islam. There has been no clan system or lineage system in the West. No ancestor worship has existed; and individuals, not families, have been held responsible for crimes. Elders have arranged marriages—but youngsters have had a greater voice in the final choice, partly because (except, perhaps, for the Latin upper strata at divers times and places) young women have not been segregated from young men, even when kept under the scrutiny of a chaperone. Child marriages have never been the ideal or the statistical average. There has been an ideal (still held, but never strong) that a large kin group should live under one roof; but the dominant pattern—which caused marriage among farmers to occur late, on the average—has been that a young couple should have land enough to support themselves independently before marrying. No regularized concubinage or polygyny has been known. The leader of the family has not been even ideally the eldest male, however much deference he was paid.[22]

Moreover, the Protestant Reformation sharpened these differences. It seems more than fortuitous that Henry VIII's break with Rome was precipitated by his insistence that he had the right to make an individual choice about his marital future; and it seems not merely a matter of chance that, a century later, it was a Puritan who made the first serious modern plea for the right to divorce. Our ample documentation of the extraordinary role which ascetic Protestants played in the early development of science, industry, and capitalism should not obscure their less direct, but perhaps not less weighty, influence on an emerging philosophy of anti-traditionalism, freedom of speech, egalitarianism, political liberty, and individualism. Their contribution to the ideology of the conjugal family, a transformation of that philosophy, seems equally important; but historical inquiry has not yet delved into it.[23]

The Puritans conceived of the husband-wife relationship as a loving one. This concept emphasized much less the partner's place as merely a link in a kin network. Even during the early period of colonial settlement in the United States, the Puritans' children began to insist on free marriage choice. In his religion, as in his work philosophy, the Puritan was responsible for himself as an individual; he was not merely an ascriptive part of a kin group. His family attitudes fitted him for the opportunities of a new industrialism and capitalism.

Even if this general notion cannot be demonstrated, it is at least indicative of family differences that English workers did not resist factory mechanization because they ranked the values, roles, and enterprises of the extended family higher than the opportunities of the new era. When they did resist, it was on very different grounds—such as wage levels and threats of unemployment. In contrast to the situations reported in some less industrialized countries today, English factory owners rarely had any problem of labor supply. Some investigators have claimed that most of the English opposition to mechanization actually came after it was well under way, and that it was due to the impact of mechanization on the internal structure of the individual family unit, not its impact on the kin network.[24]

It seems, then, that it might be fruitful to inquire whether, in the early phases of Western industrialization, some changes in family patterns had already occurred that prepared certain strata for the new system.

An interesting modern case in point is the Communist attempt to undermine the old Chinese family, and to go *beyond* the conjugal family, in order to accelerate industrialization. If our earlier theoretical analysis has been correct, some variant of a "communal family" pattern would answer the demands of industrialism better than a conjugal family could. Plato's variant was more radical than the Chinese blueprint; but in both, as in the kibbutz, the goal is to weaken kinship obligations, whether between parent and child or between spouses.

Western criticism of China, like earlier attacks on parallel systems in Russia, has largely ignored the possible industrial efficiency of a communal family system. The appraisal has been focused on the totalitarian control over the young, on indoctrination. However, when the objective is rapid industrialization, the older Chinese family (in its post-Manchu form as well) is a definite hindrance; and even the Western conjugal family is not so efficient a structure for permitting individuals to take jobs where they are needed, on the basis of individual achievement. Allocation by achievement violates the family values of all other systems, for it is ultimately *individual* in character—talents and skills are individual, not family, traits. Rapid industrialization, as an all-embracing goal, would, therefore, require family ties to be reduced as much as possible.

We are not denying the costs of such a system. Had Plato established his Republic, the competitive atmosphere would have been at least as psychologically destructive as that of, say, New York. No such system has ever evolved naturally, without political direction and revolutionary fervor; both Israel and Russia have retreated somewhat from the ideal; and the Chinese have had to de-emphasize certain elements in their

248

campaign (e.g., by reassuring the young Chinese they still owed their parents some care)[25]—these facts suggest that industrial and technological criteria are not entirely prepotent, and that the amount of energy required for a family pattern which is even less binding than the conjugal may be excessive.

SOME WORLD CHANGES IN FAMILY PATTERNS

If family variables are indeed independent (and they may be overridden, even though independent, under certain circumstances), we can assume that the *direction* of change for *specific* family traits, such as rate of divorce or age at marriage, might be very different from one industrializing system to another—though all of them might be generally moving toward a conjugal pattern. For example, in the broad matrilineal belt of Central African societies, the power of the father is increasing, in contrast to the movement toward female egalitarianism and weakening patriliny in most of the world. However, in the same area, the divorce rate is probably not changing (it has always been high) and will doubtless eventually drop somewhat, in contrast to China, Europe, India, or much of the rest of Africa. In Japan, the divorce rate has been dropping since the turn of the century, in contrast to the other great industrializing areas; and it has also been dropping among the Algerian Moslems.

Lengthy explication of each of these trends would be necessary for adequate exposition. However, we may succinctly, if cryptically, say that each high or low rate in the pre-industrializing or early industrializing phase was the product of specific family patterns. These earlier patterns begin to move toward some conjugal family variant; and thus the rates fall or rise, according to their previous level. In much of Africa, for instance, it seems highly likely that, as the family systems approximate a conjugal form, the marital fertility rates will *increase*, the age of females at first marriage will rise, and the age of males will not change greatly. We cannot make any predictions, without prior empirical observations, about which elements will resist these pressures more or less. And, since no accepted classification of *forms* of industrialization exist, we cannot yet predict how different forms will affect different family systems.

It might be worthwhile to omit the consideration of the theoretical and empirical bases of many of these changes, and merely list some of the major ones.

1) Freedom of marital choice, with the following concomitant changes:
    a) Marital bargaining is taken from the hands of elders;
    b) The young couple must be economically independent;
    c) The age of females at marriage is likely to drop in Japan, but to rise slightly in China and substantially in Arab countries and

249

India; the age of males depends on several additional variables; at a minimum, there develops the notion of a "proper maturity at marriage" for both;

d) The pattern of class homogamy does not change greatly;

e) In cultures where there was nearly universal marriage (India, Japan, China), there may be a slight diminution in the percentage ever married; and

f) Age-discrepant marriages, i.e., between spouses of very different ages, diminish.

2) Marriages between close kin (e.g., between cousins) decrease.

3) The dowry or bride price begins to disappear.[26]

4) Illegitimacy rates increase in systems where most marriages have been consummated between children (e.g., India—but *not* China and Japan). Since most civilizations seem to have various forms of marital unions which are not fully legitimate, the movement toward a conjugal system may (as in Japan) actually reduce the illegitimacy rate.

5) Concubinage and polygamy decline.

6) Theory cannot predict whether fertility in a conjugal system will be high or low—but fertility will be controlled in the interests of the couple, and not of the kin group. Under industrialization, of course, the rate usually falls. And any movement toward a conjugal system reduces the *size* of *household*—even in Africa, where possibly the marital fertility ratio may be increasing.

7) Infanticide decreases—though we have no firm numerical data with which to measure its past rate in those countries where it allegedly once existed (India, Japan, China, and the Arab world).

8) Matriliny weakens—although here our Western bias may exaggerate changes in lower-caste Indian or Central African systems; i.e., because the system seems strange, we are more alert to changes in it.[27]

9) The divorce rate will be high, but the *trend* in any given culture will depend on its prior level. It may drop if the rate was already high and the new system yields some new elements of stability (e.g., the removal of the Japanese parents-in-law's right to send the bride to her parents).

10) Remarriage after divorce or the death of one's spouse becomes common in areas where it was rare. Here, stereotypes confuse somewhat, since divorce was certainly more common in some countries (e.g., China) than commonly supposed, as was remarriage of the widow or widower (as in China and Japan).

CONCLUSION

Rejecting evolutionism in its nineteenth-century form, we have created no theory of social change of comparable scope. However, we have returned to a more sober appraisal of the detailed facts of social change. We are both aided and hindered by the nearly universal pressure of industrialization upon human societies in this era. The visible presence of industrialization often obscures the independent effect of other ranges of variables upon the total process—or, indeed, upon industrialization.

The analysis of family change is especially difficult, since reliable descriptions of systems of even a few generations ago are so rare. The classical family of Western nostalgia is a myth—a myth which perhaps has its mythical counterparts in most civilizations—and to measure change by that base line usually leads to error.

In addition, theoretical analysis must take account of the fact that the conjugal family, toward which industrialization is thought to be pressing all family systems, is primarily an ideal-type construct. It is, second, a set of ideals; and, third, it is an observable pattern of behavior. We must examine each facet independently if we are to understand changes in the modern world.

In general, the ideal type of the conjugal family demonstrably does fit the central demands of an industrial system. On the other hand, there are necessary strains between the two, and there are theoretical and empirical limits on the adjustment between them. Moreover, we can not neglect the question, "To what extent does industrialization meet the needs of the conjugal family?" A number of differences in the adjustments of various class strata to the patterns of industrialization suggest the independence of family variables and the strains between two great sets of processes.

In addition, we clearly do not yet know just *how*—i.e., through which processes—the two interact. The achievement or merit occupational systems, in China, and in Europe during the High Middle Ages, imply that variables we have not yet distinguished may be operative.

In the contemporary world, there is an important set of forces in the ideology of the conjugal family, which is structurally similar to that of economic progress. Both have important radical roots and appeal to the disadvantaged, to women, to the young, and to intellectuals—even when they do not fully accept the ideology or are unable to conform to it in action. The ideology enters into political and legal debate and into court decisions, thus furthering a number of changes toward a conjugal pattern.

It would be worth-while to investigate whether the Western family systems, for many centuries, have been better organized than others, to take advantage of industrial opportunities; and whether shifts in family attitudes may be attributed particularly to the Puritans, whose ties with industrialization are well documented. The independent importance of this adjustment is discernible in the campaign of the Chinese to go "beyond" the conjugal family to a communal system which would be even better suited to the needs of industrialization. Although such a system would create new strains—some of which have already been observed—it would solve some of the problems of strain between the conjugal system and industrialization.

Family and industrial variables are independent though interacting. Hence, even when most family systems move toward some conjugal form, specific indexes of change will move in different directions, depending on the state of things at the inception of the new era. We have presented a number of examples of such differing trends. In addition, we outlined a list of many of the major trends characteristic of most of the world's population. How far they will go, or how rapidly, we cannot ascertain as yet.

1. For a concise statement of nineteenth-century family theory, see René König, "Familie und Familiensoziologie," in W. Bernsdorf and F. Bülow (eds.), *Wörterbuch der Soziologie,* 1955, pp. 114-26.

2. E. B. Tylor's judgment on most matters was extraordinarily good for his time, but his "method" for ascertaining the past was a triumph of imagination over common sense. "On a Method of Investigating the Development of Institutions: Applied to Laws of Marriage and Descent," *Journal of the Royal Anthropological Institute,* XVIII (1888), 245-72.

3. See George P. Murdock, *Social Structure* (New York, 1949), pp. 226-27. Eskimo groups vary among themselves, of course; see Charles C. Hughes, "An Eskimo Deviant from the 'Eskimo' Type of Social Organization," *American Anthropologist,* LX (December, 1959) 1140-47.

4. "Horizons in Family Theory," in Robert K. Merton, Leonard Broom, and Leonard S. Cottrell (eds.), *Sociology Today* (New York, 1959), p. 180.

5. Robert F. Winch and Linton C. Freeman, "Societal Complexity: An Empirical Test of a Typology of Societies," *American Journal of Sociology,* LXII (March, 1957) 461-66.

6. William J. Goode, *After Divorce* (Glencoe, Ill., 1956), p. 3. Cf. Ernest W. Burgess and Harvey J. Locke, *The Family* (2d ed. New York, 1953), chap. iii.

7. For comments on the classical Chinese family, see Rose Hum Lee, "Research on the Chinese Family," *American Journal of Sociology,* LIV (May, 1949), 497-504; Francis L. K. Hsu, "The Myth of Chinese Family Size," *American Journal of Sociology,* XLVIII (May, 1943), 555-62; Maurice Freedman, *Lineage Organization in Southeastern China* (London, 1958), pp. 176 ff.

8. They will be published in my *World Changes in Family Patterns* (Glencoe, Ill., forthcoming).

9. I shall use the term "conjugal," since "nuclear" should refer to a structural unit made up of father, mother, and children, which may exist relatively independently (conjugal), or be bound up with other such units to form extended family systems (polygyny, through a common father; polyandry, through a common mother), or various lineages through certain blood relatives.

10. Max Weber, "'Objectivity' in Social Science and Social Policy," in *The Method-*

ology of the Social Sciences, trans. Edward A. Shils and Henry A. Finch (Glencoe, Ill. 1949), pp. 89 ff. See also the brief summary in William J. Goode, "Note on the Ideal Type," American Sociological Review, XII (August, 1947), 473-75.

11. For additional variables important in comparing family systems, see Goode, "Horizons in Family Theory," pp. 178-91.

12. The term is Max Gluckman's.

13. See, for example, Raymond Firth (ed.) *Two Studies of Kinship in London* (London, 1956); Michael Young and Peter Wilmott, *Family and Kinship in East London* (London, 1957); Elizabeth Bott, *Family and Social Network* (London, 1957). Unpublished research by both Morris Zelditch and Eugene Litwak have shown the importance of many kin links in the United States. See Eugene Litwak, "Occupational Mobility and Extended Family Cohesion," *American Sociological Review,* XXV (February, 1960), 9-21.

14. A good analysis from field data is made in Wilbert E. Moore's study of traditional family patterns and industrial demands in Mexico, *Industrialization and Labor* (Ithaca, N.Y., 1951), especially chaps. ix-xi. See also Herbert Blumer, "Early Industrialization and the Laboring Class," *Sociological Quarterly,* I (January, 1960), 5-14.

15. Both were, it should be remembered, "primitive capitalisms." See Margaret Mead, *New Lives for Old* (New York, 1956); and H. G. Barnett, *Being a Palauan* (New York, 1960).

16. Numerous studies over the past generation have shown that mothers work extremely long hours. See Mirra Komarovsky, *Women in the Modern World* (Boston, 1953), chap. iv; also, Marx, *Capital* (New York, 1936), p. 405.

17. See Theodore M. Caplow, *The Sociology of Work* (Minneapolis, Minn., 1954), chap. xv. For France and Belgium, see *Sociologie comparée de la famille contemporaine* (Paris, 1955), p. 68; and *La condition sociale de la femme* (Brussels, 1956), pp. 53 ff.

18. The enclosure movements were different in kind; and the degree to which they were important in creating a labor pool is debatable. However, from the fifteenth century on, there was a floating labor supply. The late eighteenth century (when the agricultural revolution displaced many agricultural workers) was a period of war, colonial emigration, and urban migration—i.e., it was characterized by loose ties to family and locality. See G. R. Elton, *England under the Tudors* (London, 1955), pp. 78-81, 201-07, 230-33; and T.S. Ashton, *An Economic History of England: The Eighteenth Century* (London, 1955), pp. 36-47.

19. By now, the data on this point are extensive. Robert M. Marsh, in *The Mandarins* (Glencoe, Ill., 1961), has summarized these data. In the Ch'ing Dynasty, the amount of mobility was somewhat less than that in the United States, according to certain criteria. P'an Kuang-tan and Fei Hsiao-t'ung restricted themselves to the examination system alone, and decided that it was not a significant mobility ladder. Cf. the analysis in Robert M. Marsh, "Bureaucratic Constraints on Nepotism in the Ch'ing Period," *Journal of Asian Studies,* XIX (February, 1960), 117-19.

20. William L. Kolb has argued that those who inveigh against romantic love as a foundation for marriage often use anti-democratic principles in "Sociologically Established Family Norms and Democratic Values," *Social forces,* XXVI (May,

254

1948), 451-56. See also my "The Theoretical Importance of Love," *American Sociological Review,* XXIV (February, 1959), 38-47.

21. Arthur Phillips has written a useful summary of the influence of Western ideology on family decisions in native law; see "Marriage Laws in Africa," chap. ii, Arthur Phillips (ed.), *Survey of African Marriage and Family Life* (London, 1953). Revisions of Chinese codes after 1911 were especially influenced by the Swiss Code.

22. For relevant, though not conclusive, data on certain of these points, see George C. Homans, *English Villagers of the Thirteenth Century* (Cambridge, 1941); Josiah C. Russell, *British Medieval Population* (Albuquerque, New Mexico, 1948), chaps. vii-viii; K. H. Connell, *The Population of Ireland 1750-1845* (Oxford, 1950), chaps. ii-iii; Louis Henry, *Anciennes familles genevoises* (Paris, 1956); Regine Pernoud, "La vie de famille du Moyen Age à l'ancien regime," in Robert Prigent, (ed.), *Renouveau des idées sur la famille* (Paris, 1954), pp. 27-32; and G. G. Coulton, *Medieval Panorama* (New York, 1955), chaps, xxv, xlv, xlvi.

23. For a good analysis of the Puritan family, see Edmund S. Morgan, *The Puritan Family* (Boston, 1944). Milton's "The Doctrine and Discipline of Divorce" was first published in 1643.

24. Neil J. Smelser, *Social Change in the Industrial Revolution* (Chicago, 1959), chaps, ix-x.

25. Feng Ting, "Love and Support of Parents Also a Necessary Virtue of the Socialist Society," in *Chung Kuo Ch'ing Nien* (*China Youth*) XXIV (December, 1956); translated and reprinted in *Extracts from China Mainland Magazines,* LXV (January, 1957), 17-20; and Yuan Po, "What Attitudes Should One Take Toward One's Parents," *Chung Kuo Ch'ing Nien* (December, 1954), translated and reprinted in *Survey of China Mainland Press,* CMLXXIII (January, 1955), 30-32.

26. Its persistence even in urban Africa is based primarily on the lack of an accepted ceremonial substitute for the validation of a marriage.

27. A matrilineage is in any event somewhat difficult to maintain. See the excellent analysis of its structural peculiarities in David M. Schneider, "The Distinctive Features of Matrilineal Descent Groups" (Mimeographed. Berkeley, California, 1959); also (with Kathleen Gough), *Matrilineal Kinship,* Berkeley, University of California, 1961.

PART VI

Education and Communication

CHAPTER 13

The Impact of the Educational System
on Technological Change and Modernization [1]

C. ARNOLD ANDERSON

University of Chicago

INTRODUCTION [2]

Education receives only passing reference in most of the now vast literature on technological change, modernization, and economic development. A few writers accord it major importance, but they only occasionally amplify on their reasons.[3]

Attempts to identify the role of education in these dynamic processes are handicapped by the failure of economists and political scientists to reach consensus on basic issues. Writings in these areas have a sectarian flavor, as is to be expected when policy questions are so urgent and the phenomena so intertwined. If, for example, the appropriateness of large- versus small-scale investment were specified for different situations, the educational implications could then also be specified. If the level of tolerance for foreign technicians in new nations could be forecast, local educational programs could be planned more definitely. If the different "mixes" of high- and low-level skills required for assimilating various technologies were known, the structure of schools could be designed accordingly. In view of the inchoate state of the literature on these topics, any discussion of the place of formal schooling must explore alternatives.

We can rely upon historical precedents only to a limited extent. To be sure, since educational structures are more malleable than industrial systems, there is even less necessity in the former case for a new nation's repeating the experiences of the pioneer nations. Yet, among these earlier experiences, there are precedents of great potential value, if only they could be identified. One may suggest, in passing, that the Soviet model is of no more utility than the West European; Japanese experience is probably more pertinent, but the documentation is meager. In most of the earlier cases, the economic takeoff was associated with nationalism emerging against a feudal background. There was an indigenous educated

259

elite, and there was much international exchange in educational practice. However, there was nothing of the overlay of colonialism that generates so many complexities in the newer nations today.

A writer who concentrates upon one aspect of economic development (such as capital formation or agricultural technology) tends to magnify the contribution of that particular factor in the total growth process. When such a specialist exhausts his analysis, he is inclined to confer unwarranted importance upon some residual factor—typically, education—that is outside his framework. Among writers dealing specifically with schooling, there are similar preferences. Some find the key in higher technical and professional training;[4] some, in general university culture; others, in secondary vocational schools, in mass literacy, or in elementary schools. One could argue persuasively for each of these alternatives.

We must look at complexes of factors in order to ascertain how each form of schooling plays its respective part in different sectors or stages of development. Simple notions of "more" or "less" education tell us little. The critical question is *how* each kind of education affects different economic processes or different chains of technical adaptation, and what roles individuals with different forms of training play in the economy and in cultural life. One might, for example, trace the impact of divers sorts of schooling upon supply curves for different grades of labor, upon preferences for risk-taking, or upon ability to deal with problems in economic rather than in provincial political terms. We must study the diffusion of technical practices and economic actions, and their interaction through time.

EDUCATION AND THE BASIC ECOLOGICAL DIFFUSION PROCESS

Economic development and the implanting of technology are examples of social change. Social change may fruitfully be described in a framework of ecological distributions (including the vertical dimension of social status) that result from and in turn generate processes of diffusion. The thesis of this paper is that education has a critical role in development to the extent that it is integrated into this ecological structure of diffusion.

When non-economists deal with economic development, they commonly emphasize the resistances and the cultural inhibitions to economic behavior. Frequently, they apparently assume that there are strong built-in "irrationalities" of non-response to economic incentives. It might be argued that it is the *absence* of certain "growth institutions" and of certain technological experiences, rather than the presence of resistances to new patterns of economic behavior, that should receive emphasis.[5] These two

260

interpretations are not mirror images. There is abundant evidence that material living patterns have intrinsic appeal and that they are adopted readily when presented appropriately. While their not being adopted may be due to inertia or ignorance, it is more often due to definite economic costs of shifting. We need to put "economic man" back on the stage. Resistances melt when net inducements toward novelty are strong. We need more scrutiny of effective incentives rather than ethnographic studies of inhibitions.[6] These two approaches are complementary; but a focus upon incentives facilitates analysis of diffusion and fits better into analyses of growth.

The importance of schooling for growth in the short run may be quite minor; yet, in the long run, schooling may be decisive by virtue of its role in sustaining the broader milieu that favors change. Seemingly there is much merit in the position that availability of capital is less important to new countries than a cultural pattern favorable to the rooting of new technologies. For example, the cultural climate of the inferior and backward rural schools in the state of South Dakota a generation or more ago was probably much more conducive to economic development than is the climate of the high-standard grammar school in Accra that trains pupils so successfully for a British university.

Economic development, like other social changes, occurs in nodes, in centers displaying high rates of change and of interchange with other centers above and below in the ecological hierarchy.[7] These influences spread in gradient patterns. Development requires that clusters of people who have developed a stake in the new nourish the new.

In other words, sharp demarcations (in political parlance, these would be called "inequities") between strata and localities are indispensable for development. Their appearance is, in any event, inevitable. Their encouragement, within a framework designed to implement the spread of established gains, would seem to be good policy. Appeals for fairness and equality are potent, however, in the nations recently risen from colonial status. Obviously, it is only just to establish uniform social services and to assist backward areas to live "decently." Yet such equalization may be a luxury—to be indulged only in prosperous countries, and not to be insisted upon if rapid development has priority. No nation, even today, has attained uniformly accessible, high-quality primary schooling for all its regions or communities, not to mention social strata.

We believe that educational policy will make its maximum contribution to development if it is integrated with the ecological gradient structures and with the stratification gradients of emulation and diffusion. This implies, for example, that the responsibility for financing of schools should not be taken from local communities; it should rather, be manipulated in such a way that it spurs on those localities manifesting high aspirations

261

while giving only foundation aid to lagging areas. The hinterland schools will remain inferior; this is the obverse of the rapid construction of superior training facilities in the economic centers. Such a pattern of schools fosters economic development because it works with, rather than against, other processes of change.

Acceptance of this viewpoint also entails acquiescence in widely differential acceptance of educational norms among sub-populations as a normal feature of social change. In some areas in the United States, after a century of strenuous efforts to improve schools, the residents still have no clear norms for the schooling of their children.[8] In other areas, definite norms have existed for two or three generations, and their level has risen steadily. The leading position of some groups in accepting higher norms has, indeed, been one means of stimulating the aspirations of laggard groups or areas. What Kuznets infers for income differentials may well be valid for schooling also: the initial period of development is accompanied by widening differences among strata and localities, only later to be replaced by narrowing differentials. Educational norms diffuse downward in the social hierarchy at the same time that they diffuse outward along the lines of ecological gradients.

It is a corollary of the above argument that, in the new nations, individual financing of secondary and especially of higher education should, for some decades, rest primarily upon loans and fees. Free stipends are, in many respects, dysfunctional in early stages of development. Given the existing variability of readiness for further schooling among areas and strata, the pupils who win stipends will come, for the most part, from families able to pay fees or repay loans. This distribution of appreciation for the higher levels of schooling will change; but to alter it drastically and rapidly will entail heavy expenses that, perhaps, are not advisedly assumed at present. We should also like to recommend that private-venture schools be given wide scope in new nations; this could be another device for keeping the school section of the public budget within manageable limits.

Development will be advanced by tolerating variations in educational standards from community to community and from school to school. Under such a permissive policy, a continuum of standards will emerge, instead of the familiar distinction of recognized and substandard schools. This flexible situation is conducive to the diffusion of schools, and is more realistic than plans demanding rapid universalization of high standards. To eliminate quality differences among schools would, in practice, either be enormously expensive or inevitably involve severe narrowing of standards and a limitation upon the scale of educational operations. If there is wide local and private option, variations in quality will correspond roughly to the aspirations of parents in different localities, to the level of

262

preparatory schools, and to the levels of needed qualifications as measured by labor markets.

As appreciation of the practical (or symbolic) value of better schooling becomes more widespread, incentives to raise standards in the lagging schools take hold. Some schools will never catch up, for the top is steadily rising; but diffusion of higher standards continues apace and is facilitated by the absence of rigid categories. It is not an accident that the local school is the pride of so many thousands of American communities; and this widely shared pride is related to the rapid spread of virtually universal secondary education during the past half-century.

The United States has, in fact, followed this sort of policy for more than a century.[9] Whether measured by later incomes or jobs of the graduates, by the books in the homes of students, or by the proportions of graduates going on to college or professional school, individual secondary schools and coleges have always varied to an astonishing degree. When one considers the kind of educational system we would have had for the past century if Harvard University graduates had determined national educational policy, one may—with more reason than merely national pride—conclude that the benefits of this loose system have outweighed the costs that would have been entailed in making standards uniformly higher.

When these various issues are considered from the viewpoint of how the national elites function, the importance of the ecological processes is underlined. Gradient patterns of educational opportunity, combined with diffusion of cultural norms, encourage the development of well-knit localized clusters of elite persons in the main ecological centers. Because they are lively clusters of leaders, they are motivated to co-ordinate the skills of the several special elites in the local scene for the advancement of their center and their schools. If propensities for national centralization do not swamp these growing points, accelerated diffusion of practices is fostered.

Undeniably, this permissive policy can generate some serious dilemmas. The pull to one or a very few centers may be so strong that it aggravates locational differentials of development and impedes further change. Geographic and status discontinuities may become, or be made, so wide they obstruct diffusion. The economic and educational "multipliers" may be choked by restrictions or by inefficiencies arising from undue concentration. When well-distributed centers have not arisen, there is a case for planned facilities in power, highways, and schools to create them. We are not advocating ecological parity, and any such attempt would fail. But we do recognize the need to stimulate development at appropriate localities so that they may function as diffusion centers.

Appropriate spatial relations among ecological centers are not enough. Neither is a policy of encouraging development of geographic and status continua in standards, and their transformation and diffusion through time. I believe that such patterns can best be realized and maintained only in a situation in which there is flexibility with regard to role allocation of men and women of assorted educational backgrounds.

Many, especially persons inclined toward central planning, have asserted that, in an appropriately designed program for development, schooling should be closely articulated with occupation and income. The civil service pattern of graded jobs and salary categories appeals to the planner's sense of the fitness of things—a new version of "the great chain of being."

To be sure, men with the best schooling tend also to have the best jobs and the higher incomes. The few data available at hand for undeveloped countries indicate that these attributes are connected quite loosely; and this continues to be true in most if not all the advanced countries. There is a tight connection only at the extremes. Pons's data for Stanleyville,[10] for example, reveal that the unskilled typically have no schooling, while most people with at least six years of school had clerical jobs or better. Yet less than half those without schooling were holding unskilled jobs; and over one-fourth of those with at least six years' school were manual workers. Men in each occupational category were found at all levels of the income distribution, though the unskilled were bunched in the lower brackets and the white-collar workers usually had high incomes. The self-employed seldom had much schooling, but they often had relatively large incomes. The Sofers' data for East Africa reveal a similarly loose association of occupation, education, and income.[11] It is noteworthy that the Stanleyville Africans were recruited from the hinterland inversely to distance; one infers that they migrated by stages along the ecological channels. Occupation not only reflected a man's schooling; it was also strongly influenced by whether or not his father had worked for Europeans.[12] Mercier reports that in Dakar, intertribal marriages were more frequent among the Africans in the better occupations.[13] There is evidence that the better-educated individuals substitute social class for tribe as a criterion of status and friendship.[14]

Apparently, a loose connection among these attributes of the labor force conduces to development; a close connection would be a manifestation of the rise of inhibiting rigidities. Many qualities contribute to vocational success or productivity. Individuals differ in what they learn in school and in what use they can make of that training. Teachers cer-

264

tainly are fallible judges of their pupils' potentialities for economic productivity. School certificates or job titles tell little more. Skilled artisans are worth more to a society than inferior physicians or briefless lawyers. A few gifted enterprisers are literally worth their weight in gold annually. Yet in some countries, there are signs that a premature development of respect for formal schooling in "recognized" schools threatens to introduce dysfunctional rigidities into the occupational structure. The wisdom of encouraging the mystique of titles, certificates, and formalized qualifications is dubious.

In this, as in many other situations, difficult choices must be made. Where roles have hitherto been allocated on a familial basis or where nepotism flourishes, there is undeniably a need to inject some clear-cut impersonal rating system into the new bureaucracies. And it is difficult to establish suitable criteria without relying upon certificates or another narrow set of specifications. Moreover, too complete a displacement of ascriptive allocation would strangle those strata-centered valuations of education that can play so large a part in generating diffusion of education. Indeed, up until now there has probably not been any general displacement of particularistic selection. Familistic criteria often dictate who gets the training or the certificate as well as who gets the job. An ostensibly impersonal merit system frequently is only a façade superimposed on the traditional modes of selection that really dominate the schools. Meanwhile, the system becomes cramped by the adulation of certificates. All in all, a loose-textured relation among education, income, and occupation may well provide a better framework for the transition from particularistic to universalistic role allocation than can be achieved by a neat program of manpower assignment.

In at least a few of the new nations, the intelligentsia, the foreign-educated elite, are already being superseded in leadership by more charismatic and demagogic political leaders.[15] In one sense, then, the training of the former group has apparently been wasted—as is often the case when they have rigid job preferences. However, these rivalries are improving the chances for the half-educated, who are pushing ahead by means of electoral choice and patronage. This process may, in fact, build bridges between sections of the social structure (a function whose importance will be discussed below). The new leaders are likely to prove more sympathetic to flexible and experimental programs for schools—although, on the other hand, they may be inclined to spread the meager school funds so thinly that these become useless.

If the Dakar data are typical, the occupational strata in the new nations are quite unstable—healthily unstable. Urban workers are, of course, disproportionately recruited from families who have been long-term residents of the cities, as are men in white-collar vocations compared to manual workers. But some of the sons of professional men have begun to slide down the scale, while some farmers' and workers' sons are quickly working their ways into relatively high positions.[16] In both older and new nations, a good schooling facilitates upward mobility; but in both, formal schooling does not seem to be be decisive—luck, drive, and talent remain important. Educational arrangements that implement appropriate occupational mobility, without introducing new rigidities into selection, encourage the flexibility essential for development. These arrangements are not achieved by spreading school funds broadcast nor by making certificates a cherished preserve; they evolve when schools of varying standards are integrated into the other dynamic economic and cultural developments.

THE ELUSIVE CONTRIBUTION OF EDUCATION TO PRODUCTIVITY

Elementary education is sometimes alleged to serve primarily in altering consumption habits without exerting much influence upon production skills or attitudes. This allegation seems too narrow. Apart from conveying specific skills of language and number, elementary education develops social habits that facilitate group organization, and thereby enhances external economies.

Development involves roundaboutness which is favored when men's horizons extend beyond the village. Even a modest schooling makes people more alert to opportunities and equips them to articulate their ideas over a wider range of topics. The greatest significance of general education may rest in the kind of world it opens to the literate. This new world in the early days of European economic development (and also in the curiously Victorian atmosphere of the Soviet Union) may well have been distinctive. In past centuries, literacy often led the individual into the world of Enlightenment, into a world of moral norms stressing individual activity, and into the Puritan philosophy of work. Since the surrounding society was permeated with these values—but, let us remember, in locality and strata clusters—the contribution of the school needed only to be complementary. Increasingly, the world into which literate men move has become one of collectivistic values, marked by skepticism about the values that accompanied earlier economic changes. Perhaps it would be unduly sanguine to expect schooling to have the same impact on productive life today that it had in earlier centuries.

When contacts expand beyond the face-to-face kind, as they do in urban centers, literacy becomes essential. Specialized and impersonal contacts multiply where economic activities increase; they constitute a large part of the ecologically patterned influences so significant in the diffusion

266

of economic practices. Large, bureaucratic organizations of business, government, and private associations are at the head in economic foci. Hence the advantages accruing to literacy are realized more promptly in urban centers, and more rapidly generate incentives for moving beyond literacy.

The Stanleyville data indicate that family traditions of education, good jobs, and sustained contact with Europeans have gone together. Commitment to newer economic ways—as distinguished from mere recruitment to European firms—is concentrated in the local centers and social strata where the emoluments of being literate have been most assured. It is in the latter that literacy per se swiftly becomes of minor value.

A "multiplier" process operates in diffusing attitudes and practices favorable to economic development. Schooling plays a key role in this process. The clusters of families who have had longer contact with Westerners, Western schooling, and Western ideas will continue to have a large lead over other families. From these favored families come key business people, key civil servants, and manipulators of power—though the same processes steadily draw new members into their midst. For this among other reasons, the multiplier process works most vigorously in the ecological centers.

Policy-makers have to make difficult decisions that will encourage or inhibit this multiplier process. In the name of justice, pleas will be made to raise the backward sections to the same level, to lift depressed strata, to spread welfare benefits. The problem is to design policies that conform to contemporary ideals—while simultaneously both continuing to encourage the centers and strata evincing progressive educational aspirations, and stimulating the diffusion of these aspirations and practices.

There are political as well as economic returns from elementary schooling. A literate populace is more capable of checking up on the operations of the elites. Bridges between sections of the social structure cannot be erected by a handful of devoted intellectuals and technicians. Few elites constantly keep the interests of the populace in mind. All these considerations have implications for the relative emphasis upon lower, middle, or higher schools—though no one has yet made these implications explicit. I maintain that effective elementary and middle education should be sustained in the dynamic centers—even at the expense of remote villages. Secondary schooling should be provided on a sufficiently large scale to filter graduates into many occupational levels. I believe that the preservation of "standards" in higher education should be conditional upon the demonstrated willingness of university graduates to relate themselves to other segments of the society, and especially upon the proved power of higher schools to stimulate the widespread expansion of secondary education.

The new nations are striving for economic development during a time when ideologies of the welfare state and of an active civil service are strong. Skepticism about the virtues of autonomous economic forces, and suspicion of unwatched, decentralized decision-making are prevalent today.[17]

In an earlier age in the West, the efforts of thrusting groups to implement their economic programs generated struggles for power. In the more socialized and nationalistic new states, power has a tighter organization, and economic forces have less scope for action than they had in the less efficient states of the past. Today, the civil services have their pride in education combined with their power to control. The capacity of less valuably educated men to make appropriate decisions in their own small worlds is less respected. The new nations demand that their political survival be safeguarded on their own terms and expect also that other countries will guarantee economic development. Development policy has become a "sensitive" issue.

The proliferation of a centralized civil service has several implications for the contribution of education to development. Certificated officials determine the destiny of business firms, through labor laws, licensing, etc. Officials favor their own kind of men in non-government agencies, though the connection between proficiency and formal education may be quite tenuous. Frequently, business must function under conditions dictated by men with literary training, many of whom are antagonistic to economic behavior on principle. The concentration of trained manpower and of the right of decision within these new civil services represents a poor allocation of decision-making in relation to the existing capacity of men to decide.

Efforts to achieve balanced development through central planning and budgeting generate other constraints, though they also have many effects conducive to development. As an illustration, let us consider schools. If their cost is loaded on the central budget, schools must compete with other central services for funds. The consequence may be that education does not achieve optimum development. There are many arguments in favor of decentralizing school costs, relaxing the tendency toward ministerial policing carried on by measuring against factitious standards, and establishing inducements for localities to be responsible for their own schools.

The beneficial influences of education on development are affected by the character of the relations among the leaders of a nation. When the several elites (legislative, business, administrative, intellectual) enjoy considerable autonomy, trained people and creative individuals have more opportunity to insinuate themselves into those parts of the system where

268

opportunities or needs are most vital. If, however, these elites are well ordered under the benevolent tutelage of a ruling party or of the civil service, much trained manpower is usually wasted, and the trained sensitivity of specialized cadres finds less scope for initiative. Civil servants disparage the efforts of amateurs or of the uncertificated. They do not appreciate enterprising people, who, by definition, prefer not to work in channels.

The directorates in the new nations have accepted the humanitarian values embodied in the ideology of the welfare state. They are more sensitive to evil than they are alert to novelty. They desire enlightenment, health, and prosperity; at the same time, they are inclined to restrict the unequal distribution of development so naturally manifested in the ecological structures. They do not always encourage the fruitful inequities represented by zealous families and communities striving for education and rapid development. They dread the social costs of development that are the price of flexibility. They overlook the costs arising from botched central plans, excusing them as tactical adjustments.

In education, neatly planned developments eliminate the crasser barbarities of popular control; but ministerial plans are not always best suited to encourage development. Funds are frittered away when schools are introduced in localities where parents will not allow children to remain in school long enough to become literate. Voluntary or proprietorial schools may be discouraged on the ground that their graduates are not "well trained." Meanwhile the educational ideologies fostering the unemployed intellectuals are bolstered by official approval.

Civil service control over educational policy sometimes exacts a high price for the many services it performs. There are two reasons for this. Central services are usually manned by co-optation; but Ghana may not need officials of the quality demanded in Britain. Then, too, civil servants dread the disorder of growth, with its seemingly chaotic and often sordid processes. The intrinsic orderliness of spontaneous structures like the ecological structures is not always appreciated.

RIGID STANDARDS MAY BLOCK THE RESPONSE OF THE SUPPLY
OF EDUCATION TO THE DEMANDS

The supply of schooling usually corresponds to the demand, unless factitious standards of quality are imposed. Once the pattern of formal schooling has been accepted by leading sectors of a population—particularly when they are trying to attain economic development and modernized technology—conditions are propitious for this equilibrium.

But, in some new nations, certificates and examinations multiply un-

269

duly. One sympathizes with the aspiration to turn out graduates of metropolitan quality, and these graduates are a joy to meet. However, prematurely high standards can be dysfunctional. The concern for standards easily becomes a preoccupation with token certificates: the parent wants his child to get the certificate that opens (or once did open) the way to esteemed jobs.

Second, educational systems with firm standards and central supervision are usually conservative in curriculum. We must be wary of attributing economic significance to school curricula as such; still, conservative curricula do discourage freewheeling by teacher or pupils. Too often, the cry is, "the syllabus, the syllabus." In actuality, the satisfaction and incentive gained by "completing" a course of study may be more productive of diligent manpower than what is learned therein.

Third, we know little about the standard of proficiency that is "needed" in newly developing economies. Presumably, a finely graded series of graduates, with different proficiencies and abilities, will most closely fit the complex job markets. Insistence upon rigid standards aggravates inelasticities in the supply curves of labor. The preferable system is one in which individual schools, of varying quality, graduate such students as they can, using flexible standards, and then let their graduates find their levels in the job markets.

It is apparently utilitarian to encourage a wide diffusion of aspiration for schooling and other training—of whatever quality. Conceptions of "adequate training" vary with ecological location and in different strata. Uniform standards have more heraldic than economic utility. Until nations become economically mature, they will be unwise to permit a mandarinate to scrutinize each pupil. Parents, teachers, and pupils, in the dynamic centers and in the more educated strata, quickly learn that higher standards are attainable and that it will be rewarding to strive for them. Meanwhile, people in more isolated regions are acquiring their first taste for schooling of a quality appropriate to local public values and employments.

The above comments are especially relevant to the training of teachers.[18] Fiscal restrictions often dictate a policy that is, in terms of diffusion, relatively efficient, given judicious location of schools plus wide scope for local initiative. It is questionable that the marginal gain that accrues when the quality of teachers is raised matches that gained from raising the quality of engineers or enterprisers. What is taught to pupils may have little relation to what they learn, except at the extremes of quality. It is said that "the best land gets the best farmers," and one suspects that the "best" communities and schools recruit the best teachers. This may be unjust, it may be inefficient in some ways, and it certainly seems disorderly. But teachers are not a free good.

Citizens of the United States, of course, are biased on many of these questions; yet it is more than a figure of speech to say that this nation was built on the one-room rural school taught by the barely-literate farmer's daughter. High standards were established, in a few localities, early in our history; but they were incorporated into few schools until recently.[19] Even today, laggard schools are racing to match the standards reached by other schools two decades or more ago. Americans are prone to regard certificates more as trophies than as entrance tickets. Meanwhile, we have had a steady and generally adequate supply of better-trained individuals flowing out of the most varied sorts of schools. The American economy would have come to a halt if we had excluded, from the labor force or from key positions, all men who had not received schooling of "certificate" quality. The assorted schools, when classified by quality or by the backgrounds of their pupils, have been distributed inequitably in the familiar ecological pattern. Diffusion of higher aspirations and attainment of higher standards have constantly advanced—yet fanciful standards have never been allowed to obstruct the supply of competent workers.

WORLD COMPETITION AND "KNOW-HOW VS. KNOWLEDGE"

It is possible that the nations now launching upon development must make more extensive and explicit use of formal schooling than did the nations that developed previously. Certainly, training for the use of radio and combustion engines is essential now, though these skills were needed only recently in the West. However, it does not follow that the efficient way to provide this training is through schools; placing tractors in school gardens and playgrounds might obviate the need for tractor-driver schools.

The argument that new nations need more education is sometimes based on the assumption that, when the Western industrial revolution occurred, nearly all workers were illiterate. In fact, although the mass educational situation was quite varied among the Western nations in their earlier stages, a large fraction (or even a majority) of the industrial laborers were, by the first part of the nineteenth century, "literate."[20] Planned development of human resources was important even in Tsarist Russia and in early post-restoration Japan, as well as in other leading nations. England did not have a good system of elementary schools until she had almost reached her zenith of industrialization; the northern United States had a fairly good system at least a generation before industrialization bloomed. Historical precedent, then, is an uncertain base for speculations about the scale of education requisite for economic development.

Today, the minimum education required to support development may be higher because there are a different sort of competition and a different

271

organization of industry in the international economy. The forms of production now being borrowed by underdeveloped nations are complex; and an organizational revolution has occurred that is as central to development as the technical revolution. Literacy is necessary for communication and flexibility; but literacy will not engender the higher levels of "know-how." Nonetheless, literacy is not needed for a large proportion of jobs.

Knowledge is what the schools can most readily convey; but that learning forms only a small part of productive skill. Know-how requires direct experience. As special skills become more complex, part of the job experience can be transferred to a formal school setting; engineering has thus been undergoing transformation in the West. But the know-how that gets new plants running and "digs out the bugs" is expensive, and it can only partially be taught in schools. This fact emphasizes the need to import working teams to serve as nuclei from which this know-how can spread to the members of the native population who have sufficient formal training to assimilate it.

There is perhaps no more critical question than this one, with its implications for integration of formal teaching, importation of human capital, and on-the-job experience as a core around which to build a high-level diffusion process. The growing lists of successes and failures in transplanting new firms illumine this problem. Nor is the importance of high-level know-how limited to industry. It is increasingly relevant for agriculture, and made more urgent by the population explosions. The Ford Foundation report on India shows that simultaneous change in a number of agricultural practices is necessary if increase in productivity is to repay expenditures.[21] The required changes are not brought about by campaigns to distribute fertilizer this year, better seed next year, and so on. Neither can new methods be taught in scattered elementary schools. A cadre of extension workers, who bridge the gaps between the economic centers and the hinterland are needed. Among the masses, the readiness to act upon the results of demonstration projects depends on some prior literacy and "Westernization." Hence good elementary schools should be clustered with pilot project areas. Once again, diffusion is not the same as equality —diffusion involves a dynamic innovating center that leads, and the location of this center is significant.

FUNCTIONAL EDUCATION AND TECHNOLOGICAL CHANGE

To understand the present and prospective roles of education in newly developing countries, one must examine what education does and has done for the individuals receiving it. Three complaints are frequently made

272

about the responses of indigenous peoples to educational opportunities. One complaint stresses the apathy of ignorant rural families, who discourage their children while they are in elementary school and cause most of them to lapse into illiteracy. A second concerns the "oversupply" of academically trained persons who are unable to find jobs "suited to their station." A third complaint, related to the second, focuses on the prevalent lack of interest in vocational and technical training.

Apathy and the resulting illiteracy may involve more than the waste of the resources invested in the schools. They can actually retard the diffusion of educational aspirations. Yet this disinterest is not irrational; if semi-literacy does little for the child's prospects, and education has not itself become a consumption value, to pursue it would be imprudent. Within the context of traditional social relationships, a little education may be highly dysfunctional, since it creates misfits unable to function in the "new" society. Too great a concern for distributional equality, when neither adequate resources nor readiness to assimilate expanded schooling exists, produces just such dilemmas.

The problem of the oversupply of academically educated persons has several facets. We can clarify these by viewing behavior in relation to expectation patterns. The oversupply may be a transitional dislocation, or it may reflect inappropriate extension of past expectations. In one guise, this is manifested in a preference for the liberal arts kind of higher education that, in the past, suplied incumbents of high positions in many Western societies and their colonies. But even in India—the most often cited case—surveys among the educated reveal that unemployment occurs mainly at the intermediate levels. In a large proportion of cases, the unemployed decline to work far from the metropolis—and remote from income from their families. A study of Primary V and Primary VI leavers in Uganda indicates a similar situation.[22] In the parental generation, a given level of schooling (higher in India than in Uganda) sufficed to qualify one for high-status job. This is no longer true: there is a lack of co-ordination among job opportunities, job preferences, and supplies of skills.

The supply of middle-school graduates does not automatically engender an adequate supply of jobs for them; and this lag creates at least transitional problems. On the other hand, the growth of a cadre with such intermediate skills lays a foundation for a rate of economic development not otherwise feasible. The problem results partly from the proclivity of graduates to apply an opportunistic economic criterion to their whole training, although some of it should be viewed as valuable in itself. Some nations were fortunate in that, prior to their industrialization, literacy had become widespread for its religious and civic value as a good in itself.

The demand that education become more technical and that elites be disabused of their disdain for manual work is a commonplace. This

273

proposition is rarely questioned, though the difficulties of effecting such a conversion are duly recognized. Some technical training is essential to support a technologically advancing economy. It does not follow that this training should be provided through the establishing of specialized vocational schools fitted into "the plan." In some new nations, technical schools stand empty, because the public do not appreciate their function or see no market for their graduates—or else can obtain satisfying jobs with more conventional types of training. It is difficult to determine which of the skills that can be produced in schools are needed in a given economy.

Thus technical training in Ghana did not take hold until recently—now, suddenly, the demand strains the facilities. In response to newly perceived job opportunities, such education is becoming regarded as purposeful. A dual readiness has emerged: job outlets, on the demand side; and sufficient numbers with general education, on the supply side. In this kind of situation, as with transitional oversupply of university graduates, there is a timing problem in the diffusion process and in co-ordinating economic and educational developments. However, it is difficult to anticipate correctly the timing and magnitude of popular acceptance of technical education. Hence, the generous use of imported teachers for such programs when they become timely is justified.

It is equally difficult to achieve a balance between school training and on-the-job training. The significance of this equilibrium is underlined by the intricate network of growth processes, the great importance of know-how, and the need to integrate educational and economic changes. These adjustments have been considerably more crucial in Western countries than we usually acknowledge, but they have been made in diverse ways. More recently, the turns and twists in Soviet vocational programs have had an appearance of planned integration between the demands of training and those of labor force. There were, nevertheless, major miscalculations; and it is by no means certain that Soviet planners achieved any better adjustments than were realized through more decentralized arrangements elsewhere.[23]

If vocational schools are combined with apprenticeship of various sorts, complex problems arise of co-ordinating wage structures with scheduled estimates for assorted manpower categories. Unrealistic wage policies for modern enterprises have emerged in some new nations; the existence of such regulations makes it possible to experiment in linking wage patterns with provisions for training.

However, some countries will probably make a series of poorer choices. There is a growing trend toward discouraging expatriate technicians. In some countries, racial attitudes make it less possible to import skills than it would have been a century ago. At the same time, ministries set such

274

high standards for schools that they often limit supplies of trained persons or restrict their use. Employers cannot always set wage structures; yet the assortments of skills becoming available for employment are distorted by conservative educational practices.

No one is in a position to be dogmatic about the relation between schools and the creation of an appropriate skill hierarchy. For example, we do not know the extent to which the importation of skill embodied in modern machinery makes it possible to by-pass the evolution of skill structures reflected in historical developments in the West. These uncertainties are valid reasons for allowing maximum flexibility to all agencies that affect the supply of skill. There are two choices possible. Vocational training can be made increasingly formal—incidentally absorbing a large share of the best-trained manpower. Alternatively, managers and employers can be given inducements to train more workers and to develop policies of promoting. Tax policy and other incentives can make it possible to capitalize on localized decision-making in vocational training, thereby enabling job markets in the ecological network to exert their maximum influence.

CONCLUSIONS

This paper has been both analytical and policy-oriented. It has emphasized the importance of diffusion processes through ecological networks for both educational and economic development.[24] "Natural" developments are not adequate; important social processes should be exploited to introduce modifications that work with, rather than against, these processes. I have stressed flexibilities that permit continuities of variation in educational standards and job allocations, and the dynamic ecological centers where educational and economic changes may produce multiplicative impact and from which both sorts of innovation may spread. Decisions on these topics are continually being made, by intent or by default; I propose that they be made with the ecological gradients clearly in mind.

In view of the fundamental position of agriculture in underdeveloped economies, the question of schooling for farm children is central. A rise in labor productivity in agriculture is essential; hence something beyond migration to towns is needed. Impressed by the Ford Foundation report on India and by Hardin's report on Pakistan, I advocate the training of qualified agricultural extension workers and the simultaneous development of pilot communities where basic education is used to generate readiness for change. If these communities are related to economic centers, the market processes that always play a key part in changing farm methods can be exploited.

Intensive attention to educational programs in the ecological centers

275

does not imply sacrificing either quantity to quality, or wide coverage to training an elite. The influences radiating from ecological centers should be relied upon to extend educational opportunities in an ordered fashion.

The diffusion process does involve stress on quantity after the minimum education sufficient to insure literacy has been achieved. Educational centers should be numerous and appropriately located. Any social facility based on mass participation recruits clientele approximately in accord with the inverse square law. A mediocre secondary school for each 100 Km^2—assuming a given level of educational aspiration—will stimulate more rapid diffusion of schooling and of attitudes conducive to technical change than would a superior school serving 1000 Km^2. A similar logic suggests the establishment of many small teacher-training colleges is preferable to gathering trainees into a few select urban schools—even at the price of less well-prepared teachers.

The foregoing discussion also implies that entrance into or passage from one level of school to the next should be made relatively easy, so that there may truly be an educational stairway. The interested public will quickly recognize differences of quality among schools, and their graduates will be treated accordingly; this is no more surprising than the fact that some schools win most of their cricket games. If many schools of assorted quality are established, and located in centers of corresponding "rank," the matching of talents or aspirations to training facilities can be accomplished more precisely, and the output of skills will be maximized.

Finally, a functional approach to education requires attention to the relation between formal education and other training. Schools spread the basic sort of knowledge that encourage flexibility in later occupational roles and stimulate countrywide communication. Apprenticeship in various forms is essential for the creation of that kind of human capital we call know-how. In all these contexts, a loose structure without sharp boundaries implements the adoption of a functional program of education and its rapid diffusion.

1. This paper remains in the form in which it was laid before the Conference. If the writer were to revise it now he would lay considerable stress on the conflict between political demands upon education and the economic aspects that are discussed here.

2. I am particularly indebted to Philip Foster, Instructor in Comparative Education at the University of Chicago, for illuminating discussions on African education.

3. A distinct exception is W. Arthur Lewis, *The Theory of Economic Growth* (Homewood, Ill., 1955), pp. 183 f.

4. For example, F. Harbison, "High-Level Manpower for Nigeria's Future," *Investment in Education* (Lagos, Nigeria, 1960).

5. See Lewis, *op. cit.*; and C. Wolf, Jr., "Institutions and Economic Development," *American Economic Review*, XLV (1955), 867-83.

6. S. Rottenberg, "Incentives in Underdeveloped Economies," *American Economic Review*, L, No. 2 (May, 1960), 73-83.

7. F. W. and R. C. Young, "Two Determinants of Community Reaction to Industrialization in Rural Mexico," *Economic Development and Cultural Change*, VIII (1960), 257-64; W. E. Moore, *Industrialization and Labor* (Ithaca, N.Y., 1951), pp. 216-60, 295.

8. See C. A. Anderson and M. J. Bowman, "Educational Distributions and Attainment Norms in the United States," Session 27, *1954 (Rome) Population Congress*.

9. In 1926, in the United States, the minutes per day of schooling in the sixth grade in cities ranged from 240 to 420. Among rural communities, the weeks per school year ranged from twenty to forty; in villages, from twenty-eight to forty and in large cities, from thirty-six to forty-two. C. H. Mann, *How Schools Use Their Time* (New York, 1926), pp. 127, 137.

10. V. G. Pons, "The Growth of Stanleyville," in International African Institute, *Social Implications of Industrialization and Urbanization South of the Sahara* (1956), pp. 251 f.; I. M. Wallerstein, "The Emergence of Two West African Nations: Ghana and the Ivory Coast" (Ph. D. dissertation, Columbia University, 1959), pp. 237 f. These linkages are surprisingly loose in the Soviet Union; see

A. Inkeles and R. A. Bauer, *The Soviet Citizen* (Cambridge, Mass., 1959), chaps. iv, vi.

11. C. and R. Sofer, *Jinja Transformed* "East African Studies," No. 4 [Kampala, Uganda, 1955].

12. Pons, *op. cit.*, p. 641.

13. P. Mercier, in International African Institute, *op. cit.*, pp. 518 f.

14. P. Clement, in International African Institute, *op. cit.*, pp. 368 f.; A. L. Epstein, *Politics in an African Community* (Manchester, 1958), p. 240.

15. Wallerstein, *op. cit.*, pp. 244 f.

16. Mercier, *op. cit.*

17. S. N. Eisenstadt, "Social Development and Political Stability in Non-Western Societies," in *The Challenge of Development (Jerusalem*, 1958).

18. See John Vaizey, "L'économie de l'éducation et les pays sous-développés," *Tiers-Monde*, I (January-June, 1960).

19. It has been estimated that the median days of schooling of Americans were, in 1800, eighty-two; in 1840, 208; in 1860, 434; in 1880, 690; in 1926, 1360. It was a modestly educated population that conducted our development. See Mann, *op. cit.*, p. 49. Merle Curti and his co-workers have demonstrated how rapidly educational norms "took hold" on the northern frontier (Curti *et al., Making of an American Community* [Madison, Wisc., 1959], pp. 394 f.).

20. Representative historical statistics for England are given in R. D. Altick, *The English Common Reader* (Chicago, 1927).

21. Ford Foundation (sponsor), *Report on India's Food Crisis* (Delhi, April, 1959); see the mimeo report by Professor Charles Hardin on agricultural education in Pakistan.

22. S. Elkan, "School Leavers in Uganda," *Comparative Education Review* (October, 1960).

23. A. Kahan, "Soviet Vocational Education," *Comparative Education Review* (October, 1960).

24. Fundamental explanations and fresh research on the diffusion process can be found in the works of the human geographer, Torsten Hägerstrand, at the University of Lund, and of the sociologist, Elihu Katz, at the University of Chicago.

CHAPTER 14

The Role of Communication in the Process of Modernization and Technological Change

ITHIEL DE SOLA POOL

Massachusetts Institute of Technology

COMMUNICATION AND THE SOCIAL SYSTEM

Communication is an all-pervading aspect of our social environment. Unlike government, education, the church, or the market place, it is not a social institution. However, almost every social act in every institution involves some communication. Hence the consideration of communications is one particular way of considering society.

A social phenomenon of such ubiquity might seem important—it undoubtedly is important in some respects. But let us not form conclusions too quickly. If a phenomenon's relevance to policy-making is the criterion by which we measure its significance, then that which is ubiquitous at all times may not be of any interest. Communication is significant if it acts in a variable way upon the social events of which it is a part, not if it appears as a universal constant with no operational effect upon the inter-relations of other social phenomena.

Let us consider, for example, the banal observation that the intelligentsia of colonial countries dislike imperial domination. Every important term of this proposition may be interpreted as referring to a communication phenomenon. The fact of a "colonial" relation, for instance, is a set of assertions made by rulers and the ruled under certain recognized circumstances. If we try to imagine what it would be like for a tribe of totally wordless and signless Martians to conquer a nation and establish a regularized system of rule, we find it hard to conceive. Whatever the Martians' behavior, it could hardly have the character we call "colonial." Yet the fact that the relationship "colonial" comprises a myriad of verbal events of fixed character does not necessarily make communications a meaningful variable for its study. Under any set of communications circumstances plausible for a human society, the proposition at the beginning of this paragraph would hold. It is true that the intelligentsia of colonial countries dislike imperial domination, whether there is a free press or a censored press, high literacy or low literacy, television or no television, good literature or poor literature. No change in the communication system affects the validity of the proposition.

The insensitivity of that phenomenon to variations in the communication system implies that the messages constituting the fact of colonial rule or of being disliked are enormously redundant. They are repeated far beyond the possibility of their being suppressed by the elimination of certain media. They are repeated in every available medium. The communication system can, therefore, be treated as a constant, and disregarded. We can predict that colonial rule will breed resentment; one need know nothing about the particular communication system that is present in order to make that prediction without hesitation.

However, the operative irrelevance of communication variables does not hold for all propositions. There are some things which will happen under one communication system that will not happen under another. It is such communication-sensitive events which concern us here.

Some scholars, including myself, like to describe the social process by reference to its communications aspects—just as other scholars prefer descriptions in terms of power relationships, and still others, descriptions in terms of resource allocation. Since each of these aspects of human behavior is quite ubiquitous and pervasive, it is feasible to use any one of them as a way of describing society, and the choice between them is aesthetic and heuristic. But the selection of one of these terminologies is not the postulation of a proposition. The propositions about communications and modernization that can be tested are those which assert that the relationship of something else to modernization is different under one communication system than it is under another. Daniel Lerner asserts that personal desires relate differently to political policy in high-literacy and low-literacy societies.[1] The literate person who, through the literature he reads empathically, experiences conditions of life very different from his own, is able to formulate opinions about what policies government ought to follow, and he can do so in terms relevant to a government. However, an illiterate can express only his immediate needs. Literate rationalization is more indirect.

If modernization is the transition to participant society, then the direction of change in public communication is toward a constantly expanding opinion arena. The significant mode of participating, in any network of human communication, is by sharing a common interest in the messages it transmits—i.e., by having opinions about the matters which concern other participants.[2]

Here we stress that the transition to participant society hinges upon the desire among individuals to participate. It grows as more and more individuals take leave of the constrictive traditional universe and nudge their psyche toward

280

the expansive new land of heart's desire. The great gap is passed when a person begins to "have opinions"—particularly on matters which, according to his neighbors, "do not concern him."[3]

Lerner's proposition, valid or not, is a testable assertion that the communication system makes a difference to human behavior; it is not just the use of communication metaphors.

The literature contains few propositions like this that relate communication systems and modernization; and most of those, like the one just noted, concern literacy. Literacy is widely assumed to be the *sine qua non* of modern society. An additional assumption is apparently that, if the literacy requirement is met, communication systems adequate to the need will evolve when modernization demands them. Everett Hagen, among others, has suggested that, if certain other conditions of modernization are fulfilled, the development of communication systems will somehow automatically follow.[4] The necessary knowledge of technology, and the necessary postal, telephone, telegraph, radio, and printed channels, will emerge. Ideas for modernization will be sufficiently diffused to be available if people wish to adopt them. Those who hold this view do not believe that the communications media can be the bottleneck that obstructs modernization. In this paper, we shall explore and criticize their assumption.

First, we must briefly establish what we mean by "modernization" in this paper. We shall not define a "modernized" society, or a sector of a society, in terms of GNP per capita or of proportion of the population engaged in industrial endeavor, but rather in terms of certain values and modes of behavior shared by the inhabitants. These values—e.g., high achievement motivation, secularism, functionally specific relationships, mobility, etc.—do exist in high GNP countries. Their empirical relations with modernity, measured under different definitions, are high.[5] But for analytic purposes, we can conveniently define the word in such a way that we can classify as "modernized" both industrially advanced countries and regional enclaves and educated groups which have only recently acquired the cultural prerequisites of industrialization—those which, while still poor, are on the road to an urban, modern way of life.

1) The norm for the modern man is to work with high aspiration level, energy, and discipline. He does not necessarily work harder than the peasant who breaks the baked crust of the earth under the tropic sun. But the work norm accepted in modern society is that of striving, by mental effort, system, and hard work, for successively higher levels of achievement.[6]

2) The modern man has strong secular aspirations—in particular, aspirations to improve his material condition.

3) The modern man computes strategies on a broad stage. He considers policy for the nation, or even for the world. If he is an entrepreneur, he thinks about wide markets and the management of vast enterprises.[7]

4) The modern man calculates his strategies with relatively little inhibition by custom. Taboos are vital to any society, modern as well as traditional; but the modern man enjoys a greater freedom of means and goals. He is more free about where he lives, whom he marries, how he earns his living, and which faction he supports. Over considerable areas, means-ends considerations supersede fixed traditions.

5) As modernization prevails, ascribed status becomes less, and functional role becomes more, significant in interpersonal relations. The way a man is treated is largely determined by the job he is doing, rather than by his family origins. Since jobs in modern society can be reassigned according to criteria of expediency, emphasis on functional role promotes social mobility.[8]

6) All these factors make it possible for the device of organized association to be used extensively in modern societies. There are voluntary associations, business firms, and the state bureaucracy—each has the characteristics of a body of members organized in a hierarchy of ranks who, though free in their private lives, owe certain voluntarily assumed obligations of discipline in restricted portions of their lives. These organized associations are tree-connected. Decision-making of a medium or high degree of generality is assigned to specific persons; and all other persons act under the guidance of these decisions as they are transmitted by intermediaries responsible for leadership of specific portions of the body social.[9]

7) There is, subject to retrieval, information covering advanced science and advanced technology somewhere in the society.

These seven generalizations fit what we ordinarily think of as "modernized" societies—whether in the Communist or free world, whether in entire nations or in urban enclaves, whether in industrial societies or among European agricultural settlers abroad.

Our inquiry concerns the extent to which, and the ways in which, the functioning of any of these seven features of modern life is sensitive to the kind of communication system which exists in a country. As noted, there is not inevitably any relation. For example, there is no *a priori* reason to believe that need for achievement is better inculcated by one media system than by another—at least, among the media systems actually available as options in the contemporary world. The kind of early child training which produces or inhibits it may be as easily normalized by word of mouth as by paperbacked manuals or television. If, as his paper in this volume suggests, David McClelland has really discovered a relationship between mass media development and the inculcation of achievement motivation, he has come upon a significant and by no means self-evident relationship. There are only a limited number of such relationships. We shall attempt to examine some of them—i.e., some of the ways in which the character of a society's communication system may affect the aspects of modernity listed above.

Before beginning our investigation, we must emphasize that we are not presupposing that modernization is always a good thing. On the contrary, ambitions to impose vast goals on a world scale, coupled with the discarding of the customary inhibitions of the religious heritage, have produced the macabre aberrations of totalitarianism—to cite one example. We are going to consider some conditions of modernization; but that is a limited intellectual task. It seems a worth-while task, because some forms of modernization are undoubtedly both desirable and inevitable. But there is no ground for assuming that whatever is found to promote modernization is, *ipso facto*, to be advocated as policy.

COMMUNICATION AND DEVELOPMENT

Of the many development plans which have been adopted by modernizing nations in the past decade, only a few have given investment in a mass communication system the emphasis it deserves. In India, for example, the First Five-Year Plan allocated two-tenths of one per cent of total outlays to development of radio broadcasting. Actual expenditures on the Plan as a whole turned out to be fifteen per cent less than anticipated; but those for broadcasting were forty-five per cent less than the initial very low total. Thus, in practice, outlays for broadcasting were somewhat over one-tenth of one per cent of the total. They were, in fact, 1.7 per cent as much as the outlay for education, and less than seven per cent of the outlay for post and telegraph. The Second Five-Year Plan gave the development of broadcasting no greater role. Again, it was allotted two-tenths of one per cent of the expenditures. Present thinking about the Third Plan will reduce this to less than one-tenth of one per cent.[10] In Guinea, the government, as a matter of policy, prevented the establishment of any newspapers. The Guinean government was not unaware of the role of communications— it developed an extremely efficient so-called "democratic centralist" political party whose cells, operating on the model of the Communist parties, provided an efficient channel for communication and command throughout the land. Nonetheless, the attempt to modernize a country without allowing the existence of a press is extraordinary.

In some countries, newsprint has been rationed to conserve foreign exchange; in others, television has been excluded for the same reason. Television exists in sixteen underdeveloped countries in the Eastern hemisphere—the largest number of sets in any one of them in 1958 was twenty thousand. Newsprint consumption per capita in South and East Asia is only 0.3 Kilograms—less than one per cent of the per capita consumption in the United States. Telephone systems work poorly in most countries of the world; telephone sets are often connected only after long delays.

In short, the development of a mass communication system has seldom been regarded as a priority measure toward modernization, comparable in significance to steel mills, roads, railroads, electric power, etc. Only literacy has been given comparable priority.

There are a few exceptions to these generalizations. The exceptions occur mostly in Communist countries, and concern largely a rather limited range of hortatory and didactic communications. Ever since Lenin's day, the Communists have been acutely cognizant of the advantages accruing from a mass media system. The circulation of newspapers in the Soviet Union grew from 2.7 million in 1913 to 9.4 million in 1928, to thirty-eight million in 1939, to forty-four million in 1954.[11] An *Agitprop* organization of two million members was built, functioning in interminable meetings. In China, too, investment in wall newspapers, political drama groups, and public-address systems has been given high priority. Of course, this effort was devoted to propaganda; but it was also for purposes of modernization and development. Much of the output was exhortation to hard work, production, punctuality, and efficiency; there was an overwhelming demand for achievement and surpassing of norms.

In non-Communist countries, also, when the mass media have been put at the service of development efforts, the operative hypothesis has usually been that they should be consciously educational. Entertainment, movies, commercial radio, etc., have often been regarded as detours from the immediate national task.[12]

This Puritanical view is probably a mistake, since it neglects two factors which we should discuss at some length. The first factor is the necessity of developing attention and motivation among a very wide mass audience before the process of self-sustaining growth can become effective in a democratic society. The second factor is the role which image formation —as distinct from skill-training and exhortation—plays in the process of modernization.

The third characteristic of modernity listed above was a willingness to plan and operate on a large stage. Wide markets and vast enterprises require the unifying and organizing facilities provided by mass media. Industrial produces must be able to advertise to a large proportion of a large population all at once. National development planners must advertise their programs to audiences of even greater comprehensiveness. Publicity serves to create broad markets. National daily dissemination of commodity price quotations makes market mobility possible. It undermines traditional dependent relations between rural producers and village traders. Universal prompt knowledge of sanitary countermeasures similarly helps a nation to cope effectively with human and agricultural epidemics. Village education plans or village sanitation plans—or any such plans that involve persuading, within a relatively short period, several thousand different village communities to want or do the same thing—must rely on more than bureaucratic channels. A number of people in each village must be reached repeatedly by the same or similar exhortations. This makes necessary the use of mass media of communication. Furthermore, common concerns with foreign developments and with national political activities, as covered in the newspapers, contribute to the growth of a national consciousness. Mass media, especially radio, movies, etc., tend to promote homogeneity in language, and a shared popular culture, in contradistinction to sectional and group ones. They help make possible nationwide parties and voluntary associations—instruments for action on a countrywide scale. It is extremely difficult to conceive of the possibility of organizing large masses of persons over large areas on a continuing basis without a system of mass communications. A mass media system which reaches all strata of the population is part of the social overhead capital for the creation of a nationwide arena of action.

However, not all mass media systems can fulfil this function. The problem of the mass media is to capture the interest, attention, and respect of a large audience. A mass medium provides, at best, a pale surrogate for the personal leadership which it can quantitatively, but never qualitatively, surpass. Studies made of even such a media-dominated society as the United States have shown that personal influence is a decisive ingredient in both political and purchase decisions of ordinary citizens.[13] There is a complex relationship between the media system and personal influence that Katz and Lazarsfeld have called "the two step flow of communication." A mass media system disseminates information which is picked up on a wide scale by individuals already interested in and attuned to particular items. These persons become "opinion leaders." Others may see or hear the same things; but they will not accept, or act positively on them until the desirability of doing so is confirmed by the opinion leader.

If this is true even for buying in as advertising-saturated a society as the United States, how much more true it is in traditional society with its strong personal bonds![14]

Paul Neurath's study of village radio programs in India provides a clear illustration. Programs that were heard by individual villagers had no discernible effect. When they were heard by organized listening groups which then discussed them, they produced dramatic changes toward adoption of new agricultural methods. The mass medium had to enter into

285

the decision process of an actively functioning group before it could have real effect. It did not act on individuals in an isolated anomic fashion.

A mass media system, if it is to be effective in promoting modernization, must be designed to provide organs of expression and mobilization for those groups which have significant functions in development and change. Modernization, as we have noted, implies mobility in function and in the influence derived therefrom. This is facilitated if access to media of mass expresion is readily available to persons who are organizing modernizing activities.

In free societies, the press has this characteristic. Where private enterprise flourishes, a commercial press based upon advertising evolves. It supplies a link among entrepreneurial organizations, and between them and their customers. On the other hand, in societies where nationalistic and other political movements are the chief instrumentalities of change, a party press is likely to evolve. Because, in most countries, the press must seek support where it can find support, it tends to connect itself rather well to the significant functional groups in society.

Radio, however, has more often been established as a subsidized monopoly. In many parts of the world, it has, therefore, tended to operate in a political vacuum. Frequently, a few intellectual officials in charge of broadcasting dictate that what they think is good goes out on the air. It is often expressed in an idiom that only educated persons in the capitol understand. Even agricultural information broadcasts are sometimes in the "good" form of the language. Furthermore, the national radio is generally kept from serving the special interests of selfish groups; both commercial advertising and politically partisan programs are often either severely restricted or prohibited. The radio is reserved for supposedly national purposes.

Operationally, the results of this policy are frequently diametrically opposite to the intended effects. The special interest groups who are denied access to the instrumentality of radio are the groups which, in any society, provide the meaningful reference function to individuals. Much as national leaders may regret it, something as broad as the nation is not a primary reference group. Opinion leaders are scattered among the citizen body; and, if the citizen body is genuinely to be mobilized, these natural leaders must be utilized. Hence if broadcasting rights are denied to special interest groups they are denied to the opinion-leading elements and thus, most significantly, to those few dynamic groups in any society which are the organizers of change.

Of course, if leadership of the process of change is considered to be a monopolistic prerogative of a single group—e.g., a ruling party, as in a totalitarian society—such exclusive control of mass media makes sense. But if initiative for innovation and development is to be encouraged

286

in a variety of sources in a society, then mass media facilities must be made available to the centers of initiative. Whether the decentralized sources of initiative be private investors, village councils, political parties, co-operatives, school systems, or all of these, mass media control and facilities should be at their command.

We reach a similar conclusion if we consider the problem from the point of view, not of the opinion leaders, but of the mass audience itself. While mass media alone seldom serve to provoke audience action, they do have vital contributory effects—some of which we have already discussed, and others of which we shall discuss below. These effects all depend upon the audience's caring about the media. The audience must enjoy the content of the medium, understand it, and find in it characters with whom they can identify and topics that bear on their own lives—in general, they must find it so interesting that they will continue reading and listening with absorption.

Commercial media can be depended upon to cater to audience interest —indeed, they often do so to the point of cultural debasement. Competition leads them to build as vast and absorbed a clientele as they can. It is the so-called "educational" media, or media of public "enligthenment," that may fail to educate or enlighten, because they do not bother to gain an audience.

Among the Western liberal and socialist ideas that have diffused to and been widely accepted in developing countries is a somewhat snobbish contempt for commercial media. Western ideas have been taken to other areas by intellectuals who tend to transmit the Western intellectuals' criticisms of those aspects of Western society that do not express their own values. These views are adopted by intellectuals in developing countries. At the UNESCO-sponsored meeting on Development of Information Media in South-East Asia,[15] for example, there was a bitter attack (led, not by left-wingers, but by a Pakistani delegate, supported by Thais and others) on commercial radio and television as degrading. A resolution was proposed against the intrusion of commercial broadcasting into the South-East Asian area. The proposal was not adopted only because it seemed to be an attack on those countries—particularly the United States —which use commercial broadcasting. The prevailing opinion—that commercial radio is an object of suspicion—was expressed in the resolution which was adopted, that commercial radio, if allowed at all, should serve the public welfare.

Would a positive communication program for developing countries contradict this opinion? What measure is likely to accelerate the modernization of a country so fast as the introduction of large-scale commercial advertising on press, radio, and television? The demand for soap, toothpaste, aspirin, or bicycles generated by advertising will not conform

287

to any officially ordained schedule of priorities. But the desire for new ways of life is generated rapidly indeed when profit-seeking enterprise does as much as it can to stimulate this desire. One of the cheapest ways to impel a country to strive for modernization would be to blanket it with subsidized cheap television sets and then to permit commercial telecasting. Such a program can be validly opposed in terms of other values. But if the goal is the transformation from traditional to modern society, is this program not as effective as anything one can do?

Our opinion that commercial mass media can be a powerful stimulus to modernization is vulnerable on two grounds. It can be opposed on the basis that the barrier to modernization is not insufficient popular awareness of the good things industrialization can bring; the obstacle is, rather, the lack of means for obtaining the good things. Further, it can be argued that, to acquire these means, developing societies need to increase savings —to curb, not stimulate, consumption. This viewpoint contends that villagers around the world are not traditional by choice. They want bicycles to ride and medicines to cure their ills. What they lack is not desire, but a Puritan ethic that urges systematic self-denial on behalf of productive thrift. Accordingly, a demonstration effect which comes from contact with industrial civilization is a barrier to development. Such contact generates unsettling, unrealistic demands for immediate consumption —demands which cannot be satisfied.

In the last analysis, this theory, however plausible, is invalid. It tries to make development planning operate more appositely and tranquilly by eliminating the dynamic motivational force that can set masses in motion. While there are relevant economic issues (although we must pass over them here), social-psychological considerations make it doubtful that such a sanitized program can ever work.

First, villagers and illiterates around the world do not clearly conceive of a modern industrial life as their desired good life. Of course, they want more food, better houses, easier transportation, and cures for their ailments. But these desires are old. To equate them to a desire for the goods of industrialization is to equate the magic of potions to the techniques of science and industry. To want cures for disease is not the same as wanting pasteurized milk, chlorinated water, sterile hospitals. A great deal must be learned about germs, asepsis, vitamins, and balanced diet before the desire for health becomes a set of desires for the practices and equipment of modern hygiene. The wish for more food is not yet a longing for canned goods. A desire for advancement is not yet a demand for mathematics courses in the schools. The shape of the good life needs to be delineated.

Then, too, even when desires for modernity exist, there may not be enough willingnes to pay the price. Ambivalent desires are not enough.

288

Villagers who want schools may still be reluctant to have their children abandon village ways. Villagers who desire more food may still be unwilling to violate taboos. Modern things must be wanted—but they must be wanted enough so that people will be willing to change their way of life to obtain them. And in addition, the desire for a better life must be strong enough to provide an incentive for systematic savings and investments.

Indeed, the notion that savings and investments will be higher in a society that does not have the driving inducement of burgeoning consumer wants is an odd one. Capitalist investment has always expanded and flourished where the market for the products seemed to be growing without limits. Socialist development plans too have had to hold the promise of more consumer goods as a goal, sometimes postponed, always in the forefront of consciousness.

The propaganda for modernity contained in commercial media such as the press, movies, and commercial radio is not just a plea that the audience buy a particular brand of soap. That plea may support the operation; but the medium, and the plea, would have no audience and no effect if the medium did not supply a far richer fare of enlightenment and excitement. The request for a particular purchase preference is only a small part of a plea in favor of a whole modernized way of life. Media which are committed to expanding the market for new products, new interests, and new enjoyments also portray new kinds of men in new kinds of environments. The entrepreneur, as Marx pointed out, is a revolutionist, although he may not intend to be. It is the mass media—traditionally the press, but now others too—which make what would otherwise be wistful dreams of a few modernizers into the dynamic aspirations of a whole people.

At this point, we should review our argument. Earlier, we pointed out that mass media seldom induce action except as adjuncts to face-to-face opinion leadership. Yet now we are stressing the power of the mass media. How can we resolve this apparent contradiction?

The development of a mass media system—as Katz and Lazarsfeld, among others, have shown—does not replace or destroy the age-old system of direct communication. The network of personal contact remains important—for, contrary to much in older sociological writings, modern society is not anomic, depersonalized, or free from primary-group controls. The development of a mass media system embeds traditional channels of contact within a new system of intercourse.

The new system, superimposed on the old, results in giving communication in a modern society four qualities not present, in comparable degree, in communications in traditional societies. (1) It keeps accurate and permanent records. Newspapers, films, books, magazines, and magnetic

289

tapes are available for reference and verification years later. (2) It is extraordinarily rapid—it can report major events, within hours after their occurrence, all over the world. (3) It extends the scope of men's empathic comprehension beyond the compass of their firsthand experience. Newspapers and radio enable people to conceive what it is like to be a ruler, or a foreigner, or a millionaire, or a movie-star. (4) It co-ordinates the groups which constitute the personal contact network. To each of the opinion leaders of the various groups in the society, it gives similar clues and it conveys to the members of these groups similar images. By establishing a common record of mutually understandable information simultaneously available over large areas, a mass media system welds the segments of the personal contact network into a whole, capable of integrated action.

The ways in which the mass media matrix operates on the interpersonal structure of society are varied. Katz and Lazarsfeld have shown that guidance by face-to-face leadership is usually necessary to induce social action. But action is only one consequence of communication—and, perhaps, the one which requires the maximum stimulus. Persons do many things mentally before they can be impelled to change their conduct in life.

In addition to inducing action, the mass media contribute to the imparting of skills, disseminating of facts, creating of images, and establishing of identifications. A short-sighted view of the role of communications in modernization might focus on persuasion to act and treat each of the other effects of communications as but intermediate steps to action. That is the view of the advertiser or policy-maker who is interested in his chances of obtaining a specific result from a set of persuasive messages he originates. But, in the long run, the character of a society (e.g., its modernity) may be more deeply influenced by the distribution of skills available in it, or by the goals in which it believes, than by any single action its members are persuaded to take.

Let us consider the effects of the existence of a mass media system on a society in terms of each of the consequences of communication that we have listed. We have already noted the limited role of such a system in impelling action—it implements co-ordinated action, on a national or even wider scale, by providing guidance to opinion leaders who are the instigators of action in face-to-face groups.[16]

We know less about the role of the media in imparting skills, but there seem to be some similar restrictions on their impact. Ordinarily, the personal direction of a teacher seems to be essential for the difficult process of learning a new art. Studies of television courses or agricultural extension courses indicate that the media do not impart much learning unless they are aided by discussion groups, teachers, etc. Child training manuals and cookbooks may ostensibly have greater success; but they, too, usually work only when they are reinforced by personal advice and confirmation from friends and relatives.

But in teaching facts and creating images, the mass media present a different picture. They reach beyond the leaders of face-to-face groups, and directly influence the people as a whole. The media create a picture of the world; and, in a modern society, we all learn this picture from what we read and hear. Study after study has shown that the media have small effects on attitudes and actions, but far greater effects on images. Hilda Himmelweit found, in England, that television (especially when there were several channels among which to choose) had little effect on the values, attitudes, and cultural accomplishments of children; but it had a profound impact in imparting images.[17] Western films, for instance, usually did not demoralize children or change their attitudes toward violence. They did, however, supply the children with an image of what a cowboy was like, or how a town of the American West looked and felt.

The images people have of the world around them are the realities in terms of which they act. Such images have an abiding significance far greater than that which the concept "image," with its ethereal connotations, suggests.

The process of modernization is, very largely, the process of acquiring new images. For example, there is the image of life as subject to deliberate change. The peasant who perceives the failure of his crops as resulting from the operation of a jealous purposeful fate against which man is impotent can acquire, instead, the image of events as subject to technical manipulation through knowledge and organization.

Another image is that of the possibility of economic growth. Malayan Communists, as described by Pye, had acquired a rudimentary image of modern life; they had not yet perceived the available good things as being essentially limitless because subject to creation. They saw a static consumption economy in which there were a certain number of good things —most of them possessed by the West. Communism was a way to redistribute the wealth by taking from those who had and giving to those who had not. Modernization means, among other things, the acquisition of an image of limitless progress and growth as the normal character of life.

A third image is of what it is to be cultured and educated. This has reached millions of young men and women, and has filled them with the aspiration to be literate, to know the names of the great writers and artists, to practice the marvels of science, to work as professionals and intellectuals.

The sectors of the world not yet modernized have an image of the modernized portion of the world. The "revolution of rising expectations" is the phrase most often used to describe the awareness, reaching all the world's peoples, that diseases can be cured, that people can drive automobiles, etc. The point is frequently made that knowledge of technological possibilities comes on the wings of the mass media and vastly outdistances people's willingness to do the things necessary to achieve these possibilities. Essentially, this is what we are trying to say here—in forming images, the media reach right down and change the people directly; action comes only by the more tortuous processes of social organization.

Identification with the objects whose images the mass media convey does not follow automatically. It is a somewhat more complex phenomenon than imagery itself. It clearly depends in part on interpersonal leadership, but not so much as action does. People do learn to identify with characters whom they have met only through the media. The little world of friends and relatives who are the subjects of village gossip is replaced by the world of film stars and party leaders encountered through the mass media. The media audience member puts himself into their places and begins to consider what he would do in their circumstances. He approves of some of the new members of his circle of experience and is against others. Psychically, he has become part of the great society before he is asked to to participate actively in it.

The psychic initiation of vast numbers of people is an essential step in the process of modernization. The modernizing actions which any developing society must call upon people to take are so many and so varied that they canot be prescribed by central authority alone. Punctuality, good work habits, investment, readiness to change to improved methods, confidence about manipulating machinery, moving to new residences, adopting personal hygiene, tolerating new liberties by one's wife and children, etc., are all acts which millions of individuals must perform in billions of specific circumstances. The experience must be psychically rehearsed many times before the acts can be performed. Personal leadership is often required as the final impetus to such actions; but it can operate only after the media have first made these actions familiar and understandable.

That is why the development of a modern communication system is an important part of a well-conceived development plan. Many things are needed. Among them are expanding the manufacture of newsprint, the building of movie theaters, the promotion of literacy. Radio and television are particularly important because they by-pass literacy. The government of Malaya has wisely waived tariffs on low-cost receivers. It would be good to see the production and wide diffusion of a four- or five-dollar long-lived battery radio or of a comparable, though somewhat more expensive, television set. Technologically, such sets are feasible if manufactured in large quantities.

Measures to raise the professional status of mass media personnel would also be helpful to modernization. One cannot expect the cast-offs of better-paid professions—frequently unemployed intellectuals, men without security—to provide a constructive, responsible national voice. The values, aspirations, and quality of media personnel will be translated into the character of a nation's development process.

Modernization would also be facilitated by a mass media system which consciously set out to raise the level and knowledge of the populace, by means of advertisements, exhortations, education, and purposeful effort.

The media have a great responsibility, and one which they cannot fulfill by preaching alone. The mass media system must be linked with the face-to-face organization of the population. Listening groups, clubs, village workers, co-operatives, etc., cannot be replaced by the mass media nor can they be substitutes for them. The two kinds of communication must parallel and reinforce each other.[18]

Let us close by noting one contribution which the *world*'s mass media can make to the democratic modernization of a country. As the limits of a people's awareness grow to include foreign countries, and especially the industrialized ones, the people become curious about the ways other nations view them. Indeed, universally, the foreign news which interests people most is foreign news about themselves. Each of us likes to read about others' attitudes toward ourselves.

Thus, the world view of a nation's performance becomes a significant sanction toward good and progressive performance. During the Blockade, the Berliners needed, for their morale, assurance that the world was watching them and understood the sacrifices that they were making in the cause of freedom.[19] So, too, when a new country holds its first election, and millions of people go to the polls peaceably and responsibly to choose their own government, the approving attention of the world can provide an important reinforcement to democracy. Every nation wants to be recognized as modern and advanced. Shame is an important factor in undermining many deep-rooted customs which run counter to modern values—e.g., customs in the treatment of women, in denying equality on the basis of social origin, in the use of magic, etc. Shame is felt also for the very fact of poverty or for lack of political order. Pride is felt in development plans, in new schools and hospitals, in steel mills (the temples of industry), and in the emergence of the arts of culture and progress. A very positive contribution can be made to modernization if foreign peoples turn their spotlights on the admirable and fordward-moving steps which a modernizing country takes, and if the mass media inform people how much and with what respect others are watching their successes.

1. Daniel Lerner, *The Passing of Traditional Society: Modernizing the Middle East* (Glencoe, Ill., 1958), pp. 60-62.

2. *Ibid.*, p. 71.

3. *Ibid.*, pp. 72-73.

4. Everett Hagen, *On a Theory of Social Change* (Homewood, Ill., 1962).

5. Center for International Studies, M.I.T., *Economic, Social and Political Change in Underdeveloped Countries and Its Implications for United States Foreign Policy* (Washington, 1960).

6. David C. McClelland *et al., The Achievement Motive* (New York, 1953); McClelland (ed.), *Studies in Motivation* (New York, 1955).

7. Lerner, *op. cit.*

8. Talcott Parsons, *The Social System* (Glencoe, Ill., 1951).

9. H. H. Gerth and C. W. Mills (eds.), *From Max Weber* (New York, 1946), pp. 196-240.

10. While any attempt at comparison would be very artificial, it is interesting to note that comparable United States percentages would be higher by a factor of two or three.

11. Figures for 1913-39, from Alex Inkeles, *Public Opinion in Soviet Russia* (Cambridge, Mass., 1951), p. 144; figures for 1954, from UNESCO, *Basic Facts and Figures* (Paris, 1956).

12. Only five underdevelop countries in the eastern hemisphere have commercial television; these five include the two where television has developed most rapidly. Of fourteen Latin American countries, only one has excluded commercial television. Television has developed much more rapidly there.

13. E. Katz and P. Lazarsfeld, *Personal Influence* (Glencoe, Ill., 1955).

14. For an illustration of the dependence of political choice on personal allegiance in an underdeveloped area, see Lucian Pye, *Guerilla Communism in Malaya* (Princeton, N.J., 1956).

15. Bangkok, January, 1960.

16. This is true of Communist as well as of democratic development programs. Clamorous exhortations for achievement have had only limited direct effect. People gradually become cynical about and immune to repeated appeals. But

morale and discipline are maintained by the party structure, vocal agitators, and myriad organizations, whose leaders are guided by the daily and periodical press. One of the leading magazines in Soviet Russia, e.g., is *Agitators' Guide-book*, which is addressed to the vocal agitators.

17. H. Mimmelweit, A. Oppenheim, P. Vince, *et al., Television and the Child* (London, 1958).

18. For further development of this point, see this author's "Mass Media and Their Interpersonal Social Function in the Process of Modernization" in Lucian Pye, ed., *Communications and Political Development* (Princetown, N.J., 1963).

19. W. Phillips Davison, *The Berlin Blockade* (Princeton, N.J., 1958).

PART VII

Summary of Substantive Findings

CHAPTER 15

Industrialization and Social Change

WILBERT E. MOORE
Princeton University

INTRODUCTION

Two decades ago, there was little scholarly interest in the social transformation going on in the economically underdeveloped or newly developing areas. Some anthropologists, it is true, were turning their attention from the reconstruction of pristine tribal systems to the observation of such systems under the various kinds of external impact. A very few economists and sociologists, and even fewer political scientists, exhibited an interest in economic development and its non-economic concomitants.

No doubt a principal source of the interest in "underdeveloped areas" has been practical. Responsible governing officials in these areas have sought rapid economic transformation and have engaged in divers official measures to achieve it. These measures have included obtaining "technical assistance" of several kinds and forms, both through the United Nations and its associated specialized agencies, and through national programs of assistance—e.g., those of the metropolitan governments with respect to colonial or associated territories, and those of the "Point Four" and successive agencies of the United States government. For these programs, first economists, and then other social scientists, have been called upon to study and advise.

Some developments within the social sciences coincided with these practical concerns, and it would be unduly cynical to link those developments entirely to outside forces. With slow and faltering steps, the several social scientific fields have been moving from an exclusively "static," cross-sectional or equilibrium approach to a growing interest in transformations in social systems through time. Again, economists appear to have taken the lead, but other disciplines have also shown renewed interest in historical processes and in conceptions of systems that considered tensions and inherent sources of change. For this theoretical evolution, a

299

major empirical facet of the modern world offered ample materials for study—the rapid transformation of societies under the impact of induced economic change.

In the United States, by 1950, there was a sufficient accumulation of scholarly interest in economic development to warrant the establishment of the Committee on Economic Growth of the (American) Social Science Research Council, with an interdisciplinary membership. The conferences and other projects sponsored by that Committee have been concerned both with the continuing dynamics of industrialized societies and with the processes of change in areas just beginning modernization. The comparison of historical and contemporary industrialization is, indeed, a recurrent theme in the study of economic development—although scholarly specialization occasionally gives the impression that the subjects are quite unrelated.

The study of economic development has a number of advantages: it is theoretically challenging; it is potentially practical; it offers abundant material for empirical study in both familiar and exotic places; and it virtually requires interdisciplinary co-operation.

All these virtues have been exemplified in UNESCO's consistent interest in the subject. This interest has been manifested in special issues of the *International Social Science Bulletin*,[1] in bibliographical essays in several numbers of *Current Sociology*,[2] in research publications and international conferences,[3] and in the support UNESCO has given to regional research centers in the social sciences established to investigate this subject.

This report is based in part on a series of regional surveys sponsored, directly or indirectly, by UNESCO.[4] This chapter summarizes the principal results that have emerged from the many relevant studies made by scholars around the world. If it is to be properly interpreted, this summary must be prefaced by several comments.

1) The survey is limited primarily to studies of the newly developing areas. The relation of these results to the contemporary and historical experience of the most industrialized countries is not a primary task of this summary, although such comparisons are noted at various points. In some instances, however, as in the reports on Japan, parts of Western Europe, Poland, the Soviet Union, and Canada, the data concern countries recently and incompletely industrialized.

2) Because of language difficulties and sheer accessibility of materials, regional reports have been prepared for the areas of the world where they have been published as well as for the areas of empirical concern. There are, thus, some minor duplications in the original summaries. On the other hand, the intensity of the respective reviews prepared for different regions is quite unequal. Because of the disposition of financial and scholarly resources, a few countries have accounted for a majority of the

300

studies undertaken outside their own boundaries, in less developed areas. The exceptional volume and coverage in area and subject matter of the North American literature preclude making repeated references to that survey. Summary statements not credited to other regions may be assumed to derive from the North American materials.[5]

3) The volume of material to be reviewed presented problems in this report, and these problems were met by a series of compromises. Among the several regional reports our major attention was devoted to the most recent literature. Where summaries of particular topics already existed, these were treated as primary rather than as secondary sources—an expedient that, unfortunately, necessitated the exclusion of many extremely valuable studies. This summary is almost entirely undocumented, except for reference to the regional surveys. It can only be hoped that the scholar interested in pursuing various topics in greater depth will take the necessary steps of using the "intervening" sources—the individual regional summaries and their principal bibliographical sources—as a guide to the original studies.

4) We are chiefly concerned here with the social implications of changes in productive technology, summarized as "industrialization." This is a broader definition of "industrialization" than is implied in the ordinary use of the term, as it includes "technification" of agriculture and even of services, in addition to fabrication as such. On the other hand, "productive technology" is not intended to incorporate various social techniques, such as administrative organization, "human relations," or advertising and public relations. Where these social techniques have been related to productive technology, they are treated as implications under the proper rubric provided in the outline. Although somewhat arbitrary, this procedure seems preferable to an unduly complex and heterogeneous concept of productive technology.

5) The phrase "social implications of industrialization" does not imply any rigid economic or technological determinism. The problem is posed in this way because changes in productive technology are being fostered in most of the underdeveloped countries, and because some limits and focus are important to facilitate analysis. This denies neither the possible reciprocal influence between cause and effect, nor the probable connections among the different social implications or effects. Research done with sufficient temporal perspective might have results, for example, that establish the functional interdependence between productive technology as such and the administrative technology of job specification. It might thus be possible to demonstrate how a given form of productive technology is followed by increased standardization and routinization of manual tasks, giving rise to new substitution of mechanical for muscular action. Similarly, it may be possible to show that a new demand for factory

workers not only leads to rural-urban migration, but also that this migration has a direct effect on family structure and on fertility rates. Or again, it may be possible to establish the way in which new manufactured products affect both the level of consumption and also the style of life of the family—as when the radio or television encourages members of the family to remain together for their recreation.

6) The importance of avoiding technological determinism is emphasized by the existence of impediments and resistances to the impact of industrialization. These are as truly implications of the process of socioeconomic transformation as are the more clearly dependent variables.

7) Still other restrictions and limitations will occur to the student of economic development. Industrialization or changes in productive technology are not necessarily simple, homogeneous processes. A small-scale, labor-intensive, decentralized plant that fabricates consumer goods for a strictly local market may not have the same social implications as a large-scale, capital-intensive, urban plant that produces machine tools for the whole country and, even, possibly for export. Although no absolute rule will exactly answer all doubts, a general principle has guided the survey of social implications: Generalize whenever scientifically possible; particularize whenever necessary. In other words, the *particular* variety of industrialization to which social implications are traced may or may not make a difference. The *relevance* of variety should be neither exaggerated nor overlooked.

8) The same considerations apply to a type of economic regime, including degree of public and private direction and initiative, particular property institutions, etc. It may not be possible in fact to generalize about implications without stipulating the economic regime as a condition; but both social science and the transferability of research results to other places will benefit if differences in economic regime are treated as questionable rather than automatic variables. This is a question of fact, not of ideological doctrine. For example, one summay (VIII) * states categorically: "In socialist society technology contributes to the reduction of the work day, whereas in capitalist society its use prolongs it [the work day]." As this is contrary to all evidence, it must be discounted as a limitation on generalization. The difference between social science and irrational ideology consists in the predilection of science for facts.

9) The more heterogeneous the actual details of social phenomena are, the more "abstract" will be any generalization comparing them. That is, more information is lost in the process of generalization; and more information must be added to progress from the general to the particular—the particular that often concerns not only the policy-maker, but also the

* Hereafter, all regional summaries will be designated in the text by the numbers given them in note 4.

careful observer of the peculiar intricacies of social situations. At numerous points in the following pages, the relevance of variable social conditions will be noted, as restricting the richness of the highest level of generalization or, perhaps, precluding that level completely.

10) A different but related question concerns the interpretation of causal sequences where rapid economic development forms part of a general revolution in political and social structure (I). Centralized economic and social planning attempts to foresee, implement, or control the various social implications of industrialization. This situation presents difficulties in distinguishing the social consequences of economic transformation per se from the general revolutionary changes that surround the change in economic structure. A paradox is evident here. Many social changes are deliberate rather than unplanned and often unintended consequences. On the other hand, the plans themselves obviously rest upon a kind of theory of necessary and interdependent alterations in social systems—i.e., the explicit application of general principles to particular goals and situations. Thus social theory becomes the basis for social action; but, in the process, real differences in both time and social mechanism are introduced.

Like the surveys upon which it is based, this report is organized under four major topical headings, each of which has several subdivisions. The four major headings are "Productive Organization," "Economic Structure and Institutions," "Demographic and Ecological Structure," and "Characteristic Aspects of Social Structure."

Functional interrelations make any attempt at a serial list of social implications somewhat arbitrary. However, we adopted the plan to aid in making research results comparable. Apparent linkages and concurrent effects have been noted. Differences in views about linkages and sequences provide challenges to theory, raise questions concerning the transferability of research results from one society to another, and help to illuminate critical research needs.

There is a kind of rationale both for the order of the topics and for the topics themselves. Starting from changes in the productive system, the discussion moves through economic, demographic, and ecological changes to transformations in the wider reaches of societies and cultures. Some social characteristics are either omitted, because of their hypothetically minimal linkage with economic transformation, or treated in connection with other topics. The resulting organization is not proposed as the only correct one, but as one possibly sensible approach to the genuine complexity of the real world.

PRODUCTIVE ORGANIZATION

The first, or at least the most apparent, alteration of social systems that accompanies industrialization is in the productive organization itself. If industrialization is viewed narrowly as the multiplication of human effort through the use of inanimate sources of power for production of goods, the resulting changes in human activities become implications or consequences.

In presenting the various aspects of these changes, we will note first the implications for a "typological" situation of factory or farm mechanization. Then the significance of various ranges of variation will be recorded, since wide variations actually do exist both cross-sectionally and through time or "stage" of industrial development.

Work Relationships

The mechanization of non-agricultural production (including some forms of food-processing) involves a spatial juxtaposition of workers and fixed machines for daily or continuous operation. This bare, ecological fact has a number of consequences that contrast sharply to those of other productive systems. If the production worker is the point of reference, the consequences may be identified under the general rubrics of relations to machines, to fellow-workers, and to supervision or management.

The outstanding characteristic of factory work is the extent to which the timing and sequence of activities are regulated by the machine. Of course, the anthropomorphic view of the machine that is a feature of much of the critical literature on industrialism is to be avoided. The pace and rhythm of work are determined partly by machine designers, partly by decisions of management, partly by the interaction of machine characteristics and maintenance work. Yet, for the worker, the proximate impulse does come from the machine. To a point, increased mechanization increases the super-ordination of the machine by reducing the decisional or optional procedures available to the worker, and especially by shortening the repetitive cycle in both time and distinct motions. Beyond that point, in automation the worker regains his mastery. (This is strongly emphasized in the report on the Soviet Union [VIII].)

In a factory producing a given type of product, and of specific size and state of mechanization, different employees have quite different relations to machines. Typically, the least skilled workers (for example, sweepers) are not so closely regulated by the machine as are those directly involved with production. The assembly-line worker is more precisely paced by the machine than are materials handlers, although the latter have rather narrow margins of timing. Machine designers, installers, and maintenance men have a more super-ordinate relation to the machine—as, obviously, do supervisors, executives, salesmen, or accountants.

Short-cycle repetition, as such, differentiates factory work from most, but not all, non-industrial work. Some kinds of agricultural work, and certain types of "gang labor" in road-building and other construction, also involve monotonous routine. The crucial difference is that factory work involves machine-pacing.

A very considerable proportion of the relations among workers are, in the first instance, technologically determined. That is, in a particular technical organization, various kinds of reciprocal and sequential services constitute the workers' required relations. In extreme cases, these relations may require no oral communication at all after each worker has been informed of his duties by a supervisor. Repeated observation demonstrates, however, that continuous, face-to-face relations among limited numbers of workers produce the necessary and almost sufficient conditions for additional interaction. This informal organization may simply supplement and amplify the minimal required interaction; but it is likely to develop codes of conduct somewhat at variance with official expectations.

Where the technical organization of production has resulted in over-specialization, work teams or "brigades" that exchange jobs may appear —with or without managerial approval (VIII, XII). Their appearance assumes a much greater versatility than in fact prevails among many workers with scant industrial experience.

If we broaden somewhat the view of the industrial work force, we can perceive the norms governing relations among workers as constituting a set of closely related ideal prescriptions. The required work relations are supposed to be: (a) functionally specific, i.e., confined to the particular duties; (b) impersonal, i.e., relating to the jobs or functions and not to the persons performing them; and (c) affectively neutral, i.e., demanding neither personal identification nor loyalty. Positions are presumably filled on the basis of merit or competence, and workers may appropriately exhibit deference or accord prestige to those more highly placed than themselves, and esteem superior, as opposed to inferior performance, for any position. Except as modified by the norms of legitimate authority (as we shall discuss presently), the workers' relations with employers are appropriately contractual, and sharply delimited by the terms of the contract.

This normative complex stands in fairly sharp contrast to most of the canons of conduct accepted in non-industrial societies. Indeed, it is in contradistinction to some necessary institutional characteristics of any society. Accordingly, violations of these norms are not remarkable as such—both because other principles of conduct intrude, and because the work environment itself provides the potential conditions for modification (as noted with reference to informal organization).

The interesting questions about work relations, particularly in newly developing areas, concern the occasions for compromise with traditional canons of conduct; the effect of these on efficiency, the extent to which

305

such compromises impede full social transformation; and the alternative possibilities for less austere (and, perhaps, more realistic) normative presumptions.

In Japan (III), for example, after decades of industrial expansion, labor recruitment and employment relations are still highly particularistic, especially in the numerous small plants. Wages often reflect seniority only, rather than task or skill.

In so far as workers are recruited on universalistic criteria—i.e., without reference to any previous relationships with each other or with managers—the novel norms may be approximately fulfilled. Paradoxically, high inter-employer mobility increases the probability of impersonal relations. Yet such mobility, as in Africa and India (VI, IXA), is more likely simply to represent an uncommitted and transitory labor force. Situations where the norms of merit recruitment and highly impersonal relationships prevail possibly provide the first of many examples of the typological extreme of the industrial system that occurs early, rather than late, in the sequence of socio-economic transformation. Later modifications do not re-create the pre-industrial society; they do conduce to the development of "relaxed" normative codes within the industrial sphere itself. Where the acceptance of the codes can be assumed, their enforcement may be less severe.

The worker is, in addition to his relations to the machine and to fellow-workers, related to the productive organization in other ways. He has a financial relation, through the payment of his wage or salary. He is likely to be the object of various staff services. Above all, he is subject to a structure of authority. Whether the "ultimate" claim to legitimacy of authority rests on proprietary, delegated political, or even elective political, grounds, specialized activities are co-ordinated and organizational decisions are made by supervisors and managers. This authority is nominally bound by the same restrictions as other interpersonal relations; but it still has a different quality by virtue of its being explicitly graded or hierarchical.

Where workers are also nominally co-owners, as in socialist economies, the principal distinction in actual work relations is in the greater responsibility of workers, through unions or councils, to share in the determination of work standards (I, VIII).

Since social inequality is universal, the mere fact of inequality or even of direct authority is not the critical problem in social transformation. The problem is that the basis of authority is novel and, ironically, that it is highly restricted. The worker who tries to transfer allegiance from a traditional leader to a plant foreman or superintendent is likely to find that his allegiance is rebuffed in all ways except those relevant to work (VI). Since new employment often means a radical change in way of life

306

both outside and at the work place, the worker may seek a wider and more passive dependency on the employer than that to which the latter is prepared to respond (IV).

Deviations from strictly delimited authority and compromises with the non-industrial environment are numerous. The outstanding ones involve the special problems posed by foreign managers who use native intermediaries as supervisors. The supervisors may have few talents except being bilingual (VI). They may "abuse" their positions by being, simultaneously, recruiters for the employers, employment agents for workers seeking jobs, and actual supervisors and disciplinarians. The ensuing situations invite the promotion of high labor turnover to enrich the foreman.

When the many "cultural" differences between managers and workers are solidified into a policy of systematically excluding indigenous workers from higher positions—an extreme example is the "color bar"—the legitimacy of the system of authority rests in part on technically irrelevant grounds. It is extremely doubtful that such arrangements can endure, chiefly because the equity of the system cannot be sufficiently institutionalized to secure the willing compliance of those barred from promotion and managerial responsibility (VI).

The different reactions to foreign or racially exclusive management provide a series of lessons in the ways that reactions to grievances need not inevitably lead to "ideal" solutions. Certain countries that have long been politically independent, especially in Latin America, have legislatively imposed quotas of native personnel in management. These quotas prevent one kind of discrimination and impose another if qualified native managers are not, in fact, available. Some of the newly independent countries of Asia and Africa have reacted to previous grievances against the metropolitan power and its citizens or racial colleagues by systematically withholding positions of responsibility from them. Again, the policy appears to be emotionally rather than technically founded. Where the color bar still prevails, as it does in some places in Africa, its upholders support political policies and legislation to make inequality official—thus revealing that the supposed "natural" inequality is actually spurious. If colored workers were, indeed, biologically incapable of learning and performing skilled trades, there would be no need to make rules prohibiting them to do so. The exclusion of natives from various responsible positions tends to keep the rates for unskilled labor low. However, it is likely to be rather costly on balance, because it results in the inflation of wages and salaries of "superior" workers who are exempted from the need to maintain their superiority against competition.

The discussion of work and authority relationships has revealed a number of ways that typological and ideal patterns are modified in practice. There remains the task of specifying some of the principal modes of variation in the industrial system itself as they are relevant to the organization of work. These may be identified as the type of production, the degree of mechanization, the size or scale of units, and the stage in the industrialization sequense. These four sources of variation are interrelated.

The picture of the machine-paced worker best fits the production either of relatively simple and uniform consumer goods (e.g., textiles, clothing, electric lights) or of more complex products with standardized parts and sequential assembly (bicycles and automobiles, watches and weapons). Chemical and metallurgical production is usually either a "batch process," with consequent lengthening of the work cycle, or "continuous flow," with low quantitative labor requirements but with the workers exercising high levels of skills in the manipulation of complex instrument panels, or high levels of responsibility in checking for deviance and failure. Mechanized agriculture chiefly involves mobile machines, as do most forms of mechanized transportation (excluding conveyors and similar methods of handling materials), and clearly involves more machine "mastery" or direction than it does "servitude" on the part of the operator.

In part, then, variations in type of production are variations in appropriate technology. But they are not synonymous. The economics of technical innovation are such that the same or similar products may be produced simultaneously in the same country by techniques invented or introduced as much as fifty years apart. Technical innovation may be related to new products or to standardization and quality control; but a principal incentive for, or at least consequence of, technical innovation has been the substitution of capital for labor, or of machines for men. The degree of mechanization is, accordingly, a major variable to consider in appraising the immediate consequences of industrialization for work organization. To the point of true automation, increased mechanization is likely to be related to short-cycle repetition, highly fractional interaction among workers, and impersonal, distant supervision, because very few matters must be referred to superiors for decision. Automation both substitutes machines for the already-mechanized worker, and radically changes the character of skill levels and work relationships. (It is interesting to note that mechanization of agriculture may greatly reduce the drudgery of farm work, often without the intervening step of extreme routinization; although other processes, such as vegetable-harvesting, may require routine labor comparable to that of the worker or the assembly line.)

Since the course of technological innovation in the most advanced countries has generally been labor-saving, it follows that most of the underdeveloped areas, which are rich in labor and poor in capital, should, on grounds of economic "rationality," import old-fashioned technology. For political and other ideological reasons, they often do not do so. This

308

compression of history thus makes it possible—indeed, necessary—to consider the entire spectrum of technological intensity in appraising the social implications of industrialization in newly developing areas.

The types of work relationships that follow from industrialization vary, not only with the type and degree of technological innovation, but with the closely related variable of size. Size as measured by capital, units of product, or labor force is not the same thing, since these are independently variable. But short of the push-button factory, these (and other) measures have a crude correlation.

The ideal norms of workers' relations to machines, to other workers, and to management are more likely to be approximated in large-scale than in small-scale production. This is partly because of the obvious difficulty of maintaining personal relations with vast numbers of functionally heterogeneous co-workers, and the usual association of impersonal bureaucracy and large scale. It is also because size is rather precisely correlated with specialization of tasks. In a large-scale productive organization, specialization usually greatly exceeds any division of labor known in the non-industrial economy. (We shall discuss the implications for the understanding and evaluation of occupational roles in the community and society in connection with "Social Stratification" later in this essay.) This fact has implications for work relations, since it supports a narrow specification of work-relevant interaction.

For this and other reasons, advocates of geographically decentralized, small-scale production units have argued that the transition to an industrial mode of production would be facilitated by avoiding the historic errors (or at least the example) of the West. Japan is commonly cited as a case in point. However, the exploitation of labor, common in early stages of industrialization, is ordinarily exaggerated rather than reduced in such enterprises (III). We may rephrase this generalization by stating that the intrinsic economic disadvantages of small-scale enterprises are largely borne by workers who not only lack the latitude offered by urban labor markets, but are also entrapped by inappropriate and unrequited loyalties to family-type enterprises.

The picture of the industrial worker is not the portrait of the whole man—this can be painted, if at all, only after tracing through his other social involvements and incorporating them. Available data do not demonstrate that the attempt to engage more of the personality in the productive organization itself helps anyone—and perhaps it helps the object of sympathy least of all.

Organization of Productive Units
The use of industrial technology imposes minimum, but not exact, requirements on the organization of productive units. Some have been

noted in our discussion of work relations. Here, we are concerned with questions of administration.

Historically, the principles and practices of administrative organizations were evolved chiefly for governmental agencies, both civil and military. They can be applied to industrial organizations because of the common problem of large-scale co-ordination of highly specialized tasks. Thus, aside from such technical innovations as the many business machines and modes of rapid telecommunications, the links between standard industrial organization and industrial technology are indirect, operating chiefly through the intervening variable of size.

The appropriate size of productive units is a function of various technological and economic considerations—e.g., size of markets, transportation costs and facilities, the technological divisibility or indivisibility of capital installations—as well as of social considerations like the availability of competent administrators and the motivational problems of highly formal procedures.

Presupposing that industrial development involves at least some large-scale productive units, we may briefly note some of their leading attributes.

The geometric representation of the hierarchy of authority in administrative organization as a pyramid has a simple arithmetic base. Given a limited span of control (i.e., number of direct subordinates) by any manager, the height of the structure (i.e., the number of echelons of authority) is directly related to its width or volume (i.e., the total personnel). The span of control is a function of the degree of specialization of tasks and of the closeness of supervision or co-ordination demanded. Thus, an organization comprising relatively homogeneous units may be less high than one with great diversity of tasks. Increasing specialization requires either that administration increase or that greater latitude be allowed to the subordinates in making operating decisions. However the co-ordinators are selected, and whatever the ultimate source of legitimacy of their authority, there is apparently no other realistic alternative. (Administrative co-ordination could be abolished only if the goals and subgoals of the organization were perfectly established and static, perfectly understood and translated into tasks perfectly performed—i.e., a system requiring neither decision nor discipline.)

Administrative decisions are regulated by the norm of rationality, even if other criteria of choice are involved. This means that information appropriate to decisions will be sought. Complex organizations that operate in a complex and variable environment thus, as a rule, develop various staff functions for the expert supply of information. These staff officers perforce impair the "omniscience" of executives; this is one reason that some form of line-staff tension is an endemic characteristic of administrative structures.

310

Another leading and commonly noted characteristic of large-scale organizations is the complex communication network that necessarily exists. Although pious preachings about "good communications" often imply that "everyone should get the word," this is patent nonsense. If all communications reached all parties, the result would simply be noise. Policies must be elaborated into prescriptions for action appropriate to particular units. Information must be digested and generalized before it is manageable for use in assessment and decision. Relay points and translators must be established throughout the organization. Not only the language, but also the habits of thought and the approaches to problems, differ by occupation and organizational position.

Of course, the standard communication problems are greatly aggravated when even the basic language is not common, and there are radical differences both in level and in type of education.

Perhaps the most common complaint about bureaucracies is directed against their internal regulatory structure. Although a ritualistic and mindless following of rules, regardless of ends or consequences, is a pervasive pathology in administrative structures, the elaborate regulations are essential for organizational operation. Like all norms, bureaucratic rules insure predictability of social behavior. Their special importance in complex organizations arises from the combination of heterogeneous personnel and of the fine specialization of duties. Rules permit co-operation between strangers or even potential enemies. The rules allocate duties to their appropriate places and persons; following them enables one to avoid the twin dangers of under-performance and over-performance. Making the rules independent of particular persons insures organizational continuity, despite the normal expectation of turnover in positions and offices. Finally, the rules establish the basis of discipline—the powers and limits of constituted authority.

The "bureaucratization of the labor force" that is characteristic of all industrialized societies provides transitional problems in developing areas. And it is not simply the uneducated factory recruit, without industrial traditions, for whom this transition is troublesome. Family and class favoritism, personal rather than organizational loyalties, and whimsical administration, are sufficiently common among the elite groups from whom industrial managers are usually drawn to make the establishment of an efficient administration a halting process. This is not just a problem of the prevalence of sin. There are genuine differences in the appropriate values; and these instrumental values (i.e., those connected, not with economic development, but with the procedure for getting there) may be among the most difficult to establish.

Much of the industrialization of Japan (III) has taken place in small shops, whose work forces largely consisted of relatives of the owner. In

Africa (VI), native workers are not expected to become full-fledged members of the modern productive organization, since it is assumed that they will retain tribal affiliations and partial dependence on the subsistence economy. In Singapore (IXB), rationalization of production is impeded by the small scale of units and by a host of countervailing conditions. In India (IXA), the long-standing shortage of capital and managerial personnel has led to the establishment of "managing agencies," some of which administer highly diversified business interests with doubtful efficiency but undoubted concentration of economic power. New administrative forms are now being fostered. For some societies that have no significant familiarity even with a monetary market system (e.g., the islands of Oceania [VIIB]), co-operatives have been suggested as a kind of transitional economic form.

The effect of industry on the non-industrial sectors of the economy is interesting. Unless elaborate international trade is involved, an industrial population requires an agricultural surplus, and thus a previous or concomitant reorganization of agriculture. But continued industrialization tends to lead to further technification of agriculture, often with considerably higher productivity per worker. The rapid attainment of these results has been a principal aim of collectivization of agriculture in the Soviet Union and other Eastern European countries, and of the "popular communes" in China (V), which have also linked small-scale and part-time manufacturing to agricultural reorganization. In much of central and southern Africa (VI), an essentially subsistence agriculture persists in tribal areas, supplemented by the money incomes from migratory male workers. If substantial underemployment is prevalant, reorganization of tasks on the reserves may maintain previous levels of production. This reorganization is said to be easiest in patrilineal groups. It is, however, doubtful that a system that relies on migratory labor to bridge quite disparate economic systems will be stable in the long run (XII).

The implementation of modern industrial administration does not resolve all organizational problems. Any administrative organization offers ample opportunities for various pathologies, such as the ritualism already noted, or corruption in the form of substitution of personal for organizational goals. Minimal, rather than optimal, performance is common. Because objectives are often hazy and conflicting rather than clear and ordered, and because appropriate procedures are less than perfectly validated, internal conflicts about such matters as policies, budgets, and jurisdictions are "normal," in both the statistical and the theoretical sense.

We have indicated that size or scale is a major variable affecting the form of industrial organization, or, at least, its approximation to the pure bureaucratic type. But, even for large-scale organization, it appears doubtful that there actually is one invariably correct mode of management.

Three conditioning variables seem especially relevant: the state of technology, the state of the labor force, and the state of environing interests and controls.

The state of technology, which varies according to industry and to economic considerations, has obvious implications for the type of production personnel needed; consequently, it is relevant to the type of supervision needed. Some actual technological innovation—particularly in new, alternative processes of production—may occur in developing areas. Generally, however, "research and development"—which accounts for substantial budgets and personnel in advanced industrial countries— has minimum importance, in new nations, in industrial organizations. Borrowed technology, with minor adaptations, is common. Though the role of the technologists is ostensibly lesser, it is in fact crucial, and their influence within new enterprises usually actually greater than it is in industrialized countries.

Certain recent and contemporary theories of administration have strongly advocated administrative decentralization, the flattening of the structure of authority. They argue that the morale of subordinates will thereby be improved, and that it will increase efficiency if decisions are made where problems arise. One principal consequence would be that the managerial role would be purely co-ordinative, and the co-ordinator would be less expert (and possibly less valuable) than his subordinates, each at his own specialized functions. Surely, however, such an administrative theory is relative to the state of the labor force actually employed or available for employment. It assumes that a highly centralized and authoritarian administration does not fully utilize the skills of subordinates. Although participation in decisions seems to be a positive inducement to employee commitment and performance, it is not likely to be either efficient or motivationally effective if the decisions (and concomitant responsibilities) are beyond the subordinate's capacities.

The appropriate principles of administration thus appear to be conditioned by the general and specialized education of employees, their acceptance of the general value and legitimacy of their mode of employment, and the financial (and other) incentives offered. Where anti-native personnel policies have been in effect, and where no attempt has been made to modify and utilize pre-existing craft or managerial skills, talents are clearly wasted or not well utilized; but the major personnel problem in developing areas is the shortage of appropriate skills. This means not only that the most "modern" theories of administration may not be appropriate; it also indicates that considerable managerial effort must be devoted to actual education rather than to giving orders or enforcing discipline—to say nothing of chairing strategy meetings of subordinates.

Finally, the relevance of differences in environmental interests and controls must be noted. The sharpest differences are along the range from strictly free enterprise, through various modes and degrees of centralized planning, to the socialistic control of productive processes. The differences should not be exaggerated, of course. The plant manager in a large multi-product corporation may occupy a position not radically different from that of the manager of a plant in a socialist state. Moreover, the degrees and channels of influence may differ more than the kinds of influence do. The productive unit must maintain relations with suppliers of materials and components, with sources of capital, with customers or at least channels of distribution, and with administrative agencies of government. Statements to the effect that, in the Soviet Union, "The administration is controlled by workers' collectives," or that "All disputes that take place between workers and the administration are resolved in favor of the workers" (VIII) are simply not persuasive.

Maintaining appropriate relations with different significant elements in the environment is likely to require specialized staff services at some point in the structure. A relatively wide margin of managerial autonomy will not necessarily decrease the importance of these functions, since both the boundaries and the character of the interests impinging from beyond them may be uncertain and troublesome. Most of these functions are not economically measurable, nor are the functionaries economically accountable. As a result, there is no clear evidence indicating either the "proper" kind of organization or the factors that do, in fact, account for observable variations.

Motivation and "Enterprise"
Implicit in the requirement of new work relations and forms of productive organization is the necessity of subjective attitudes and objective incentives favorable to novel jobs and conditions of employment. More empirical research and theoretical work have probably been done on this aspect of industrialization than on any other. The results, however, yield more in identifying pressures, barriers, and incentives regarding labor recruitment than they do in more complex propositions where many forces operate concurrently and even discordantly.

The pressures for industrial employments, in the widest sense, include: (*a*) the decline of alternative economic opportunities (deteriorating man-land ratios in agriculture, displacement of handicrafts by cheap manufactured goods, and the impairment of trade and similar employments); (*b*) the incidence of political pressures (direct coercion, and indirect coercion through monetary taxation); and (*c*) the escape from social pressures (evasion of religious and magical controls, of familial and other obligations, of punishments for infraction of codes in the traditional village).

314

There are, however, barriers which must be overcome by either negative or positive incentives. Among the barriers are: (*a*) ignorance—the lack of knowledge of alternatives—which has sharply decreased, in recent years, in most areas of the world; (*b*) the "discontinuity" in social systems (loss of traditional forms that give security, lack of appreciation of the new status system, and various qualitative differences in occupation and source of income); and (*c*) opposition to mechanization (including loss of "freedom" as an independent producer, loss of socially recognized skills, and failure to accept machine-pacing and new work rhythms).

Some other barriers to labor recruitment, or full commitment, have been observed. One interesting discontinuity is represented by the African worker's failure to comprehend an "employment contract" within his traditional framework of services for a patron (VI). In many areas, and particularly in Africa, India, and Japan (III, VI, IXA), the industrial worker "keeps one foot" in his village. He may then become a "target worker," with a fixed and definite demand for money. Higher wages may then cause him simply to work less time. Similarly, a high labor turnover (I, VI) may be a manifestation either of a high sensitivity to minute differences in wages or working conditions, or, more probably, of a relatively low involvement in the whole industrial labor market.

The barriers and antipathies between competing social systems may be extremely strong. L. A. Costa Pinto (X) refers to the "structural marginality" that accompanies partial modernization (see also VIIB). The worker's maintenance of some traditional elements in the pattern of life while he participates in a novel work environment depends upon the relative insulation or "role segmentation" possible (II, VI). Disenchantment with new forms of social organization can lead to withdrawal, hostility, or a conservative reaction on the part of the non-industrial population (VIIA). At times, this assumes distinctly religious forms (as will be discussed in a subsequent section).

Nonetheless, a crude shortage of labor is rare. Labor surpluses are common, as demonstrated by demographic calculations and also by the workers seeking employment. Unfortunately, few workers have usable skills and their presence in the industrial labor market is more often reluctant than enthusiastic.

The most obvious and essential positive incentive is financial. However, the abundance of labor usually leads employers, public or private, to a low-wage policy. Such a policy has negative effects on any attempt to expand effective consumer demand. It may also result in various "vicious circles" with respect to labor productivity and morale. A barely noticeable difference in effective income is unlikely to convert the short-term target worker into a committed worker. At the extreme of low wages, sheer malnutrition can affect productivity. In any situation less

315

extreme, the problem is more psychological—and still real. The poorly paid worker does not usually excel in performance, and poor performance usually confirms the policy of poor pay.

Of course, the effectiveness of wages is linked to the development of markets that offer goods and services within the worker's scheme of needs and wants. Within that scheme, the newly recruited worker is likely to approximate the pure type of "economic man." The values and non-financial rewards of the new productive system have little appeal within the traditional value system. Moreover, many non-financial rewards and amenities actually do cost the enterprise money; they are very likely to be meager in struggling concerns with low productivity.

Various other positive work incentives have been reported here and there. National prestige and divers collective goals have been offered as inducements to co-operation. "Socialist emulation" (I, VIII) may be coupled with ideas of mutual aid among workers and with the popularization of advanced procedures among the less advanced workers (VIII). Aspirations for individual mobility, voluntary social relations, and new experience may be effective in recruiting workers or in improving the productivity of those on the job. Broadening the basis of creativity (VIII, IX) may provide a sense of participation not otherwise afforded. The difficulty in appraising the research results is the virtual absence of experimental data about the *relative* efficacy of various incentives under constant conditions. Yet when a number of incentives, including wages, lead in the same direction, they may serve as mechanisms for securing commitment.

Commitment involves both the performance of appropriate actions and the acceptance of the normative system that provides their rules and rationale. Whether such full commitment is or can be achieved in a single generation is debatable. The dispute hinges in part on the interpretation of the relative significance of early (childhood) and adult socialization. The empirical evidence is not very helpful, since the kinds and degrees of incentives capable of quickly capturing loyalties to new productive forms are rarely offered.

Labor surpluses can lead managers and scholars alike to minimize the importance of commitment. But the uncommitted worker is likely to quit or to perform minimally, and to require much supervision. These probabilities have economic costs as well as implications for the long-run viability of industrialization measures.

The shortage of skills that may be hidden behind labor surpluses, particularly in primitive technology, is sharply disclosed in the case of technicians, engineers, accountants, and administrators. These shortages derive not only from poorly equipped educational systems, but also from problems of motivations and occupational choice. Indeed, a number of

316

developing countries have no absolute shortage of people with advanced education—but they are prepared for traditionally honorable occupations rather than those most urgently needed in industrial enterprises (e.g., V). Planned or socialistic economies may attempt to gear educational production to employment demand by using centralized control of schools, and pressures and rewards for individuals. However, even these methods do not completely resolve the difficulty of orienting people to occupational achievement in largely unfamiliar fields of work. And the person who is overtrained, relative to actual employment or promotional opportunities, may present motivational problems as serious as the lack of commitment by the untrained (II).

If all or substantial segments of the economy are left to free enterprise, the shortage may be precisely in "enterprise." Pessimists note the relative scarcity of persons willing to take the risks entailed in economic innovation. Even the absence of the Protestant ethic is not a completely dead issue. The influence of the teachings of Ghandi that favor cottage industry, for example, have had a considerable but undetermined influence on thought in India (IXA). Optimists, on the other hand, feel that risks are taken if the possible rewards are sufficiently great. Political instability and uneconomic political policies are blamed for discouraging incipient economic risk-taking. Again, the available data provide no or little substance for a controlled comparison that would help to resolve these issues. There is, however, some evidence that schools, by maintaining a competitive system based on achievements and rewards (honors), operate not only as a mechanism for education as such, but also as a value-forming environment for the development of achievement orientations, if not of actual entrepreneurial endeavors.

ECONOMIC STRUCTURE AND INSTITUTIONS

Economic development requires a variety of changes in the structure of economic activities and in the norms governing them. Some of these are pre-conditions—e.g., the establishment of a monetary system of exchange, rational cost accounting, communication and transportation networks, and modes of transfer of property. Others are consequences—e.g., changing occupational structures and labor mobility, the movement of goods and services through the market, and changing patterns of consumption. We will not try, to make rigorous distinctions among the economic pre-conditions, accompaniments, and consequences of industrialization, since the functional interplay, through time, of different components of an economic system can be very complex. We shall summarize both typical and variable features of the structure of economies undergoing industrialization, but pay only intermittent attention to sequences.

Occupations

The outlines of changing occupational distributions are much more easily traced than the details. Industrialization involves the transfer of many workers away from food production (with subsidiary attention to clothing, shelter, and various handicraft products), into manufacturing and services. The familiar classification into primary (agriculture and mining), secondary (manufacturing), and tertiary (services) production requires modification, but it conforms crudely to the sequence of transformation of occupational structures.

In many underdeveloped areas, we must initially distinguish between the subsistence sector of the economy and the commercialized sector. The latter may include agriculture—in parts of Africa, Latin America, and South Asia, for example, it does so prominently. But commercialized agriculture is organized on different principles from those prevailing in subsistence economies. Persons exclusively or primarily engaged in subsistence production are not part of the labor force, in any precise sense; and the lack of economic exchange outside the subsistence sector makes it have minimal real—although possibly greater potential—significance for the national economy.

In some areas—especially in sub-Saharan Africa (VI)—temporary labor migration forms a bridge between the subsistence economy and the labor market. The probable instability of this arrangement is less economic than social. Subsistence agriculture is normally marked by underemployment, and migratory workers can add cash income without seriously affecting subsistence production. The probable source of the instability is the gradual "detribalization" of the migrants and their growing acceptance of the norms and expectations appropriate to wage-labor. Even in India, where a monetary system has long affected village-based peasant agriculture, the urban labor force is still highly transitory (IXA). However, this may reflect the miserable living conditions of the poor in the cities as much as any unbreakable bond with the village.

The importance of the initial step from subsistence production to *any* commercialized production is indicated by the estimate that a majority of African producers south of the Sahara are still in the subsistence sector.

Peasant farming that is commercialized—at least to the extent of trading agricultural surpluses for other goods and services—is clearly closer to the urban-industrial economy than is subsistence production. However, in terms of labor mobility, the movement from the subsistence sector into the labor market is more probable than is the early departure of peasant cultivators. Aside from the differences in relative economic advantages in the two types of mobility, the work organization in tribal societies often offers closer parallels to industrial organization than does family farming.

318

The peasant cultivator and his family will not be unaffected by industrialization, however. Although classified as "agriculturalists," the productive units are usually also engaged in handicraft production and part-time trade, at least in marketing their products. Greater economic specialization and the manufacture of consumer goods, such as textiles, generally turn the peasant into an agriculturalist or farmer, strictly speaking.

Even if economic modernization is heavily concentrated on agriculture and the processing of agricultural products, there will eventually be a substantial movement of workers away from farms. This is caused both by the lower labor demands resulting from rationalized productive techniques and capital equipment, and by the many services, including transportation, finance, and distribution, that a commercialized agriculture requires. (The prosperous "agricultural" economies of Denmark and New Zealand employ well under half of the labor force in agriculture.) Continued rationalization and technification of agriculture results in substantial occupational specialization within even that productive sector—including highly trained and even professional skills (II).

Industrialization, then, implies an increased proportion of workers employed in manufacturing and services. As a rule, early industrial establishments tend to be fairly labor-intensive unless economically non-rational investment decisions have been made. In any event, greater capital-intensity means not only a reduction of gross labor inputs per unit of output, but also an "upgrading" of the required skill levels in manufacturing employments.

Various leads and lags can create social problems in the relation between labor supply and demand. Cheap manufactured products may displace handicrafts more rapidly than industrial employment expands, with consequent increases in overt unemployment or hidden unemployment in inefficient family farms. This situation, coupled with a demographic growth of potential workers that is more rapid than the expansion of non-agricultural employments, may actually result in a larger *proportion* of the population's being "gainfully occupied" in agriculture. This occurred during the recent past in Pakistan (IXA), and, somewhat earlier, in India. The displacement of handicrafts causes the loss of supplementary incomes for peasant families (V). Traditional craft guilds underwent considerable disorganization in pre-Communist China, but there is some indication of a revival of handicrafts in co-operatives (V). Among the Maori of New Zealand (VIIA), the earlier loss of handicraft markets has been partially offset by an explicit "cultural" revival.

Surpluses of unskilled labor may coexist with acute shortages of skilled labor for the new technology.

The long-term upgrading of occupational distributions is associated with technological changes and their implications for man-machine relations. They are also connected with the growing importance of highly educated persons in the administration of enterprises and the operation of complex economic systems. Mechanization engenders the dissolution of some skill combinations and the need for other, new combinations. Automation generally requires many new technical and administrative skills (VIII, XI). However, it may lead to the employment of a lower proportion of the labor force in all occupations associated with manufacturing, a shorter work week, and a transfer of workers to various "services" outside manufacturing. If the displaced workers are to retain their earning and skill levels, adult retraining may be necessary.

Not all services expand with economic modernization. Domestic servants tend to escape into less menial and more highly rewarded occupations. But a myriad of new services appear. Some of these simply represent the transfer of traditional duties and reciprocities to the market or governmental mechanisms. Others are types of activities closely associated with economic production—for example, various financial, clerical, and informational services. Others reflect the allocation of increased resources to such cherished objectives as health, education, and recreation.

The key to changing occupational structures is mobility. The mobility manifested in shifts among economic sectors indicates nothing about the most common meaning of mobility: namely, status changes between generations or within occupational careers. Broad occupational shifts are not always—even in a "pure" labor market—responses to the lure of greater returns and opportunities (positive status mobility). Inevitably, some movements represent escapes from deteriorating earnings and prospects—as is often the case with the reluctant factory recruit.

Status mobility is both a functional necessity for an expanding economy and an important incentive for those involved. It contrasts vividly with both the realistic expectations and the norms of most non-industrial economies (e.g., VI). Too little ambition results in the failure to seek training and to expend money and effort to secure advancement. Too much ambition results in frustration and either apathy or revolt. No industrial system has uniformly matched aspiration with realization.

The amount of status mobility discerned depends in part on the fineness of measurement—both in the number of gradations taken into account and in the avenues of mobility observed. Thus a simple hands-head division of occupational status may disclose little status mobility, while finer occupational and income gradations reveal a great deal. If one concentrates solely on mobility subsequent to entrance to the labor force, one may neglect the crucial sorting process performed by schools prior to this entrance. (The educational system is, in fact, the normal link between generational and career mobility.)

Some other aspects of labor mobility are worthy of note. As a general

320

rule, the transferability of skills from one detailed occupation to another decreases with skill levels, because of training time. Thus a considerable amount of genuine occupational mobility may represent slight if any net changes in status; it may simply reflect changing factor allocations as determined by the market or by administrative decision. Because un-skilled labor is predominant in early stages of industrialization, such labor mobility may assume fairly large proportions (VI, VIIA, IXA). The transition from the farm to the factory involves a change of sector, occu-pation, and employer, but possibly no essential shift in status.

"Lateral" occupational shifts often involve changes of employers also. These shifts are often made for minute, fictitious, or whimsical reasons, especially by essentially uncommitted industrial recruits. (In southern Africa, for example, the fact that workers mill around among employers compounds the difficulties of making a statistical appraisal of the perma-nent, compared with the temporary, migratory labor force.)

We should make several additional comments about status mobility, which has stirred up the most concern among scholars and social critics. Wide status changes, whether generational or within careers, are, and have always been, relatively rare in all societies. High-level managers rarely come from the ranks of production workers (e.g., II). One signifi-cant cause is the fact that the work experience itself is not an adequate means for acquiring the necessary skills. Educational opportunities for adults to upgrade their skills while employed naturally increase chances of promotion (VIII).

The rate of economic growth is a differentiating variable in the poten-tiality of upward mobility, both among various sectors and career lines within economies and between societies. There are, of course, elements of risk and chance in career choices, and elements of uncertainty in gearing an existing educational system to meet a somewhat indefinite future demand for trained talent. Precise co-ordination would require a more sensitive formal and informal training and selective system than any society has had.

Occupational differentiation does not necessarily produce either sharper or more numerous status differentiations. Status differentiation tends to be sorted into various contexts of valuation, such as neighborhoods or work organizations; and there is usually low transferability between them. In other words, if "difference" means generalized social rank, then an industrial system of occupational allocation results in many distinctions without a difference. Indeed, some contemporary societies, like China and the Soviet Union (V, VIII), have not only cultivated breadth by the constant expansion of workers' skills, but have also minimized status dif-ferences by the temporary assignment of "head" workers to factory and agricultural jobs.

Industrialization involves gross changes in occupational structure by economic sector and finer changes by the relative demand for skills, and also by a degree of occupational specialization that is unmatched by any other labor system. All developing economies, old and new, manifest a secular trend in increased specialization. This specialization has important real consequences for the real world of work. In addition, it has consequences for the observation, measurement, and interpretation of occupational structures and mobility rates. The analytical utility of any simplified occupational classification made according to a few categories by sector of status steadily deteriorates, through time, by losing more and more information about the allocation of workers to functions.

Savings and Investment
It is banal to observe that the principal economic problem of the underdeveloped areas is the shortage of capital. However, some aspects of the problem are far from elementary; and there is ample theoretical and empirical reason to doubt that large capital supplies would automatically solve the remaining difficulties of economic development.

Substantial savings cannot be expected in tribal or other subsistence economies; however, peasant and other agrarian societies may have considerable "frozen" savings not put to productive use. The shortage of developmental capital may thus derive largely from the lack of confidence in the safety of investment and in the stability of currencies, and from the lack of reliable channels of investment for the small investor (IXA). Existing investment channels, if available and utilized at all, may be overly conservative or may divert savings to relatively unproductive uses (IXB).

Socialist states can attempt, more or less effectively, to capture and utilize all savings by collectivizing all forms of production and taking all profits either directly or through taxation. Other economies must find alternative ways to induce savers to become investors rather than hoarders.

In free enterprise systems, business profits become a principal source of capital accumulation through being reinvested in the same or other activities. Profits, however, may simply be spent on increased current consumption by their recipients. In many underdeveloped countries, increased luxury consumption has negative effects on the economy, since it is likely to involve luxury imports. This provides no effective increased market for domestically produced goods, and uses up scarce foreign exchange needed for capital imports. Foreign investments pose a special problem, for the profits may be neither spent nor invested locally, but instead be repatriated for the benefit of the investors, to spend or invest in the country supplying the original capital.

322

Even high profits may not be sufficient to divert savings from one economic sector to another, e.g., from agriculture to industry. The risks may be judged as disproportionately higher. In addition, unfamiliar organization and technology are involved. These possibly rational considerations are often supported by non-rational ones. This is particularly true where ownership of land involves the principal basis of both security and prestige in the traditional social structure (V), while newer economic activities at best provide only wealth but not aristocratic social standing.

Large-scale industrial production normally requires capital beyond the means of even wealthy families. There are three fundamental alternative ways of getting the necessary capital: from a large foreign corporation; from a domestic corporation that will pool the resources of many investors, or from the government, which uses its taxing or borrowing power to acquire the funds. There are, of course, many varieties and mixtures of the means of assembling savings and directing them toward investments consistent with continuous economic growth. The machinery of investment is itself a necessary counterpart of the organization of production, whether or not it can be identified as a consequence.

In newly developing areas, investment for expansion as connected to rising demand for current consumption is a critical probem. Even if there were no population growth—and population growth multiplies the problem in many areas (e.g., IV)—the poverty that is a major incentive for economic development is also a major deterrent to rapid growth. For the private investor in the oldest industrial economies, savings represent deferred consumption. In the meantime, he receives additional income, in the form of interest, dividends, or trading profits, from investing his savings. The desperately poor are unlikely to afford voluntarily the luxury of postponing consumption, unless this is somehow linked to familial obligations toward their children.

The desire for speed and centralized coherence in development measures is not, alone, the reason that governmental action is greater in the newly developing areas than it was in the older industrial systems. In the new nations, the state, either directly or indirectly through fiscal policies, is the only source of power sufficient to extract savings from an economy that provides very low levels of per capita income.

According to one doctrine of historical interpretation, economic growth in capitalist countries was accomplished by the exploitation of workers in order to extract profits. But apart from the different dimensions of the demographic problems in developing areas, and the desire for rapid growth, another unique quality in the new nations discourages historical repetition. It seems fairly clear that the effective per capita income, *before* the industrial revolution in the West, was substantially higher than is characteristic of underdeveloped areas today. Hence, if exploitation is

323

the method of capital accumulation, its relative dimensions must be greater today than in the past.

Both socialist and capitalist modes of assembling and directing savings provide for multiple involvements in the economic system. In both systems, one's employment or occupation is the principal source of one's private income. In both, however, the worker also is usually an investor —although not usually a risk-taker. The investor in a socialist economy may have little or no choice about the dimensions or the direction of his savings. In a capitalist economy, he probably has more choice about the dimensions of his savings; but he may well leave their direction to banks, insurance companies, and other financial institutions.

Distribution and Consumption

Aside from military considerations, the principal aim of economic development is presumably to secure a rising real income per capita. Unless some of this income is reinvested, continuous growth is impossible, and production and therefore income will eventually decline because of the obsolescence of capital equipment. An additional part of national income will be expended for governmental services rather than remaining available to the household consumer. It is that remainder, however, that chiefly determines average and differential levels of living.

Industrialization does not require that a "pure" commodity market, in the classical economic sense, complete with "consumer sovereignty," be established. Production quotas may be established by administrative decision rather than by guesses at consumer demand. Goods may be rationed, or allocated to different clases of consumers, or sold at different prices to different consumers. But it does appear impossible to operate a large-scale industrialized economy without some variant of a monetary system of exchange.

One principal implication of industrializaation, accordingly, is the establishment of monetary exchange where it did not previously exist, and the expansion of market organizations already in existence (III, VIIA).

In the extreme case of production of raw materials for world markets, the expansion of domestic consumption as such does not inevitably foster economic growth. In any moderately balanced economic development, the expansion of demand is the principal excuse and incentive for increased production.

Apart from socialistic economies, departures from market purity are numerous in developing areas. These departures range from the persistence of traditional terms of trade in money-mediated barter, despite shifts in relative supply and demand, to the persistence of particularistic trading relationships, despite disadvantages in price and quality.

324

In economies where commerce has long been established, a stubborn problem in distribution is the preference of merchants for high unit profit on small volume instead of low unit profit on high volume. Until and unless competitive price-cutting occurs, this will seriously retard the expansion of consumer demand.

In industrialized economies, marketing and distribution systems become very complex, even if they are centrally administered and unencumbered with competitive strategies, advertising, and market prediction. Markets are only one factor considered in locational decisions—and, for many types of production, they are not the critical one. Thus storage facilities, methods of packaging, and an accounting and record-keeping system are all necessary. Since none of these ancillary services is free, they too are subject to pressure for technical innovation that will improve efficiency.

Commerce, or at least distribution, is a major sector of the labor force in all advanced economies. In capitalist economies, there have been discernible tendencies for employment in sales and distribution to rise in relation to actual production. This correlation is due partly to the fact that the latter has been more mechanized, and partly to the fact that there have been genuine increases in the variety, quality, and convenience of services provided to consumers by distributors.

Commerce also constitutes a major sector of the labor force in many developing areas. In several situations, this does not represent a genuine increase in commercial services so much as it reflects a minute division of the services rendered among a number of underemployed participants. This pattern, characteristic of much of Latin America and South Asia, is generated by extremely rapid urbanization without a corresponding expansion of opportunities for truly productive employment. The rural migrants, and especially the recent ones, eke out an existence either by performing a variety of personal services for which there is little genuine demand (as porters, guides, shoe shiners, car watchers) or by engaging in forms of petty commerce (as street vendors, operators of tiny newspaper or tobacco shops, hawkers of lottery tickets). At times, the income of these marginal workers seems to be more private charity—but without the ultimate degradation of outright begging—than a return for productive services.

There is remarkably little precise information about consumer budgetary behavior in any society, but certain broad features can be discerned. "Engels' Law," that the proportion of income spent for food is inversely related to the magnitude of income, was originally stated in terms of cross-sectional income differentials. It can be roughly translated into temporal terms, however. Food, clothing, and shelter are universally the necessities for the consumer, until they are supplied at some acceptable standard (V, IXA, IXB). (It is not surprising that textile production figures so prominently in early industrialization, since it is usually not only labor-intensive but also geared to potential domestic demand.)

Some anomalous expenditures appear in budgetary behavior. Indebtedness is common among Indian workers, and paying debts and usurious interest lowers an already low level of living (IXA). In pre-Communist China, poorly paid workers still sent remittances to rural relatives and spent part of their tiny resources on travel expenses for visits in their native villages (V).

As economic development continues, other manufactured goods are added to the consumer's budget. No generalization about the sequence in which new products are adopted seems to hold. Imitative consumption and the ready adoption of high-prestige products have been widely observed. And since the goods are mainly "borrowed"—as are the techniques for their production, if they are locally produced—products need not be adopted in the same order in which they originally appeared in the advanced countries. One fact does stand out. "Luxury" items that figure generally or repeatedly in consumer budgets quickly tend to become necessities, and their purchase is no longer really discretionary.

The shift of productive resources from manufacturing to services naturally has its counterpart on the consumption side. The expansion of the variety of services and the proportions of income spent for them are marked in all industrially advanced countries. Some of this is caused by the decline of non-market reciprocities and the "movement of services into the market." However, much of it is a genuine increase of expenditure for health, education, and experiences, rather than for continuous accumulation of goods. But rising wage levels and expanding alternative employment opportunities tend to make domestic and other essentially menial service progressively more expensive or luxurious.

Within the productive system itself, goods and services move by market principles or by administrative direction. A developing economy demands at least a correlative growth in the interdependence among units of the economic system. This interdependence, which is analogous to a complex division of labor, is simultaneously a principal source both of the superior productivity of the economy and of the vulnerability it has to failure in any of its parts. Assured regularity of supplies is thus a foremost goal of any producer or distributor.

DEMOGRAPHIC AND ECOLOGICAL STRUCTURE

Two quantitative trends of the contemporary world—and, in fact, of most parts of it—involve numbers of people and their distribution. Both the "population explosion" and the rapid rate of urbanization are connected with industrialization, although in part circuitously and indirectly. A considerable portion of the growth of population is due to the falling mortality rates made possible by improved public health and medical technology, which are in turn largely a consequence of industrial development. The movement to the cities is partly a response to the services and amenities that cities offer as a result of economic modernization, and partly a quest for economic opportunities better than those in rural areas —even if those opportunities are not realistically available.

We shall summarize the implications of industrialization for demographic and ecological structure here in fairly broad outlines, without attempting to recapitulate detailed statistical regional information.

POPULATION SIZE AND GROWTH

It is customary to begin a discussion of the demographic situation of developing areas by referring to the "demographic transition" in the West. The broad empirical generalization is that pre-modern populations were comparatively stable. High and relatively constant fertility rates were offset by high and variable mortality rates. With modernization, death rates were reduced; and fertility rates were reduced considerably later, with the result that there was rapid transitional growth. The transition is presumably completed when low and relatively constant mortality is matched by low and variable fertility.

A set of explanatory principles have been developed for each of the variables and sequences. These are not all essential for present purposes, but two are of considerable importance. First, it is argued that mortality rates fell before fertility rates because death is always a negative value, whereas fertility is, in most societies, a positive value. Second, it is argued that fertility eventually declines—crudely, this is attributed to industrialization and urbanization; more precisely, it is attributed to the fact that high fertility is inconsistent with aspirations for mobility within single careers and between generations.

The validity of the transition theory as a historical generalization has been increasingly criticized—especially its validity as a model for contemporary developing areas. Its explanation of declining fertility is particularly important. Clearly, knowledge of contraceptive techniques was a relevant but probably not crucial variable. (An apparent diffusion of contraception from upper economic to lower groups, and from urban to rural areas, implies that sheer accessibility of knowledge and contraceptive materials was relevant, however.) The crucial issue involves attitudes towards deliberate fertility control, however achieved. Most reinterpretation of the historical generalization continues to center on some variety of "economic" motivation—for example, avoidance of uneconomically small, fractional agricultural holdings in France; famines and limited land in

Ireland; displacement of rural populations by the enclosure laws in England; urban residential congestion and decline of urban child labor in all industrializing countries. In other words, the "mobility" explanation has been challenged as too generalized. By the same token, the possibility has been accepted that attitudes conducive to fertility reduction, if they appear at all, are correlated with variable values and circumstances.

Meanwhile, the slowness with which mortality declined in the West need not be recapitulated in the new states. Improved transportation of food from areas of surplus to areas of shortage, improved sanitation, innoculations, the control of disease-bearing insects, all result in very rapid mortality reductions (I, IV, VIIA, VIIB, IXA, IXB). The fact that fertility has not fallen proportionately and concurrently—indeed, it has not fallen at all in most underdeveloped areas—seems to provide a kind of gross confirmation of at least part of the transition theory.

The initial introduction of contraception may have little effect on aggregate fertility rates, since it may be practiced only by those women who already have "too many" children. Since these are the comparatively more fertile women, they may have higher average fertility rates than women who do not try to limit the sizes of their families (IV).

As the practice of limiting one's family's size becomes somewhat more widespread, the historical fertility differentials in the West will probably be more or less repeated in the developing areas. That is, urban professional, business, and managerial groups will probably lead in fertility reduction. Consequently, there will be an inverse relation between fertility and indexes of socio-economic status. This expectation obtains whether one follows some variant of the mobility hypothesis as the attitudinal factor in family limitation, or simply considers the greater exposure of elite groups to Western ideas and practices. The variables affecting acceptance of family limitation have been tested in India (IXA), and the results confirm both the "standard" differentials, and the additional variable of a desire to have male offspring prior to any limiting of family.

If history approximately repeats itself further, a narrowing of fertility differentials will follow. If and when fertility limitation becomes common, and most child-bearing voluntary, a positive relation between income and family size may appear. Children will then become something like consumer goods, to be conspicuously displayed.

Any substantial difference in net reproduction among status or other segments of the population will change their relative proportions through time. They will most probably provide a demographic basis for mobility from one generation to another.

Family limitation and particular contraceptive techniques are, of course, the subject of much religious controversy. However, it can scarcely be disputed that the rates of actual or potential population growth in the areas attempting modernization threaten to counteract completely or seriously retard the possible rates of economic growth.

Another subsidiary part of transition theory that is subject to question is the assumption of the universality of high-fertility values. In at least some countries of the West, it is doubtful that the ideal of the small family was an invention that followed the industrial revolution. Field studies in other areas have indicated that in terms of "ideal size of family," the resistance to family limitation may have been exaggerated. If, however, the desire to limit family size is present, although not very strong, questions of cost, convenience, and mutual acceptability to both spouses assume special significance. One recurrent finding is noteworthy—namely, that males feel a greater enthusiasm for annual child-bearing than females do.

Changes in Demographic Composition

Fairly stable fertility and mortality rates and conditions will result in a population that, as successive birth cohorts are gradually eroded by mortality until all have died, is relatively pyramidal in age structure. Major discontinuities in rates or migration will alter the shape of the age-sex structure. Some of the principal types of alterations relevant to the demographic characteristics of developing areas should be noted.

Improvements in mortality conditions are unlikely to affect the age-specific mortality of all groups equally. (Only very recently has there been any substantial decline of death rates for those over fifty in the most advanced countries.) Where sanitary and other health conditions are very poor, improvements are usually most marked in the reduction of infant mortality rates. These reductions have the maximum effect upon the average expectation of life at birth; in addition, they have other consequences for the average age of populations (they become younger) and for the ratios among the several age groups.

The consequences of changing age compositions may be considered in terms of the ratio of "active" to "dependent" populations. Old-age dependency (i.e., the proportion of the population over sixty-five) is usually higher in advanced than in underdeveloped countries. This is because more people live to become aged, and also because the somewhat lower birth rates mean that the very young account for smaller proportions. Youthful dependency, on the other hand, is very much higher in most underdeveloped areas—and more than enough so to offset the slight advantage they have in lower old-age dependency.

The unfavorable ratio of active to dependent sectors of the population means that productive segments of the population have greater dependency burdens in areas where productivity is in any event low. It also means that endeavoring to improve the educational facilities for the young in areas where these facilities are meager is relatively more difficult.

Large numbers of children would bolster the demand for all sorts of products, if the means for purchase were available. Similarly, if the children survive to adulthood they add to the effective labor force—if useful employments are available.

Sharp short-term changes in either fertility or mortality have long-term demographic consequences—theoretically, through generations. "Bulges" and "hollows" in the age composition of the population, the heritage of past influences, have no necessary relation to current labor force needs or social services and facilities.

Migratory patterns also have clear effects on age-sex composition, as migrants are rarely representative of either the area of origin or the area of destination. Thus mining and some industrial centers have greatly disproportionate concentrations of young adult males (VI, IXA, IXB). Other urban centers show substantial majorities of females, chiefly as a result of clerical and service employments (XI). Radical disproportions in sex ratios usually present problems for "normal" marital and family relationships, as well as for residential patterns, community services, and the like.

Migration

Labor supplies are generally not a decisive consideration in the location of productive enterprises. Other factors in production (raw materials, power, capital) have different significance for location according to type of production and to conditions of technology and transportation. They all usually have greater deciding weight than labor availability, which is assumed to be fairly unproblematical—potential workers simply respond to employment opportunities by appearing where needed. Moreover, in a free enterprise system at least, labor is the one factor in production that is not assembled at the employer's expense. Migration in response to differences in economic activities and opportunities is, accordingly, a nearly universal characteristic of industrialization.

The exceptions to these generalizations are, of course, not insignificant. The self-selected work applicants may not match the employer's skill demands, and thus there must be more positive recruitment or training at the employer's expense. Private economic or pubic welfare policies may place some types of production, not heavily restricted by other locational considerations (e.g., light consumer goods manufacturing), in areas of substantial unemployment or underemployment. When new forms of enterprise are established in an environment totally untouched by a labor market system, workers may *not* simply appear. In Africa, especially, active labor recruitment and transportation were initially linked with such indirectly coercive measures as making the head or hut tax payable in cash, which was generally obtainable only by entering employment for wages (VI).

330

Internal and international migration does occur for reasons other than differences in economic opportunity. Although such migration—most of which can be included in the term "refugee"—presents problems of economic assimilation, it is not of primary concern in a summary of the social implications of industrialization.

Migration that is a consequence of differences in economic opportunity, real or imagined, may be conveniently divided into three types: temporary, permanent-voluntary, and administrative transfers.

Temporary labor migration accounts for a substantial volume of movement of people in various parts of the world. One of its general characteristics is that it provides a mode of bridging otherwise separate systems of production. Seasonal migration usually matches labor supplies with the highly uneven demand for manpower in diverse forms of commercialized agriculture. In Africa, commercial farmers hire natives from tribal economies during peak seasons. In both West and East Africa, the employers, as well as the employees, are often indigenous. Seasonal laborers on farms in Uganda and the Sudan come not only from the major labor-supply territory of Ruanda-Urundi, but also from as far away as French West Africa. In other cases, e.g., the tea plantations of India, differences in the timing of peak labor demands permit peasant farmers to work for wages on the plantations. Seasonal Italian workers in Argentine agriculture take advantage of the reversal of seasons north and south of the Equator. In other instances, the seasonal migrant can find only intermittent and marginal employment off season.

The longer-term, but still actually or nominally temporary, migration has had a considerable history in various forms of indenture. Indian and Malayan descendants of indentured workers exist in many parts of the British Empire, and contractual workers from China were common in South-East Asia and some Pacific islands before World War II. Today, the principal area utilizing large numbers of annual or longer-term contractual migrants is Africa. Several millions of persons are concerned in these migratory movements, which often involve great distances and elaborate international agreements.

The migratory labor system in Africa links the typical subsistence agriculture of the native village with the demands for unskilled labor in mines, factories, farms, and households. The employers are mostly European in origin. The development of a permanent labor force has been slow or non-existent, and in some areas it has been actively discouraged as a matter of official policy (VI). Nevertheless, there has been a gradual accretion, in urban locations, of detribalized natives who are wholly dependent on the commercialized and industrial sectors of the economy for their livelihood. Although the opinions of experts differ, it appears that the migratory labor system in Africa is transitional; the subsistence

331

economy is being slowly eroded by increasing intrusions of monetary exchange, and the native workers will probaby not always be content with their marginal status and income.

Another type of temporary migration is of slight statistical significance, but it may have strategic importance in the geographical matching of the supply of and the demand for services. This kind is illustrated by the mobile crew or team, such as operates in some types of constructon— it may or may not have a "home base," but is mostly employed at short-term jobs, often widely separated in distance. Although such migratory groups are probably more characteristic of advanced economies, with their elaborate economic specialization, they are not unknown in newly developing areas, where teams of technicians may stay in one place until they complete a project or until local people can complete it (V).

Much of the migration associated with economic development represents the voluntary movement of workers and their families to places of supposedly greater economic opportunity, and with no intention of return to the place of origin over the short term or perhaps ever. Most of the rapid growth of cities, discussed further in the following section, is attributable to this permanent-voluntary migration.

Statistical data on internal migratory movements are scanty everywhere. For the most part, they must be inferred from the differing growth rates of regions, the growth of cities, and fragmentary information about the directions of migratory flows. Nevertheless, an "economic interpretation" apparently will account for the directions, if not the dimensions, of such migratory movements.

Permanent-voluntary migration does not preclude making repeated moves. Young adults are usually most mobile—if for no other reason than the obvious ones of minimal property and community ties. Men are generally more mobile than women, except where women have gained considerable social and economic independence. Unskilled workers, with their wider transferability by type of industry and occupation—and, probably, their smaller stakes in particular jobs—are usually more mobile than the highly skilled (although the demand for the latter may more frequently bring them competing offers of employment).

The question of selectivity of migrants has wider ramifications. In particular, the quality of rural out-migrants compared with the quality of those who stay behind has been inconclusively debated. One view of the migrant is that as a rule he has superior qualities, including ambition; the concomitant inference is that talent is systematically drained from rural and directed to urban communties. The contrary view is that the migrant is a misfit or even a failure, who moves because either economic or social reasons make it necessary.

Since scattered evidence can be adduced in support of either position, varying conditions must be taken into account and only lower-level generalizations should be attempted. One clearly relevant variable is the accessibility of opportunities. The rural "misfit" may be such precisely because he has talents inappropriate for the opportunities available, which may be limited by systems of hereditary privilege. The qualities and varieties of opportunities may be so different that the ambitious and talented outmigrant is no more a misfit than are some of those who remain behind, but in quite different types of performance or leadership. Finally, several selective processes may operate concurrently. The village boy who has a college education may find no employment suitable to his training in his home town. In the city, he may well be joined by the village scoundrel —who has not only found it healthier to leave the village, but finds that the city offers wider opportunities for his anti-social activities.

The third major type of labor migration is the administrative transfer. Administrative transfers may be quite extensive in controlled economies, with their many restrictions on voluntary transfers. They are of smaller statistical importance, but still of strategic significance, in other areas. Wherever large enterprises have geographically scattered operations, transfers among these operations are probable. There are several causes for these transfers, and in any particular instance more than one may be operating. The most obvious sources of transfers are the establishment of new plants or other operations, or shifts in intensity of operations among existing units when the local sources of appropriate personnel are inadequate. Where different locations are of unequal desirability, even at equivalent ranks and salaries, a temporary tour of duty may serve to soften the differences. Temporary assignments may also serve, deliberately or unconsciously, to minimize local separatism and deviation from prescribed procedures through the periodic breaking up of informal patterns of performance and personal relationships. Finally, temporary and diversified assignments may be used as a training device, making the employee with broadened experience available for broader administrative responsibilities.

Administrative transfers are of minor importance in many newly developing areas—except, possibly, for the succession of foreign administrators. Yet, in the United States, it is possible to identify residential communities largely composed of such involuntary nomads. And in controlled economies, both workers and managers may be transferred to establish "pioneer" settlements at outposts of what they consider "civilization." The opening of virgin farm lands and of new industrial centers in the Soviet East has resulted in major migratory movements (VIII).

In identifying types of migration related to industrialization, we have largely ignored the conventional distinction between internal and international movement. The distinction may be significant chiefly because of the sources of statistical data. National boundaries are real, and they are steadily becoming less traversable by the individual voluntary migrant. Quantitative and qualitative restrictions abound; even countries that are seeking migrants want only certain types. Thus, administered migration, involving official international agreements, is increasingly common. The international migrant may fit any of the three types discussed, but he is somewhat always more likely to present problems of social assimilation than the native. Even internal migrants pose some problems of assimilation, whose magnitude and nature may, where sharp ethnic or other cultural distinctions exist within the national territory, be very like those raised by foreign immigrants (e.g., VI, VIIA).

Urbanization

Although urbanization and industrialization are associated in many ways, they are independently variable. Urbanization can take place without industrialization; at least small-scale industrialization is possible without urban agglomerations. Nevertheless, the economic advantages of concentration and, indeed, congestion form one of the connections between industries and cities. Even the small factory town has social characteristics more similar to those of the city than to those of the rural village.

In developing areas, cities have usually grown at a rate surpassing both the expansion of employment opportunities and the expansion of urban public services. The ecological structure of American and some European cities, consisting of a growing circle of commuters' residences whose value increases with distance from the city center, is not at all the pattern in the burgeoning cities of Asia, Africa, or South America. The cities in the new nations are characterized by suburban slums, whose dirt, health hazards, and congestion often are even greater than the impoverished conditions in rural villages (e.g., IXA).

Why, then, do people migrate to the cities? The answers are speculative more than they are precisely grounded in research. Some, and probably most, of the new migrants undoubtedly overestimated the economic advantages of the city. But that does not account for their staying if there is any way they can leave. However miserable the living conditions, urban public and municipal services are usually superior to those in rural areas. Since the opportunities in the cities have benefited some in the past—and even some in the present—the misery may be regarded as temporary. The flight from the form is caused by changed knowledge and aspirations of rural dwellers and, in many instances, by genuinely deteriorating economic opportunities and returns in agriculture (I, V, IXA, XI).

Rapid urbanization confronts poor countries with serious economic and social difficulties. The demand for houses, streets, water, lights, and sewers necessarily diverts resources from the capital investments which

334

might lead to the very employment opportunities sought (and, eventually, to the income to support expanded urban services). The problems of social integration and control will be discussed below in the section on "Community Organization."

Even in urban centers, the rates of growth may not correspond with economic realities. In much of Latin America, the capital cities are growing far more rapidly than provincial cities—which may offer greater opportunities in new enterprises. However, in the capital cities the "cultural" advantages of urban life are more evident, and direct relief or emergency employment measures are more likely. In fact, the national government may derive a major amount of its political power from the economic and political manipulation of the impoverished inhabitants of capital cities.

The over-urbanization of principal cities (e.g., IV, IXA) creates the probability of a reverse urban-industrial influence. In a sense, cities may become the cause rather than the effect of industrialization. That is, the aggregation of unemployed and underemployed people who have already broken with rural ties (and traditions?) may conduce to locating plants where the workers are. Some countries have tried, with varying success, to achieve deliberate geographical decentralization of industry. Attempts at rural reconstruction also fare unequally. Village development schemes, in India and elsewhere, have retarded the flight from the land, the rural exodus; but they have not stopped it.

Rapid population growth partly accounts for urbanization, because absorptive capacity of agriculture is limited, particularly where it is already super-intensive (e.g., IV). In much of Latin America, however, there are undeveloped agricultural potentials. The limitations there are chiefly those of ownership, capital, transportation, and markets. They tend to have the same consequences as actual land shortage. In much of Africa, the land distribution is very unequal, especially between Europeans and Africans. Traditional modes of cultivation, and stock-grazing on smaller areas with growing populations, have resulted in the deterioration of the absolute as well as the relative carrying capacity of the land. These circumstances alone account for considerable African urbanization, whatever official attempts have been made to retard or prevent it.

Urbanization is not only a demographic and ecological fact; it is also a way of life. Some aspects and problems of the urban way of life will be summarized in relation to "Community Organization." Here, it is important to note that changes in the social structure, initiated in the city, have wider ramifications. Some rural areas are incorporated into metropolitan complexes and lose much of their rural character. With rapid communication and transportation, the isolation and self-suffficiency of villages are steadily eroded. As agriculture becomes more and more incorporated into the commercial industrial system, the differences in the qualities of life may become very narrow. The country bumpkin finally disappears from all but the carefully preserved mythology of popular humor. And no amount of nostalgic regret is likely to preserve or restore the qualities of rural life, if economic growth persists and proceeds.

CHARACTERISTIC ASPECTS OF SOCIAL STRUCTURE

Anthropological and sociological analyses usually regard the structural components of societies as being so closely interrelated that a change in any part of the system would have repercussions in all other parts. Indeed, if a model of extreme functional interdependence is adopted, the characteristics of any component of the system should determine the characteristics of all others.

This analytical model, although useful for certain theoretical purposes, is clearly contrary to fact. The integration of societies is often more functional than structural. Functions essential to the survival of societies *are* performed—but by patterns of action (structures) that have considerable variability, from one society to another, or from one time to another in the same system. The general functional requirements for the persistence of any society set only very wide limits on the appropriate structural ways of accomplishing those requirements. This may be called "the principle of structural substitutability," which is the counterpart of the principle of structural suitability.

Of course, the specification of the divers component social structures narrows the range of possible variation in other structures. Were there no such relation among various aspects of social behavior, the conception of a social *system* would be untenable. The several patterned ways of social behavior would have to be regarded as simply randomly variable with respect to each other. This notion also is contrary to fact, since societies are integrated both by common understandings and values and by a vast network of relationships among structures or patterns of action.

The point of our theoretical discourse is not to deny the functional interdependence of the elements of social systems. Were there no such interdependence, industrialization would have no social implications. However, we are avoiding the endeavor to account for every variant in patterned social behavior by reference to the rest of the social system. In other words, the specification of parts of a social system (say, its characteristic economic organization) delimits possible variation in other parts; but it does not determine their exact form in all details. We may call this "the principle of autonomous variability."

With these cautionary principles in mind, we can proceed to try to trace the consequences of change in societies. The repercussions of a change in one sector of society depend upon the magnitude of the change —i.e., both the degree to which it differs from preceding patterns and the extent to which it is adopted—and upon the mode and amount of its linkage with other aspects of the total society.

The descriptive literature on social change is replete with examples of major consequences of minute changes. Thus a change from wooden to steel hoes or plows has obvious effects on agricultural productivity and on the durability of tools; but it may also degrade the social status of displaced toolmakers, and possibly upset magical rituals associated with the mere technical production and use of the displaced tools. Descriptions like these display the virtuosity of functional analyses at their best, and must not be taken lightly. However, there are myriads of minute changes that are not reported, precisely because no such connections and consequences can be traced.

These strictures apply less to the study of industrialization—which is likely to be a major change wherever it occurs, even if it is not extensive —than to the attempt to trace detailed implications of every other feature of social life, implications which may not in fact exist. If the industrial mode of productive organization does become common to all parts of the world, we may realistically anticipate a growing similarity of cultures in a variety of other respects. These similarities are summarized in the several sections of this final part of the report. We should not, however, expect the resulting patterns of action and systems of beliefs and values to be alike. Indeed, the ways in which they differ become crucial points of potential conflict.

Family and Kinship

Family and kinship organizations are apparently universal structural features of human societies. Whatever other functions they may perform, they always involve legitimate procreation and the early socialization and social placement of children. Whatever kind and extent of broader kinship systems exist, the nuclear family, comprising parents and immature children, is invariably an identifiable structural unit.

Beyond these generalizations—which are not insignificant—the variety begins. Modes of mate selection, the permissibility of plural unions, the place of residence, the durability of unions, the ways of tracing lineage, and the character of internal role relationships—families differ in these and other ways. The differences are not random with reference to other structural characteristics of the divers societies. Since the family always has some economic functions, the variety is related to new forms of productive organization.

Although family and kinship systems are more thoroughly recorded in research literature than almost any other aspect of culture or social structure, the results offer only scattered data on the significance that particular kinship variables and their combinations have for economic modernization. This inadequacy is, in part, a consequence of the inclination of ethnographers to report ideal and traditional kinship systems rather than actual and current patterns. Most discussions of the impact of industry have tended to lump all kinship structures in non-industrial societies under the single rubric of "extended kinship," in comparison with the "small-family" system of urban-industrial societies. With the aid of that dichotomy, the generalization is commonly accepted that industrialization is an undermining influence on extended kinship systems. This generalization is valid only if the type, degree, and speed of change are subject to question, and it is not assumed that the transformation is global and immediate.

The principal cause of the breaking of large kinship organizations is the extensive mobility required by industrialization. This mobility is geographical, involving a concomitant physical separation of kinsmen. It is also social, thus involving the separation of kinsmen in social status and styles of life. The respective fates of adult siblings—to say nothing of cousins—may be very different in competitive economic placement. Perhaps even more damaging to the notions of lineage is the expectation of inter-generational mobility—hereditary, ascribed social status is widely superseded by status assignment made on the basis of individual qualities and achievements (VI). Despite the justifiable cynicism about the extent of "equality of opportunity" in industrial societies, some inter-generational mobility is essential for the establishment of any industrial system, as well as for the continuous changes in occupational distributions that continuing economic growth requires. The demand that all kinsmen "share and share alike" would set impossible restrictions on an industrial system of labor allocation and mobility.

All this seems clear. But it does not follow that the significance of kinship reciprocities beyond the primary family disappears. "Corporate" kin structures, as integrated economic units and as primary agencies of social control, are not likely to survive (VI, VIIA). Less formal modes of mutual aid may; and there are many intermediate and transitional situations.

In India, the joint family apparently survives as an operating unit in all ways except residentially (IXA); urban workers retain their rural kinship ties. However, this appears to be related to the low general commitment of the industrial worker—a commitment that is low for reasons besides the barrier provided by the kinship system.

In China, the traditional extended family was more ideal than actual among peasants and the urban lower classes. (In post-revolutionary

338

China a radical reduction of kinship responsibilities is evident, most clearly in the communes [V].)

In Japan, the legal persistence of the traditional family, with male primogeniture, permitted urban employments for daughters and younger sons, but held the kinship unit responsible for their reserve security (III). (Actually, there was a gradual but steady undermining of strict kinship responsibilities, particularly in the cities [III].)

In Egypt, the nuclear family is the norm among urban workers. However, the nuclear family maintains social ties with kinsmen in the villages, visits them, and often extends them financial aid (IV).

In the islands of Oceania, money derived from agricultural production is usually distributed within the kin group according to traditional norms; but urban wages lead to the economic separation of nuclear family units (V).

In short, as the social transformations accompanying economic modernization proceed, many kinship relations become permissive rather than obligatory; and the number of situations in which they are at all relevant decrease (VI).

There is a weakness, however, in the institutionalization of the isolated primary family. It is asking a great deal of parents, children, and siblings, to demand that they spend years in intimate, affective relations and then, when the children have reached adulthood, treat one another as strangers. The real significance of more distant relatives may or may not be radically reduced. The importance of the principle of descent usually precludes the complete disappearance of the identification of kinsmen as somewhat different from other persons. There are substantial strains and ambiguities in the norms governing kinship obligations in all industrial societies. Since some of these strains are intrinsic, they cannot be considered as simply anachronistic.

The weakening of kinship bonds is one of the principal social costs that disturb some thoughtful people in areas undergoing industrialization. Some of these costs appear to be inevitable, unless the productive system is to be inflexible and highly inefficient. Yet their worries may have been aggravated by the common failure of scholars to distinguish more precisely the exact nature and degree of social transformation required by industrialization.

The evidence about particular marriage and kinship variables is even shakier. Nevertheless, we may hazard making certain hypothetical generalizations.

The minimization of parental control has a number of implications, both for courtship and marriage customs and for the internal structure of the family. The independence of young adults is quite inconsistent with any but a voluntary system of mate selection (V, VI), and with specific

339

economic transfers (bride prices [VI], dowries) as a part of the marriage agreement. Similarly, a unilateral descent principle is usually undermined —it becomes weaker in its status-fixing significance and is superseded by increasingly bilateral kinship organization (VI). The intensity of interaction usually increases *within* the primary family as it decreases with other kinsmen (VI).

If children are to achieve adult independence, the authority of the father during childhood will be diminished. Since schools provide a leading agency of social sorting that is largely independent of the family, children tend to gain an independent status in school. Indeed, the expansion of knowledge and the growth of specialization lead to the situation in which the child knows more than his father about some or many things. The young are, in any event, much more likely than the adults to accept novel norms and forms, and thus to challenge the traditional basis of parental authority (II, VI, VIIA).

Other variables in marital practice also usually change. Plural marriage —never common even where permissible—is likely to decline further, both because of the economic strains if there is a single, male breadwinner, and because increased economic alternatives to marriage for women change their relative social position (VI). Residence becomes, at least ideally, neolocal; i.e., it becomes separate from either parental family. This is consistent not only with geographical mobility and urban residential crowding, but also with the social separation of the generations.

Within the family, there is a relative decline of parental authority. Since age usually loses significance as a primary basis of adult social placement, the significance of birth order within the family may be reduced. Prospective ability may outweigh seniority as a preferential principle.

Even if the economic position of women is not markedly improved, their authority within the family is likely to increase, if only because of the absence of the father. And, since production is no longer a family affair (the so-called "loss of family economic functions"), the mother's duties are usually to be reduced, so that she may have greater independence of movement and of disposition of time. The loss of her traditional economic and social functions may actually, if temporarily, reduce the relative position of the urban wife (VI). However, greater freedom and alternative economic opportunities for independent employment are likely to compensate for this (I, V, VI).

The family only partly "loses" its economic functions. In all industrial economies, the family is the basic unit of consumption; market principles of distribution end at the household door. The shift in marital role relationships usually means that wives have considerable control over deciding purchases for the household. This factor is also likely to diminish the extent of male dominance.

340

One common problem engendered by industrialization is the rise of "family disorganization." Of course, if family organization is judged by the traditional standard, the changes made in response to industrialization represent disorganization by definition. By the same token, the persistence of traditional practices may be regarded as anti-social by new standards. But this dismisses the matter too lightly. Deviance from old norms does not automatically involve the development and acceptance of new ones. The loss of traditional controls may result in sexual promiscuity and irregular unions that are contrary to any established institutional order. The reduction of parental authority may simply lead the children to delinquent conduct rather than to self-directed responsible behavior. The greater emphasis on the affective relations between spouses, combined with declining emotional support and social control from outside the immediate family, and the changing status of wives, may produce a great increase in marital conflict. The greater intensity of interaction within the family, and the concomitant emotional strains, are much more important sources of marital instability than is the supposed loss of familial functions.

At least some of these problems are intrinsic to or persistent in the small-family system, and not simply transitional phenomena generated by the confrontation between different systems of values and conduct.

Community Organization and Problems
Industry is located somewhere. And whether that location is a long-established town or city, or a rural and possibly uninhabited area, problems in industry-community relations immediately arise. Industry presumably provides new avenues of employment and new sources of revenue, both public and private. It may also supply leaders who are capable of supplementing or challenging the leaders in existing communities, and are almost certain to be major influences in community life in new ones. Some types of production involve difficulties like air and water pollution, noise, unsightly wastes, and various hazards to life and health. The dependence of a community on industry varies according to the relative size and the simplicity or diversity of the economic structure. Yet, once new productive facilities have been established, the community is extremely reluctant to give up the economic advantages of their continuation.

The small mining or industrial town may become essentially an enclave within a predominantly non-industrial environment. If most of the labor force is recruited locally, many non-industrial social patterns may persist. This may make it difficult to secure a social transformation adequate for efficient operation, as when workers take jobs temporarily and then leave them to return to farming (VI) or persevere in observing large numbers of traditional holidays. It is, however, in the industrial city that the problems of community organization arise most strongly.

341

Cities tend to throw into juxtaposition persons of different tribal, regional, or even national origin. In Israël (II), cliques based on different national origins persist; but social disorganization is greater if they are partially incorporated in the new community. In Africa (VI), tribalism is frequently transplanted to the city, though in a modified and often restricted form. Tribal divisions may mark relations among Africans, but not figure in the dealings of Africans with Europeans. Then African solidarity may be cultivated; and the union or the political party is clearly the appropriate instrumentality rather than the (divisive) traditional structures.

Urbanization may well proceed more rapidly than the provision of public services. The specialization of the city means that the place of work is often quite far from the place of residence, and strains on transportation and traffic congestion ensue. When municipal planning is attempted, the planners may lack the necessary controls to implement their ideas and the necessary speed to plan rather than merely to react to developments. In some places, local political boundaries were established before cities expanded; in consequence, difficulties arise in any co-ordinated planning or control for the metropolitan area as a whole.

It is the rapidity of urbanization that especially strains the capacity of the urban community to "absorb" (in all senses) the migrant through adaptation and organic growth (I, VI, VIIA).

Even without over-urbanization—i.e., migration to cities in excess of expanding employment opportunities—slums appear to be a nearly universal feature of city life.

The fundamental cause of slums is poverty. But ethnic discrimination adds another basis for residential congestion and uneven health standards and public services. Slum clearance usually requires public housing subsidies—i.e., income redistribution by governmental action. Similar public action is usually necessary to obviate private prejudice.

Slums are one (but not the only) environmental source of a number of problems of social control in urban communities. Poverty, when mixed with other urban characteristics, engenders acute strains on obedience to formal laws and to informal standards of social conduct.

To many, one of the most appealing features of cities is their anonymous congestion. There are crowds without true social interaction. Segmental and even transitory interaction abounds. So-called "secondary" relationships are nominally features of employment relationships, and are actually characteristic of many others—the teacher and the parent, the public official and the citizen, the landlord and the tenant, and, in extreme degree, the buyer and the seller.

In these circumstances, the maintenance of "primary" social controls is difficult and occasionally impossible. In a "normal" social structure, social codes are internalized early and are constantly reinforced by rewards and punishments (approval and disapproval) from "significant others." Exclusive theoretical concern with early socialization neglects the possibility that new values might be internalized at any time in life; in the same way, it is misleading in its neglect of demoralization. Without the support of family and friends for maintaining moral conduct, and faced with all sorts of conflicting standards and many opportunities for anonymous transgression, the individual may well become a social deviant.

Frustration, value conflicts, and loss of emotional security from significant others are likely to lead to various symptoms of apathy or alienation. Thus alcoholism, drug addiction, and mental disorders have a higher proportional incidence in cities, even after all due allowances have been made for statistical errors (e.g., VI, VIIA, IXA, XI, XIII).

Crime and juvenile delinquency are also disproportionately urban. The very impersonality of urban life, together with a possible decline in primary social controls, may lead the individual to reject accepted standards of conduct (e.g. I, VI, VIIB). A cynical, instrumental view of social conduct is conducive to law obedience only when the perceived risks of being detected in transgression are high. Crimes against property are especially marked in cities. Personal violence is, perhaps, no more common than in rural areas, and then often in connection with robberies.

The counterpart of the possible decline of informal social controls and the greater opportunities for deviant behavior is the growth of formal controls in cities. Arrests by the police are substituted for scolding and gossip. At the extreme, the varieties of tolerated behavioral differences and the lack of any apparent common value basis of conduct result in austere, impersonal disapproval of behavior, but not in moral outrage. The efficiency and integrity of the police are questioned, legitimately or not; but personal responsibility for maintaining order and decency is radically reduced.

We have oversimplified in order to illuminate the sources of deviant and anti-social behavior in urban communities. Statistically, conformity with social codes is still the norm. Most people obey most rules most of the time. For many, urban residence is incidental to the maintenance, or constructive adaptation, of customary codes of conduct. Either maintenance or adaptation is difficult where the transition is rapid and the resulting agglomeration brings together people of distinctly heterogeneous social backgrounds.

Education and Science
Although factory production or commercialized agriculture may be introduced with an illiterate and largely unskilled labor force for manual operations, at least a minority must have higher education and technical

skills. As industrial or agricultural operations become more complex, rising levels of general education are needed.

Literacy is by no means common in the underdeveloped areas, and technical skills are often in very short supply. The expansion of education is both a cause and a consequence of economic development.

There are moot questions of social strategy involved in formulating educational policy for developing areas. The possibility of utilizing abundant unskilled labor—even if wastefully and with outmoded technology—leads some experts to emphasize the initial provision of technical, professional, and administrative skills. Others argue that such skills can be imported or that people can be trained abroad; that available resources should be used for the widest possible extension of general education.

A system of universal education provides a more effective system of identifying, sorting, and cultivating latent talents than any alternative system of social selection. The uneducated are doomed to poorly paid and low-status jobs, whatever their potential talents.

The proponents of mass education add political and social considerations to the economic ones. Full participation in community or national life is scarcely possible for the illiterate workingman or housewife (I, V).

In a developing area, the role of the school in providing literacy—and, for some, more highly trained skills—is supplemented by its effectiveness in forming achievement orientations and an approach to situations very different from those of most traditional cultures. Secular education encourages a rational, problem-solving habit of mind, rather than an unquestioning acceptance or explanation in terms of non-rational categories (VI). This is, perhaps, the crucial difference between workers with industrial traditions and workers without them.

The correlation of educational supply with manpower demands is not perfect anywhere. Schools are imperfectly matched with the current occupational needs, and occupational choices are made on grounds besides objective rewards and opportunities. In addition, the schools must train people for an uncertain future. This leads to the troublesome issues involved in general vs. specialized training. The latter may be more quickly and exactly related to current manpower needs; but it is vulnerable to obsolescence if changing technology, markets, or administrative policies remove the need for the skill. General education to a fairly high level presumably lays the foundation for short specific training in many fields and for relatively easy retraining as needs and opportunities change; but it is always in danger of being regarded as useless for any specific purpose (IXA).

Because educational curricula and school graduates are incompletely matched with manpower needs in the economy, the employer, whether public or private, must devote some organizational resources to personnel training. In underdeveloped areas, the short supply and/or poor quality of the output of the schools make on-the-job training both even more essential and more difficult, since the supply of qualified managerial personnel is severely enough limited before training is added to supervisory functions.

The pursuit of pure science in underdeveloped areas is difficult for several reasons: the limited quantity and quality of appropriately educated people; the limited resources available for scientific work; and the urgent need for applied science in current technological and other problems. The last is by no means least. In some centers of old cultures, long traditions of scholarship in the humanities are currently preserved with pride. No one requires humanistic scholars to be practical. But in the natural and social sciences, the need to utilize scarce intellectual resources for the solution of urgent problems discourages attempts to pursue possibly useless knowledge. This situation is regretted by the international brotherhood of scholars; but it is likely to continue as long as the countries are poor and are borrowers, rather than inventors, of knowledge and techniques. The line between "pure" and "applied" is not absolute; important additions to abstract knowledge may result from action-oriented research. However, these essentially accidental contributions are not likely to loom large in the general progress of knowledge.

Communication and Popular Culture

Perhaps the single most important technical product of modern industry, in terms of the number of people directly affected in their everyday lives, is the radio. Very few areas of the world are not reached by radio broadcasts—if not over private household sets, then over public loudspeakers in village squares. Newspapers depend upon a considerable technical organization and a literate public. Television is too expensive to reach most people in the underdeveloped areas. Radio, however, has neither handicap. For many, it provides their first and only substantial contact with events and ideas in the world outside their village. The cinema has had a somewhat similar impact, but with a more restricted diffusion (IXA).

Economic development tends, sooner or later, to bring all areas and sectors of production into a national, if not international, economic network. The process may be slow and uneven, however. The mass media of communication, and particularly radio broadcasts, supply the technical basis for the formation of a national public and a widespread, if passive, participation in political events and policies, popular drama, and music.

The extent to which radio standardizes political attitudes or musical forms, even when broadcasting is governmentally and centrally controlled, is still debatable. Radio clearly serves most reliably simply in communi-

345

cating information. In many areas, its chief additional effect may be to make villagers arrive at the rather revolutionary realization that village life is not isolated and autonomous. It is possible that the development of a mass or popular culture, only recently recognized in the older industrial countries, is rather rapid in developing areas (e.g., I, II, V, VIII). Thus the eventual outcome of a long chain of technical changes in communication, as a consequence of industrialization, may well precede any substantial economic transformation in the underdeveloped areas.

It is precisely the standardization and possible degradation of ideas and tastes that most concern the critics of mass culture. In some instances, a distinctly snobbish attitude is discernible: popularity is equated to vulgarity, even if there has been no change in, say, the art forms involved. Thus musical classics, on radio or on records, are regarded as having lost quality by the mere fact of having wider circulation.

The debate is a little hard to transplant to impoverished areas that do not have a national market for best-selling books or equipment for playing high-fidelity recordings; yet, in slightly altered form, the policy debate does occur. One of the worries about the supposed standardizing consequences of industrialization concerns the charge that much of the cultural variety that existed within and among non-industrial cultures will be lost. The radio and cinema are considered as substituting passive entertainment for traditional dances, fiestas, and other modes of recreation and expression.

For reasons not directly linked to industrialization as such, the alarm would be inappropriate—even if it were valid to assume that new entertainments are uniformly inferior to old. The growth of nationalistic sentiment that accompanies programs of economic development often leads to the preservation, restoration, or adaptation of elements of folk culture. Nor is this necessarily anachronistic. Esthetic and expressive forms and canons are, of all aspects of culture, least intimately connected with other elements in social systems (VIII). In other words, their functional autonomy is relatively high. The essential truth of this assertion is not damaged by the recognition that preservation of exotic crafts and rituals may be encouraged as a tourist attraction. The motives of the participants may be mixed; but it does not follow that the cultural forms are radically transformed by commercial considerations.

Folk customs may be preserved, or only partially lost and modified, in cultural enclaves within burgeoning cities. All experience to date evinces their hardy survival power, even when they confront the undeniable standardizing influences and the growth of commercialized, often passive recreation (e.g., the cinema and spectator sports). For some frustrated, footloose, and discontented urban dwellers, escapes may go to anti-social extremes or lead to personal disorganization, as illustrated by the bums

346

in many large cities. Gambling may introduce pleasant uncertainty into lives otherwise all too predictable and routine.

One matter that excites the attention of social critics in the advanced countries has a qualitatively different significance in underdeveloped areas —the problem of leisure. Leisure is a problem for the unemployed and underemployed. But their principal problem is to gain an adequate income, not to decide what to do with their involuntary freedom. The problem of leisure in the advanced countries is what use to make of time that is a consequence of productive efficiency and prosperity—i.e., one's non-working hours while one is "fully" employed.

It would be too glib to say many underdeveloped areas wish that they had this problem. Working hours may in fact be shortened—not because of the high productive efficiency achieved, but as a measure to spread employment. Socialist states try to find devices to assure full employment, and also devote a great deal of attention explicitly to providing leisure activities, ranging from work brigades to doctrinal study groups (VIII). And, where leisure is less organized and controlled, the urban environment and the products of industry afford opportunities for adult self-directed recreation. The problem is often one of attitude, not of opportunity.

Interest Groups and Associations

The multiplication of organizations is one clear consequence of industrialization. Some organizations, like unions and occupational groups, are directly related to new forms of work. Others represent new involvements in national political life. Still others are organized manifestations of the potential multitude of interests that become involved when the notion of deliberate social action has taken hold. Finally, associations may simply reflect the common expressive and recreational interests of their members. In a sense, they all represent substitutes for the multi-functional structures that constituted the traditional basis of village life.

The industrial system of production introduces new occupations and new forms of organization. These are inevitably accompanied by new tensions in work relations, new bases of distinction and allegiance. At least four possible bases of identification by workers are potentially operative in industrial and related employments. The worker may identify with the employer and thus become a "loyal" employee. By doing so, he may also identify with the industry or sector of the economy—for example, when the new recruit becomes committed to the modern, as opposed to the subsistence, sector of the economy; to factory, rather than agricultural, wage-labor; to steel, instead of aluminum, for construction (because his skills and livelihood are bound up with the market for steel). As an employee—as distinct from an employer or a manager—he may identify with other employees of similar status. As a worker in a particular occu-

347

pation, he may identify with people who have similar training and skills and, possibly, similar economic interests.

It is an academic or ideological prejudice that any one of these interests is more "normal" than another. Since they are all actually or potentially operative, strains among them as competing bases of allegiance are intrinsic, not abnormal. Generalization about the "predominant" form of interest group organization is hazardous unless other conditions are stipulated. If union organization and membership are more or less voluntary, and the bases of allegiance are somewhat competitive, then something approximating the following sequence evolves. The new recruit is usually not interested in unions at all. Union membership is indicative of at least partial commitment to the new forms of labor. Early unions are likely to be composed exclusively of skilled craft workers, because of their strategic power and greater sophistication—or, if the unions are organized on a broader basis, they are led by such workers. The appearance of status-conscious industrial or general unions manifests a realization of the actual disparities of status and career opportunities for managers and workers.

The broadly based union, however, does not dispel other bases of allegiance and division—especially those that revolve around distinct occupational interests. The steady increase of specialization and the growth of technical and professional groups combine to undermine the common status interests and to impel occupational organization. These organizations either form cliques and parties within a general union or constitute separate organizations. In either event, coalitions among them may operate for particular purposes but prove unstable as interests and events shift in a dynamic society.

In socialist states, unions are controlled; rival unions, whether based on competing claims or on competing principles (craft vs. industrial) are not ordinarily tolerated. In these circumstances, the strike is not available to unions as a bargaining device. However, unions apparently retain functions of collective representation and protest. Centralized control is tightest at the national political level. Locally, the managerial organization, the political organization, and the union are discrete, if interdependent, agencies. Some leverage on the system of social organization is thus possible. At the same time, the labor organization is expected to participate actively in technical innovation and improved worker productivity (I, VIII).

Unions in underdeveloped areas are sometimes characterized as agencies for the "management of protest." Their management may be incomplete if freedom of association does not exist, or if the avenues of legal protest are very narrowly restricted or totally prohibited. The prominent political interests and activities evinced by unions in many countries

348

(e.g., IXA, IXB) seem to derive from two sources. One is the fact that party and other kinds of political participation may be incompletely developed—indeed, the franchise may be denied by various kinds of voting restrictions. The other source is that the "economic" power of unions must, sooner or later, rest upon their political legitimacy. Until that legitimacy has been established by legislation, the employer's position is buttressed by courts, administrative agencies, and the police.

Membership in a union does not necessarily imply rejection of "the system." The uncommitted worker does not join in labor protest, except under pressure from his fellows. An industrial system institutionalizes conflicts and tensions; it does not eliminate them.

Unions, then, become agencies of change. Viewed restrictively or negatively, they cushion the impact of change or alter the conditions under which change occurs. But in at least some instances, labor organizations take the lead in fostering change, through acting as labor recruiters for new industrial employments and even through exhibiting active concern for the living conditions in industrial communities and for the working conditions in industrial plants. Mexico provides vivid illustrations of labor unions that participate actively—and impel their members to do so —in social transformation and in resisting some features of employment policies. In Israel, the general confederation sponsors productive enterprises (II).

Political participation may be organized around either unions and other occupational groups, or a variety of other interests and loyalties. A single-party system seeks to minimize political division, but not political participation.

The relationship between economic development and increased political participation is less apparent than some other social consequences, but the connection can still be discerned. The tensions produced by widespread, fundamental social dislocation engender efforts to control or modify the situation through political action. If legal political action is thwarted, the activity then becomes criminal or rebellious. Like the union, the political party may become an agency of protest—effective or impotent. When linked to anti-colonial or other nationalistic movements, political organization mobilizes sentiment and action on behalf of governmental policies, and incidentally diverts criticism from the internal weaknesses and strains in the social order.

The economic and cultural interests able to form the basis of political action are very diverse in any society. A single-party or two-party system does not dispel such divisive interests; the interests simply necessitate more elaborate compromises and coalitions to be formed within the party, rather than between parties, in order for the party to be able to legislate and govern.

As all sorts of social functions become conducted by specialized organizations—like welfare agencies, hospitals, schools, and consumer co-operatives—voluntary associations are frequently formed to promote, support, and control those organizations. Associations may also be formed to promote or prevent a host of undesired actions. The most striking common feature of the many associations that are inclined to emerge with urban industrialization is the idea that purposive social action is possible and appropriate. This idea is comparatively uncommon in traditionally organized societies. Although the heady idea of social betterment or prevention often generates a multitude of rather ineffectual groups, their members do at least manifestly accept a rather revolutionary change in the proper relation of the individual to the social order (VI).

Studies of associations and their members are not far advanced anywhere. Obviously, a major conditioning factor is the legal code—i.e., whether freedom of association is broadly interpreted or virtually non-existent. A closely related condition is the extent to which some associations, like political parties or unions, are genuinely multi-functional, which quality avoids the degree of multiplication of separate organizations observable in some countries.

Where freedom of association is extensive and membership is largely voluntary, patterns of differential participation recur. The "joiners," or "good organization people," are generally not those who ostensibly would benefit most by social action or seem to be most in need of being diverted after frustrating routines at work. Rather, associations are usually composed of successful, often upwardly mobile, elements in the population. The persons who apparently derive high work satisfactions from their jobs also seem to have time and energy for other organized activities (XI). Differential participation can be understood not in terms of the range from frustration to success, but in terms of the range from apathy to positive self-confidence.

In a subtle sense, freedom of association may be inconsistent with voluntary participation. The interests promoted by an association may have negative consequences for others. Therefore, once an interest group has become active, its collective effort may call forth the formation of associations to protect the interests it threatens. Thus the freedom not to join interest groups may be exercised only at the risk of losing ground, relatively or absolutely. This is as true of associations to promote, e.g., wild-life preservation as it is of the more obvious case of the partial but economically successful union organizations that result in the relative deterioration of the economic positions of workers who are not organized.

We shall now consider the associational counterpart of popular culture. Fraternal associations, although they often have political or religious overtones, probably serve more nearly recreational functions, as do amateur

350

sport organizations, musical groups, collectors' societies, and the like. One encounters differential patterns of participation, partly caused by the actual costs (dues, equipment, financial resources for collecting). It is also probable, however, that the apathy and discontent felt by poorly paid and marginal workers are general attitudes that do not conduce to their involvement in "cultivated" leisure activities.

A caution should be given here. Its flavor is conveyed by the aphorism, "The pub is the poor man's club." Some of the differential participation may be a statistical manifestation of the fact that formal associations have constitutions, bylaws, and membership lists. Non-joiners may find their recreation in genuine groups which lack formal trappings. Time-budgets of behavior would give more precise dimensions to our knowledge of voluntary social activity—but that research instrument has never been adequately refined or used.

Religious Organizations and Beliefs

More speculation than study—and not much of either—has been devoted to the precise relevance of religious ideologies for economic development. The notion that the Protestant ethic is a prerequisite for economic modernization is no longer taken seriously in its crude form. Governmental action can be substituted for private, individualistic enterprise. And collectivist ideologies may assume religious overtones, promising, among other things, that worldly immortality can be gained by developing the economy on behalf of generations yet unborn. Nationalism and patriotism always have religious elements—whether linked to traditional religious beliefs or not.

Subtle questions remain, however, concerning religious beliefs. As we noted briefly when discussing motivation and enterprise, the achievement orientations encouraged in some parts of Protestant Christianity may be either absent or less socially disciplined in other religious systems. Does the other-worldliness of Hinduism or Catholicism, combined with an emphasis on acceptance and adaptation instead of active improvement, preclude economic development? Does the somewhat more hedonistic other-worldliness of Islam, coupled with an authoritarian view of worldly power, have similar negative effects? The questions multiply; but the answers do not.

Here and there, clear evidence of economic activities differential according to religious affiliation leads one to suppose that religion itself makes a difference. These data do not always indicate a full explanation of the relationship.

One type of religious manifestation has a close association with rapid social change generated largely under external impact. Pagan cults rarely survive when confronted with one of the great organized religious systems,

351

although the latter not uncommonly adapt to the former. More significant are the situations where new religions spring up or, more precisely, are invented. In various parts of the world, ranging from the southwest United States to Africa (VI) and the South Pacific (VIIA), new cults have appeared that often involve combinations of Christianity or Islam with old beliefs and practices plus some novel additions. Such cults apparently flourish best among those people who, while exposed to Western religion, goods, and political rule, have not been fully incorporated into a "modernized" social system. These phenomena are interesting in the present context, not as religious aberrations, but as manifestations of the rejection of alien influences. They are—in the non-evaluative sense of the word—reactionary.

Possibly the most outstanding effect that industrialization has on religious organization and belief is secularization. At its extreme, secularization involves an active rejection of traditional religion, and the substitution of a new set of essentially religious beliefs for old ones. In its less extreme forms, secularization involves a reduction of religious control over everyday life, the possible growth of agnostic positions toward theological doctrine, and the substitution of rational for ritual action (XI, XIII).

As new forms of social activity appear and the close integration between religion and other elements of traditional social organization declines, the church ceases to pervade the life of the community and becomes a special interest association. The role of the clergy or other religious leaders is restricted, especially in matters now identified as mundane. Religious leadership becomes functionally specific rather than functionally diffuse, as does, usually, the social behavior of the laity. Indifference may be a greater danger than active opposition, since the latter tends to challenge believers to take defensive action.

As a problem, secularization is, perhaps, strongest in the challenge of science. Science has no significance for religious beliefs of a strictly supernatural character—e.g., the metaphysical explanation of the meaning of existence, and beliefs in immortality. But almost all concrete religious systems have sacred writings that purport to be partly historical, in the secular sense. More important, most religious systems provide supernatural explanations for, and claim that supernatural powers may be used to alter the course of, empirical events.

Science may have no enlightenment to offer about the nature of heaven —but it can teach about what causes weather, about the way of getting better crops, and about what keeps boats afloat. In technical social science analysis, a distinction is made between religion and "magic"; the latter refers to the use of non-rational powers and procedures to produce or avoid empirical events. Although the very fact that much of magic is embedded in religious systems gives it a considerable immunity to chal-

352

lenge, it does not survive rational challenges over the long run. For example, the magical rituals of the New Zealand Maori (VIIA) have succumbed to rationalism. The situation in Africa is less clear-cut, since some magic and witchcraft may survive because of the very uncertainties and anxieties in the new environment (VI). Since magic is vulnerable, its union with religion implies that the strong defense of magical practices incurs the risk of general alienation from religious doctrines.

The universal function of magic is to eke out the difference between rational prediction and control, on the one hand, and the felt need for control, on the other. As rational techniques are improved, they become accepted as more efficacious than magical ones. Nevertheless, the uncertainties of human existence are, and are likely to remain, such as to provide opportunities for old and new magic. The derogation of magic as "superstition" indicates the relative success of rational orientations; but the persistence of magic despite derogation must also be noted. The secular attitude is not wholly satisfactory for confronting many of life's problems. However, it is likely to spread to many aspects of human activity, as part of the habits of thought encouraged by technical change and problem-solving orientations. In the process of diffusion, some established religious rituals will either be modified or fall into disuse.

Social Stratification
Industrialization inevitably provides a new set of social positions and new criteria of social placement and valuation. At the very least, therefore, it must result in the "complication" of systems of stratification. More commonly, it gives rise to competing systems of stratification, since its criteria of placement and valuation contrast sharply with traditional modes of assigning status, power, and prestige (II, VI, VIIB).

The possible integration of the non-industrial with the industrial stratification system depends not only on their degree of similarity, but also on the scope, extent, and speed of economic transformation. A highly commercialized economy, with comparatively open competitive opportunities, may set few barriers against new modes of market entry and placement, and be able to use simple income tests for some aspects of social valuation. This was the situation, in varying degrees, before the industrial revolution in the oldest industrial economies. We do not mean to deny either the short-run or, certainly, the long-run differences, but only to note that competitive placement and financial rewards were not startling innovations. In many developing areas, however, they are.

A slow and limited change may permit considerable adjustment and compromise between the old and the new. One can imagine, and possibly find, a direct transfer of quasi-feudal relations between landlords and tenants

353

to similar relations between factory owners and workers. If the change is sufficiently limited in kind, even rapid alteration of production may be absorbed into the traditional structure—e.g., in the case of the "familistic" organization of small shop production in Japan (III). Over the centuries, the caste system of India has been able to adjust to new occupations by forming sub-castes; a slow and very limited industrial development could possibly have challenged the caste system less sharply than has actually been the case (IXA).

These situations are significant but exceptional. The industrial requirements of merit recruitment, mobility, technical division of labor, and limited authority relationships do not fit well into other systems of social placement.

During early industrialization, few and sharp distinctions in social status emerge. During this stage, the differences in social origin, education, and power of managers and workers are likely to be widest—even in countries where the status of managers is not that of owners, as it is in socialist economies. Welfare considerations protect the worker from exceptionally harsh bargains, but the lack of competition among employers may give him no opportunities for improving his situation. However, the fundamental fact of radical disparity in social position remains.

As industrialization advances, the skills of manual workers become more differentiated, and still more kinds of managers, technicians, and professionals are added to the productive organization. These developments multiply the ranks based on position in the occupational structure. Within a single productive organization, the distinctions may be fairly clear; and the absolute differences in income, for example, may go to greater extremes than in the less complex organization of small factories. The first point to be noted, however, is that these distinctions cannot be meaningfully equated with "class"—unless the "class" system is to duplicate the number of distinct levels; if it does not, the dividing lines are likely to be arbitrary.

We have stated this point as it obtains in the simplest possible case, where a single and rather clear-cut gradation of occupational positions is available. However, we cannot generalize that such a gradation exists in every industrial system. The kinds and gradations of occupations are frequently somewhat peculiar to the industry, perhaps to the particular firm. The multiplication of occupations and the fact that, except in terms of income (and, less reliably, training time), they are comparable only to a low degree, may heighten the importance of occupational distinctions within the work context, while reducing its validity as an indicator of general social status. Broad income-and-occupational categories may become conventionalized as classes, but without any sensible criteria that precisely determine their number or boundaries.

354

This, then, becomes the class system of an industrialized society. According to all available evidence, such a society can be made classless only if "class" is arbitrarily defined as resting upon the private ownership of productive property, and such ownership is then abolished. Differential effective control of productive instruments is not thereby eliminated (e.g., II).

Within this common framework, there are significant variations. These variations include the range of differences in status on a single scale (which may reduce to effective income), and the degree of mobility within careers and between generations, which is related to the degree of equality of opportunity. As opportunity is a multiple and not, except in income terms, a single variable, it entails critical questions about modes of occupational assignment and choice.

Research on these questions has produced crude and fragmentary results, because the instrumentation of research inquiries is difficult, and because the questions themselves have not been correctly identified. Generally speaking, because of the reasons noted above, phrasing the questions in terms of "class" status and mobility dooms the answers to imprecision and low transferable predictability.

The complex organizational structure of industrial societies, and the multiplication of relatively discrete contexts of social action and attitude, necessarily increase the contexts in which stratification or differential valuation is relevant. Economic position provides the best single set of variables for determining general social position. But the contexts in which general position is a significant component of social action may be narrowly restricted—even when that position is clearer than it usually is.

Two aspects of the problem of status determination and its predictive consequences must be distinguished clearly. One aspect relates to persons (or families as the normal unit of general social status). The other relates to contexts of action. An industrial system assigns positions and rewards in the economic system in such complexity that precise status is difficult to convert to general status, except in crude and arbitrary generalizations represented in notions of "class." The detailed criteria of status determination in the work context, other than income, will not yield a rank-order scale. At best, they yield "occupational prestige groups," which tend to have a high correlation with income and educational attainments, but with arbitrary boundaries and heterogeneous internal composition. (This, incidentally, appears to be true even among African workers [VI], who behave as a "class," if at all, only with respect to Europeans.) The notion that there is a single scale of occupational prestige that can, without resorting to income criteria, reliably rank all occupations, is pure myth.

This imprecision in the comparison of the general status of persons is intrinsic to an industrial system of occupational divisions. It may be

355

reduced, or, rather, defined away, in the extreme case of a complete bureaucratization of the labor force under a single, centralized control, with a simple and uniform system of assignment of bureaucratic rank to occupations. This would provide, by administrative fiat, an "occupational status group"—but it would not insure that the occupations were comparable in any other respect.

Hence, it is extremey difficult to compare the general social status of persons, even if only economic indicators are used. The difficulty is compounded by other criteria of evaluation, since the same person is involved in different, and perhaps many, contexts of action.

In any pattern of behavior or context of social relationships in which varying degrees of "ideal" behavior can be approximated, differential valuation is made of the individuals involved. Indeed, such valuation may be placed on qualities and conditions over which the individual has no control—e.g., on seniority, lineage, or ethnic origin (VI, VIIA, XIII). The criteria of social valuation may be highly particular to variable contexts. They may, like the criteria of "race," have repeated or general relevance.

The critical empirical question here is the degree of "status coalescence" or status consistency in a social system as a whole, or differentially for various categories of persons. Economic or occupational criteria can be taken as primary determinants of "genera" status; but how predictive are such criteria for social valuation in other contexts? An economic and social system under extreme centralized control is likely to provide greater status consistency in many contexts of life than is a system that permits a great deal of autonomy in organizations and in private lives. This fact is partly due to the probability that formal bureaucratic rank is "carried with" the individual, and partly due to the probability that all or most aspects of social life will be made part of a relatively coherent social plan in a centralized system.

The probability of status inconsistency—or, at least, of independent variability of positional contexts—leads to the possibility that "primary" criteria can be influenced by "secondary" ones. This is readily recognized when ascribed qualities and conditions aid or hamper achievement. It can also be discerned in a "reverse" transfer of non-occupational prestige, in, for example, family entertaining, community activity, or success in amateur sports, to enhanced occupational position.

Although the preceding paragraphs have implied the context of fully industrialized societies, the analysis need not be so delimited. The fact that industrial modes of status allocation in developing societies are set in a context of other criteria of social placement enhances the probability both of status ambiguity in the comparison of persons and of status inconsistency as applied to individuals. And sometimes not even the

356

universal solvent of income is an appropriate, if rickety, bridge from one system or context to another.

Organization of the State

The historical and contemporary variety of state organization in industrialized societies manifests the fact that there is considerable independent variation between economic and political organization. Indeed, at first glance, it seems impossible to make a generalization concerning the political implications of industrialization. However, careful scrutiny discovers some common elements and characteristics.

These common elements are more readily identifiable in the administrative than in the strictly political structure of the state. All contemporary states use a similar administrative structure for carrying out public functions—the "bureaucratic organization." We need not recapitulate here the essential features of bureaucratic organizations, in terms of gradations of authority, the matching of power and responsibility, clear-cut functional specialization, merit placement, etc. It seems unlikely that any other mode of conducting regular public functions could achieve the required reliability and accountability of action.

Administrative structures differ in detail, and in their relative magnitudes in the society as a whole. Specific agencies and their relative importances vary from one country to another, as does the mode of relationship between administrative and political authorities. Experts agree that the efficiency and reliability of administration are greatly impaired if it is not established as a permanent civil service, rather than being staffed through patronage and subject to detailed political interference or turnover. Similarly, efficiency is presumably impaired by any form of particularistic placement, such as nepotism, even if not politically inspired. And corruption—in the technical sense, i.e., of substitution of individual for organizational ends—is a potential problem in all bureaucracies. Corruption may range from a conflict of interest between the official's public responsibilities and his private, otherwise legitimate, interests, to outright graft. If personal moral standards are not taken into account, graft can be regarded as usually related to slow, complicated, and unreliable administrative action and procedures.

Modern public administration is fairly novel in some of the developing areas; and it is not surprising that it is often judged to be inefficient, if not corrupt. The difficulty of securing technically qualified administrators represents part of the problem; and competing demands from commerce and industry will do nothing to improve that situation. However, the acceptance of a somewhat novel normative system is also involved. This acceptance requires either widespread changes in individual attitudes, or the imposition of exceptionally rigorous discipline "from the top down."

357

The connection between the economy and the polity can best be approached in terms of minimum and maximum degrees of state regulation of economic activities. The minimum is apparently determined by the necessity of preserving order, enforcing institutional rules (including those relating to various business practices), and the public provision of financial and fiscal responsibility. Even such a minimum presupposes the development of efficient public administration.

The preservation of order is, of course, a primary function of any state. But an industrial system is more vulnerable to civil disorders than other modes of economic organization and activity. It operates with fixed capital installations, and normally depends upon a fairly elaborate and reliable transportation network to assemble the factors of production and to move goods to markets. Even in the absence of outright civil disorder, an industrial organization must have reasonable confidence in the law, in its administration, and in its judicial interpretation. Plans and commitments of resources must often be made well in advance of actual operations. If the rules of procedure are subject to uncertainty or rapid change, if agreements on supplies and services can be violated with impunity, the situation may be too economically perilous for the private enterpriser or too politically perilous for the publicly employed manager.

The maximum effective control by the state need not be total. The planned and controlled integration of an entire complex economy may have to leave margins of uncertainty and individual choice. One reason for this incomplete control is the impossibility of having perfect advance knowledge of the outcome of the interaction of many, partially uncontrolled, variables. In addition, the administrative costs of perfect, detailed control may be much higher than the cost of some margin of individual variability.

Between the minimum and maximum, what will determine the degree of economic control exerted by a state organization? Obviously, the major variable is ideological, as is most vividly illustrated by the extreme positions of the single encompassing socialist state, and of the limited state in a "pluralistic" society providing wide areas of functional autonomy to economic or other organizations.

Even where the ideology of a pluralistic society prevails, however, the factual role of the state is substantially above the minimum. This is especially true in countries seeking rapid economic development and willing to use the power of the state to foster it (e.g., IXA).

The "liberal" state is likely to intervene in economic organization and policy for a number of fairly standard reasons. For military and defense production, the role of the state is paramount. In addition, the state often intervenes to redress balances, either cross-sectional or temporal. Thus, the state will try to reduce or eliminate sharp fluctuations in the level of

358

economic activity, but also to reduce or prevent inequities in competitive positions or income distributions. Where centralized economic planning is a prominent feature of economic policy, the balance and sequence of economic activities are partly guided by national, aggregative considerations, and not entrusted to the preferences of managers or investors. Similarly, in any economic system—and especially in one undergoing rapid development—the government tends to intervene to break bottlenecks if private action is unable or unlikely to do so. The more functionally interdependent the economy, the greater the potential number and strategic importance of such bottlenecks.

These considerations help to account for the trend for the role of government to expand in all industrial societies—to expand absolutely, if not relative to the growth in complexity of other aspects of the societies. More generally, the state is essentially the "residuary legatee" of unsolved social problems; regardless of political ideology, it will sooner or later intervene if private solutions are not forthcoming. Cynical critics of state expansion are approximately correct in alleging that, except for some clearly identified "emergency" measures, a function taken on by the government is rarely released.

The probability of increased political participation in industrializing societies has been noted in a previous section. But it is not possible to say that industrialization inevitably engenders "representative government"—or, at least, to get any agreement, across ideological lines, about the essential structure of representative government. The probability of increased nationalism has also been noted. Emotional adherence to national policies may serve to gloss over strains involved in rapid transformation, conflicting interests, and the substantial cultural diversity within some states.

Clearly, the increasing similarity of the technology and even of the organization of production has, if anything, a negative relation to political and ideological rapprochement. Industry provides weapons for external war and internal terror. It has not yet produced substantial and reliable restraints on their use.

The Social Implications of Industrialization and Technological Change: Concluding Comments

WILBERT E. MOORE
Princeton University

The world is full of revolutions. This is true at least in the language of scholars and journalists, and quite possibly also in fact. Advanced industrial countries are said to be experiencing their second, or perhaps third, industrial revolutions. The underdeveloped countries are said to be in the midst of a "revolution of rising expectations," and on the verge or in the early stages of a first industrial revolution.

If we accept a common-sense meaning of "revolution" as rapid, extensive, and fundamental social change, the social implications of industrialization are indeed revolutionary. The character of the change, its depth and direction, its rate and sequence, are extensively illuminated in the several preceding chapters. There remains the task of identifying some of the leading theoretical, practical, and "professional" issues that appear in the technical papers and prompted discussion at the Conference for which they were originally prepared. Some conclusions, partially substantive and partially hortatory, will be presented at the end of this summary.

SOME DISCUSSION HIGHLIGHTS

No attempt will be made here to summarize the rich detail of the technical papers prepared for the Conference, or even the critical discussion that the papers elicited. Rather, some highlights have been selected for special comment, compressed, but in a sequence that follows the general order of the preceding chapters.

Conceptual and Theoretical
The discussion of the two papers dealing with general concepts and with the general patterns of social change brought to the fore several related

360

issues. (*a*) Dichotomous classifications of variables, leading either to "polar types" or, in combination, to "ideal types," may be empty theoretical constructions or have considerable heuristic value in testing theoretical relationships. (*b*) Such modes of analysis present problems of operational identification in research, and of mensuration when the mixed situations of empirical reality are approached. (*c*) General concepts of structural change—e.g., differentiation, integration, and disturbance—share with structural types the problem of the canons for empirical identification. (*d*) These concepts are perhaps more useful in identifying processes of social transformation from *given* causes than in explaining the origins of change or in accounting for the temporal order of changes.

Particular Social Implications

The discussion of the specific social implications of industrialization started with what some regard as the fundamentals: the human motivation for making constructive innovations. Entrepreneurship was discussed as a reaction to conditions of uncertainty that permits strategies to capitalize on risk-taking. The disputed points involved such matters as the conditions for innovation under bureaucratic organization or in situations where the major impulses to economic growth are channeled through government. Particular conceptualizations were challenged as having a too stringently limited historical relevance, and the need for testing historical generalizations in currently developing areas was strongly emphasized.

The variable incidence of high achievement orientations as between societies and sectors of societies led to the interpretation of this psychological attribute as crucially important in economic transformations. The principal controversies, aside from methodological criticism of the evidence, revolved around questions of psychological or institutional primacy in determination of behavior, and the minimal significance attached to the possibility of adult personality transformation or attitudinal change.

Some of this concern for significant variation in motivation was also brought to bear on problems of savings and investment in developing societies. Traditional forms of investment (e.g., in land) may be economically non-rational; and some uses of savings (e.g., paying for ceremonial occasions, or pure hoarding) do not lead to substantial increases in economic productivity or welfare. Although there was some disagreement in the interpretation of the evidence, it was strongly argued that neither savings nor investment were impeded by other-worldly orientations as such, but, rather, by various traditional reciprocities and modes of maintaining status that do not permit rational investment.

On a more strictly structural level, the significance of rising income was

361

related to shifts in economic structure. Increases in income for whole economies is accompanied by a rising *proportion* of non-agricultural income, despite the probable concurrent rise of income in agriculture. Much of the discussion turned on the meager information concerning detailed shifts in consumers' budgets and the extent to which these follow a common pattern.

From economic performance and its motivational base, the discussion shifted to political and administrative organizations. Here again there was controversy about the proper use of analytical elements and constructed typologies. In view of the apparently wide range of variability in political structures associated with seemingly successful economic growth, predictive propositions seemed more likely to result from linking a few variables than from complex types as such. One type, the bureaucracy or rational administrative structure, ostensibly has a wider generality than political organization and ideology. The appearances may be deceiving, however, as bureaucracies in new states are expected to be agencies of social transformation while operating within environing conditions that impede, distort, or constrain their activities. Where changes in loyalty are involved, as in new economic activities and the emergence of new regimes, the problems may be approached in terms of "interest groups" and their conflicts. However, it was noted that social science conceptualization has not always made the distinction between groups with preclusive membership and groups with overlapping memberships that may make competing or incompatible demands on individuals.

Conceptual problems plagued even those analyses based in part upon "hard," quantitative data. For example, in a study of urbanization, a geographic-demographic delineation of the city does not satisfy all needs, any more than do looser concepts like "urbanism." The extremely rapid physical urbanization in underdeveloped areas was accepted as a basis for discussion, which indicated the need for closer analyses of both historical and contemporary evidence on reasons for migration and the selective characteristics of migrants. Although the role of social scientists as policy advisers was not universally conceded, it was noted that those in such a role must consider balanced rural-urban development as a way of restraining the drain on economic resources involved in social overhead for rapidly growing cities.

The concept of over-urbanization was akin to that of over-population. In both cases, the problem was discussed in terms of growth rates inconsistent with optimal allocation of resources for economic growth. It was noted that there is a generally inverse relationship between current levels of living and the prospects for population growth. The moot issues revealed by the discussion included the prevalence of a desire for family size limitation, the speed with which contraceptive practices can be accepted, and the extent to which concern for future welfare enters the decisions of any family about its optimum size.

The discussion of the demographic implications of economic change conversely led naturally to a consideration of family structures. Strong support was expressed for renewed attention to types of relationships between family and economy. Extended kinship relationships may become voluntary rather than compulsory under conditions of industrialization, but they do not necessarily therefore disappear. Indeed, family and kinship structures appear to have greater independent variability with reference to productive organization than conventional analysis has conceded.

The position of education as an instrument of economic change was contrasted to its position as a "consumption good." A number of issues were sharply joined, but none resolved: (a) broadly based elementary education vs. selected training of strategically important skills; (b) the "aggregative" effect of education vs. its "micro-effects"—i.e., on the mobility patterns of individuals; and (c) the effects of education in rising aspirations for consumption or higher employment vs. the effects of education in increasing productivity and employment opportunities.

Finally, the significance of new modes of communication (the mass media) was noted. Here again, the inconsistency between the possibly rapid change in aspirations and possibly slow changes in the means for their realization was manifest. There was some dispute about whether "wants" now need to be cultivated, compared with, say, attitudes toward productivity and investment. Whatever the purpose and sponsorship of mass communication, however, it was accepted as a possible substitute for formal modes of education where resources are radically limited.

Summaries of Research Surveys

As part of the general UNESCO program of which this Conference was a component, an attempt was made to appraise existing knowledge for each of the world's major regions. Those surveys more or less followed a uniform outline and presented selected bibliographies. Several such regional surveys, or summaries of them, were discussed at the Conference, and others formed part of the background documentation.

For these surveys and the summary of them presented here, the crucial problem was the comparability and generalizability of social situations and their analyses. Over-generalization leads properly to complaints that general propositions are abstract or banal and, in any event, meaningless. On the other hand, failure to attempt to construct predictive propositions is an abdication of the claims and hopes of social science. Individual preferences run toward particulars or generalities. One point of agreement may be noted: the fair amount of ignorance about both the details and the principles.

Research Resources, Strategy, and Application

The problems of the practicing social scientist, especially in the less developed countries, raised some additional issues. One view was that basic research, or even ordinary scholarly work, was impeded by a paradoxical combination: a distrust of social science and an insistent demand for its practical advice. Another viewpoint regarded policy issues as urgent, and the social scientist as obligated to aid in their solution. Although the respective proponents of these views remained unconvinced by their adversaries, there was general agreement that in either role the social scientists need a relatively secure position and access to the international community of scholars for both stimulus and validation of scholarly work.

International communication was also involved in discussions of the programs for exchange of scholars, problems of texts translated not only in language but also in terms of local applications, the need for training indigenous experts at home or abroad, and the varied activities of the UNESCO Department of Social Sciences.

Finally, communication of all sorts was proffered as the key to making social science acceptable as well as merely usable. This did not entirely subdue the critics of "social engineering," but it did serve to confirm the common feeling that considerable progress had been made on a difficult and important subject.

CONCLUSIONS

It seems justifiable to draw from the papers and the discussions certain conclusions about research strategies and procedures, and about major gaps in reliable knowledge.

Research Strategies

1) The Conference demonstrated the utility—and indeed the necessity—of an interdisciplinary approach to the complex phenomena of economic development. The problems, whether theoretical or practical, are mostly "undisciplined." Any attempt to deal with them within the strict confines of a single discipline is thus likely to result in sterile formulae and impractical advice. For many purposes, interdisciplinary research teams are essential. However, there is also growing need for "interdisciplinary individuals"—i.e., students of economic development and its social implications must expand their conceptualization of research and their operating vocabularies in order partially to encompass the approaches of neighboring disciplines. This expansion of the talents of scholars is facilitated by interdisciplinary conferences, and further encouraged if scholarly contact is frequent and durable.

2) Social scientists often show strong predilections for *either* theory *or*

364

research techniques. The discussions of the Conference repeatedly demonstrated the need to mingle research precision *and* intellectual order. Two questions must be asked: What do we want to know? How shall we find out? The construction of conceptual schemes may result in meaningless name-calling if the concepts cannot be converted into research designs. The elaboration of research tools may result in useless precision if they are not designed to answer significant questions. A set of working hypotheses tends to minimize both dangers.

3) Because of the actual diversity of social situations and the wide range of scholarly and practical interests underlying research programs, they are substantial problems in achieving comparability in research results. For many areas of the world, and especially for the economically underdeveloped ones, the most elementary statistical information is not available at all, is extremely unreliable or is out of date. The United Nations and its specialized agencies endeavor to improve the quality and comparability of data, and to indicate approximate reliability in their publications. Research institutes, professional societies, and even individual scholars can encourage governmental officials to improve collecting and reporting information. In actual research design, the quest for "originality" in concepts and procedures has further aggravated the difficulties of comparability. The generality and applicability of some relationships between economic and social forms can be determined only by replication of research under varying conditions. Such repeated testing of relationships is generally the closest approximation to genuine experimentation that the social sciences permit.

4) Since the total scholarly resources for analysis of the social implications of industrialization are small, it is appropriate to note that some intellectual disciplines not usually represented in conferences and research teams may have valuable contributions to make. Economic, social, and intellectual history may permit wider testing of relationships, and also help to solve the troubled questions of order and sequence in change. Economic and human geography may aid in assessing the role of variable resources and also the total ecological or spatial setting of social relationships. Law, particularly comparative law and public administration, may contribute to appraising the significance of variable conditions, legal philosophies, and actual administrative procedures.

5) The resources for research on the social implications of industrialization are, of course, most meager in the underdeveloped areas. Trained personnel requires teachers, texts, and equipment. Even if adequately trained, the social scientist may be under either economic or political pressure to participate in current action programs—perhaps to the total displacement of basic research. Granted the urgency of immediate programs and the correlative need for professional guidance on them, it is hoped that some resources will be found so that some social scientists may remain free from distracting day-to-day policy involvements. In this connection, the value of research efforts and expenditures may be enhanced if centers can be established for continuous, longitudinal observation of change. Such centers would both aid in the problem of keeping data current and provide an accumulating record of sequences, on which present knowledge is indeed scanty.

6) "Social engineering," i.e., the application of social scientific principles to practical problems, is urgently requested by political leaders in many countries. The obstacles to conscientious and successful effort are substantial, and must be noted. (a) Ultimate values are not scientifically given or derived, and such value problems cannot be entirely neglected by the practitioner. (b) In many instances, the reliable scientific principles simply do not exist. Optimists argue that the social scientist has a better chance than the lay official in guesses as to procedures. Pessimists argue that, in the absence of long-term and basic research, the guesses have little chance of being right, and that failure will cast lasting discredit on scholarly endeavor. (c) In any event, application requires "adding in" information previously lost in the process of abstracting to achieve generalizations. Often, several principles are relevant to a particular case, along with many particulars. The "engineer" needs "art" and "judgment" as well as scientific training. Nevertheless, it may be maintained that social scientists will be asked to advise on policy, and that in doing so they will begin to develop a body of case experience which may be partially transferable and thus, in a sense, contribute to the enrichment of general knowledge.

Some Major Gaps in Knowledge
The technical papers for the Conference, the international survey of research results, and the discussions of this documentation, indicated some significant gaps in relevant knowledge. Some of the leading *lacunae* are noted below. We have not attempted to assign research priorities. Such priorities in projects must be determined by evaluating their respective scientific interest, feasibility, the practicality of results for economic and social planning, and, not least, the wandering or vagrant predilections of individual scholars.

1) Widely varying views of appropriate priorities in educational expansion revealed the inadequate state of knowledge about the educational implications of economic development. This applies to both educational prerequisites and consequences. The problem of matching levels of training and aspiration, on the one hand, and realistic employment opportunities, on the other, needs exploration. Conference participants were encouraged by the evidence of closer co-operation between the Education

366

and Social Science Departments of UNESCO, particularly in connection with educational needs for economic growth.

2) Despite the historical connection between industrialization and urbanization, the two are somewhat independent. In many underdeveloped areas, urbanization is occurring much more rapidly than the expansion of industry or other employment opportunities. Although valuable research results are accumulating, there still appears to be a strong need for comparative study of urban structures—ecological, economic, administrative, social—and of the causes and characteristics of urban migration. The Conference noted with pleasure that there is to be a major emphasis placed on problems of urbanization by the United Nations and its specialized agencies.

3) Much more analytical work must be done on the interrelations between rates of population growth and the age-sex structures of populations, on the one hand, and the economy—both as productive organization and as the aggregate of consumers—on the other. The situations, now and in the future, differ greatly from one country to another. No simple assumption of overpopulation, or its opposite, is likely to fit these variable situations.

4) Psychologists are inclined to consider human personality and its motivation as the basis of social action and institutions; other social scientists are inclined to regard personality variables as dependent. Proponents of both views are likely to concede interplay between the variables, but more comparative research must be undertaken on deep-seated motivation, the conditions for its creation, the conditions for its manifestation, and the possibilities of motivational alteration consistent with new forms of social action.

5) The common assumption that the hierarchically arranged administrative organization is the single best way to co-ordinate specialized activities must be carefully scrutinized. "Bureaucracies" (administrative organizations) have much in common regardless of differences in function or even in ultimate control. But we do not really know how much of this common organization is intrinsic to the task and how much may be simply imitative of historical and comparative models. The empirical range of feasible organization for work is not systematically recorded, and theoretical alternatives have not been systematically explored.

6) The generalization that industrialization is destructive of extended kinship systems has been subject to considerable question and modifications. Comparative studies must be made to determine more precisely the necessary and probable implications of industrialization for family and kinship, as distinct from the independent or undetermined variability in these universal social structures. It now appears that there may be a number of institutional compromises between familial forms and functions,

367

on the one hand, and productive organizations, on the other, within the "tolerable" range of the criteria for economic efficiency. It is doubtful that any compromise will remove all sources of tension and strain. (The perfectly integrated society is a theoretical myth, not just an actual one.)

7) Research, or at least theoretical analysis disciplined by research considerations, is needed to sharpen decisions on what kinds of analytical variables, and of their combination into typologies, will be most efficacious in ordering data and permitting high-level generalization. Where social phenomena are very heterogeneous, the highest level of generalization may be too "abstract," that is, result in loss of too much information on differences and details. This situation ordinarily calls for lesser generalizations involving sets of manageable variables, or typologies permitting partial generalizations for a class of phenomena. Social scientists interested in conceptualization have not uniformly considered research operations or even the problems of realistic generalization and prediction.

8) Finally, the scientific purposes in the study of the social implications of industrialization will be enhanced to the degree that functional and dynamic relations are correctly intertwined. This will require identification, in varying historical contexts and contemporary situations, of several distinct or distinguishable problems; (a) the necessary social correlates of economic change, without temporal ordering; (b) required temporal sequences—prerequisites, concomitants, and consequences at some remove but still determinate; (c) ranges of structural substitution, whereby types of correlates are specifiable but not exact structures within the tolerable range; (d) ranges of sequential substitution, i.e., limited alternative paths of change, with some consequences perhaps determinate after initial options have been exercised or drifted into; and (e) degrees of probability of consequences that are likely but not precisely determinate. This view of social dynamics neither abandons the useful functional view of human societies nor is submerged by some of the implicitly static conventions of that view.

Some scholars will of course emphasize pure research, and others the practical social problems; some will be discretely descriptive and others indiscreetly general; some will sharpen the tools of research and others will polish their analytical models. There is, however, some hope that these variable types, like the representatives of distinctive disciplines, may prove to be educable and co-operative in the continuous quest for knowledge.

1. See "Social Consequences of Technical Progress," *International Social Science Bulletin,* IV, No. 2 (1952); "Factors of Economic Progress," *International Social Science Bulletin,* VI, No. 2 (1954).

2. S. C. Gilfillan, "Social Implications of Technical Advance," *Current Sociology,* I, No. 5 (1953); Georges Balandier, "Social Implications of Technical Advance in Underdeveloped Countries," *Current Sociology,* III, No. 1 (1954-55); Lyle W. Shannon, "Social Factors in Economic Growth," *Current Sociology,* VI, No. 3 (1957).

3. Banton, *Social Implications of Industrialization and Urbanization in Africa South of the Sahara* (Paris, 1956); Philip M. Hauser (ed.), *Urbanization in Asia and the Far East* (Calcutta, 1957). A similar regional survey of Latin America is in preparation. In addition, UNESCO indirectly sponsored, through the International Social Science Council, a symposium on *Social, Economic and Technological Change: A Theoretical Approach* (Paris, 1958).

4. This summary has drawn upon the reports listed below, which were sponsored by, and are distributed by, the Research Office of the International Social Science Council. In the text, references to each of these reports is made by the parenthetical indication of the Roman numeral assigned to the report in this note.

    I. Jan Szczepanski, *Les Implications sociales de l'industrialisation dans les recherches des sciences sociales en Pologne.*

    II. S. N. Eisenstadt, *Social Consequences of Technical Innovation: Report on the State of Research in Israel.*

    III. Chie Nakane, *Research Survey on the Social Implications of Industrialization in Japan.*

    IV. Hassan El Saaty, *Research on the Social Implications of Industrialization in the United Arab Republic.*

    V. Jean Chesneaux, *Les Implications sociales de l'industrialization: Rapport regional sur la Chine.*

    VI. M. Banton, *The Social Implications of Industrialization in Africa South of the Sahara.*

    VII. Ernest Beaglehole, *Social Implications of Industrialization.*
        A. The New Zealand Maori Case.
        B. Southeastern Oceania.

VIII. G. Osipov and N. Ignatiev, *L'Importance sociale du progrès technique en U.R.S.S.*

IX. C. N. Vakil (ed.), *Survey of Research Results on Social Implications of Industrialization in South and Southeast Asia*; in three parts, with combined bibliography).

    A. India, Pakistan, and Ceylon (under the editorial sponsorship of the UNESCO Centre at Calcutta).

    B. Malaya, Singapore, and Borneo (by A. F. Wells).

    C. Philippines (by Ruben Santos-Cuyugan and Ofelia Regala Angangco).

X. L. A. Costa Pinto, *The Sociology of Development in Latin America.*

XI. Series of annotated bibliographies of relevant European literature and several brief summaries. Prepared under the general direction of S. Groenman.

XII. W. E. Moore, *Research Survey on Social Implications of Industrialization: Based on North American Literature* (This report is mainly a classified bibliography).

XIII. Stuart Jamieson, *Survey of Recent and Current Research on Social Implications of Industrialization and Technological Change in Canada.*

5. An extensive coverage of the relevant materials—although still not complete concerning the range of topics discussed here—is to be found in Wilbert E. Moore and Arnold S. Feldman (eds.), *Labor Commitment and Social Change in Developing Areas* (New York, 1960).

Appendices

Problems of Establishing Valid Social Research in the Underdeveloped Areas

GINO GERMANI

University of Buenos Aires

The problems raised by research on the social implications of industrialization and technological change are not clearly separable from those which relate to social investigation in general—"social investigation" being defined as based on methodological principles of a scientific character, and using advanced technical procedures adequate for the subjects with which it deals. In the study of the effects of technological change, problems often arise that are related to the type or "style" of social research to be employed, or the most appropriate techniques, or the order of priority to be given to the different subjects suitable for investigation. However, these problems constitute only one aspect of the general questions about the possibility and development of social reseach in less advanced countries. Some of these questions are probably very general. Others are endemic to certain areas characterized by common cultural features or similar levels of socio-economic development. After having examined briefly some of the general conditions presumably linked to social research, we shall refer more particularly to Latin America.

The social conditions which affect the possibility and development of scientific knowledge in general, and of social research in particular, have been considered in different discussions. Here, we shall recall only certain general aspects of these discussions, remembering that the theoretical and practical problems which arise with social research in the underdeveloped countries actually have their place within this broad frame.[1]

Scientific knowledge can occur only in societies in which the process of secularization has advanced sufficiently. The socio-cultural structure, in particular, must include—at least as regards science and its institutions, its roles, and status system—the institutionalization of change, action by choice regulated by reasoning (in place of traditional action), free examination, and permanent control of scientific propositions. The process of growing specialization of institutions must be in a fairly advanced stage, where science is clearly distinguished from other activities by its values, its social organizations, its system of roles and status; and where there is a further internal differentiation by which the *social* sciences (and their organization) have been clearly designated and are recognized as an autonomous and legitimate sphere of scientific endeavor.

Another necessary condition for the existence and growth of science, in the modern sense, is that there must be an operative form of recruiting scientists on the basis of efficiency and achievement. This involves a system of stratification in relatively open classes.

The type of political regime also exerts a considerable influence on the social sciences, since the predominance of officially established ideologies impedes, in one way or another, the development of scientific activities in this field.

The fact that social change is produced unevenly in different parts of the socio-cultural structure has, moreover, particular relevance for social research. The pattern of scientific knowledge is applied very late to the social sciences. The legitimacy of this application is not only correspondingly delayed; it also meets special obstacles deriving from possible, real, or supposed clashes with other parts of the structure—e.g., with institutions, norms, and values which are considered to be traditionally linked to the integration of society and even essential for its survival. This type of problem has arisen, and still exists with greater or lesser intensity, in countries which have now reached a high level of development. It acquires particular significance in less developed countries. In this respect, the recent history of the development of social research and its possible practical applications in advanced countries is relevant, because underdeveloped nations often confront the same type of problems.[2]

Certain other factors are of special importance in less developed countries. In the first place, modern science is the product of a particular historical and cultural context, and the particular *ethos* of this context has excercised a powerful influence on its development. To the extent that the underdeveloped countries do not partake of this cultural pattern—or else include value systems somehow opposed to (or not favorable to) the development of science, and of the institutional background and the corresponding motivations and attitudes —the possibility that social research will expand adequately is curtailed. Moreover, because of the particular relation of social sciences to the socio-cultural context—a relationship which is unanimously recognized as being closer than is the case with the natural sciences—the relative dependence of the culture becomes even more serious. This dependence tends to limit externally the development of the social sciences, while at the same time it affects the kind of social science that is most likely to evolve and prosper. In spite of the powerful unifying tendencies of recent years, we must realize that, especially in the field of sociology, we are still quite a long way from a unification comparable to that obtaining in the natural sciences. The conflicts of "diverging styles" of sociological work[3] are manifested not only in the selection of subjects and in the opposition of theories, but also (and specially) in the relative heterogeneity of methodological patterns prevailing in investigations. Often this conflict results in considerable insecurity and controversy about the standards to be applied in social research, and about the evaluation of its results since there are no universally accepted norms. This has a much more serious impact in those countries which are just being initiated into social research. They do not have a firmly established scientific basis, and in them, the influence of the socio-cultural structure can often be unfavorable to the development of social

374

science. Thus, the intellectual and academic traditions firmly rooted in the type of culture and social structure of a given country may contribute to the adoption of certain styles of sociological thought and social research and to the exclusion of others. Sometimes, the theoretical and methodological controversies, which characterize the social sciences in their present state, at an international level may have unforeseen repercussions in underdeveloped countries—repercussions which, in certain cases, seem to escape the logical framework of the original controversy.

Then, too, the considerable discontinuities characteristic of the process of change are manifested in all their intensity in the underdeveloped countries. Several types of contrasts are discernible. Geographically regions of very different social development coexist within the same country. In the sphere of social organization, institutions evince equally great contrasts in their respective greater or lesser fitness to the model of modern industrial society. The discontinuity is also apparent in the sphere of the concrete social groups, in mentalities unequally fitted to the new type of emerging social structure. Finally, all these conflicts, which manifest themselves with particular intensity in the sphere of values and of ideological struggle, have repercussions on intellectual activity, on the material organization of scientific activity, on teaching, and on research. In this way, they can affect, to a greater or lesser degree, the possibilities and character of social research in each country.

Another feature which probably characterizes all the underdeveloped countries must be indicated. We are concerned with countries which have only recently achieved their national independence or which, even when they have had a century or more of independence (as is the case with the majority of Latin American countries), still remain in a state of greater or lesser economic and cultural dependence. In the intellectual sphere, this real or perceived dependence usually manifests itself in different and at times contradictory ways. They generally assume the form of an imitative, uncritical tendency, or the opposite shape, an exclusive nationalism. The supranational character of the natural science shields them, to a great extent, from these problems; but the same cannot be said of the social sciences. Because of the many controversies in the social science disciplines, these conflicting positions are often brought into opposition with one another in conflicts which thus assume clear extra-scientific connotations. The danger that ideological elements will infiltrate the social sciences is too obvious a point to be considered here. However, we must mention that this danger is greater in the underdeveloped countries, because the most advanced centers in the scientific or intellectual fields are also centers of world politics. They are not only exporters of the products of that culture (including the modern social sciences), but also centers of economic, political, and military power. Above all, they are protagonists in the struggles and tensions which take place in the international arena. It is, therefore, inevitable that all sorts of misunderstandings should arise—sometimes justified, sometimes unjustified—about the meaning and the significance of the importation of theories, methods, and techniques in the field which is the object of the most intense controversies and ideological conflicts.

We have, in the previous paragraphs, discussed in general terms some of the problems relating to the possibility and development of social research in the less developed countries. In the remainder of this paper, we shall be concerned more specifically with Latin America.

The most serious obstacles to the development of social research are: (*a*) insufficient supply of scientific personnel; (*b*) insufficient material resources; and (*c*) inadequacy of the organizations devoted to research. Though these problems are extremely important, they also constitute the expression of the social context. The process of resolving the "practical problems" mechanically —through more financial resources, foreign experts, etc.—has, perhaps, a limitation inherent in the general conditions of the social context itself. Even without adopting a rigidly deterministic scheme, one cannot forget the obvious fact that the impediments to social research in underdeveloped countries are precisely a function of their insufficient development. Even if it were possible to employ a special strategy to overcome such obstacles, some limiting conditions might remain whose modification was more dependent on the change of the whole social structure.

The social structures of the countries of Latin America do not present a uniform picture. On the contrary, sharp contrasts may be observed both among and within the different countries.

In some nations, the process of urbanization and industrialization began toward the end of the last century and has achieved progress, at least in its social effects. This has been true in the three countries in the southern extremity, Argentina, Uruguay, and Chile. Their systems of social stratification, degrees of urbanization, demographic structures, levels of instruction, standards of living, and other indices are nearer to those of Western industrial society. In addition, their populations are totally European or Europeanized in type of culture. Other Latin American countries are at the opposite end of the scale. They are almost totally rural in character; their systems of stratification are still very near to the traditional pattern; and large proportions of the indigenous population are not, or only partially, integrated to the European culture. Most of the countries present vivid internal contrasts. Thus statistical data referring to the whole country can be somewhat misleading; for example, Brazil includes some of the more intensely urbanized areas of the entire continent, yet its national figures put it in the lowest range as a predominantly rural and less urbanized country.

In the last thirty years, extremely rapid change has been taking place. This is reflected in the great internal migrations which have led to the intense growth of the urban centers; in the transformation of the social structure and the stratification system, with the emergence of a considerable middle class and an urban proletariat; and in the rise of massive political movements. The last may, in general terms, be described as an manifestation of the rapid integration of large sectors of the population to the national community and modern culture.

The contrasts evinced in the degree of development of Latin American countries are superimposed on a certain foundation. Their common Hispanic heritage can still be perceived in spite of the extreme diversification produced by the differing tempi of development, the contrasting influences of indigenous cultures important in some cases, and inexistent in others, and European immigration (in some countries considerable, and in others negligible).

In general, the interpreters of "Latin American culture" (in so far as one can generalize in this respect) emphasize, of the particular features still noticeable in the different countries, those traits which may be considered as unfavorable to the development of modern social research. These traits include the accent on aesthetic rather than on practical values, on the humanities rather than on science, on the manipulation of verbal symbols instead of the experimental manipulation of things, etc. Other features of the social structure have been stressed—especially its "particularism," in comparison with the universalism necessary to the development of science.[4]

The general features must be remembered. The political instability and the presence of authoritarian regimes impede or in certain cases annul the development of the social sciences . On the other hand, the intelligentsia tend toward "politicization —i.e., the frequent involvements of scientific institutions and of scientists in ideological controversies—whether because of their own attitudes or because this is the way they are perceived by the public or by other intellectuals. Although it must not be inferred that this politicization always and decisively acts as an obstacle to social research, there is no doubt that it is a relevant factor in the conditions affecting it.

These are the elements—an uneven rhythm of development, traits from a common cultural heritage, political instability and authoritarianism, politicization—which constitute the social context which must be taken into account when evaluating the possibilities and the problems of social research in Latin America. These elements combine in a unique way in each country, according to the historic situations and intellectual traditions peculiar to the country. We shall now try to determine the way in which these conditions impinge upon certain aspects concretely related to social research.

In contrast with many underdeveloped areas, most Latin American nations have academic organizations that are often more than a hundred years old. They also have an established tradition of social studies, mainly concerned with Latin American societies and the changes they have undergone since becoming independent. Both these factors, in conjunction with the early development of law schools (in particular, of political law), and with the predominance of positivist tendencies from the middle of the last century to the beginning of the present century, facilitated the acceptance of social sciences by academic circles as much as among the intellectuals, politicians, and educated people in general.[5] These circumstances, which one would expect to conduce to the development of social research, and especially to the increasing study of the social effects of technical change, have acted and are still acting in a contradictory manner. In the past, they contributed substantially to the understanding of the social processes unfolding within Latin American societies. In addition, they helped to create a conscience about the problems raised by the social changes and showed the need for adopting a favorable attitude toward research and the social sciences. Sometimes, however, they seriously hindered modern social research from developing to the point of undertaking the study of the social processes in an age of technological change. The tradition of social studies, and the fact that the social sciences were institutionalized within the academic framework at a relatively early date (prior, at least, to the development of modern social research methodology), have had certain negative effects which we shall briefly indicate.

They have helped to create a "deformed pattern of scientific endeavour in the Social Sciences"—a pattern which still exists and thus hinders the adoption of adequate methodological principles.[6] This pattern exhibits the influences not only of an obsolete view of social research but also of certain features of Latin American culture. In these "impressionistic" studies, the preoccupation with literary expression takes on a detached form and the theme is not treated in a systematic manner. The treatment is almost exclusively historical-sociographical, and it rarely has a theoretical background or a connection with theoretical problems. Finally, within this tradition, the necessity of maintaining evaluative neutrality so far as possible is not clearly recognized; on the contrary, many social studies have at the same time an open ideological and political content.[7]

This type of study is far from what is today considered to be social research. Nevertheless, it retains considerable prestige among intellectuals and the academic world. In addition, to a certain extent it continues to represent "social research" to the lay public; and this public includes those people or groups who occupy power positions in the community or in academic organizations and are thus able to exert influence in questions of fundamental importance to the development of the research. The prestige accorded to, and the validity attributed to these studies as suitable models for social research persist for a number of reasons. For one, these studies are related to certain tendencies and values implicit in Latin American culture. Then, too, many earlier social studies were works of great value for the interpretations of Latin American societies and their history. In many cases, the works were of substantial literary importance.[8] Finally, these works had political and historical significance through their profound and lasting influence on the elites.

The fact that the social sciences (or at least some of them) were accepted at an early date within the academic organization has become, in the present, the cause of very serious obstacles to the evolution of modern social research. The hindrances are of various types, but all of them tend to reinforce the deformed pattern of social research. The problems are well known and have been analyzed thus: (a) the principal preoccupation of the academic body is teaching and not research; (b) there is a shortage of full-time personnel; and (c) the research institutes and research itself are conceived around the idea of the isolated research worker and armchair study. In addition, the shortage of scientific personnel of advanced training is crucially important—the shortage is a result of the factors to which we previously referred and, at the same time, the reason that they persist. In Latin America, as in many European countries, the old academic organization has either not yielded, or has yielded in a limited way and with much resistance, to the formation of scientifically prepared centers suitable for the new types of social research, especially in sociology. For a long time, even schools of economics were dedicated solely to training accountants—and this is still so in many cases. In sociology—a subject which

378

began to be taught in Latin America during the nineteenth century, and which is now represented by hundreds of professorial chairs within the region [9]—the content of teaching has frequently remained uncorrelated with the developments of the last thirty years. With certain exceptions (Brazil, for example, where the situation is notably better) it is only during the last five or ten years, as schools specializing in sociology have been created, that improvements have been discernible.[10]

This fact must not be related solely to the tradition of social studies nor to the relationship with philosophy, political law, and other intellectual influences which conditioned the teaching of sociology. There are other factors associated with the absence of recognized professional standards.

It is not merely that there is no adequate conception of social research. The majority of professors and practitioners in sociology or social research have had no formal training, as a consequence of the lack of specialized, professional schools in the field. Thus all sorts of "amateurs"—with little or no training of either the formal or the selftaught kind, can enter the field. This situation appears to be widespread in Latin America. Speaking about Brazil, a country more advanced than the rest, Costa Pinto talks of the "random assortment of adventurers" who invade the field of social research.[11] Campo Jimenez in Costa Rica, Arboleda in Colombia, and Silva Michelena in Venezuela all agree on this point.[12] In Argentina and other countries, the situation is apparently the same.[13] It is aggravated by the fact that, under the impact of the rapid process of change, there is an increasing demand for "applied" social research—even when the public are still completely unaware of the conditions, limits, and characteristics of this application. New employment opportunities for social scientists are opening both in public administration and in private enterprise. Nevertheless, there is still a lack of institutions designed to impart adequate professional instruction. Still more serious is the fact that it is not considered necessary that a social scientist have special training equivalent to that required for the other professions.

As Costa Pinto notes in his analysis of the situation in Brazil, these are typical problems encountered in the course of establishing a new profession.[14] In Latin America and elsewhere the new status and its corresponding roles have only recently begun to acquire definite shape; in fact, they can nowhere be found clearly established within the occupational framework. In Latin America, this is aggravated by the vagueness that embraces not only the field of application of social research, and thereby the professional role of the social scientist as a practitioner, but also his role as an investigator and teacher. In other words, this vagueness occurs in just those departments which everywhere have the responsibility of fixing a scientific standard within each speciality and of evaluating, by reference to this criterion, the products of scientific activity and of the work of the scientists themselves. In addition, this situation contains elements which operate to hinder its modification. Thus the absence of scientific standards in social research diminishes the necessities recognized for a rigorous professional training, for the creation of institutions to give that training, and for the adoption of norms guaranteeing that its practitioners and advisers will receive a minimum of specialized training.

We have insisted on this point because the situation described obviously exerts a substantial influence on social research and on the conditions in which it must evolve in the majority of the countries under discussion. The lack of specialized personnel, and the inadequacy of scientific tradition and public attitude, have not only acted as factors *limiting* the possibility of quantitative expansion; they also have had a qualitative effect on the content of the studies and on methodology. It is possible to demonstrate that many of the problems confronting the social research worker in Latin America arise precisely from the situation described above.

In most Latin American countries during the last few years, a small number of social scientists who have modern training on a good professional level have appeared. These people invariably work under conditions in which the habitual mechanisms of evaluation and control of scientific work are non-existent or insufficient. Their usual procedure is to use as models the work of the most advanced international centers; but they cannot eliminate certain endemic aspects of the situation.

In the first place, Latin American social scientists are subject to a sort of double standard. On the one hand, there is the "international level," which is the frame of reference they usually adopt. On the other hand, there is the situation prevailing in their own country—a situation informed by obsolete conceptions of social research, by the common-sense expectations of the public and the potential "consumers" of social research, or, even worse, by the activity of the amateurs in teaching positions in the universities and in jobs as practitioners or advisers in government and private agencies.

The international level by no means offers a unified frame of reference. On the contrary, it offers several, often contrasting, models of social research. Hence methodological controversies that originated in scientifically advanced centers are transferred to a new context containing elements which tend to modify their original significance.

Then, too, the organization and material conditions under which research is evolving in Latin American countries are very deficient. This fact alone makes the social scientist face difficult decisions, where the hope of maintaining a high scientific level in technique and methodology conflicts with the need to complete research. Another negative factor is relevant to these decisions: the shortage of what we may call the background of established social knowledge —caused by that same lack of prior research, insufficiency of official statistics and data, and generally the unorganized or inaccessible (if existing!) documentation. In addition, the possibility of choosing research subjects that will have maximum scientific value, both in content and in method, is much smaller than it is in those centers where research is well established. In Latin America, the selection of subjects and methods is subject much more to accidental factors: the occasional support of the academic authorities, or the often unforeseen and irrational demands, by public and private agencies, for "applied" social research. The scientific and ethical problems of social scientists are thus aggravated by ignorance of the nature and scope of social research—and this is most serious in countries with less scientific tradition.

Finally, the scientists of Latin America are in a unique situation because of the lack or inadequacy of the means of communication between them, despite the similarity of language, problems, and general situation. This is usually attributed to organization and material problems—insufficient or inadequate, professional organizations, or scientific meetings. But it must also be considered to be a result of the fact that the professional social scientists are inclined to familiarize themselves with information originating in advanced centers outside Latin America and to mistrust information from inside the region. This tendency is explained by the absence of recognized scientific standards and mechanisms of evaluation and control in training and scientific activity. The reference group to which Latin American social scientists often turn is that ideally constituted by their colleagues in the United States, England, and, to a lesser extent, France.[15]

Certain discussions held recently in Latin America illustrate these circumstances. In a congress in 1953, the following resolutions were proposed: (a) That sociology in Latin America must be occupied only with that research which can contribute to the development of the different countries, in order to improve their living conditions and to assure the integration of their inhabitants to materially and culturally more advanced forms of life. (b) That, because of underdevelopment, "it is inadvisable to use funds for research on details of social life." Rather, funds should be applied to "the formulation of generic interpretations of total and partial aspects of national and regional structures." (c) That, in using sociological methodology, sociologists should remember that the need for refinement and precision depends on the "level of development of the regional and national structures." Sociologists therefore must not use sophisticated methods and techniques of social research evolved in more advanced countries until these methods and techniques have been adapted to the lower level of material and technical resources and to the lower cultural level of the population.[16] These proposals were supported by a considerable number, though not the majority. Their author added that only if the policy they outlined were adopted would it be possible to "cut the umbilical cord which has transformed Latin American Sociology into an abortive by-product of European and American Sociological thought."[17]

This is an extreme position containing statements which few or no professional social scientists would accept. Nonetheless, it manifests the complex ideological undertones of such questions in Latin America today. It also reveals some of the possible reactions to the problem. For example, this position proposes nothing less than the renunciation of the level of refinement and precision permitted by the most advanced methodology. Another position advocates—often without consciously wishing to do so—the pattern of impressionistic historical-sociographic studies. A third attitude is what Fernandes calls a "compensatory type," which leads social scientists to adopt the kind of methodology that appears more "scientific."[18] According to Fernandes' Brazilian example, mathematical formalism and pure theory can be divorced from research. According to another Latin American sociologist, "abstracted empiricism" may be adopted as a model—a danger in some countries where the "first buds of scientific Sociology" concern research of limited scope and dealing with subjects "which usually have little theoretical or practical relevance."[19]

381

TABLE 1

	birth rate*	death rate†	national per capita income (U.S. dollars)‡	inhabitants in cities of 20,000 and more§	per cent of active population in primary activities#	per cent of active population in urban middle strata**	per cent of literates††	university students per 1,000 inhabitants‡‡
Argentina	24	10	−400	48	25	28	85	7.7
Uruguay	(24)	(8)	−400		22	21	85	5.2
Chile	40	15	300–400	37	35		80	3.9
Cuba	35	15	300–400	43	44	21	75	3.9
Mexico	45	15	300–400	24	59	(13)	60	0.9
Costa Rica	45	15	250–300	18	57	14	75	2.3
Paraguay	45	15	−100	15	54	12	66	1.3
Venezuela	45	20	−400	31	44	16	53	1.3
Panama	45	20	250–300	22	55	15	68	2.6
Colombia	45	20	200–250	22	58	12	53	1.0
Brazil	45	20	200–250	20	62	13	50	1.2
Honduras	45	20	150–200		76	4	38	0.7
Peru	45	20	100–150	14	60		48	1.8
Ecuador	45	20	100–150	18	51	10	57	1.4
Bolivia	45	20	−100	20	68	7	32	2.0
R. Dominicana	50	20	150–200	11	70		43	1.2
Nicaragua	50	20	150–200	15	71	(7)	38	0.7
El Salvador	50	25	150–200	13	64	9	38	0.5
Guatemala	50	25	150–200	11	75	6	28	0.1

* United Nations, *Report on the World Social Situation* (New York, 1957).

† *Ibid.*

‡ Ecla, "The Structure of Employment in Latin America". *Economic Bulletin for Latin America* (1957).

§ "Demographic Aspects of Urbanization in Latin America", in UNESCO, *Report by the Director-General on the Joint UN/UNESCO Seminar on Urbanization in Latin America* (Paris, 1960).

Ecla, *op. cit.*

** Germani, "The Socio-Occupational Structure of Latin America Based on the Census of 1950" (in preparation).

†† *Anuario Internacional de Educación.*

‡‡ *Ibid.*

Thus, frequently problems which are current on the international level are discussed in Latin America in terms which are not the most appropriate ones for reaching a rational solution to the needs of research. This kind of question does not appear to be confined to this region or to sociology. Haberler has pointed out that the teaching of economics provides an example of the "demonstration effect" in the "very last theoretical innovations," irrespective of their usefulness as instruments of scientific analysis in a given situation.[20]

Before examining other problems involved in social research in Latin America, let us see how the level of methodological refinement, and the scope and type of themes selected for research can be considered on a plane more free from extrascientific implications.

Although the level of methodological refinement should be as high as possible, the particular circumstances which condition social research must be taken into account in setting it. It would be absurd "to lower the scientific level to the level of development of the social context." On the other hand, the social scientist should avoid going to the opposite extreme of what has been called "methodological inhibition"—which, in Latin American countries, would be even more harmful than in others. In this case, there would be a risk in following Fernandes' recommendation that the social scientist select his objects of inquiry only from among those for which existing conditions allow research to be conducted in accordance with "the most rigorous norms of scientific work."[21] On the contrary, in the selection of subjects the evaluation of the conditions in relation to the level of refinement possible must be made a function of the significance and importance of the problem itself—whether as a part of the process of accumulation of scientific knowledge in the relevant sphere, or in terms of its general theoretical importance. Although a clear view of the limitations of the results must be maintained in every case, they cannot be evaluated in abstract terms being measured against an absolute ideal level.

The evaluation of concrete conditions is, universally, a requisite when the social scientist is deciding whether the working conditions or the problem itself is a promising or unpromising kind. The nature of social studies itself imposes, at least at present, certain bounds on the social scientist's legitimate aspirations to methodological perfection. Thus the social scientist must make a type of decision for which abstract formulations and general methodological norms can help only as background (and then in a limited manner) in so far as a permanent relationship to concrete circumstances is required. This generalization obtains in two contexts. First, it applies when methodology, theoretical techniques, and conceptual constructs developed in other social conditions are to be adapted to the particular conditions of the region. Second, the abstract formulations and methodological norms indicate the *optimum* scientific level to be attained, witihin the limits prescribed by material needs, personnel, information, and previous scientific knowledge, on the one hand, and the urgent need for progress in research, on the other.

But this too generic statement may seem deceptive to the person seeking a precise orientation for the social scientist. It may be convenient to indicate the conditions which can help separate difficult decisions that must be confronted in the present circumstances in Latin America from irrational or extrascientific connotations. These conditions—which arise directly from the situation analyzed in the previous paragraphs—can be summarized as pointing out the necessity *to promote the emergence and functioning of mechanisms for evaluating and controlling scientific work; these mechanisms, in turn, must be based on the adequate application of the requisites of the international level to concrete local conditions.* For these requirements to be fulfilled, many factors must be modified.

a) The general environment in which professional social scientists must work must be improved. The level of understanding of the public, and especially of the academic world and of the heads of public and private entreprises, must be raised, concerning the characteristics of modern social research and its needs for a specialized professional training, type of organization, material resources, and a clear definition of its possibilities and limitations in the actual conditions obtaining in Latin American countries.[22] In particular, efforts must be made to educate the public to the point where they realize the necessity to maintain a suitable professional level within each specialized sphere of the social sciences—above all, in those that have appeared most recently, like sociology—equivalent to the level existing in other professional and scientific activities; at the same time, the deformed perception of social research that now predominates must be corrected. During the last few years, international and other agencies have reiterated the need for social resarch. This repetition is not, by itself, sufficient—in fact, it can be harmful unless it is accompanied by a careful exposition of the basic requisites and conditions necessary to complete an adequate program of research. It is this which must be emphasized, instead of the need for research; the latter is clearly recognized.

b) The communication between professional social scientists in Latin America must be improved, so that the interchange of information and criticism about the work conducted in each country is insured. To this end, regional seminars or symposia about problems of method and techniques of investigation (similar, e.g., to the seminar held in Asia by the Calcutta Centre) would now be appropriate.[23]

In Latin America, instruction in social research methodology (which is just beginning, in some countries) is seriously hindered by the fact that it must be taught with texts whose examples and illustrations derive exclusively from experiences in the United States. Social scientists must try to preprare a textbook of methodology that, while including technical advances already made, utilizes Latin American experience as much as possible—or at least adapts norms and techniques to the social context and concrete conditions among which Latin American research must evolve. Perhaps the present time is not appropriate for the conclusion of this task; but there is no doubt that cooperative efforts in that direction should be started now.

It is obvious that the numerical increase both of personnel with advanced scientific training and of research centers are the essential prerequisites for all other measures. Nevertheless, the possibility of escaping from the characteristic vicious circle which impedes social research in its first stages depends also on factors like those indicated above.

The issues relevant to the type of subject to be selected and to the priority assigned to each sphere of research are not unrelated to the problems of method we have discussed. There are frequent disputes between the theoretical and the substantive meaning in social research. Also, the "ascetic" attitude in methodology can encourage the study of excessively circumscribed and over-simplified subjects; while subjects of much greater scope are—because of their complexity, the number of variables, and the scale of the units constituting the object of inquiry—often chosen by social scientists whose methodological scruples are less rigid.

However, the problem of the *optimum scale* of the study subject is not related only to the level of methodological demands. Another problem—closely linked to it, but discrete—involves the debate between the alternative of conducting studies on a national or equivalent scale and that of engaging in vastly reduced—whether from the geographical point of view or in accordance with other criteria—investigations. In addition, the question arises of whether preference should be given to inquiries with a theoretical, systematic purpose and of a very general and abstract nature; or to sociographic studies dealing primarily or exclusively with a geographically or historically determined area (national, regional, or local) without regard to the comparability of the results or the possibility of their use in theoretical systemizations. Finally, there is the choice between "applied" research, directed to the immediate practical use of the results upon which to base a program of social action, and research which has no "practical" purpose but adds to theoretical, systematic or sociographic knowledge.

The ostensible alternative scales of the research units are not real. The interest in fact is in the range of the generalization that can be made from the results of a given inquiry and its significance within a larger context. In part, it is a sampling problem; in part, it depends on its connection with the theory. However, the apparent alternatives do reflect an element which cannot be disregarded. In a situation where there is an extreme shortage of studies that are conducted with a sound scientific methodology, *it seems reasonable to grant priority to those research projects which*—regardless of their scale—*contribute basic knowledge on Latin American societies;* i.e., which help to lay the necessary foundation for later inquiries.

When it is necessary to assign priority among theoretical systematic studies, sociographic studies, and applied studies, the usual recommendation is to try to effect a reconciliation among the different purposes. In principle, this is possible and should be tried; but the fact remains, and should not be concealed, that such a reconciliation may detract from the value of an inquiry. It might be essential to promote greater understanding in those people who somehow control or condition the selection of social scientists—and especially important to establish an open state of mind about the significance of the distinction among the three types of research. Many people have no idea of the part played by empirical research in verifying a theory. In the same way, they do not properly distinguish between applied and basic research. This confusion is not prevalent only among the lay public; it occurs in sociological texts, articles, etc. These misunderstandings usually cause pressures to be exerted on social scientists to give precise answers that will be easily applicable to the social problems which, it is thought, can be resolved by the social sciences. Here, again, there is an urgent need to clarify the issue by informing the public about the limits and conditions of social research.

Only by doing these things can social scientists become a little less constrained by the demands from ill-informed quarters that tend to make the adequate selection of study subjects even more difficult.

The problems discussed above can be expressed as a single one—a problem of crucial importance for social research in Latin America, namely to ensure the optimum distribution of the scarce personnel and material resources available for research. Of course, this is a universal problem. However it is aggravated in a country whose research is still almost embryonic and whose resources are scarce, and where there is little or no prior information on which the research worker can base rational decisions. We may, in this connection, suggest some ways to provide for a better distribution of available resources and thus to ensure a more rational approach to social research.

a) In this context, the problem of bibliographic documentation is vitally important. In Latin America—partly as a result of the lack of communication among social scientists, and associated factors—it is notoriously difficult to be informed about the research work published or conducted out in the region, especially if the authors are Latin Americans. Everyone works in a profound isolation and receives only fragmentary and unreliable information about the work that is being done on similar problems, sometimes within the same country. Scientific works, particularly any dealing with the impact of technical change, are very scarce. Nonetheless, some material capable of being utilized does exist. Ways of mobilizing and integrating all these elements must be found. Some proposals have been advanced and deserve to be studied—e.g., the creation of documentation centers, the publication of abstracts, etc. Work of this sort has been begun (for example, through the efforts of the Latin American Centre for Social Research in Rio de Janeiro); but it must be much more complete and systematic if it is to bear fruit.

b) The use of existing data and documents in social research should be stimulated as much as possible. This is especially significant because in Latin America (as sometimes in other areas), there is a growing trend toward over-estimating the value of data obtained in surveys or field studies. However, many social scientists recognize the advantages accruing to the use of existing sources—an otherwise traditional form in sociology—in that they supply one with information before one begins an inquiry, and also provide a means of obtaining worthwhile results solely on the basis of the data they contain. For example, the census of the Americas made in 1950 apparently has not generated the analyses that one would expect could be made on the basis of the data collected here. All efforts tending to promote the better use of census data and other existing statistics (however deficient they may seem) should be encouraged. As illustrations of such effort, we may cite the recent seminar in Chile concerning the use of census data; and the publication, by the Inter-American Statistics Institute, of the data of the 1950 census in a co-ordinated and comparative form.

c) In Latin America, more than elsewhere, national and continental co-ordination must be promoted in the formulation of research plans and in the adoption of the methods to be employed. Advancing such co-ordination would be the most direct way of making certain that the scanty available resources woud be fully utilized. In addition, it is possible that this would bolster the position of the social scientists when they were confronted with the various factors which somehow tend to introduce extrascientific elements into their decision-making. As we have already observed, joint meetings and discussions among professional research workers are a great factor in the establishment and functioning of the mechanisms of control and evaluation in scientific inquiry within the region. Of course, such a co-ordination is not easy to accomplish. Nevertheless, by using intelligently the existing regional centers (e.g., the Centres at Rio or the Flacso), while simultaneously concentrating on an effort at achieving co-ordination in only a few existing principal research agencies in the region, real advances may be made. Some cases of close co-operation already exist; and the experience gained in them should be extended further and also within each nation. In addition, if plans and the results of meetings were published, it would engender a greater understanding of the problems, suggest fruitful lines of research, and designate priorities. All these results would substantially assist the individual and organizational formulation of research projects throughout Latin America.

We shall now examine some of the ideological problems that affect social research in Latin America. The less obvious conditioning factors able to help or hinder research have already been mentioned; although the discussion of them is by no means sufficient, we have not the space here to deal with them at greater length. Instead, we shall consider to problems which are manifested in more evident and direct ways.

One of the most common sources of the ideological problems affecting social research is the fact that the degree and extent to which people and institutions are politically involved are much greater in the scientific field than elsewhere. Thus in most countries the universies are vulnerable to the risk of becoming involved in ideological conflicts.

There are diverse reasons for this. One derives from the fact that many universities were created at a time when the traditional pattern of social stratification predominated, and higher education was available only to members of the "traditional families." As the social structure was gradually transformed and a growing middle class appeared, the universities underwent a profound change—caused largely by student-led political movements. For example, the *Reforma*, a students' movement which began in Argentina in 1918 and rapidly spread over the entire continent, caused the "modernization" of the organization for higher education, and particularly the assurance that teachers would be recruited by open methods and that a type of instruction more fitted to the transformations occuring in the social structure would be used. The political tradition of the *Reforma* was also prolonged because the universities frequently took the role of vanguard in the process of transformation of Latin American societies, in liquidating institutions and values attached to the old traditional and colonial structure, and in creating forms more closely approximating those of modern industrial society. Since such a process of

387

change takes place amid great conflicts, it is not surprising that the universities often find themselves involuntarily surrounded by ideological disputes. In addition, the political instability of the majority of Latin American countries contributes not a little to the politicization of the universities, which were often attacked by the authoritarian governments which so frequently wielded power in many Latin American nations. In some countries, stability was much greater and direct interference from the political power was correspondingly less. Nevertheless, in some cases—one extreme example is Argentina—the rise of a totalitarian state meant the virtual destruction of the university as it was and its replacement by an organism with clear ideological objectives.

The intellectual elites played a significant role in the process of national integration, which is part of the transition from traditional to modern forms in the social structure. It is not fortuitous that the tradition of the *Reforma* is very closely connected with anti-imperialism. In general, student movements, which have always maintained political importance in Latin America, were characterized by their nationalism—almost invariably a democratic nationalism. Despite the efforts made by the faculties and boards of the universities to remain aloof from political commitments, they did not succeed. Thus the notion existed that there was a political significance in the action and comportment of the universities—even when a given action had no political or ideological connotations. Also in many Latin American countries, students participate directly, through their representatives, in the government of the universities.

The situation of non-university institutions is very similar to this, when they are public agencies in which direct political influence is exerted. In most cases, these institutions are even more vulnerable to the fluctuations of the political parties and the different administrations which succeed to power. As a rule, this causes a great deal of discontinuity in the organizations and activities of the scientific centers which are directly dependent on the public administration; but these repercussions have less effect on the university, which in general enjoys a high degree of autonomy.

In many Latin American countries, a special effort has yet to be made that will cause certain subjects to be treated in a scientific spirit—and that will help people become accustomed to the idea that such a treatment is possible, or that it is at least possible to make conscientious attempts to realize the ideal of impartiality. The elements of politicization, and the still strong tradition of "social studies" (all with ideological bases), make it more difficult to impose habits of self-criticism that would tend to insure a greater scientific neutrality, or, at worst, the realization that neutrality is an essential condition of research.

To the greater degree of political involvement on the part of scientific personnel and institutions in Latin America, we must add other elements deriving from the special situation of countries in the process of rapid development. These elements have been mentioned earlier; in this chapter, we shall examine their concrete aspects.

a) In underdeveloped nations it is more likely than in advanced countries that certain people and groups exist who mistrust social research and consider that the application of scientific methods to the sphere of human activity threatens certain values, the stability of existing institutions, and the integration

388

of society. Although there are no data available to substantiate it, we can state with confidence that such situations exist in Latin America. Their concrete manifestations vary in accordance with local circumstances, which are sometimes of a historical character and sometimes purely accidental. Thus in some instances (e.g., in Argentina), a type of sociology devoted to German irrationalism or to Neo-Scholasticism may be accepted, while a modern kind of sociology might be attacked because, for example, "certain spheres of human behavior should not be submitted to scientific study."[24]

An important Latin American newspaper severely criticized a research project, conducted in the University of Buenos Aires, that was designed to establish the social origins of the students, their motives for entering the University, their selections of careers, and other connected factors. The questionnaire used was similar to those utilized in analogous inquiries in France, England, and the United States; it was described as a "lengthy and minute interrogation of a police type."[25] In Uruguay, a similar investigation provoked a violent argument in the newspapers, which were aligned according to their respective more liberal or more conservative political attitudes. In other cases, a purely scientific discussion of psychoanalytic concepts, of studies about the organization and function of the family, of the social psychology of adolescence, etc., has been branded "anti-religious," "destructive," and the like. Uruguay is unique and curious in that no population census has been taken since 1908, although statistics about other things (e.g., agriculture) are quite up-to-date; this is usually attributed to individual idiosyncracies and to suspicion of administrative interference in private life.[26]

However, resistance to research apparently does not invariably originate in the population in general; rather, it seems to be generated by certain ideological groups. The university research projects in Argentina and Uruguay did not meet obstruction or refusal from the people interviewed; the conflicts about them were instigated by groups who, for one reason or another, utilized the projects as weapons in arguing for their own objectives. Thus the real or perceived politicization of the universities and the intellectuals can affect a purely scientific and neutral activity.

b) Collaboration with foreign experts and foundations, especially in certain research subjects, can engender misunderstandings. Thus the Point Four program is particularly liable to ideological involvements when its application is connected with plans in which the universities must intervene. In general, any association with the United States is distrusted in Latin America. The feeling is that, although plans for co-operation can be successfully terminated, particular care must be exercized by all persons and organizations concerned —national and foreign—to remain alert to prevent the entry of bias.

It is relatively easy to make the mistake of adopting valorizing positions when formulating problems concerning economic development, since research on economic development presupposes a very careful analysis of unseen valorizing implications. Precautions must be taken against this everywhere, but they are particularly essential in dealing with a situation like that in Latin America. Foreign agencies and experts collaborating in research projects in Latin American countries must be careful to remember this. Misunderstandings are not always

389

caused by definite ideological proclivities or by the excessive politicization of the Latin American students or social scientists; at times, they are generated by the equally biased conceptions of the foreign experts. It is much to be desired that the latter be very sophisticated about the sociology of knowledge, that they be capable of analyzing the implications of their own theories, and that they be aware of the ways that the local social scientists and public may perceive these or interpret them. Completely assured scientific character and neutrality of concepts can often mask unexpected ideological implications.

This paper has been concerned primarily with the conditions under which present social research in Latin America should develop. We have advanced some suggestions which might help to improve these conditions. However, we have not dealt with the more strictly methodological and technical aspects of research. We have omitted them because of the features of research in Latin America that we have been discussing. Research is lacking, particularly on the subject of the social impact of technological change. In addition, because of the low standard of communication among social scientists, the methodological experience gained remains dispersed and relatively inaccessible. The most urgent requirement for social research in Latin America is that greater co-operation between the people and centers working on the continent be promoted. Only this co-operation will make it be possible to apply appropriately any plan tending to improve conditions in general and to expand research in the field, while maintaining an acceptable scientific level.

NOTES TO APPENDIX 1

1. See Talcott Parsons, *The Social System* (Glencoe, Ill., 1951), chap. viii; R. K. Merton, *Social Theory and Social Structure* (Glencoe, Ill., 1958), Part IV; B. Barber, *Science and the Social Order,* (Glencoe, Ill., 1957); R. K. Merton and D. Lerner, "Social Scientist and Research Policy," in D. Lerner and H. D. Lasswell (eds.), *The Policy Sciences* (Palo Alto, Calif., 1951).
2. Barber, *op. cit.,* chap, xi; Merton and Lerner, *op. cit.*
3. C. Wright Mills, *The Sociological Imagination* (New York, 1959), chap. vi; R. K. Merton, at the first session of the World Congress of Sociology (Stresa, 1959).
4. Traits of Latin American culture that are considered to be detrimental to the development of a scientific attitude in the social studies have been emphasized by many observers. See H. Godoy Urzua, *Orientación y Organización de los Estudios Sociológicos en Chile* (Santiago, 1960); also see G. Germani, "The Development and Present State of Sociology in Latin America," *Proceedings of the Fourth World Congress of Sociology* (London, 1959), and the bibliography given there.
5. Germani, *op cit.*
6. F. Fernandes, "O Padrao de Trabalho Cientifico dos Sociologos Brasileiros," *Rev. Bras. de Estudos Politicos* (1958).
7. *Ibid.*; H. Godoy Urzua, *op. cit.*
8. See L. A. Costa Pinto, *Las Ciencias sociais no Brasil* (Rio de Janeiro, 1955), p. 43.
9. According to F. Azevedo, only in Brazil are there more than one hundred and fifty chairs in sociology (quoted in Costa Pinto, *op. cit.*).
10. Germani, *op. cit.*
11. Costa Pinto, *op. cit.,* p. 41.
12. C. A. Campos Jimenez, *Las Ciencias Sociales en Costa Rica* (Rio de Janeiro, 1959) pp. 54-57; J. R. Arboleda, *Las Ciencias Sociales en Colombia* (Rio de Janeiro, 1959), p. 58; J. A. Silva Michelena, *El Estado Actual de las Ciencias Sociales en Venezuela* (Rio de Janeiro, 1960), p. 41.
13. Germani, *op. cit.; idem, La Comunicación entre Especialistas en Sociología en América Latina* ("Publications of the Institute of Sociology," No. 20 [1960]).
14. Costa Pinto, *op. cit.,* pp. 39-51.
15. Germani, *La Comunicación.*
16. G. Ramos, *Introducao Critica a la Sociología Brasileira* (Rio de Janeiro, 1957), pp. 77-81.

17. *Loc. cit.*
18. Fernandes, *op. cit.,* pp. 45-51.
19. Godoy Urzua, *op. cit.,* pp. 49-50.
20. J. Medina Echavarria, "El Papel del Sociólogo en la Tarea del Desarrollo Económico," *Aspectes Sociales del Desarrollo Económico* (1959), p. 16.
21. Fernandes, *loc. cit.*
22. This need for clarification has been especially stressed by A. E. Solari, *Las Ciencias Sociales en el Uruguay* (Rio de Janeiro, 1959), pp. 165-66.
23. UNESCO Research Centre on the Social Implications of Industrialization in Southern Asia, *Regional Seminar on Techniques of Social Research* (Calcutta, 1959).
24. Public statement made by an organization of law graduates.
25. "Cuestionarios Universitarios," *La Prensa* (Buenos Aires), October 10, 1958.
26. Solari, *op. cit.*

The Uses of Social Research in the Developing Countries

FRANCIS X. SUTTON
The Ford Foundation

INTRODUCTION

My aim in this paper is to say something about the place social research has had and may in future have in the developing countries. The subject invites a very general treatment but my acquaintance with the concrete problems of development is largely confined to Africa. I shall therefore develop much of the discussion in African terms. I hope the analysis will have wider relevance but I suspect that it will need correction and revision for other situations.

While I shall be concerned with some of the things that need to be known, particularly about the development of human resources, I shall not try to suggest a program of research. Rather I seek an understanding of the likely and possible place of research among the various influences that actually guide developments efforts. I begin with some general and elementary observations on this subject.

GENERAL RELATIONS OF SOCIAL RESEARCH AND GOVERNMENT IN DEVELOPING SOCIETIES

Social research, like other sources of facts and ideas, affects what happens in a society in diffuse ways but particularly through those institutions that have a significant role in directing and regulating the course of the society's development. Government is most prominent among these institutions though it is not the only one, and a discussion of the relations of research and social action could be pitched somewhat more abstractly than I here attempt. But given the very great importance of government in the developing countries today, the losses in holding to an easier level of discussion do not seem serious.

In order to function, any government must be able to mobilize a great deal of knowledge about what it is doing. Much of this knowledge is of little interest or utility beyond its relevance in particular courses of action, and it is typically generated by a process of familiarization or investigation on the part of those who actually run the government. Some of the knowledge utilized by governments, may, on the other hand, come from sources outside its own ordinary structure. Or it may, like a census, be generated in a special investigation and have a broad utility and interest.

The range of considerations and the depth of fact that are taken into account in any particular course of action will depend on the government's structure, in particular on the specialization of function and competence that exists. A well-developed government usually contains various positions or agencies whose responsibilities are to assemble facts and information. Statistical services are familiar and obvious examples. They usually have continuing responsibilities not closely tied to particular problems or courses of action of a government. Staff positions may also exist for *ad hoc* investigations of particular subjects, and some investigations may be regarded as within the normal competence of administrative officers. In the past, specialized research training has usually not been required; except for statistical services, there has been relatively little demand for formal qualifications based on training in the social sciences. The qualifications for civil servants have been a certain level of general education as in the British tradition, or an essentially legal training as on the European continent. Africa, and, I presume, most of the rest of the underdeveloped world, has followed these patterns. They obviously have implications for prevailing conceptions about the character, uses, and necessity of research.

Any role in government, and in particular any executive role, carries with it a presumption of knowledge. For example, in the colonial governments of British Africa, district officers were presumed to know a great deal about conditions in their districts; a large range of decisions were made on their assessment of conditions subject to no checks by more specialized officers. Some subjects more manifestly require technical knowledge than others and recourse to the advice of specialists may be normal. In economic, and more emphatically in social questions, need for such recourse has not been easily conceded. It is probably normal in any working government that possibilities of expertise are recognized beyond that of the people whose assessments of situations are ruling. But a basic acceptance of the going pattern of information and conclusion is implied by the fact that governments work at all. Social researchers with experience of administrators need not be told that there are resistances to conceptions that the normal judgments of adminstrators are insufficiently based in fact or familiarity.

I thus emphasize that any government is characterized by a stock of knowledge about what it is doing, and institutionalized patterns of having or not having recourse to expertise and research in making decisions.

My observations thus far have been concerned with the established patterns of a government at any given time. But governments are always subject to influences that define their aims and reshape their normal patterns of operation. These influences are very diverse in character. Among them are ideas of all sorts, some derived from lowly sources, others tracing to research, scholarly inquiry, or some other form of systematic intellectual deliberation. It is notorious that ideas often ramble over long and round-about courses from their origins to the minds of political leaders. In the Western world, we live

394

with many ideas that had their beginnings in research well-removed from any immediate executive responsibilities. Marx over a British Museum reading desk, Keynes in a King's College study, and number-chasers at the National Bureau of Economic Research have ultimately shaped the course of normal thinking in government offices. In Africa, the decade-old articles of Professor Greenberg on linguistic classification are now being pulled out of the *Southwest Journal of Anthropology* to shape the ideology of African nationalism.[1] This sort of ultimate reverberation is perhaps not commonly the deliberate aim of researchers and research institutions; indeed, its uncertainty hardly makes it a good target for rational ambition. But freedom of academic research from the confines of urgent practical problems, and the pursuit of generality and conceptual novelty, give chances that research will have deep and distant consequences, in shaping development efforts as in other matters.

Any society guided by more than chance accumulations of ideology deliberately mobilizes its intellectual resources in various ways. The fostering of social research is only one way and probably not the most important in most countries. We are familiar in the Western world with strongly defended traditions of independent discussion in the press and elsewhere; also, with investigating bodies, study committees, and more continuing formalized institutions for study and advocacy on various ranges of problems. (In this country we have even had a recent Presidential Committee deliberating on our national goals!) Some of these commissions and investigating bodies have a fairly intimate relationship to governmental problems in a particular time and place. But there is a spectrum of sources of ideas and influence, ranging from direct responses to current problems all the way to remote and detached institutions free from any immediate responsibilities.

The underdeveloped countries are familiar with these various devices and institutions through their long history of contact with the West. They have the strategic problem of developing their own devices and their own ways of using what they can get from the outside world. What place they may give to social research institutions is only one of their problems, although perhaps one of considerably greater importance than in Western countries with their more varied and longer-developed intellectual resources. The resources they will have to draw on from other countries, the international co-operation that may be attained, and the focused and diffuse ways in which the results of research are spread in these societies—all of these are important determinants of the influence research may have on the strategy of development. Scientific progress in the understanding of development may have direct technical application in the problems of government. But there are many large questions in which the influence of research is likely to be diffusely mediated through ideology and general habits of thought.

These are the broad relations of social research and development that I want to keep in mind in examining the experience and prospects of African territories. To repeat, they include the place of research in the normal operations of government, particularly in building the stock of knowledge on which it operates, and the influences of research in shaping governments and their programs.

395

The notion of development is so familiar that one is tempted to leave it without preliminary comment. But the view of it that guides the later exposition in this paper ought to be made explicit.

Seen in its broadly human aspects, development poses two orders of problems. The first is the elaboration and manning of a modern occupational system. There is, no doubt, some measure of increase in national product possible within older types of social structure. But certainly outside agriculture, development takes place within functional specializations that approximate increasingly to modern occupational roles. Even within agriculture, the move from local subsistence to involvement in a money economy is a considerable move toward the patterns of modern occupations. "Industrialization" is a term that often seems to imply a dubious weighting of development priorities, but if it only means movement toward the sort of social structure that is the productive core of a modern industrial society then "development" and "industrialization" are properly synonymous.

The second order of problems is less easy to describe clearly because I leave it in the looseness of residual definition. It comprises the sprawling domain of adjustment problems occasioned by the intrusion of a new social structure. It is concerned with the costs and concomitants of constructing an occupational system on or out of an older, indigenous social system.

This statement of the development problems puts the accent on manpower problems, or problems in education and the development of human resources —an emphasis well suited to Africa and a discussion of social research.

GOVERNMENT AND RESEARCH IN RECENT AFRICAN HISTORY

I distinguish three periods in recent African history: (1) an earlier colonial period in which African development was slow and not viewed with urgency; (2) the latest period of colonial control in which substantial development efforts became normal; and (3) the current period of beginning African independence and urgent pursuit of development. Each of these periods has had characteristic needs and practices in the matter of research.

The Earlier Colonial Period
Before the development urge got hold on African territories they were manageable with thin governments, limited knowledge, and a sluggish flow of new ideas and techniques. Governments sought to maintain order, administer justice, and collect enough revenue to balance the territorial budget; there was not much margin left for deliberate developmental efforts and the populace did not irresistibly force it. Where a European settler movement was envisaged, a considerable urge to economic development might be present, but this did not evidently pose complex problems of social change among the African population.

The paucity of ordered knowledge about the territories that has been compatible with this old style of functioning is notorious. Liberia, evading colonialism through American indifference and inhibition, has been a particularly dark spot. I am told by specialists that there is still no accurate map of Liberia;

post-war U.S. technical assistance could supply topography with aerial photography but not place-names or tribal distributions. Liberia has never had a census but in this it need not be grievously embarrassed in comparison with its neighbors. Sierra Leone has had various efforts at a "census" since 1802 but they have been so approximate and incomplete that it is very questionable whether they deserve such a respectable label.[2] For Ghana many of us have confidently cited the 1948 census but I was recently shaken by a researcher[3] who found that the total population of a village as estimated in this census was less than the recorded school population drawn from the village at that time. Let us hope that this year's census is better![4]

Once serious development efforts have begun, these deficiencies in basic knowledge become glaringly apparent. The grave difficulties the Eastern Region of Nigeria encountered when it tried to introduce free universal primary education in 1957 were in part caused by ignorance of the school-age population. An investigating commission appointed to study the situation after the scheme had been withdrawn in 1958 had to busy itself with efforts to repair this crucial deficiency. Similarly, a commission appointed in 1957 in Nyasaland to study the needs for adult education in the territory (the Hadlow Commission) found itself crippled because it did not know how many people it had to plan for or where they were. The want of statistics is, of course, not confined to population alone. To cite just one recent complaint, Professor D. T. Jack in his 1958 *Economic Survey of Sierra Leone* says:

In conducting this investigation one outstanding difficulty was experienced. There is still a 'lack of fundamental information about the country.' These words were used in Mr. Child's 'Plan of Economic Development for Sierra Leone' (1949) and though there has been some improvement since that time the lack is still great.[5]

(One of his urgent recommendations is that Sierra Leone establish an office of statistical services; it now has nothing of the kind.)

To emphasize a paucity of ordered knowledge is not to say that colonial administrations were ignorant of the territories for which they were responsible. Practical familiarity related to the demands of administration was often very good. Mr. Arthur Gaitskell is fond of making the point that colonial administration provided a continuity of personnel and a depth of experience that modern assistance is finding hard to match. The old style colonial administrator with thirty years in the Sudan, Tanganyika, or the Congo certainly had that intimate knowledge of conditions in these territories to which I have alluded above.[6] His sort of familiarity was not evidently ill-adapted to a situation in which there was conceived to be ample time for practical and sensible men to observe, understand, and guide the slow changes underway. Government was not so complicated or well-provided with funds that systematic planning of its efforts evidently went beyond the capacities of simple central administrations.

Insofar as special needs for study were recognized beyond what the ordinary staff could "pick up" in exercising its functions, they centered on knowing the African populations. Motivations to study African populations were in part intellectual and disinterested. Where they were practically related to the problems of government and the demands of development, they grew out of certain special needs or special difficulties in the execution of policy. Special needs arose through the British policy of indirect rule with its demand for study of African political structure, and very generally through the problem of developing local government. They appeared in any policy affecting African marriage arrangements, succession, and land tenure. They also arose when riots and disturbances, or other kinds of resistance to government authority seemed to depend on African conditions that were obscure to the administration, and in any case demanded that "something be done."

Until shortly before World War II there were no special institutions for social research in Africa south of the Sahara except in the Union. Special posts there were. Seligman was engaged as early as 1909 to do an ethnographic survey of the Sudan. Rattray and Meek were made into government anthropologists in the Gold Coast and Nigeria in 1920 and 1921. Other posts followed and there were numerous investigations that involved field research among African populations. But on the whole, limited demands, thin budgetary support, and the prevailing conceptions of government kept the effort limited.

The educational and training problems which were later to take such a central place in the preoccupations of governments were given modest attention and research related to them was rare. Partly this was due to the limited responsibility of governments for education—at the end of World War II 96 per cent of the pupils in the British African territories south of the Sahara were still in mission schools. After the famous Phelps-Stokes Fund report on African education, general policies began to be formed; the British Advisory Committee on Education in the Colonies was formed in 1924 and made its first policy statement in 1925. Wisdom and experience beyond that presumably available to education officers in the territories was sought, and doctrine was formulated on how educational systems should be "adapted to the mentality and traditions of the various peoples."[7] But systematic research on what education of various sorts in fact did to the various peoples was not instituted. Again, this is not to say that there was not a great deal of accurate observation and creative initiative among those who actually taught Africans. The efforts of V. L. Griffiths and his collaborators at Bakht-er-Ruda in the Sudan was a notable example. They faced most energetically and imaginatively the problems of developing a suitable curriculum for a rural and underdeveloped society, of training teachers so that they would not find village life intolerable, and of combining academic, practical, and "character" education. This splendid effort, beginning in the early 1930's and continuing today under capable Sudanese is agreeably and modestly described in Griffiths' book, *Experiment in Education.*[8] But those made hopeful of systematic research by the word "experiment" in his title will be disappointed. The men who made the Institute of Education at Bakht-er-Ruda and the Sudanese system of elementary education assessed their work like practical men, who were primarily trying to get something done. To my knowledge, there has never been a study of their work by anyone who took his primary task to be research.

A dearth of research on the "educated Africans" who became so much a problem to colonial governments as early as the 1920's is not surprising. There

398

was then, in European contexts at least, little conception that specialized researchers should regularly be put to work on such problems. Colonial administrators had usually some anthropological and linguistic training for their work. They were prepared to think that special students of African peoples and institutions might be needed. But to think that government policy and the impingement of European institutions might take more than the scrutiny and reflection of "experienced" men who "knew the situation" would have been radical modesty. Perhaps it was just as well; one wonders where researchers might have been found.

Late Colonialism and Beginning African Nationalism
After World War II, favorable world economic conditions, a new conscience among the colonial powers, and pressures from newly aroused African populations brought a new pace and urgency to development. Relatively much more money became available to governments and more people could be engaged to spend it. New policies were aimed toward educating and training Africans and expanding African economies. Earlier, there had been a comfortable sense that decades of slow and reluctantly accepted change lay ahead. Now, hastening governments were always harried by African demands.

A notable expansion of research accompanied the new tempo of development. In the British territories new institutions were fostered by Colonial Development and Welfare funds, grants for individual research multiplied (from this and other sources), the university colleges provided new centers for research, and government research agencies were considerably strengthened. Of a total of nearly £20 millions allocated for Colonial Development Research since 1940, some 8 per cent has gone to social and economic research, about half of it to Africa.[9] In the Belgian Congo and Ruanda-Urundi, the establishment of IRSAC (Institut pour la Recherche Scientifique en Afrique Centrale), and in the French territories, the development of IFAN (Institut Français d'Afrique Noire) and subsidiaries of metropolitan organizations marked comparable developments.[10]

A remarkable increase in the scientific literature on Africa has resulted. But this increase has occurred at a time when the faster tempo of change and a greater range of governmental efforts imposed rapidly increasing demands for greater knowledge. Much of the increase has not been concerned with the areas and problems of most interest and urgency—as administrators often complain. Thus, in Ghana we have better recent monographs on peoples in the Northern Territories than in the more developed forest and coastal areas; in the Sudan, we know the backward south from classic monographs, but have relatively little to read on the changing north. Despite a new interest in studies of urbanization, knowledge of the African populations most intimately involved in social change has remained thin. I remember a visiting professor at the University College of Ghana a couple of years ago telling me with scowling seriousness and some indignation that "nothing is known about this country." By normal standards for Western countries his rhetoric was justified and in recalling it I do not mean to point a finger at Ghana; it is indeed one of the better studied African territories.

Lord Hailey thought that anthropologists had proven their utility in studying why development efforts go wrong and had yet to show their uses in the positive construction of policy. The judgment may have something to do with the special characteristics of professional anthropologists but it probably also reflects a continuing practice of bringing in social research after starts have been made on the basis of pragmatic estimates. In recent years, with much being tried in Africa, there have been plenty of difficulties to scrutinize. Some very pretty studies—like Dupire's and Boutillier's on checks to the reorganization of palm oil production in the Ivory Coast [11] or Marris's study of traders' discontents with slum clearance in Lagos [12] have resulted. Such studies have uses beyond explanation of the particular difficulties to which they are directed (where they indeed often come too late and without enough remedial prescriptions to be of much help in administration and policy). They may serve to alert governments to social considerations that need to be included in any realistic planning. But the acceleration of development in Africa seems to have outpaced the growth of such studies and the enlarged awareness of social factors in development that might have been based on them. To cite examples from only one important territory, it seems clear that the large efforts of the Office des Cités Africaines in building new housing and communites, and of the government in establishing *paysannats* throughout the Belgian Congo were not much guided by sociological and anthropological work—the discontents revealed in the urban riots of the last year and a half, and the uneven success of the *paysannats* might have been less striking had architects and agronomists been more constrained by social considerations.[13]

The strength of a government is, of course, not to be measured simply by the resources in research that it can command. Increased governmental establishments and a new kind of contact with African populations gave post-war colonial governments in Africa improved means of coping with their new responsibilities. But the situation had changed profoundly from the earlier colonial period where, as I have suggested, experience could be slowly accumulated. In the new tempo of effort and change, there have been relatively fewer men of long experience and the problems they have faced have been more complex and subtle. Even within stable political conditions the new scale of effort would have posed new problems in planning and co-ordination. But there were added the sharp changes in assumptions imposed by African nationalism.

The development urge in Africa has been a great, fuzzy, and disorderly passion. It has been generated out of changes in awareness and aspirations among large numbers of people that gave irresistible strength to African nationalism but imposed heavy burdens on the new leaders in defining coherent and realistic programs. Once African development became a massive movement of social change, its problems could not be readily understood either by Europeans or Africans on the basis of their own past experience. A new order of need for factual knowledge, guiding ideas, and planning has arisen which evidently offers new opportunities for using research. The needs could be illustrated in various fields, but it seems better to concentrate on the problems of education and the development of human resources.

The new thrust for development in recent years in Africa has pushed the problems of education and manpower development into the forefront of governmental pre-occupations. This has been as much a consequence of social pressures from individual aspirations as of national policies aiming toward autonomy and self-government. Voracious appetites for education seem normal in developing societies. That they have grown so sharply in Africa over the last decade and a half is one of the better indices to the development that has gone on in the continent. I have sometimes called African nationalism a "populist" movement to stress its concern for the claims of all the people. The educational corollary is a pressure on governments to get as many children as possible into school. The resulting demands on territorial resources are severe. The Eastern and Western Regions of Nigeria have been devoting about 40 per cent of their budgets to education (a percentage only possible because some governmental responsibilities are discharged by the Federal Government). The government of Upper Volta in 1959 devoted 23 per cent of its budget to putting 6 per cent of the territory's school age children in school. Even rich territories like Ghana and the Ivory Coast have been hard-pressed in carrying out their spectacular expansions of recent years.

The demand for education as an individual right has not been easy to combine with policies for education as national investment for development. Some sort of attention has, of course, had to be given to producing the competences needed for running an independent country. This became inescapable once public expenditures on secondary, technical, and higher education were called for. But until recently in Africa, these considerations have not in fact led to much careful planning enlightened by research.

The beginnings of serious planning for development in the territories of Africa came after the Second World War with the institution of aid programs from the metropolitan powers. Once the sort of responsibility implied in the Colonial Development and Welfare Acts for the British territories and in the FIDES program for the French territories was assumed, an obligation to make some rational allocation of the funds made available by the metropolitan powers was involved. This led to a series of efforts in planning that devolved for the most part on existing administrations—administrations which despite considerable expansion were very hard-pressed to meet the task.[14] Allocations as between education of various sorts and other uses of the metropolitan funds were necessarily involved. A rational basis for these allocations was, however, hard to find. Many implications of the allocations actually made were not worked out in terms of the manpower supply and demand they would involve. Thus in Nigeria, after a series of post-war development plans, there has as yet been no serious manpower survey in the country and no concrete efforts at "costing" of the development plans in terms of manpower. A similar situation has prevailed in the other British African territories. Ghana had a manpower survey conducted by a U.N. team in 1957 and has another now underway. Only one other serious effort is known to have occurred in

401

the British territories, and that only last year. French efforts may have been somewhat more serious. In Guinea, for example, when the aluminium development began in Fria in 1956, a special mission was supplied to the Guinea government to work out some of the implications of this new development, and the work of this mission involved a thorough study of the foreseeable supply and demand of manpower in various categories.[15]

Here is an obvious field for research along lines that are now technically well developed in the Western countries. At least since World War II there has been a corps of social scientists, mostly economists, with conceptions and techniques for assessing a nation's manpower. Certain competences in assessing the present state and probable development of an economy, in orderly classification of occupations, and in the techniques of empirical sample surveying, are required. These competences have not all been normally within the command of colonial administrators in Africa and have only lately been applied through the avenues of technical assistance.

The recourse to manpower surveys may prove to be a crucial step in the effective linking of social research and practical development efforts and I venture to dwell on them. An appeal beyond the resources of information possessed by the ordinary machinery of government through its ministries of education, commerce, and industry, etc., arises from various sources. One is the pressure on African governments to justify before the populace their expenditures on education in various categories. Another has been the evident slowing of development plans by manpower shortages (this has been particularly noted in West Africa). Also, there has been concern that many of the products of expensive schooling were apparently not proving to be available or effective in the occupations for which they were trained. All of these various stimuli have contributed to a recourse to special assistance in gaining a new kind of information on manpower. The consequences of one particular study will illustrate what may flow from such studies. I regret that I am not fully free to identify this study since the government for which it was performed has asked that it be kept confidential until some of its "revolutionary" conclusions have been thoroughly assessed and a government policy position on them been formulated.

This study was undertaken because of an apparent failure of a system of technical schools to produce the artisans and technicians for which they were set up. A thorough assessment of supply and demand of manpower over the next five years was undertaken through a sample survey that took in about 80 per cent of the employment above unskilled labor in this African economy. Very serious shortages were forecast in a great variety of occupations. In particular, it was evident that the system of technical education was not producing the kind of people employers in the economy wanted, and that the numbers the system was training were in any case far too small for the demand (even had all the graduates of these schools been up to satisfactory standards). The whole status of the technical education system in this territory was thus thrown into question. In particular, the deficiencies of which employers complained were ones of command over the English language and general education rather than want of particular technical skills as such. The question was raised whether the expensive technical education might not better be replaced by more general education.

The background of this particular technical education system lay in a conception of African development somewhat as follows: A need for African artisans and technicians was recognized. The normal metropolitan practice was to develop this level of technicians principally through an apprenticeship system. The opportunities for such apprenticeships in the African economy were assumed—apparently without careful empirical investigation—to be lacking. It was consequently assumed that the formal educational system would have to make up the deficiencies. To provide technical training equivalent to an apprenticeship or a substantial part of it within the normal years of schooling took the beginnings of this technical education back to a very early point in a system that used the vernacular as the beginning language of instruction. The system proved to be expensive, and as the study made painfully clear, ineffective.

The execution of this study did not immediately solve the problems of the government for which it was done. But it did serve to provide a kind of information not hitherto available. It demonstrated the possibility of a new order of intelligence to guide planning, and the government in question was persuaded that it should see that machinery for a continuous assessment of its manpower problems will be available. The analogy with national income accounting seems close. This is the sort of procedure that does not in itself solve the planning problems of a country but which makes possible their discussion from a firmer and more realistic base. One ventures to think that suitable machinery for continuous assessment of manpower needs and supply should be a basic part of the research services in developing countries.

The example given suggests an array of problems, general in character and great in their practical importance. I note three of them: (1) the numbers of people to be trained to various levels in a developing society; (2) the balance between special and general education, and the substantive character of both; (3) the possibilities of training outside the formal educational system, in particular within the occupational system itself.

Obviously, policies on all these questions must be formulated by governments and by those who guide and operate the educational system. On the first of the questions we have seen that potentially available and highly important information has typically been lacking. This has not, of course, kept African governments from formulating educational development programs in which the expansion of primary, secondary, technical, and higher education were proportioned according to some scheme. As I have noted above, a want of basic demographic information has made some of this planning costly guesswork and finding methods of providing accurate vital statistics that are within the means of African governments is an urgent problem. But beyond the technical questions of getting accurate basic data there are deep questions of the needs and tolerances of social systems on which more guidance than is now at hand might be hoped.

Educational planners now give much attention to the shape of the educational pyramid. It has been a very sharply narrowing pyramid in Africa and the enthusiasm of new African governments for more primary schools has tended to prolong the "colonial" shape. Professor W. Arthur Lewis has recently stimulated much attention to this problem with arguments about the percentages of the population who ought to get secondary education.[16] Other planners have had formulae of various sorts. From my own examination of various plans, three principal guides seem to have been used: (1) estimates of the percentages of secondary and university graduates needed for an economy at an estimated stage of development; (2) estimates of the wastage likely and tolerable; (3) and, of course, an unrationalized percentage expansion that seemed "reasonable" in terms of the past distribution of education and the likely budgetary resources. In the first of these guides, very general arguments have had to be used for want of precise manpower data, and rough proportioning based on the experience of a particular metropolitan country has been common.[17] The need for more precise fitting to the characteristics and likely prospects of the countries in question seems evident, and in principle not terribly difficult once adequate manpower surveys have been made.

But a much more difficult problem lurks in this proportioning. This is known in the British African territories as the "school-leaver" problem and it arises naturally from the narrowing pyramid and rising standards of education for employment. The lust for education in Africa is a practical lust, based on expectations of the employment and status education may bring. There was a time when a complete primary education assured a job and an attractive income. Now this is not so. In almost every African territory there is an acute and urgent problem of providing careers for those who neither go on to further education nor find a job. Since the Ashanti Survey in 1945-46 showed that 95 per cent of the students finishing primary school want no more of their traditional life but head hopefully for the towns, the problem has been clearly stated. What in fact happens to these young hopefuls seems, however, to be more familiar to politicians than to educational planners. Solutions to this problem may be among the most critical needs of African countries over the coming years. Finding them takes one through the whole gamut of economic and social development problems, but there are at least some of the essential elements toward solutions that can be quickly indicated. For rational strategies of educational development one needs an understanding of: (1) the process of social change whereby a particular type and level of education becomes reasonably stably attached to expectations of later life; (2) the duration, strains, and costs of this adjustment process; and (3) the possible adaptations of educational systems toward easing this adjustment process and contributing positively toward performance in later life.

I have tried to state all these problems in general terms which may suggest their interest as subjects for social science. They seem to me challenging and important questions as such. There has, of course, been a long history of efforts to face these problems in Africa. To make education compatible with a rural existence and thus to "adapt it to African conditions" was the concern of a host of practical educators long before the Ashanti survey; it was, incidentally, a reason why the Sudanese Institute of Education mentioned above was located in simple quarters in remote Bakht-er-Ruda and not more sump-

404

tuously at Khartoum. A great part of the present and future assault on these problems must come through the efforts of practical educators. Researchers will not suffice. But it is difficult to conceive how effective programs can dispense with their guidance.

The second problem I have stated—the relation and content of special and general education—is not merely a question for philosophers of education. It is, as I think my example has suggested, a matter of the most urgent practical importance. It is a question on which contrasting models lurk in the minds of statesmen, politicans, and educators. A certain model has been explicit or implicit in the policies and thought of colonial administrators and educators. This is a view that stresses the slowness of development of most of the competences involved in modern "civilization" or in the operation of a modern society. The European heritage, perhaps especially that from Britain, has run this way. Fear of veneers, respect for experience and for slow maturation, have been part of this tradition at home. We Americans, with a somewhat more activistic bias and a disrespect for vague general qualities, are conscious of this European disposition. When it was transported into Africa, it probably underwent a subtle sharpening and emphasis (just what has gone on in this respect seems to me one of the intriguing and important chapters on colonialism still to be written). Taken naively, the procedure of a manpower survey and the continuous assessment of manpower needs, imply a quite different model of social development. If one interprets the list of needs revealed by a manpower survey as an agenda for special training programs, the emphasis goes from a diffuse kind of development of men to providing them with readily definable competences. At a certain specialized technical level this is plausible; there are evident skills and knowledge that a machinist, doctor, surveyor, or an entomologist need. But some irreducible quanta of general education and experience are also evidently necessary. The natural bias of the emerging African peoples would seem to be towards the activistic and technical side in this choice of dispositions. African nationalism is an assertion that basically Africans have a right to and are capable of manning their own societies. Manifest deficiencies there may be at present. But it is incompatible with the driving ideology in national independence that these deficiencies be taken as diffuse and general capacities subordinating black men to white men. The differences are more readily seen as ones of opportunity in access to particular kinds of experience and training, and thus differences that Africans can erase if similar opportunities are provided, and this within a finite time.

These differences in fundamental conception on the ways of developing human resources are inescapably matters of ideology and deep-set beliefs. But they are not thereby inaccessible to rational guidance. General guidance in the recent past has largely been sought through expert advisers and special commissions. Impressive levels of wisdom and competence have been attained in the work of the Educational Advisor from the Colonial Office or the Binns and Jeffreys Commissions [18] in the British territories. But the work of such outside advisers and commissions must inevitably be limited in depth and acquaintance with the particularities of a local situation. Testimony may be gathered from students, teachers, and education officers; the data available to ministries may be marshalled; but the sort of data that patient research can supply is inevitably missing. In recent years in Africa, the development of Institutes of Education in the British territories has provided bases for research. They are not much developed yet, except in Ghana, and even in Ghana basic data on the characteristics of Ghanaian children and the special problems of their education are only beginning to be gathered. In the French territories, the development of Centres de Formation Professionelle Rapide has brought testing programs that are providing much new knowledge, and various Belgian researchers like Ombredane or Maistriaux have been at work in the Congo. But the work remains very thin and meagre by European or American standards, and little work is yet being done by Africans themselves.[19] The range of possible questions for research is enormous, from very fundamental matters of nutrition and socialization practices to the details of pedagogic technique; measured against the needs, the existing resources are, as the French expressively say, *dérisoire*.

A certain practical effectiveness in judging the results of ventures in specialization or broadening of training can, no doubt, be gained without systematic research. And certainly more things will have to be tried than can be studied. But more ventures ought to be carefully studied than are likely to be, and the results of such study extensively communicated.

Finally and briefly, I note the relations of the formal educational system and the occupational world itself in the development of competences. In the example I recounted, an apparent weakness of the particular African educational system was that it tried to do what normally is done within the occupational system. Clearly, this division of responsibility is a fundamental question of strategy in social development. The subject is one that ought to be, and in a measure is a concern of social science research and reflection. There seems in fact to be a considerable body of knowledge on what the division is in various Western countries that might, when properly abstracted, be applied. The development of African countries will inevitably depend heavily on how well men can learn jobs for which they have often very limited qualifications. The problem is particularly conspicuous and acute in the manning of governments. Normal patterns of advancement in the models of colonial tradition have been perforce abandoned. Special means of accelerated training have had to be sought, and quickly. A rough pragmatism must inevitably rule such efforts in the main, but there are abundant problems for diagnosis and prescription which research efforts might aid. To note only one example, a West African government has been complaining that its young administrative officers lack initiative; there seem to be various reasons for the complaint, among them the peculiar problems of staffing a modern bureaucracy with people from a very hierarchical African society. Pursuing this idea would seem to have obvious interest for research and such research could be a basis of strategy in training in this territory.

An exposition of this sort tends to waver toward programmatic exhortation. But hopefully, it has given some sense of the increased need for guidance by research that rapid development brings. Now let us turn to look at the possibilities that new African governments will get the guidance their problems call for.

We are in the midst of a fundamental change in the control of African societies as Africans themselves take over. This changeover is taking place after a period in which most of the territories have been in a substantial spurt of development that has had the important consequence of rapidly increasing governmental establishments and giving them more than ever to do. Newly elaborated organizations are thus being turned over to relatively inexperienced men.

The tested experience on which colonial administrations depended must for a time be largely lacking to the new African governments, except in the measure that there has been timely "Africanization" and they retain expatriate staff. A compensating factor, difficult to assess but doubtless important, is the first-hand familiarity of men with the societies in which they are native. Some things will doubtless be done right because African leaders and administrators know their people, which a colonial government could only do right through exceptional sensitivity and assiduous study. But are there not dangers that too much may be expected from general familiarity and intuitive understanding? Colonial governments were led to encourage some forms of research because they were in an exotic setting to which their common sense did not evidently apply. Africans have no such protection against overestimation of what is "obvious" about African conditions. They should, however, be less likely to be confident that they know the goals of their development efforts than were their European predecessors. They are not, after all, trying to produce societies like ones they have known elsewhere. Recognizing the newness of the African societies they are set on constructing, they are unlikely to have a simple faith that intuitive judgments and familiarity will guide them. Both the lack of sufficient numbers of technically trained people and unerased feelings of dependence make a continuing receptivity to guidance from outside likely. The emphasis in using outside assistance must be on its technical character lest there be nourishment to the fears that colonialism will persist in covert forms. And among the forms of technical assistance, research should have a neutral character and welcome place.

Receptivity to the uses of research will presumably depend on the education of African administrators. I have noted earlier that African administrators have been trained in the images of their colonial predecessors, and such training has not been specially conducive to recourse to research. The urgency of developing administrators faster than they would normally develop through experience promises much attention to their preliminary education and to schemes of in-service training. The suggested bias of African leaders toward confidence in the efficacy of specialized training also promises efforts to make administration formally teachable. British and French administrators may be

407

dismayed to discover their African offspring seduced by American beliefs in a "science of government." It may not go that far. But social science bids fair to become more prominent in the training of the men who run African governments, and an indoctrination in the meaning and uses of research is a natural part of such training.

Provided that resources in men and money are forthcoming from the outside world, the chances for major application of research to making African governments perform their tasks better thus permit of some optimism. In the short run this outside help looks to be crucial and indispensable. From the start, it should include assistance in the development of institutions of higher education and research in the African territories themselves. Effective preparation of African administrators and leaders requires an orientation to African conditions which can best be gained in local universities. The materials for such education must be based on research, and there are other reasons why research organizations with fairly basic and academic responsibilities are important to African territories. While many of the general ideas and basic principles that guide development may continue to be generated elsewhere, their application in African conditions cannot be expected to be routine. There is a great fund of knowledge and analysis of local conditions that needs to be worked up in any field of social and economic development, and much of it is sufficiently remote from direct application to make it more appropriate for independent research organizations than for working governmental agencies.

Over and above what they may contribute toward the effective technical working of African governments, institutions that carry the discipline and traditions of social research have an evident importance in the intellectual and ideological climates of these countries. Rapid development such as Africa is set upon can hardly be carried out without a great deal of deliberate effort at changing and controlling human beings. Some of this effort is likely to be crudely coercive, but it must also be well-directed and inspire voluntary effort, particularly among the elite, if it is to be effective. The directing elite must have sources of creative ideas and be inspired by an ideology in which development is of central importance. Nationalism and popular solidarity provide part of the ideological stimulus, but only a part. The ideologies that support faith in progress and development are likely to put a strong emphasis on rational effort and science. They may take various forms, including beliefs in the efficacy of planning, "scientific socialism," or a more diffuse kind of "scientism." This last has a special interest for my subject. I mean by it a high valuation of science and a persistent reference of standards of conduct and policy to the supposed best evidence of scientific knowledge. We are familiar with such references in the modern world in a great many domains of conduct, not all of them ones in which there are very firm bases for scientific guidance. We Americans have special susceptibilities of this sort and foreign observers are commonly amused (or aghast) at our efforts to follow the latest "scientific" practice in child-rearing or human relations. Any modernizing society is likely to display a good deal of behavior of this sort, the more so as it gets away from its moorings in unquestioned tradition. While some folly and excess are unavoidable in such efforts to find guidance from scientific research, the advantages over other forms of guidance available in rapidly changing societies are notable. For "scientism" puts the ultimate reference point of authority in an international professional group. The only clear alternatives would seem to be ideologies with their ultimate authorities in political leaders —as has happened in communism and fascism.[20] How far a society can resort to "scientism" will depend in part on the research that is available to be used and interpreted. Clearly, it cannot put much faith in social scientists if they are not evidently working at the problems of the society. Responsible social scientists may quail at the dangers evident in excessive faith in their works, but there are other, and probably worse dangers in too little faith. A steady and ample flow of research on African societies such as can be supplied by well-staffed institutions in Africa (and elsewhere) promises better chances of rational and humane programs of development than could otherwise be hoped.

A great deal of the research needed for the future guidance of Africa will have to do with the kinds of problems in human development I have discussed earlier. There will also be a mass of problems in the development of industry, the uses of co-operatives, or the transformation of agriculture. These are evidently the practical problems of development. But there will also be more purely intellectual and ideological concerns whose importance is not less for being diffuse and intangible. A great effort to interpret Africa's history, special "personality," and destiny is now underway. Reading a journal like *Présence Africaine,* it becomes very evident that many new books will have to be written to meet the questions and the needs of an emerging African intelligentsia. One hopes for good quality in this new literature and there will have to be good scholarship and research on many apparently remote and "impractical" subjects to assure it.

And thus I come to the end of this discourse on the uses of social research with a reminder that although useful results are likely to be important, what is important may not be evidently useful.

1. Cf. St. Clair Drake, "Détruire le mythe chamitique, devoir des hommes cultivés," *Présence Africaine* (special number on Deuxième Congrès des Écrivains et Artistes Noirs), (1959), 215-30.

2. Lord Hailey would not allow them to be called "census" (Hailey, *An African Survey* [New York, 1956]), p. 133.

3. P. J. Foster, in a confidential report. His general conclusion is that "The first step in field work must be a general demographic study of the unit since census material is notoriously inadequate."

4. It has already shown that the estimates of population for recent years based on extrapolations from the 1948 figures were grossly low. For 1958 at mid-year, the official estimate was 4.8 millions (Ghana Ministry of Finance, *Economic Survey 1958* [Accra, 1959], p. 20), while preliminary figures for the 1960 census give 6.69 millions.

5. D. T. Jack, *Economic Survey of Sierra Leone* (Freetown, S. L., 1958), p. 1.

6. The close connection between this experience and particular local conditions is important. Posting to different districts within a given territory has been frequent practice within Her Majesty's Overseas Civil Service, and this has often meant serious losses of accumulated knowledge. Thus Roland Young remarks: "Much of the essential knowledge of districts is contained in the heads of district officers, and when a knowledgeable officer is transferred this information is for all purposes lost and has to be relearned by another officer" (Roland Young and Henry A. Fosbrooke, *Smoke in the Hills, Political Tension in the Morogoro District of Tanganyika* [Evanston, Ill., 1960], p. 125).

7. "Education Policy in British Tropical Africa" (1925), quoted by Lord Hailey, *op. cit.*, p. 1166.

8. V. L. Griffiths, *Experiment in Education* (London, 1953).

9. *Colonial Research, 1958-59* (London, 1960), pp. 6-7.

10. On the substance of recent research, see James S. Coleman, "Research on Africa in European Centers," *African Studies Bulletin*, II, No. 3 (August, 1959), 1-33. On organization, see Lord Hailey, *op. cit.*, chaps. ii, xxiv; E. B. Worthington, *Science and Development in Africa* (London, n.d.), chap. xx. Also, see F. X.

410

Sutton, "Research and Development in Africa South of the Sahara," *Public Opinion Quarterly*, XXII, No. 3 (1958), 261-72.

11. M. Dupire and J. L. Boutillier, *Le pays Adioukrou et sa Palmeraie* (Paris, 1958), p. 100. This book contains a very instructive Preface by Gov. Hubert Deschamps.

12. Marris, "Consequences of the Lagos Slum Clearance Scheme" (Mimeographed. London: Institute of Community Studies, 1959). Marris has published a brief article on his work in *The Listener* and is preparing a book.

13. These remarks are based mostly on personal observation. On experience with the *paysannats,* see F. Bezy, *Principes pour l'orientation du développement économique au Congo* (Léopoldville, 1959).

14. See Barbu Niculescu, *Colonial Planning* (London, 1958).

15. Another substantial study has recently been conducted for the Upper Volta by the Société d'Études pour le Développement Économique et Social (SEDES) and the Institut Pédagogique National de Paris (mimeographed report, 1959).

16. See *The Economist* (London), January 10, 1959.

17. Interesting examples I have examined include the preliminary work on the new Plan Décennal for the Belgian Congo, planning for legal education in Ghana, and the various schemes of M. Messadi, Secretary of State for Education in Tunisia. Sometimes plans discuss a "balanced" system with no nationalization whatsoever; see, e.g. *The Kenya Development Programme 1957/60* ("Sessional Papers of 1956/57," No. 77 [Nairobi]), p. 70.

18. *African Education* (Cambridge, 1953) incorporates these reports and the proceedings of a conference sponsored by the Nuffield Foundation.

19. Except in the Union of South Africa, where Biesheuvel and his large staff at the National Institute for Personnel Research have done work impressive in quality and volume.

20. It will occur to the reader that I neglect religions. I do not think they can provide an ideology of development without becoming fully political. They have, of course, important functions of other sorts.

Research on the Social Implications of Modernization and Technological Change in Southern Asia

C. N. VAKIL

UNESCO Research Centre, Calcutta

INTRODUCTION

In preparing this paper, we adopted first the following method. A circular letter with a suitable questionnaire was sent to the different universities and other research institutions in the Asian countries to be studied. The UNESCO National Commission in each of these countries was asked to help. In spite of all our efforts, we received rather a poor response. The replies ranged from twenty-two to thirty per cent in different countries. After trying to analyze the material thus acquired, we came to the conclusion that it would not serve our purpose. This rather depressing situation reflects the backward character of the development in social sciences, since the importance of the utility of such an inquiry could not be fully realized. In consequence, we decided to utilize the following sources of information:

a) The *Research Information Bulletin* issued by the Centre since 1956;
b) The material collected for the Centre's paper on "Survey of Research on Social Implications of Industrialization" for Professor Moore, through the International Social Science Council;
c) The records and library of the Centre;
d) Other libraries in Calcutta;
e) The material obtained from the limited response to our questionnaire; and
f) Personal observations.

As we could not use this material for a direct treatment of the subject matter of the paper, we adopted a somewhat roundabout method in order to evolve a picture of the supply of resources and skills on social implications of modernization and technological change.

In this paper, we hope to indicate the main trend of the work being done in connection with the social implications of modernization and technological change. We should add that specialization in the social sciences is still in its infancy in this region. It is difficult to find institutions devoted to such specialized subjects as the social implications of modernization and technological

412

change. The Centre is concerned with this subject, but it has learned through experience that the theme is rather narrow and not adequate to stimulate interest in some countries. Therefore it has been proposed that the scope of the Centre be enlarged to include research on problems of economic and social development. In view of this, it is obviously necessary to deal with social science institutions to locate the available facilities and skills for further development in the field of social implications of modernization and technological change. We have thus tried in this paper to present a broad picture of the development in social sciences in the region, followed by a rapid review of the work done or being done on the theme.

The material thus presented indicates clearly that the countries of the region are not yet prepared to cope with the growing need for research on the various problems engendered by the revolutionary changes which are now taking place in the economic, social, and political life of the people. Hence it is necessary to think in terms of an appropriate all-round development in the different social sciences in these countries. This would enable us to see that some institutions in each country concentrate on the social implications of modernization and technological change. The same is true of research workers. If suitable young students are expected to specialize in this theme, they must receive more systematic encouragement by fellowships and grants, and by having reasonable prospects of a research career.

Among the countries of the region, there is relatively more awareness of the importance of such studies in India, Pakistan, and the Philippines. The supply of resources and skills for the purpose is comparatively greater in India, where the Planning Commission and the University Grants Commission have, in recent years, encouraged development in social science research. Support from the Ford Foundation and similar sources has also been received for the same objective. Foundation support in other countries of the region is also increasing.

This paper is divided into two parts. The first summarizes the development of social sciences in the region. The second reviews briefly the type of research on different aspects of social implications of modernization and technological change that has been or is being done.

DEVELOPMENT OF SOCIAL SCIENCES

Organized social science research has not yet evolved very far in most of the countries with which we are concerned. The universities and colleges must devote more time to undergraduate teaching. Several universities have postgraduate departments, but in most cases even these are preoccupied with teaching load. Research work consequently takes a somewhat subordinate position in such institutions. However, organized research in the social sciences has been developed to some extent in India, particularly in recent years. Though the progress in Pakistan and the Philippines is not so great, these countries also have made a good beginning in this direction. In most of the other countries, some institutions may be discerned that are trying to develop research, or some social scientists are trying to undertake research activities; but these are exceptions.

Most of the institutions devoted to social science research are attached to universities. A few, like the Nattional Council of Applied Economic Research in New Delhi (Dr. P. S. Lokanathan) and the Institute of Development Economics in Karachi (Dr. G. Ranis), are independent of universities and operate as autonomous organizations. The rareness of research institutions attached to industry and commerce seems to indicate the comparatively low degree of modernization of industrial management. The work of the Association of Indian Trade Industry in Bombay (Dr. K. R. Paymaster) in industrial economics represents a significant step taken by industry in this connection. The work of the Ahmedabad Textile Industry's Research Association (Mrs. Kamla Choudry) in this field is also significant.

Most of the universities institutions have both teaching and research functions. In a majority of cases, the teaching load is such that it limits the time and resources available for research. However, in a few instances research has a more important place—e.g., the Departments of Economics and Sociology of the University of Bombay, which started about forty years ago, have been able to devote the larger share of their time to research, since the teaching load for the master's degree has been comparatively small.* In some institutions separate boards have been created to undertake research, such as the Socio-Economic Research Board of the Dacca University (Professor A. F.A. Husain).

One of the important factors restricting the development of these institutions is the paucity of funds. Most of them have limited resources; only a few seem to be well endowed with the funds they need. As a rule, these institutions depend mainly on government for their finances. Since the universities have other activities to look after, the share that research institutions in social sciences have in their financial plans is obviously limited. The expenditure on scientific and technological research is much higher than that on research in the social sciences. Recently, some financial assistance has been received from the United Nations and specialized agencies, as well as from international educational foundations, local charity trusts, and even from industry. The Ford Foundation, the Rockefeller Foundation, and the Asia Foundation have, among others, given a great impetus to social research in several universities of the region. In India, the Research Programmes Committeee of the Planning Commission has, since 1954, encouraged a large number of research projects to be undertaken by the universities and other bodies by making suitable grants.

Whereas some of the institutions are located in appropriate buildings and have adequate space, most of them are cramped. The numbers of students seeking admission to such institutions have been increasing with the consequence that the available facilities become more and more inadequate.

Except in a few cases, the library facilities are rather inadequate for advanced research. The Departments of Economics and Sociology in the University of

---

* The author was connected with the School of Economics and Sociology of the University of Bombay from 1921 to 1956.

Bombay have, during the course of more than a generation, built up a research library of over fifty thousand volumes. The Delhi School of Economics, though of recent origin, has been able to acquire special endowments to have a suitable library. In the Philippines, the library of the Institute of Public Administration and the Orientalia Collection of the University of the Philippines are noteworthy. However, other institutions must utilize limited funds in trying to build up special libraries suited to them.

The importance of having trained librarians who can help research workers with documentation and other services has not been fully recognized. In most institutions, the library staff is at a lower level; as a result, researchers are handicapped in their work.

The use of machines and other modern devices as aids in research is still limited. Some institutions are able to use modern calculating and tabulating machines. In institutions like the Indian Statistical Institute at Calcutta, the latest machines are found—sometimes in inadequate number for the growing activities of that institution. In contrast, however, the majority of other research institutions are without even elementary facilities of this nature.

The success of research depends a good deal on the personnel engaged in it. In a few cases, the personnel is both adequate and highly qualified; but in the majority of institutions, research staff are neither adequate in number nor properly qualified for the work. However, there is a growing tendency in these institutions to recruit persons who have had research training either in India or abroad. Research training obtained in the course of working for the Ph. D. degree is considered suitable for a start in a research career. Persons with this qualification are in demand, both by government and business, and by academic institutions. Since the remuneration offered in government and business is more attractive, research institutions cannot always have or retain the services of qualified research staff. There are persons who have only a master's degree but have had considerable research experience, but their number is small, as is the number of persons who have gone to British or American universities and have obtained research training in their respective subjects. Among these few, some find other fields more attractive than the academic.

Economics and sociology are the leading subjects of research, though anthropology, education, psychology, etc., are gradually receiving more attention. Some idea of the nature of research work done on subjects bearing on the social implications of technological change and modernization will be presented later in this paper; specialization on this theme has not yet been possible, though some work on some aspects of it has been done.

This is also reflected in the publications—books and journals—issued by institutions or by individuals on social science subjects. A general look at these publications reveals that, though a large variety of subjects have been considered, there is only limited specialization—particularly on the social implications of modernization and technological change. This may be due to the fact that the available persons working on the staff of an institution are few. Even highly qualified research workers may have to handle different subjects, both for teaching and guiding research, thereby reducing their capacity to specialize in one field.

415

We shall try to present, under appropriate headings, a brief indication of the nature of research work that has been done or is being attempted. We hope that this will enable those concerned to get an impression, however indirectly, of the resources and skills available in this connection.

Social Implications of Industrialization

The most direct form of study of this problem seems to be to select an area where a new industry or factory is established, and to make an intensive investigation of the economic and social lives of the inhabitants of the area as well as of the workers employed in the factory. Professor Husain's study of the *Human and Social Impact of Technological Change in Pakistan* is a comprehensive survey carried out in Dacca (East Pakistan). A number of such projects have been undertaken, especially in India, and to a smaller extent, in some other countries. The inquiry made by the Tata Institute of Social Sciences, Bombay, under the direction of Dr. S. D. Punekar, *Survey of Mithapur*, is described as "an attempt to study the social, economic, cultural and psychological changes which came over the workers as a result of their migration from a rural setting to an industrial environment." A similar study has been made in connection with the newly founded steel plant at Durgapur (India) by the Indian Institute of Social Welfare and Business Management of the Culcutta University, under the direction of Professor T. C. Das, entitled *Present and Future Durgapur: A Study on Planned Industrialization of a Rural Area*. This is a comprehensive survey of the socio-economic conditions of the people living in the villages outside the developing industrial area. Its object is the study of the effects of industrialization on these people's social and economic life at a later date. A study conducted by the Research Council on Community Development of the University of the Philippines has investigated *Some Socio-Economic Effects of Building Barrio Roads*, where a modern transport system was introduced. A similar project, entitled the "Study of the Impact of Light Industry in Viet-Nam," is currently being undertaken by the Michigan State University Advisory Group in that country.

In addition to such ambitious and comprehensive studies, various institutions are investigating the implications of industrialization for specific aspects of industrial workers' lives. A study entitled *Factors in Migration of Jute Labour and Consequent Changes in Food and Recreation Habits* has been undertaken by a scholar in the Department of Anthropology of the Calcutta University. The UNESCO Research Centre (Calcutta) has conducted a study of "Social and Cultural Factors Affecting the Productivity of Industrial Labour" published in 1961.

Urbanization

Problems of urbanization with either industrialization or other causes present a complex variety of problems for research. In India, the Planning Commission has encouraged urban surveys by university departments of economics

416

and other organizations. Among these the four metropolitan city surveys may be mentioned, namely, those of Bombay, Calcutta, Madras, and Delhi. The approach has been chiefly economic, though some social aspects are included. In Bombay, the scope of the survey was enlarged, with the help of the Government of Bombay and the Bombay Municipality, and a large number of social topics were included—e.g., housing, education, crime, mendicancy, migration, etc.

The Statistical Centre of the University of the Philippines has been investigating various aspects of life in Manila under its project entitled *Survey of Life in Manila*. In Singapore, also, at the request of the Ministry of Labour and Welfare, a project entitled *Urban Incomes and Housing* has been completed, as a part of the larger survey of Singapore. The Institute of Development Economics of Karachi (Pakistan) is currently undertaking "A Demographic-Economic Survey of Karachi."

These comprehensive surveys will no doubt provide basic information on the social and economic life of urban population. At the same time, studies focussing on the attitudes and behavior of urban population and on the impact that urban areas have on neighbouring villages are being made. The *Influence of Urbanisation on Work and Leisure* has been studied by Professor N. K. Bose at the Ramakrishna Mission Institute of Culture in Calcutta (India). A similar investigation on the *Use of Leisure in the City of Colombo* has been made by the Department of Education of the University of Ceylon. Among other attitude studies of urban population, the ones focussing on attitudes toward family planning measures are important—e.g., the inquiry at the Department of Psychology of the Calcutta University, entitled *Study of Attitude of the Educated Class of Urban Population towards Family Planning.*

The influence of urban living on industrial workers has been investigated at various centers. The Tata Institute of Social Sciences, Bombay, has made a *Study on the Social Effects of Urbanization on Industrial Workers Migrating from Rural Areas to the city of Bombay,* under the guidance of Dr. P. H. Prabhu. Similar studies of migrant groups have been undertaken in Bangkok by an American scholar, Mr. R. B. Textor; in Djakarta, by the Institute of Economic and Social Research of the University of Indonesia, under the supervision of A. Stolp; and in Delhi, by Mr. M. B. Deshmukh. These, as well as the Dacca study mentioned earlier, were initiated by UNESCO and are available in our publication, *Social Implications of Industrialisation and Urbanisation— Five Studies in Asia* (Calcutta, 1956). In addition, quantitative aspects of the growth of urban population, from the census and other data, are investigated. The Demographic Training and Research Centre in Bombay has done considerable work in this field.

Problems of social disorganization resulting from the rapid growth of urban centers are also investigated at a number of institutions. The general urbanization studies mentioned above do cover these problems to a certain extent. However, some inquiries have concentrated on specific difficulties, such as crimes in cities, juvenile delinquency, sexual morality of migrants, etc. We may refer, for example, to *A Study of Indian Crimes* by Miss P. C. Kerawalla.

The Socio-Economic Research Board of the University of Dacca is now

417

engaged in a study of "The Problems of Social Integration of Industrial Workers at Khulna with Special Reference to Problems of Labour (industrial) Relations." Khulna is a town in East Pakistan which was a rural area before 1947 and has become an industrial town, in recent years, as industries have grown rapidly. This inquiry is being conducted under the direction of Professor A. F. A. Husain in co-operation with the Centre.

The Centre has also made *A Preliminary Inquiry into the Social Problems of the New Steel Towns in India Compared with Those of the Older Ones*. This study has indicated a large number of significant problems. We propose to follow it up by an intensive inquiry into the Asansol region, in which there is an unusual concentration of heavy industry. It is hoped that the "Steel Towns Report," when published, will stimulate further research.

Industrial Organization

The increase of entrepreneurs should be one of the major topics of investigation. One inquiry in progress in this area is being conducted at the Gokhale Institute of Politics and Economics at Poona, under the direction of Professor D. R. Gadgil: "Rise of Modern Business in India." An article, "Business Leadership in Underdeveloped Countries: Sociological and Institutional Aspects," by the present writer (published in the *UN Industrialisation and Productivity Bulletin*, II), illumines this problem. I have made another study, "The Role of Private Enterprise in a Planned Economy," will appear in the forthcoming volume, "Modern Man and His World: As Social Scientists View Them," edited by Mr. B. N. Varma of Hofstra College, New York. In Indonesia, at the Institute of Economic and Social Research of the University of Indonesia, Djakarta, the development of entrepreneurship in connection with the nationalization of import trade is being investigated by Professor J. B. Glassburner. The Institute of Philippine Culture at Manila is also studying the background of entrepreneurs in middle-size industry in the Philippines; the Institute of Economic Development and Research of the University of Philippines is planning a similar study. In Burma, Dr. Tun Thin, at the Department of Economics of the University of Rangoon, is investigating such business ventures as are undertaken with joint international collaboration.

Industrial Management

Next in importance is the problem of management of industrial undertakings. In India, recently a number of institutions and universities have started evening courses of training in industrial and business management. However, research on these topics apparently has not yet reached appreciable dimensions. The Ahmedabad Textile Industry's Research Association in India is active in this field, and has made several case studies of the management structures of textile mills. A similar study of private enterprises, both Indian and foreign, has been conducted by Mr. C. V. Rao of the Department of Commerce, Andhra University. In Burma, the Department of Commerce and Economics of the University of Rangoon has undertaken several case studies of this nature.

418

Small-Scale Industries
Increasing attention is being paid to the development of small-scale industries in some of the countries of the region. For example, in India the Office of the Development Commissioner is an organization for small-scale industries whose network extends to different parts of the country. Introduction of modern methods and techniques is the keynote of this development. The establishment of the so-called "Industrial Estates" in several parts of the country is a new device for the encouragement of small-scale industries.

The social change caused by their development is being studied in India by the UNESCO Research Centre, and, in Manila and Karachi, in co-operation with the Centre. Mr. B. G. Bantegui, Director, Office of the Statistical Co-ordination and Standards of the National Development Council, Manila, is in charge of the Manila investigation; Dr. G. Ranis, of the Institute of Development Economics in Karachi, is in charge of the investigation there.

Labor Problems
Thus far, inquiries concerning the aspects of industrial labor relevant to the researches of our interest seem to be limited. The Xavier Labour Relations Institute of Jamshedpur, the Ahmedabad Textile Industry's Research Association, the South India Textile Research Association in Coimbatore, and the Social Science Section of the Institute of Science at Bangalore in India, have undertaken a number of studies of the social aspects of life in factories, of the psychological aspects of work in factories, and so on. In Indonesia, Professor M. A. Jaspan, of the Social Research Centre of the Padjadjaran State University at Bandung, has made a beginning with his current project, "Sociology of a Factory."

Agriculture
Along with the development of industries and urban centers, a number of policy measures adopted by governments are generating changes in techniques of agricultural work. Under the influence of different planning schemes, technological change in agriculture—in which the major part of each of these populations work—is gradually taking place.

In India, the traditional land tenure systems have been changed significantly by legislative measures which affect the social structure and power relationships within village communities. Professor Baljit Singh has directed an interesting study, *Impact of Land Reform on Group Dynamics and Class Relations in Uttar Pradesh*, at the Department of Economics of the University of Lucknow. We have listed some studies of influences of urban areas on neighboring villages in the section on "Urbanization."

Community Development
The movement of community development in almost all the countries with which we are concerned helps in bringing about a number of technological changes and in modernizing the agricultural practices traditionally followed. Studies of social changes resulting from this movement, of the reactions of farmers to these modernizing efforts, and of the over-all effectiveness of these measures, would have considerable importance for our theme. In India, the

Programme Evaluation Organization of the Planning Commission conducts continuous sample surveys on the working of the community development schemes and publishes an annual evaluation report. The newly founded Institute of Training and Research in Community Development, Mussoorie, will be another center for such studies when it is fully developed. The Government of Uttar Pradesh has established the Planning Research and Action Institute, at Lucknow, which has so far conducted a number of projects, e.g., *Evaluation of the Use of Improved Agricultural Implements.* Various university departments have also been active in this field.

In Pakistan, the Village-AID Programme is equivalent to the Community Development Programme of India. The Social Science Research Centre of the University of Punjab in Lahore has engaged in the same kind of evaluation studies.

The Community Development Research Council of the University of the Philippines, which was recently established with government assistance, has begun work on a number of inquiries about various aspects of Philippine rural life. The project *Factors Related to the Acceptance or Rejection of Innovations in Poultry and Swine Production in Rural Areas* is one example.

Tribal Change

In some of these countries, a number of aboriginal and tribal groups exist. Such groups, in their contact with modern life and industry, provide an interesting phenomenon for anthropologists to study.

A study by the Department of Anthropology of the University of Lucknow (India) is representative of the anthropological research being conducted. It is entitled *Impact of Technology on Some Aboriginal Peoples of Bihar.* Such tribal groups are involved in modernizing areas besides factory employment, and studies of these developments are also being conducted. A research project on "Culture Change and Kadar Clothes" is being undertaken at the University of Madras by an anthropologist, Dr. Ehrenfels. Among other things, it is directed to the study of the Kadar community, "a food gathering group drawn into money marketing problems." Similar investigations are being made in other countries, notably in Indonesia, especially by an American scholar of Yale University. The work of the Cornell Research Centre in Thailand has substantially added to our knowledge of the changes taking place in that community.

In India, many legislative and other welfare measures have been instituted among the tribal population. Such measures, in one way or other, have a number of modernizing influences, and their impact and the response they receive provide an interesting field of study for our interest. The Government of India, as well as the governments of some states, maintain well-established anthropological research organizations, and some of them are responsible for such studies. A study of "Impact of Socio-Economic Legislation on the Backward Classes in Selected Rural Areas" has been undertaken at the Department of Economics of the Annamalai University.

The work of both the Institute of Traditional Culture in Madras and the Department of Anthropology, Government of India, is in the same direction.

Other Social Changes

The process of social change, not necessarily directly connected with a particular technological change, is proceeding in all these countries. Various social institutions, like the caste system and the joint family, as well as the habits and attitudes of the people, are fast changing. A number of institutions are engaged in studying these changes. The Indian Statistical Institute, under the guidance of Professor R. Mukherjee, is currently engaged in a study entitled "Changing Pattern of West Bengal Villages: 1951-56." In Ceylon, the Department of Sociology of the University of Ceylon has conducted such studies under the direction of Dr. S. J. Tambiah. The Institute of Social Research of the University of Indonesia in Djakarta is presently working on the project, "Village Communities in Indonesia," to study "the present-day pattern of the village communities, the structural changes taking place, the process of economic development in the villages and the factors—social, organisational and others—affecting it." In Pakistan, the Sociology Department of the Dacca University is also conducting certain investigations of rural change.

U Aye Hlaing is directing the Department of Economics of the University of Rangoon in its comprehensive "Village Studies Project," which is to "study the economic and social aspects of a number of villages with special reference to the significant economic, social and technological changes that have taken place in recent years."

The Michigan State University Group in Saigon, Viet Nam, is planning to make a similar comprehensive study of a rural community.

Methods of Promoting the Spread and Better Utilization of the Social Sciences

JOHN H. PROVINSE

Council on Economic and Cultural Affairs

Having spent most of my life in administrative or service jobs of one sort or another, rather than as a salesman, I find myself somewhat embarrassed to assume an entrepreneurial role to discuss the methods of promoting anything —let alone the methods of promoting an enterprise as ambitious as "the spread and utilization of the social sciences." Actually, the title of this paper says "the spread and *better* utilization of the social sciences." That word "better" helps me to summarize much of my paper in one sentence: "The best method of promoting the *better* use of the social sciences is to develop *better* social science." When we have that better product, the world is poised on its mark to come running.

Lacking any promotional experience, I withdrew from the library a volume dealing with the subject. According to this, it would seem that before one goes into the promotion business, it is fitting and wise to ask some business-like questions:

1) What is the product you are promoting?
2) What is your market?
3) What means are best suited to bring your product to the attention and appeal of the consumer?

First, just what is the product that we as social scientists have to promote?

THE NATURE OF OUR PRODUCT

The social sciences are bodies of knowledge, much as the separate fields of the physical and biological sciences are bodies of knowledge. But the social sciences are more difficult than the natural sciences to present convincingly as separate bodies of knowledge, because of their greater and unique functional interdependence. Attempts to promote one body of knowledge—economics, say, or sociology—without reference to and accommodation for its siblings in the larger family of social studies, are loaded with the dangers of advancing less than the whole truth, or of hedging what truth there may be with so many assumptions or conditions that the conclusions lose most of their practical relevance and almost all of their persuasion or conviction.

Despite their interdependence and interrelationship, each segmented field or discipline of the social sciences has proceeded doggedly on its own course, devising its own terms of reference and measurement, selecting its own critical observation points, and deriving generally its own specialized "laws" and generalizations. Each has become an independent and discrete endeavor; and, as its independence and separateness have grown, each seems to have developed an increasingly arrogant confidence in its own product and its own final answers—resulting in a sort of subject-matter "nationalism" that has become as sensitive to boundaries and sovereignty as have any of the new nations emerging from the colonial past.

So far has this isolationism proceeded that most students and practitioners of any specific social science discipline not only are removed in interest from the students and practitioners in other fields; they also have evolved a language of their own, so foreign to their colleagues in other fields that, were the semantic differentiations to be graded along a linguistic scale, they could well be rated as being as mutually unintelligible as English and Chinese or Bantu and French. Thus, each discipline's increasingly specialized treatment of the functional whole of human behavior, and the increasing difficulty of communication among the separate fields of study, impose a double handicap on all efforts to put our broken-down Humpty Dumpty back together again into a form that approximates societal reality or convinces any sizable number of people that we know what we are talking about.

The unhappy results of this fragmentation of human behavior for purposes of analysis and study are of great concern to many social scientists and to educators generally at the present time. I should guess that there is scarcely a campus without some kind of academic course or program designed to bring our increasingly specialized learning about social process into greater focus and integration. But most of these efforts still are acts of summation rather than of interrelationship. Each discipline contributes its meaty bit, wrapped in unique verbiage, to a potpourri of learning, rather than to any integrated weighted analysis of living situations. Having made his contribution, the specialized donor retires once again behind the intellectual curtain of his domain—a curtain even more impenetrable than iron or bamboo—where extraneous factors are not permitted to obtrude and disturb the peace and quiet. And most of the students simply postpone learning about life in any significant sense until they get out of school.

Not long ago, in reviewing an excellent textbook on economics and economic development, I was pleased, as an anthropologist, to discover in the table of contents two chapters entitled: "Cultural Factors of Economic Development" and "Psychological Factors of Economic Development." I read these first. They were excellent surveys, well documented; I would be proud to have been the author of either. But when I read the whole volume—throughout which occurred further occasional caveats about the cultural, sociological, and psychological factors of economic development—I could not discover that these observations or admonitions had really been taken into account as modifying or conditioning factors of the many "economic" judgments or generalizations which were presented.

Again, at a recent seminar in Manila a reputable South-East Asian economist, with long acquaintance in the area, gave an excellent two-hour presentation of the cultural and sociological factors of Malayan society. He covered, sympathetically and with the insights of his experience, the problems of religion, racial aptitudes and tensions, social class, political alignments. Yet, at a later session of the seminar, when the speaker reverted to his professional role in discussing plans for economic development, all the modifying and related factors he had been so articulate about in the morning were not even brought into the discussion.

I may seem to be picking on the economists. I am not. In general, the economists are probably trying harder than most social scientists to create awareness of the data and insights of the other social sciences. These examples come to me because of recent association with economists; but examples of similar specialized interpretive efforts can be cited from political science, administration, sociology, public welfare, etc.

None of this is an attack upon any social science. Because of the nature of our data, the size of the ultimate task, and the inherited methods of our scientific endeavor, we all are victims of the same isolating handicaps in trying to analyze and reconstruct the functional relationships of the social experience. I am attempting here simply to point out as urgent business this limitation as it affects the spread and better use of the social sciences. Whether or not we are fully aware of it, or whether we are willing to admit it or not, we are actually in a parts and spare parts business. This is an enterprise which, under certain conditions, can itself be a very profitable and a very useful one; but promoting such a parts business, without someone—either the consumer or the producer—having a fuller understanding of the whole assembly process, can quickly lead to no business at all.

Government offices throughout the world bulge with economic and administrative plans and programs, national and sub-national, that in their own disciplinary terms are usually unassailable. But they are still less than a substantial portrayal of a nation and its resources; and in the market place there is beginning to be less and less conviction that they are the real article. In many instances these plans have become a sort of modish costume jewelry, without which no country dares appear in public, particularly at the bank, but which go back on the shelves when the dress parade is over and work begins again.

The educational experience of preparing these economic and administrative plans is invaluable, of course, both to the national planners and to the experts associated with them in collecting and analyzing specific data; and the new understanding coming from the exercise may itself be sufficient to justify the time and money spent. But to a degree which I think most social scientists do not realize, these plans tend to create expectations of final answers and over-all operating programs beyond the potential of the plans to fulfill. Nothing can sour a customer so fast or discredit a product so thoroughly as for the buyer to find that the product is not all the seller represented it to be, or that the buyer thought it was going to be. One aspect of sound promotion that confronts the social sciences is the necessity of curbing the almost chauvinistic enthusiasm on the part of the more zealous guild members in over-promoting or over-selling their product.

A second query relevant to acceptance of the social science product is, How thoroughly have its findings been tested outside the lecture hall or classroom? Does the product stand up? Leonardo da Vinci is reported to have said: "The supreme misfortune is when theory outstrips performance." Still, today most social science is not put to a test in the everyday world; and most social scientists prefer to validate their findings about human behavior according to the thoughts and theorizing of other social scientists, rather than in the practical situation. Much social science is already so scholastic that it would appear to vary from the Scholasticism of the Middle Ages only in its basic way of deriving truth: statistical correlation has replaced revelation.

Some years ago, at an economic development seminar in Egypt, I read a paper on the social and cultural factors related to economic development. I gave what would pass among my guild members as a reasonable presentation of the need for taking into account the various factors of social organization, motivation, value system—which, as nearly all agree, are important factors, negative or positive—in the application of economic and administrative measures in most development programs. I was disconcerted during the discussion period when the chairman of the meeting asked: "As a member of the National Planning Board, I know that all our members are anxious to discover just how to make use of the cultural, socio-psychological knowledge you are talking about. Can you give us specific instances where the insights from your studies of human organization and incentive and values have been made, or can be made, a functioning part of the plans or operations of government in its attempt to raise the standards of living among our people?" The chairman was a friend, and was not, by his question, seeking to put me on the spot. Nonetheless, I had to admit that in spite of the fervor of my plea, it was still largely preachment, and that as yet little progress had been made on the problem of how to put our new knowledge and insights back into the practical world of human affairs.

If one ponders the present commanding position of the physical and biological sciences, it is evident that—even allowing for their longer history and greater share in man's intellectual attention—they have achieved their ascendancy as much by application and practice as by preaching and teaching. At present, there is little new knowledge in the natural sciences that is not being put to work. This cannot be said of the social sciences, which now possess a startling array of information about human behavior, social, economic, political, and religious; and about relationships between people, as individuals, as groups, and as nations. Yet so far the application of this knowledge is at best fragmentary, and, at worst, a threat to man's continued existence in a peaceful world. For this lag and neglect, the social scientists themselves must share much of the blame, since, with some notable exceptions, they have shunned the practical world. They have tended to reduce in professional standing those of their co-workers who did venture forth—many of whom, by the nature of the real world in which they tried to operate, have found it necessary to compromise the "pureness" of their scientific calling.

Our failure to test our product is in general responsible for the disillusionment and despair of many practical men who want to be our friends, and many of whom earnestly and in good faith would welcome the chance to use whatever new knowledge social science could furnish them. But they cannot employ the new knowledge until it has been made available to them with better understanding of where it fits in. St. Francis of Assisi once said, "A man has only so much knowledge as he puts to work." It is still good counsel, if you seek to have others participate in your discoveries.

A third question we need ask about the promotion potential of our product involves the meaningful content of the product itself. For whom is it significant? Is the commodity we are pushing something the public and the world want or need, or is it just an end product of an academic activity we ourselves enjoy doing for its own sake? Are we asking and analyzing the kinds of questions that have bearing upon the needs countless people feel for greater understanding of the world in which they live?

What are the worrisome problems in the world today? They are not really how to reach the moon, or to discover the secret of animation of protoplasmic matter. They are not really the difficulties of selling two automobiles to a family that can afford only one, or of getting more precise statistical measurement of economic and market behavior, or of making more refined, detailed studies of class, sub-class, status, and social mobility. Not that these are necessarily unimportant subjects of study, or that, through examining them, we do not advance our knowledge in substance as well as in methodology. However, our almost provincial preoccupation with them is not now giving the returns on investment that might come from broader types of inquiry. These returns might serve to counteract a growing public disillusionment about social science studies, a feeling that they may be interesting but they are actually not relevant.

One has only to review the news coverage in the *New York Times* or *The Economist* for a month to be impressed with the great variety of problems and issues involving human relationships—the stuff of social science—and to discover how few of them are being given more than cursory attention by the social scientists. Among these are critical issues and developments which demand the most objective study that the world's best minds can give them: race relations and race hatreds, religious conflict and bigotry, changing national values and national character, various regional congregations of interest or power, minority problems, the release of long suppressed but newly awakened human energy that is going on throughout the world, and the varied organizational setups (still not well understood by most social scientists) through which, for better or for worse, this energy is being channeled and directed. Despite the anthropologists, most of Western social science has not yet discovered that the world is round instead of flat.

Why is it that—as has occurred so often among the newly emerging nations— when representative democratic governments are found wanting in efficiency or integrity of performance, the people have appealed to the army to take over

426

the government or have accepted its doing so? I doubt that this is any martial conspiracy on the part of the military to rule the world. But I know of no one who is endeavoring to find out whether, in the training and organizational pattern of military life, there are elements of discipline, rule of law, organizational integrity, and higher loyalty so developed that they are able to transcend the personal pressures, biases, and group and family loyalties that inhere in the familial pattern of social organization.

Who is the "Ugly American?" Or, perhaps more important, "Why is he?" or "What produced him?" Many of the "Ugly Americans" abroad come from countries other than America. Why is it that, when most technicians and experts step off their plane or boat to work on a foreign assignment, the mere act of landing seems automatically to raise their competence to pass judgment on everything they encounter—a competence they never had, or never thought of exercising, at home? How does one nation help another nation without creating disharmony, dependency, or loss of self-respect?

How does borrowing or communication take place across cultural, subcultural, and national boundaries; and what strains and consequences are incurred? How appropriate or efficient are our Western social science techniques, hypotheses, concepts, and models for research in an understanding of another culture, and what efforts are being made to adapt them where they are not appropriate?

How many among us are trying to understand the youth movements that are as explosive as the population problem? How many are examining the changing age structure of our new world in an attempt to find a way to accommodate the needs and productive activity of countless millions of people who will live twice as long as their grandparents and are still supposed to retire at sixty-five? And what about the world's population problem—not as a Malthusian bugaboo with which to threaten human disaster in 1980 or two generations hence, but as a crucial down-to-earth factor among most of the impoverished, disadvantaged peoples of the world today? Our concern with social process, social mobility, economic status, and the like, has perhaps obscured for us the significance of the very natural process of moving from one age group to another, or from one generation to another.

I realize that some of our colleagues are studying problems of the sort mentioned. I realize also that the aim and effort of social science are to develop whatever wisdom possible that will soften the two great explosions, in technology and in population, that are going on in the world. But these are problems of the reorganization of human efforts and of the reorientation of people on such a vast scale that social science is challenged as it has never been before. If, in this large area of human relationships, the social disciplines expect to capture consumer interest in their work, they will have to devote to it a larger part of their interest and their capital expenditures than they now do. Currently, they appear to have relinquished most of their professional rights and obligations to the journalists and newspaper men, the writers of political speeches, and the demagogues. The present social science literature is full of the word "climate"—"climate of opinion," "climate of investment," "climate of politics." What we really need are more social scientists interested in weather: in the world today, there is no longer any "climate": there is only "weather," whether we like it or not.

Raising or changing the level of our sights, and increasing the scope of our inquiries, are only the beginnings of our obligation. Are we also ready to do battle for the answers we find? How many social scientists, outside the insulated classrooms, are involved in diagnosing or in assisting to cure the apartheid illness in South Africa? If this were a parasitic infection of a plant or a chicken, or a virulent form of measles, the medical or biological sciences would have their resources mobilized post-haste to do something about it, and on the spot. There are few social scientists who are professionally concerned about the civil rights issue in the American South, or in the human relationship problem which is the North African crisis. These running sores on the body politic (which is also the body social), which kill, or maim for any productive life, more people than any known physical disease, have little compelling appeal or challenge for the social scientist as practitioner. They serve most often, in fact, to fortify him in his protestations of objectivity and detachment, the shibboleths of his professional standing. Yet more of our social scientists need the chastening, often humbling, experience of participating in the trial runs that are basic to the validation of findings in the field of knowledge in which they profess competence and in which they make their living.

Who among us is trying to discover and understand what is happening to the economic, political, and the until now impregnable family organization of a half-billion Chinese? For enlightenment on what is probably the greatest social upheaval of all history—in comparison, the population explosion may assume the proportions of a firecracker in a tin can—we are now almost totally dependent upon the opportunistic, unverifiable reports of a few hard-working, often hard-drinking, journalists who live in or occasionally visit Hong Kong!

And so I suggest that a first step in promoting the spread and better use of the social sciences should be to improve the quality of our product: (*1*) by integrating its parts into a more marketable package; (*2*) by testing it more rigorously than is now done; and (*3*) by modernizing it to meet the requirements and expectancies of a jet-propelled age of social change.

MARKETING OUR PRODUCT

With some notable exceptions, the principal channels through which the social sciences reach and affect our consuming public are the colleges and universities. There has been some movement downward into secondary-school education. There has been some growth, laterally, into the general public sector through extension and adult-education work, and through the activities of clubs, study groups, foundations, and, on a more wide world basis, of UNESCO, WHO, ILO, and other international organizations.

All of these efforts, academic and otherwise, must be strengthened and expanded. It is possible to suggest here some other potential audiences or groups to which we might give more attention than we are now doing.

a) Despite the millions of graduates of American universities and colleges

428

who have specialized in social science, it is a distressing fact, even to the casual observer of American life, that few of these graduates, (except the handful who continue professionally in teaching or research) are able to make any significant connection between the social science courses they took in college and the practical lives they are now living. Perhaps the regular curriculum application came too early in their lives and before they were ready for it; perhaps the pressures of other interests have crowded out of their minds what they did carry away from college. The subject matter of the social sciences, consisting as it does so largely of human relations, social process, and institutions based on whole life spans, may actually find much more meaningful acceptance in the older and more experienced segments of the population. In any event, if the colleges and universities could begin to think of their various alumni groups not as mere *ad hoc* fund-raising organizations, but more as former students toward whom they still have an educational responsibility, then the advancement in the level of learning that, with our present techniques for dissemination of information and our facilities for publication, could be achieved in a relatively short time is exciting to contemplate.

Nothing I have seen in print recently has presented this dilemma of modern education so sharply as Margaret Mead's article, "The Coming Revolution in Education," which appeared last year in the *Harvard Business Review*. Dr. Mead reviews the background from which our current educational machinery developed, when learning was passed on in family situations from parent to child, and, in our school system, from teacher to pupil, in a vertical or "down-the-line" process. Such vertical transmission of knowledge, or education in its formal sense, which usually stops just as life is beginning for most young people, is no longer sufficient in the quickened world in which we live. The burden of knowledge presently is too heavy to be transmitted by the time the learner is twenty; and new knowledge is being discovered so rapidly that most of those who do achieve a college education soon find that their knowledge about what is going on in the world has become dated. Dr. Mead proposes more "lateral" educational opportunity, after the initial formal schooling, that continues during one's lifetime. This is not just a glorified adult extension program like those now existing in agriculture and some other areas. It is a wholly new and drastic reorganization of our present methods and tempo of transmitting knowledge and of training in rational methods of thought. All may not agree with Dr. Mead about the changes in the existing educational set-up necessary to achieve this broader opportunity; but few can deny that the need exists for broadening and extending our educational process beyond the few years now conventionally set aside for that experience.

Among this large adult group which needs to be reached by our new knowledge of human relationships are many who for the first time in their lives have interest and leisure to read, think, listen, and study with profit. Present efforts to reach this part of the population, even in those countries where the social sciences are most developed, are practically non-existent on any effective or organized basis.

b) There is another large and growing market for the social sciences—the overseas market. The revolutionary changes that are occurring in social life and organization throughout the world, particularly in the newer nations, cry out for attention. Never were insight and understanding in more demand. We must not be misled by quips to the effect that the developing countries all want to become atomic age nations overnight. There is indeed great interest in the physical sciences and in technological training; but few responsible leaders I have met in any of the new countries have placed these interests above their needs for further education in human relations and human behavior. Some of the social sciences, like sociology, anthropology, and social psychology, have gained little recognition as yet in most new national educational activities. However, in economics, political science, public administration and management, business management, and psychology (if I may dare include it here!) the promotion of interest or demand is less a problem than is the supply of an adequate product and competent teachers (or should I say "salesmen," to keep the entrepreneurial motif?).

Furthermore, it appears that time has caught up with one of social science's reiterated generalizations, namely, that change occurs more rapidly in material than in non-material aspects of culture. This may be as obsolete as some of our other premature generalizations. Suddenly confronted with the many responsibilities of national independence, almost all new nations are seeking knowledge, guidance, and the results of the experience of others, wherever they can find them. They do not want the material trappings of another society so much as the basic non-material ideas that will contribute to the smoother operation and progress of their countries. These ideas are the fundamental stock of social science; but experience is apparently demonstrating that they cannot be transplanted successfully as Western catchwords or social science jargon. They must be made understandable and applicable in terms of the social organization, motivations, and values of the receiving culture. Reverting again to the emphasis on product improvement stressed in the first section of this paper, we declare that social science, in all its different areas, should re-examine sharply, quickly, and with humility, many of the definitions, hypotheses, concepts, and generalizations that are now the working tools of a science too shallowly based in Western life and thought.

c) The thought of other nations suggests an additional neglected market area. Six million Americans (and uncounted millions of other restless people) are going abroad this year as tourists. Many, perhaps the majority, of them go to see places and things, historical or unique. However, even casual conversations with some of these travelers elicit the fact that a large percentage are interested in living people, their institutions, values, and ways of life, and are seeking to become better acquainted with these foreign groups, once far remote but rapidly becoming next-door neighbors.

Who is preparing these travelers for greater appreciation of their new experiences in the field of human relations and exchange of ideas? Let us not engage in the controversy about whether social science is or can be a predictive science; on its slow and weary way to that goal, it has no reason not to attempt to raise people's understanding of the contracting world and its many different ways of life to a level higher than the blurbs that now appear on travel folders or in Ripley's "Believe It or Not." Social science has much

430

useful material for these people with wanderlust—not only before their visit abroad, but, perhaps more important, after they return home and while their newly-aroused curiosities are still alive.

These suggestions are just that; they are probably quite impracticable ones, and they are undoubtedly marginal to our major market area, which, for some time to come, must remain our organized school system. But we must be alert to all other possibilities for increasing our audiences, wherever they may be found. Our market is a world-wide one. It is being prepared for us by the march of world events, and it is limited only by the adequacy with which we diagnose human behavior and make our diagnoses functionally intelligible. We face one significant problem in establishing campaign priorities among the various possibilities—we must decide where and how we can be most effective most rapidly, for time is running out on us. Another of our problems is the improvement and more rapid increase in our market outlets—our "authorized dealers," in business parlance. We shall make some comment on this in the following section.

TECHNIQUES OF PROMOTING

Once we have an improved product and an almost limitless market area, what about the methods of promotion? The methods for social science probably differ little from methods used in any kind of product promotion. The object is to let the people know in such a way as to increase demand. Traditionally, this is done through advertising, demonstration, sales talks, distribution of samples, research on consumer resistance, and the like. If the product already has a prestige name or status significance, like that which the physical and natural sciences have achieved, the problem is a simpler one. Since most of our products have as yet neither name nor fame to carry them much beyond campus boundaries, we are reduced to elementary levels of communication. The techniques mentioned above will undoubtedly create cold shudders in most social scientists—they do in me—for it is not easy to think of ourselves as reduced to such tawdry commercialization. But this is a paper on promotion, and these earthy terms are merely promotional lingo: it should do us no harm to examine them as tools of our promotional enterprise.

Since so much of the product of social science is composed of written words, one of our urgent problems is to increase readership, to bring our product to the attention of more people—a primary advertising function. Too much of the useful knowledge which has been developed by the social sciences still lies buried in dull textbooks or duller research reports, purposely designed, it would seem, to discourage all but the most determined scholar. There is no reason to believe that social scientists are less equipped than other scholars to make their material more attractive to readers than they now do; but there is an almost unbreakable tradition that they do not present it thus, and a powerful sanction of disdain against those who do. Instead of being encouraged to publish outside professional journals, where their findings are seen by few, most social scientists are restrained from doing so by the fear—too often justified—that their colleagues, lying in wait, will pounce upon them for any inadequately defined term or un-footnoted statement they might make. We can scarcely expect to expand our market beyond ourselves if the members of each group continue to write only for each other. Such intellectual possessiveness, bordering on the arrogant, has already stultified and practically eliminated poetry as the constructive maker of ideals and images that it might be in our modern, dysphoric world.

Overcoming our resistance to writing for readers other than members of our particular guild is but half of the problem; the other half is a task fully as difficult and perhaps more urgent. Some years ago, the respected anthropologist Robert Redfield, after returning from an abruptly terminated educational assignment in China, wrote an article for the *Saturday Review of Literature,* "America Needs a Hearing Aid." In it, he urged America to do more listening and to spend less time telling other people what to do. In the seven years since the article appeared, I have not met anyone who has read it. How can thoughtful, stimulating articles like this ever move from a journal of limited distribution into a publication like, say, the *Reader's Digest?* The reasons that they do not appear in such widely read periodicals would make an interesting research project to which some of social science's disciplined, objective efforts might be turned.

With our modern means for widespread dissemination and amplificaton, Redfield's respected voice, and the voices of countless other social scientists accorded like respect, should not be so easily stilled as they now are in American life. But they are not automatically amplified—someone must do something about it. Social science, if it is to attract public attention to its best products, must cease to depend upon the whimsical, uninformed, or biased choices of current media of communication. An offprint or reprint service for wider distribution of selected articles, otherwise read by only a few hundred, might have to be subsidized for a time; but it might, in wise hands, eventually pay its own way. No one, I think, is at present doing this job as well as the demographers and population analysts; and their experience might be valuable for others to review and copy.

In similar vein, why have so few of the social scientists ventured to develop newspaper columns, syndicated or otherwise? Surely it is not because social behavior, as it has institutionalized itself in varied forms throughout the world and is now performing incredible somersaults, does not provide extremely interesting copy. More likely, our own smug disinterest in such publishing efforts is the cause, and not any lack of interest on the part of the public were they invited to participate. True, there now exist columns on economics, on politics, occasionally on other subjects; but one could probably count on one's fingers the number of these being written by competent social scientists. Anthropologists have unaccountably neglected to develop responsible outlets for the wealth of interesting and socially meaningful material to which they have access. They have left their rich comparative data to be publicly exploited largely by run-and-write travelers, hack writers, and shallow lecturers who concentrate on the exotic and the queer.

And I shall stoop to a level which will assuredly lose me whatever professional standing I may have left among my colleagues. Why do we not have something for our young people as eye-catching as *Popular Mechanics*, which has probably done more to arouse and maintain early interest in the physical sciences than all the textbooks prepared for academic use?

In our advertising, it might be too gross to resort to full-page ads of the "Man of Distinction" type, or to produce a radio program which carries the plug, "See your social scientist regularly." Maybe there is nothing in modern advertising methods to which we dare lower ourselves; but other highly respected scientific fields do not seem to have suffered from publicizing the more glamorous activities of their members with a kind of "Man on the Spot" technique. Maybe we do not have such individuals to talk about; but surely, throughout the world, there are more social scientists in responsible places than is generally known. Our magazines and journals are full of incidents and stories reporting the success of a doctor here, an agriculturist there, an entomologist or engineer somewhere else. Social science leaders seem never to turn up in their scientific capacities, but almost inevitably in some administrative capacity that obscures their identity.

In the same Cairo conference I previously mentioned, another "friend" of mine during the discussion period put this question: "You have cited in your paper the startling statistics on the large sums of money spent in research to find out about the physical world, the atom bomb, etc., compared to the small amount spent to find out about people and human relations. You social scientists are always bemoaning the fact that you do not have money enough to do adequate social research. Just what would you do if tomorrow you were given two billion dollars, the sum which was given by government for the atomic science Manhattan Project nearly two decades ago?"

I had another bad few minutes. But I couldn't retreat twice during the same question period; so I replied that I was glad he had asked the question and that I had given some thought to such an unlikely possibility (I had, once, for about five minutes). I replied:

"First, with half of the money I would try to bring together from all parts of the world the best social scientists, including social and legal philosophers, that can be found, irrespective of national origin, and ask them to do three things: (*1*) evaluate the mass of social science material we now have and are not using; (*2*) plan and conduct such additional research as may seem necessary; and (*3*) devise means to spread the results as widely as possible."

With the second billion I proposed establishing a world-wide lobby which would work toward a five-year moratorium on all natural science research.

Not content, my friend pushed on: "Would you include medical science research in your moratorium plans?"

With my back now really against the wall, I went all out: "Yes, I would also include medical research in the proposed moratorium."

In the five years since I made this flippant answer, I have not thought up a better one—though I would be inclined now to put medical science research at the head of the list of those activities on which a moratorium might be advocated. Actually, modern science, which now rides mankind with a heavier saddle than "things" ever did in Emerson's time, seems suddenly to have become a struggle between medical science, in its efforts to keep more people alive

433

longer, and atomic science, seeking to kill off more people faster. Rather silly, really.

Anything as starry-eyed as the above should not, of course, even be suggested in a volume of this sort. I deleted it from my original draft and herewith apologize for reinstating it in my final version. I did so hesitatingly, but without tongue in cheek, for two principal reasons. First, the great lag in the world is still social or cultural, as Professor Ogburn pointed out a quarter-century ago; and the lag has assumed new and startling dimensions. We are now faced with such imbalance in the whole field of people living together that some visionary thinking about it is necessary. Second, shocking statements, even ridiculous ones, sometimes have value as promotional gimmicks; and this is a paper on promotion.

Let me return now from outer space. Are there some more immediately practical steps that social science might take to advance its various fields of knowledge and to increase its contribution to the common good?

Earlier, I commented on the segmented nature of so much of our work and on the promotional difficulties it created, since our answers to most problems are only partial answers and therefore fail to maintain public attention. A greater proportion of our social scientists should concern themselves more industriously with interdisciplinary studies. I have been impressed in the Philippines by a recent study by a political scientist (Carl Lande). He has analyzed the Philippine political situation, not solely in terms of conventional political science concepts and hypotheses, but also in terms of family patterns and relationships which, in the Philippines, have been elaborated on a bilateral basis well beyond extended family patterns as we know them elsewhere in the world. In his study, Lande projected into his analysis of the political process the hitherto undocumented bearing that the family organization, with its associated loyalties, and its overwhelming influence, has on how things do or do not get done in Philippine political life.

Another example came to my notice recently in a study projected by an FAO representative in Rome who wants to examine the critical problem of "shifting" agriculture, that foresters, conservationists, and agriculturists unanimously condemn for its wanton destruction of forest growth and the resultant erosion of good soil. Almost everywhere, legistlation has now been passed that penalizes these "slash-and-burn" practices; but the laws are successfully enforced in very few places. The FAO representative is hoping to examine the continuing malpractice not as a wilful, stubborn violation of the law, but for what it really is—a way of life, and the only way of life most of the violators know anything about.

In Malaya, an interesting attempt is being made by the government to find a solution to this problem through working more closely and sympathetically with the farmers themselves. Instead of sending in police or the army to arrest individuals who engage in the slash-and-burn cultivation, the government is now sending technicians, foresters, and others to consult and advise the forest dwellers in their strenuous way of making a livelihood. The government at the same time requests them, after crops have been harvested and before they move on, to replant the burnt-over area with new trees from nursery stock that

434

the government provides them. This kind of human approach—seeking to understand the shifting agriculturist's problems and to enlist his co-operation —may well accomplish much more effective education, in good practices and ultimately in more conservation, than all the present unenforceable legislation.

An "administrative" social scientist, broadly trained in all the social sciences, has been suggested recently as the type of person needed to bring our separate disciplines into closer relationships with each other, both in research and teaching. There has already been considerable work done by specialists working in teams, or in groups under a co-ordinator or under the single direction of a generalist—all attempts to secure greater functional integration of our special-ized data. All these efforts must be encouraged, as part of our urgent job of bringing our segmented approaches into a more comprehensible focus. England probably has developed generalists more successfully than any other country, but the content of the basic training for such well-rounded, educated persons has embraced much more study of the humanities than of the social sciences as such. This raises some interesting curriculum problems in any program designed to train social science generalists.

Apart from any academic program to prepare social science generalists or administrators, some greater efforts might be made immediately among and between our various disciplines to appreciate and make greater use of each other's knowledge. We may again cite economics as an example, since it is the basic social science. Might not more attention be paid to relating economic behavior, in a functional way, to the other facets of people's behavior? Currently, the practice is to jump from basic economic analysis to legislation, without adequate appreciation of the social machinery through which economic plans and programs must operate.

A similar tendency is found in public administration, where organizational plans are legislated into existence with too little consideration of the societal situation in which they are supposed to function. In many areas, the political scientists and public administration people can learn a great deal, particularly about local government, from the social anthropologists; but they seldom get together, and when they do it is rarely to integrate their knowledge and findings, but usually to compare notes on a sort of recreational, small-talk level. In a highly authoritarian situation, it makes little difference how much attention is given to the intermediate social machinery of human activity, since all that is needed is a well-defined goal and a strong army. However if we expect to remain effective through democratic processes which require people's co-operation and understanding, then we must take adequate account of the incentives, loyalties, and social organization and institutions of the culture we are trying to understand.

Much of the last few pages may seem too philosophical to be acceptable. My extenuating plea can only be that, so long as we labor in our specialized fields without referring our findings back to the larger framework in which life is lived, we shall have difficulty gaining acceptance in the market place for our ideas. We are being less than philosophers, but we are also being less than good social scientists. We are becoming electricians, plumbers, carpenters, and masons, with highly specialized skills; but without the indispensable guidance of the architect, our house may not stand up and the facilities will probably not function. For some, this broader approach as social philosophers or co-ordinators may mean the loss of distinguishing professional titles as "economist," "political scientist," "anthropologist," and the like. But this is probably not too harsh a penalty, if it will help to overcome the fragmented findings and fragmentary presentations with which we are now attempting to promote the work and reputation of our science.

The social scientists must also develop more rapport with, and be accorded greater respect by, the natural scientists who happen today to occupy the top spot in the scientific heirarchy. When the physical scientist becomes frustrated about the contrariness of human nature, if it worries him at all, he is inclined to make a much wider leap than even the economist or the political scientist. He skips legislation as well as social science, and goes all the way into religion, philosophy, or poetry. It is our business to bring to his attention, as convincingly as we can, the fate that people and human institutional arrangements are increasingly a critical and functional part of the world we seek to understand. In Manila very recently, one of America's top physical scientists, advising the National Science Development Board of the Philippines on its program, strongly recommended the exclusion of the social sciences on the grounds that there was not time to do everything. Yet in the Philippines—and in this respect the Philippines are not unique—there is no more crucial area of need than in the understanding of people, their organizations and institutions, and the motivations for their behavior.

Just as we must seek greater understanding among the physical and natural scientists, so must we in our own work strive for greater rapport with those interpreters of society in such fields as history, philosophy, and law. Both the natural sciences and the humanities call upon social scientists to exercise a new function with regard to these two venerable and respected purveyors of learning. This is not an easy public relations job. However, it should be somewhat less difficult for us in the present intellectual situation, where physical science has out-distanced the people and philosophy has not yet caught up with them. Is social science doing all that it can or should do to fill the vacuum?

This paper, already too long, must close with only brief reference to the many administrative problems of promotion in our colleges and universities, still the main production and distribution centers for the social science product. I can make no contribution about the ways to handle boards of regents or university presidents, or about methods of increasing departmental allocations in the fiercely competitive struggle for funds, personnel, or space. However, these problems are, in the institutional setting in which we operate, crucial aspects of gaining recognition and support, and they warrant the most able and constant administrative attention. They will not be solved by our sitting back and feeling sorry for ourselves.

I can also refer only briefly to the public, contract, and liaison relationships which the social sciences must enlarge and improve with government, business, foundations, and other distributing organizations. We are still sending out too many boys (despite their age) to do men's work—most of them chosen because they are available, or to give them experience, or simply to reward a long tenure, rather than for their recognized performance and standing. Perhaps this practice was acceptable enough in the past, while we were still growing up. But now, with the increased need for more mature presentation and with the expectancies we have created in the world, we can no longer afford to send out less than the best.

Since much of what is written here is not wholly my own, I shall close these undocumented remarks with a credit line, consistently imprecise, to my many collaborators. These have been many other social scientists who have expressed to me their worries about the future of our "science," and many non-social scientists who have expressed their concerns about the future of the world as a place for people to live and work together.